First World War
and Army of Occupation
War Diary
France, Belgium and Germany

56 DIVISION
Headquarters, Branches and Services
Adjutant and Quarter-Master General
1 January 1918 - 18 May 1919

WO95/2936/2

The Naval & Military Press Ltd
www.nmarchive.com
Published in association with The National Archives

Published by

The Naval & Military Press Ltd

Unit 10 Ridgewood Industrial Park,

Uckfield, East Sussex,

TN22 5QE England

Tel: +44 (0) 1825 749494

www.naval-military-press.com

www.nmarchive.com

This diary has been reprinted in facsimile from the original. Any imperfections are inevitably reproduced and the quality may fall short of modern type and cartographic standards.

© **Crown Copyright**
Images reproduced by permission of The National Archives, London, England, 2015.

Contents

Document type	Place/Title	Date From	Date To
Miscellaneous	Tunnel Dump.	07/12/1917	07/12/1917
Miscellaneous	Administrative Instructions No. 1. in connection with Relief of 56th Divn. by 31st Divn. Appendix I	15/12/1917	15/12/1917
Miscellaneous	Embussing Table. Appendix "A"		
Miscellaneous	56th Div. Light Railway Entertainment Table. Appendix "B"		
Miscellaneous	56th Division Location Table on completion of Relief by 31st Division. Appendix "C"		
Miscellaneous	A.Q.S. 462/1	16/12/1917	16/12/1917
Miscellaneous	Back Area Accommodation. Appendix V	10/12/1917	10/12/1917
Miscellaneous	Administrative Instructions Issued With Reference to 56th Division Order No. 144 Appendix W	20/12/1917	20/12/1917
Miscellaneous	167th Inf. Bde. Appendix X	20/12/1917	20/12/1917
Operation(al) Order(s)	56th Division. Light Railway Entertainment Table Issued with reference to 36th Divl Order No. 144 Appendix Y	20/12/1917	20/12/1917
Miscellaneous	Location Table. 56th Division. Appendix Z	28/12/1917	28/12/1917
Miscellaneous			
Miscellaneous	56th Division. Casualties for month of December, 1917		
Heading	War Diary Administrative Branch 56th Division Period. 1st to 31st January 1918 Volume XXIV		
War Diary	Victory Camp Roclincourt	01/01/1918	08/01/1918
War Diary	Villers-Chatel	09/01/1918	31/01/1918
Miscellaneous	56th Division Administrative Instructions No. 1. in connection with Relief by 62nd Division. Appendix A	01/01/1918	01/01/1918
Miscellaneous	Accommodation. Appendix "B"		
Miscellaneous	Location Table. 56th Division. Appendix "C"		
Miscellaneous	List of Area Employ furnished by 56th Division to be relieved by 62nd Division at 11am. 7.1.18		
Operation(al) Order(s)	56th Division Administrative Instructions No. 2, Issued with reference to 56th Div. Order No. 147 Appendix B	01/01/1918	01/01/1918
Miscellaneous			
Miscellaneous	Administrative Instructions No. 3, Issued With Reference to 56th Divn. Order No 147 Appendix C	02/01/1918	02/01/1918
Operation(al) Order(s)	Administrative Instructions No. 4, in connection with Relief of 56th Divn by 62nd Divn. Issued with reference to 56th Div. Order, No. 147 Appendix D	03/01/1918	03/01/1918
Miscellaneous	56th Division Location Table on Completion of Relief by 62nd Divn.		
Miscellaneous	Administrative Instructions No. 5 in connection with relief of 56th Divn. by 42nd Division. Issued with reference to 56th Div. Order No. 147 Appendix E		
Miscellaneous	Appendix "A". Supply Grouping to Take Effect As Units Arrive in Villers-Chatel, Monchy-Breton Divl. Area.		
Miscellaneous	56th Division No. G.3/807 Appendix F	07/01/1918	07/01/1918
Miscellaneous	Scheme "A". Arrangements for the Entrainment and Detrainment of the 56th Division in case a move by rail is ordered whilst in G.H.Q. Reserve.	07/01/1918	07/01/1918
Miscellaneous	Table "D" 1.		

Miscellaneous	Table "B" 2.		
Miscellaneous	Table "D" 2.		
Miscellaneous	Scheme "C". Move of 56th Division by Tactical Trains from Reserve Area to Ecurie. Appendix G	07/01/1918	07/01/1918
Miscellaneous	Composition of Omnibus Train. Appendix "Y".		
Miscellaneous	Extracts From List of New Year's Honours Gazette. Appendix H		
Miscellaneous	Locations. Appendix I	12/01/1918	12/01/1918
Miscellaneous	Locations. Appendix K	19/01/1918	19/01/1918
Miscellaneous	Locations. Appendix L	25/01/1918	25/01/1918
Miscellaneous	Reorganization 56th Div. Instructions No. 1. Issued with reference to 56th Div. G148/1, dated 22.1.18 Appendix M	25/01/1918	25/01/1918
Miscellaneous	Proforma "A". London Regiment.		
Miscellaneous	Reorganization 56th Division Instructions No. 2. Appendix N	27/01/1918	27/01/1918
Miscellaneous	Postings to be carried out by 56th Division.		
Miscellaneous	Strength.		
Miscellaneous	56th Division. Casualties for the month of January, 1918		
Heading	War Diary Administrative Branch 56th Division Period. 1st to 28th Feby. 1918 Volume XXV		
War Diary	Villers-Chatel	01/02/1918	10/02/1918
War Diary	Roclincourt	11/02/1918	28/02/1918
Miscellaneous	Locations. Appendix "A"	01/02/1918	01/02/1918
Miscellaneous	Arrangements for the Entrainment and Detrainment of the 56th Division in case a move by Rail is ordered whilst in G.H.Q. Reserve. Appendix "B"	02/02/1918	02/02/1918
Miscellaneous	Composition of Omnibus Train. Appendix "Y".		
Miscellaneous	Table "D" 2.		
Miscellaneous	Table "D" 1.		
Operation(al) Order(s)	Administrative Instructions. No. 1 In connection with 56th Division Order 149 Appendix "C"	05/02/1918	05/02/1918
Miscellaneous	Arrangements for Embussing of The 56th Division (Less Arty.) in Case A Move by 'Bus is Ordered from First Army Area Whilst in G.H.Q. Reserve Appendix D	06/02/1918	06/02/1918
Miscellaneous	AQS. 482.	07/02/1918	07/02/1918
Operation(al) Order(s)	Administrative Instructions No. 2 In connection with 56th Div Order 149 Appendix "E"	07/02/1918	07/02/1918
Miscellaneous	Refilling Points.		
Miscellaneous	56th Division Administrative Instructions No. 3, in connection with Relief of 62nd Division. Appendix "F"	08/02/1918	08/02/1918
Miscellaneous	56th Division. Locations of Units on completion of Relief of 62nd Division. Appendix "C"	07/02/1918	07/02/1918
Miscellaneous	56th Division. Casualties for the month of February, 1918		
Miscellaneous	Strength.	01/02/1918	01/02/1918
Heading	Administration 56th Division A. & Q 56th Division March 1918		
Miscellaneous	Administrative		
War Diary	Roclincourt	01/03/1918	29/03/1918
War Diary	ACQ	30/03/1918	31/03/1918
Miscellaneous	Locations. Appendix 'A'	01/03/1918	01/03/1918
Miscellaneous	Locations.	08/03/1918	08/03/1918
Miscellaneous	Locations.	15/03/1918	15/03/1918
Miscellaneous	111th Corps "Q" Your No. GS.270/89/4 of 12.3.18	14/03/1918	14/03/1918

Miscellaneous	Administrative Instructions No. 1. in Connection with Relief of 56th Divn. by 62nd Divn. Issued with reference to 56th Divn. No. G.3/92 of 19th instant. Appx C	20/03/1918	20/03/1918
Miscellaneous	56th Division Locations.	30/03/1918	30/03/1918
Miscellaneous	56th Division. Casualties for the month of March, 1918 Officers.		
Miscellaneous	Strength.	01/03/1918	01/03/1918
Heading	H.Q A&Q 46 Div Feb Vol XII		
Heading	A. & Q. 56th Division April 1918		
War Diary	ACQ	01/04/1918	06/04/1918
War Diary	Warlus	07/04/1918	30/04/1918
Miscellaneous	AQS/5. Appendix "A".	05/04/1918	05/04/1918
Miscellaneous	56th Division. Locations. Appendix "B"	08/04/1918	08/04/1918
Miscellaneous	Locations Table. AQS/5. Appendix "C"	14/04/1918	14/04/1918
Miscellaneous	Locations. AQS/5. Appendix "C"	29/04/1918	29/04/1918
Miscellaneous	Administrative Instructions No. 1. in Connection with The Possible Transfer of The Division (Less Artillery) To Another Corps by Bus.	14/04/1918	14/04/1918
Miscellaneous	Extracts from Notes on Administrative Arrangements during Recent Operations, from a Divisional point of view.		
Miscellaneous	167th Inf. Bde.	06/05/1918	06/05/1918
Miscellaneous	XVII Corps Q. 1222/265	04/05/1918	04/05/1918
Miscellaneous	56th Division AQS/582	03/04/1918	03/04/1918
Miscellaneous	Intercommunication Between Supply Echelons During Mobile Warfare.	17/04/1918	17/04/1918
Miscellaneous	56th Division AQS/609	16/04/1918	16/04/1918
Miscellaneous	AQS/582.	08/05/1918	08/05/1918
Miscellaneous	Embussing Table-Situation "A". Reference 1/100,000 Map.		
Miscellaneous	Embussing Table-Situation B. Refce. 1/10000 Map Sheet Lens II.		
Miscellaneous	Intercommunication Between Supply Echelons During Mobile Warfare.	17/04/1918	17/04/1918
Miscellaneous	Amendments To Administrative Instructions No. 1. Dated 22.4.18	24/04/1918	24/04/1918
Miscellaneous	Administrative Instructions No. 1. In The Event of The Division Relieving The 15th Division.	22/04/1918	22/04/1918
Miscellaneous	Formation of Divisional Provisional Battalion.	03/04/1918	03/04/1918
Miscellaneous	56th Division AQS/582	03/04/1918	03/04/1918
Miscellaneous	Amendment To Administrative Instructions No. 1 of To-Day. para. 7. Ordnance.	06/04/1918	06/04/1918
Miscellaneous	Administrative Instructions No. 1 in connection with relief of 1st Canadian Division by 56th Division.	06/04/1918	06/04/1918
Miscellaneous	Amendment To Administrative Instructions No. 1 of To-Day. para. 7. Ordnance.	06/04/1918	06/04/1918
Miscellaneous	Administrative Instructions No. 1. in connection with relief of 1st Canadian Division by 56th Division.	06/04/1918	06/04/1918
Miscellaneous	Administrative Instructions No. 2. in connection with relief of 1st Canadian Division by 56th Division.	07/04/1918	07/04/1918
Miscellaneous	Strength.		
Miscellaneous	Casualties. April, 1918		
Heading	War Diary Administrative Branch 56th Division Vol. XXVIII Period-1st to 31st May. 1918 Vol 28		
War Diary	Warlus	01/05/1918	31/05/1918

Miscellaneous	Locations. 56th Division.	18/05/1918	18/05/1918
Miscellaneous	Strength.		
Miscellaneous	Casualties-May, 1918		
Heading	War Diary of Administrative Branch 56th Division June 1918 Vol 29		
War Diary	Warlus	01/06/1918	30/06/1918
Miscellaneous	Strength.	01/06/1918	01/06/1918
Miscellaneous	Casualties-June, 1918		
Heading	War Diary Administrative Branch 56th Division. Period. 1st to 31st July, 1918 Vol 30		
War Diary	Warlus	01/07/1918	14/07/1918
War Diary	Roellecourt	15/07/1918	16/07/1918
War Diary	Villers-Chatel	17/07/1918	31/07/1918
Operation(al) Order(s)	Administrative Instructions No. 1. in connection with relief of the 56th Division by 1st and 2nd Canadian Divisions, issued with reference to 56th Division Warning Order no. 180 App A	08/07/1918	08/07/1918
Miscellaneous	Amendments To Administrative Instructions No. 1. Dated 8.7.18	09/07/1918	09/07/1918
Miscellaneous	56th Division AQS/675	09/07/1918	09/07/1918
Miscellaneous	Amendments to Administrative Instructions No. 1, Para. 8	10/07/1918	10/07/1918
Miscellaneous	Administrative Instructions No. 2. in connection with relief of the 56th Division. App. B	10/07/1918	10/07/1918
Miscellaneous	Area Employment to be Relieved Under Divisional Arrangements.	07/07/1918	07/07/1918
Miscellaneous	56th Division AQS/675 App C	10/07/1918	10/07/1918
Miscellaneous	Schedule-Lorries.		
Miscellaneous	Administrative Instructions No. 3. in connection with relief of the 56th Division. App D	11/07/1918	11/07/1918
Miscellaneous	Moves of Transport Columns on 15th July, 1918. Appendix "A"		
Miscellaneous	Provisional Train Arrangements for 15th July. Appendix "B"		
Miscellaneous			
Miscellaneous	Supply Grouping Table. Appendix "C"		
Miscellaneous	56th Division AQS/675.	12/07/1918	12/07/1918
Miscellaneous	56th Division. Locations on Completion of Relief. App. E	14/07/1918	14/07/1918
Operation(al) Order(s)	Administrative Instructions No. 4 with reference to 56th Divisional Order No. 182 App. F	14/07/1918	14/07/1918
Miscellaneous	56th Divn. AQS/675. Appendix B.1		
Operation(al) Order(s)	Administrative Instructions No. 5 with reference to 56th Divisional Order No. 182 App H	14/07/1918	14/07/1918
Miscellaneous	Schedule.-Lorries (2) App. H.2.		
Miscellaneous	Embussing Table. App H.3		
Miscellaneous	Appendix "A". Instructions for Move of the Division (less Artillery) by Bus whilst in G.H.Q. Reserve.		
Miscellaneous	Amendment to Appendix "A" of Instructions for Move of the Division (loss Artillery) by Bus whilst in G.H.Q. Reserve.		
Miscellaneous	Appendix "B" to 56th Divn. No. G.3/894 of 15.7.18. Instructions for move of the Division by Stretgpool Train whilst in G.H.Q. Reserve. App I		
Miscellaneous	Ref. 56th Div. No. G.3/894 of 15/7/1918, Appendix "B"		

Operation(al) Order(s)	Administrative Instructions No. 1 issued with reference to 56th Division Warning Order No. 183 App I 2	17/07/1918	17/07/1918
Operation(al) Order(s)	Administrative Instructions No. 2 issued with reference to 56th Division Order No. 184 App I 3	17/07/1918	17/07/1918
Miscellaneous	Reference 56th Divn. No. G.3/894 of 15.7.1918 Appendix "B". Table "C" (Provisional). App I4	18/07/1918	18/07/1918
Miscellaneous	56th Divn. No. G. 3/894 dated 15.7.18 App J		
Miscellaneous	56th Division Location Table. App J. 1	18/07/1918	18/07/1918
Miscellaneous	Reference 56th Divn. No. G. 3/894 of 15.7.18. Appendix "A". App k	20/07/1918	20/07/1918
Miscellaneous	Reference 56th Division AQS/677 dated 20.7.18 App L	22/07/1918	22/07/1918
Miscellaneous	56th Division AQS/677 App L I	22/07/1918	22/07/1918
Miscellaneous	Administrative Instructions No. 1. in connection with the relief of the 1st Canadian Division in Telegraph Hill Sector. App M	29/07/1918	29/07/1918
Miscellaneous	56th Division. Locations on Completion of Relief. App N.	31/07/1918	31/07/1918
Miscellaneous	Strength.	01/07/1918	01/07/1918
Miscellaneous	Casualties-July, 1918		
Heading	War Diary Administrative Branch 56th Division. Period. 1st to 31st August 1918 Volume XXXI		
War Diary	Villers-Chatel.	01/08/1918	02/08/1918
War Diary	Warlus	07/08/1918	18/08/1918
War Diary	Le Cauroy	19/08/1918	21/08/1918
War Diary	Bavincourt	22/08/1918	23/08/1918
War Diary	Blaireville	23/08/1918	24/08/1918
War Diary	Boisleux-Au-Mont	24/08/1918	31/08/1918
Miscellaneous	56th Division AQS/704/2. App. I	15/08/1918	15/08/1918
Miscellaneous	Administrative Instructions No. 1 in connection with relief 56th Division by 15th Division and the move to Le Cauroy Area.	14/08/1918	14/08/1918
Miscellaneous	Area Employment to be Relieved Under Divisional Arrangements on 16th August, 1918 Appendix "C"		
Miscellaneous	Amendment to 56th Divn. Location Table at 10 A.M. 18th August. App. II	17/08/1918	17/08/1918
Miscellaneous	56th Division. Location Table at 10 A.M. 18th August, 1918	17/08/1918	17/08/1918
Miscellaneous	Amendment No. 1. to Standing Orders for Strategic Move of Division (less Artillery) by Bus wilst in G.H.Q. Reserve. App. III	21/08/1918	21/08/1918
Miscellaneous	Standing Orders for Strategic Move of the Division (loss Artillery) by Bus whilst in G.H.Q. Reserve.	20/08/1918	20/08/1918
Miscellaneous	Amendment No. 1. to Administrative Instructions No. 1. in Connection with Thistle. App. IV.	20/08/1918	20/08/1918
Miscellaneous	Administrative Instructions No. 1. in connection with Thistle.	19/08/1918	19/08/1918
Miscellaneous	Embussing Table.		
Operation(al) Order(s)	Administrative Instructions No. 1. issued with reference to 56th Div. Order No. 193. App V	22/08/1918	22/08/1918
Miscellaneous	56th Division. Location Table at 10 A.M. 24th August, 1918. App. VI.	23/08/1918	23/08/1918
Miscellaneous		21/08/1918	21/08/1918
Miscellaneous	Lorry Table. 56th Division AQS/677/3. App. VII		
Miscellaneous	Embussing Table. (Issued with reference to Bus Move Standing Orders Para 1)		
Miscellaneous	Strength.		

Miscellaneous	Third Army "A"	16/09/1918	16/09/1918
Miscellaneous	Amended Casualties. for Period 23rd to 31st August, 1918	17/09/1918	17/09/1918
Miscellaneous	Casualties.-August, 1918		
Heading	War Diary Administrative Branch 56th Division Period. 1st to 30th Sept. 1918 Vol. XXXII		
War Diary	Boisleux-Au-Mont	01/09/1918	08/09/1918
War Diary	Les Fosses Farm	09/09/1918	27/09/1918
War Diary	Villers Lez Cagnicourt	28/09/1918	30/09/1918
Miscellaneous	Administrative Instructions in connection with forthcoming operations. Issued with reference to 56th Divn. Order 205	23/09/1918	23/09/1918
Miscellaneous	56th Division. Location Table At 12 Noon, 22nd September, 1918	21/09/1918	21/09/1918
Miscellaneous	Amendment to Administrative Instructions in connection with forthcoming operations. Issued under AQS/734/1 dated 23.9.18	24/09/1918	24/09/1918
Miscellaneous	Locations.	22/09/1918	22/09/1918
Miscellaneous	56th Division Location Table at 10 A.M. 11th Sept., 1918	10/09/1918	10/09/1918
Miscellaneous	56th Division Location Table at 10 A.M. 9th Septr., 1918	08/09/1918	08/09/1918
Miscellaneous	Casualties.-September, 1918		
Miscellaneous	Strength.		
Heading	War Diary A.A. & Q.M.G. 56th Division. Vol 33		
War Diary	Villers Lez Cagnicourt	01/10/1918	15/10/1918
War Diary	Etrun	16/10/1918	31/10/1918
Miscellaneous	56th Division. Location Table At 12 Noon, 3rd October, 1918 Appendix A	04/10/1918	04/10/1918
Miscellaneous	Administrative Instructions in connection with relief of the Division by 4th Canadian Division. Appendix B	12/10/1918	12/10/1918
Miscellaneous	Administrative Instructions No. 2. in connection with relief of the Division by 4th Canadian Divn. Appendix c	13/10/1918	13/10/1918
Miscellaneous	56th Division. Location Table. Appendix D	18/10/1918	18/10/1918
Miscellaneous	Administrative Instructions in Connection with A General Advance. Appendix E	17/10/1918	17/10/1918
Operation(al) Order(s)	Provisional Administrative Instructions issued in connection with 56th Divnl. Warning Order No. 247 Appendix F	30/10/1918	30/10/1918
Miscellaneous			
Operation(al) Order(s)	Provisional Administrative Instructions issued in connection with 56th Division Order No. 218 Appendix G	30/10/1918	30/10/1918
Miscellaneous	Reference Provisional Administrative Instructions No. AQS/753/1 & 2. Issued in Connection with Divl. Warning Order No. 247 and Divisional Order No. 218	30/10/1918	30/10/1918
Operation(al) Order(s)	Administrative Instructions Issued in connection with 56th Divisional Order No. 218 Appendix H	30/10/1918	30/10/1918
Miscellaneous	Casualties. October 1918		
Miscellaneous	Strength.		
Heading	War Diary Administrative Branch 56th Division Period. 1st to 30th November 1918 Vol. XXXIV		
War Diary	Basseville	01/11/1918	01/11/1918
War Diary	Monchaux	02/11/1918	02/11/1918
War Diary	Saultain	06/11/1918	06/11/1918
War Diary	Sebourg	07/11/1918	08/11/1918

War Diary	Fayt Le France	09/11/1918	27/11/1918
War Diary	Harveng	28/11/1918	30/11/1918
Miscellaneous	Administrative Instructions in connection with 56th Divn. C. 280 dated 1st November/18 Appendix A	01/11/1918	01/11/1918
Miscellaneous	Administrative Instructions in connection with 56th Divn. G. 280 dated 1st November 1918 Appendix B	02/11/1918	02/11/1918
Miscellaneous	Administrative Instructions No. 1. issued in connection with the March to the Rhine.	13/11/1918	13/11/1918
Miscellaneous	AQX. 1494.	13/11/1918	13/11/1918
Miscellaneous	Location Table. 56th Div. AQS/5.	15/11/1918	15/11/1918
Miscellaneous	A.Q.S.5.	16/11/1918	16/11/1918
Miscellaneous	Administrative Instructions No. 2. issued in connection with the March to the Rhine.	15/11/1918	15/11/1918
Miscellaneous	Administrative Instructions No. 1. in connection with the move to the Harveng Area.	23/11/1918	23/11/1918
Miscellaneous	Administrative Instructions No. 1. in connection with move to the Harveng Area.	24/11/1918	24/11/1918
Miscellaneous	Strength.	01/11/1918	01/11/1918
Miscellaneous	Casualties. November, 1918		
Miscellaneous	A Form. Messages And Signals.		
Miscellaneous	56th Division. Casualties for Period 1st to 12th November, 1918		
Miscellaneous	B Form. Messages And Signals.		
Miscellaneous	N.a. 21.00I N.a. 22.00 H.a.		
Miscellaneous	A Form. Messages And Signals.		
Miscellaneous	C Form. Messages And Signals.		
Miscellaneous	B Form. Messages And Signals.		
Miscellaneous	A Form. Messages And Signals.		
Miscellaneous	B Form. Messages And Signals.		
Heading	War Diary-Administrative Branch, 56th Division. Period 1/12/1918 to 31/12/1918 Volume. XXXV		
War Diary	Harveng	30/11/1918	31/12/1918
Miscellaneous	Strength.		
Heading	Headquarters 56th Division A.A. & Q.M.G. War Diary January 1919 Vol 36		
War Diary	Harveng	01/01/1919	31/01/1919
Miscellaneous	List of Awards in The New Year's Honours Despatch.		
Miscellaneous	M.S.M. Divisional Artillery.		
Miscellaneous	Mentioned in Despatches.		
Miscellaneous	56th Division. Location Table.	05/12/1918	05/12/1918
Miscellaneous	56th Division. Location Table.	25/01/1919	25/01/1919
Miscellaneous	56th Division. Location Table.	23/01/1919	23/01/1919
Miscellaneous	Strength.		
Heading	War Diary for month of February 1919 A.A. & Q.M.G. Branch 56th Division. Vol 37		
War Diary	Harveng	31/01/1919	28/02/1919
Miscellaneous	Strength.		
Heading	56th Division. A.A and Q.M.G. War Diary March 1919 Vol 38		
War Diary	Harvengt	01/03/1919	28/03/1919
War Diary	Jemappes	29/03/1919	31/03/1919
Miscellaneous	Strength.		
War Diary	Jemappes	01/04/1919	18/05/1919
Miscellaneous	Strength.		

TUNNEL DUMP. B.15.c.3.2.	(100 complete changes for Left and Centre Brigades. (In charge of Lieut. SPICER.
BATHS AT HAGGIS HOUSE.	(50 complete changes. (In charge of Baths.

17. SALVAGE.

The Divl. Salvage Dump is established at ECURIE, A.27.b.8.8. Units will return all salvage direct to this dump

18. DRYING ROOM.

A Drying Room is established at the Main Divisional Salvage Dump at ECURIE, A.27.b.8.8. Units will apply to the Divl. Salvage Officer for its use.

19. BATHS.

All men bathing at ECURIE BATHS must take greatcoats to wear whilst their Service Dress is being disinfected.

20. MEDICAL ARRANGEMENTS.

LEFT AND CENTRAL BRIGADES.

Regtl. Aid Posts.	B.12.a.4.5. B.18.c.9.7. B.24.a.7.6. B.30.a.7.8.
A.D.S. (CUTTING).	B.27.a.4.8.
M.D.S. (St.CATHERINE)	G.15.a.4.4.

RIGHT BRIGADE.

Regtl. Aid Posts.	B.30.a.4.2. B.30.c.6.1.
A.D.S. (GUNPITS).	H.4.c.5.4.
M.D.S. (St.CATHERINE)	G.15.a.4.4.

O.C. 2/1st London Field Ambce. will command the XIIIth Corps Rest Station at AUBIGNY.

O.C. 2/2nd London Field Ambce. will be in charge of Main Dressing Station at ST. CATHERINE, G.15.a.2.5.

O.C. 2/3rd London Field Ambce. will command A.D.Ss. and all Forward Posts and personnel thereof, with Headquarters at ROCLINCOURT Dressing Station, A.29.c.7.4.

7th December, 1917.

Lieut.-Colonel,
A. A.& Q.M.G., 56th Divn.

Distribution as for Administrative
Instruction No. 1.

Appendix T
War Diary T

A.Q.S.462.

ADMINISTRATIVE INSTRUCTIONS No. 1.
in connection with Relief of 56th Divn. by 31st Divn.

Issued with reference to 56th Div. Order No. 142.

---

1. **EMBUSSING.** Busses will be drawn up on the right hand side of the road. Troops for embussing will be distributed along the road side on the opposite side of the road to the busses, as follows:-
For Seated Lorries: Groups of 20 men each per 80 yards of road space.
For Omnibus: "   25   "   80   "
An Omnibus seats 25, a seated Lorry seats 20.
Officers will be distributed among the vehicles forming the Convoy.
Embussing will be supervised by an officer detailed from Divl.H.Q., to whom O.C. Units will hand an embussing state.
Embussing table will be issued to all concerned. (Appendix "A").

2. **LIGHT RAILWAYS.** All entrainments by Light Railways will be under Brigade supervision.
Entrainment Table will be issued to all concerned. (Appendix "B")

3. **LOCATIONS.** A Location Table (Appendix "C") is attached, showing locations of Units on completion of their relief.

4. **FIRST LINE TRANSPORT.**

   (a) Transport Lines and Quartermasters Stores in the Left Divl. Area (A.27 & A.28.a) at present occupied by Infantry Brigades, R.E. Coys. and Div. M.G.Coy., must be vacated by Units of this Division as soon as they are required by Units of 31st Division.

   (b) Transport Lines and Quartermasters Stores in the Right Divl. Area are allotted as follows:-

Formation or Unit.	Location.	Billets from
H.Q., 167th Inf. Bde.)		Area
1 Bn. " ")	ROCLINCOURT,	Commandant,
167th M.G.Coy.)	A.29.c.	ROCLINCOURT.
3 Bns. 167th Inf. Bde.	A.28.c.	Area Commandant, VALLEY.
H.Q., 168th Inf. Bde.)	G.9.a.	
2 Bns. " ")		Town Major, St.CATHERINE.
2 Bns. " "	G.9.c. A.28.c.	" "
168th M.G.Coy.	G.3.d.	" "
169th Inf. Bde.	G.3.d.	" " and Area Commandant, VALLEY AREA.
1 Field Coy. R.E.	G.3.b.	Area Commandant, VALLEY.
1 "	G.9.d.	Town Major, St.CATHERINE
1 "	G.4.a.	Area Commandt. VALLEY.
193 (Div.) M.G.Coy.	G.3.b.	" "

   (c) Formations and Units concerned will place Billet Wardens in any of the above lines which they do not occupy whilst the Divn. is out of the Line.

P.T.O.

5. BATHS.

    (a)   Baths in the new area will be open ready for use and stocked with clean underclothing by 20th inst., under the arrangements of the Divl. Baths Officer, as follows:-

Place.	Troops to use.
ECOIVRES	168th Inf. Bde. Group.
FREVILLERS) RECOURT) MAGNICOURT)	169th " "
TINCQUES.	Divl. H.Q. & Pioneer Bn.

    (b)   167th Inf. Bde. and other Troops remaining in the Forward Area may use Baths run by the 31st Divn. These Units must draw their own clean underclothing from the Divl. Clean Clothing Store and take it to the Baths.

    (c)   S.C. Train will arrange to deliver at each Bath House in the Back Area (except ECOIVRES) a supply of coal so that the baths may be ready for use on the 20th inst.

    (d)   The Divl. Clean Clothing Store will remain at the Theatre, G.4.c.9, until accommodation has been arranged for it at ST. CATHERINE.

6. AREA EMPLOY. Officers, N.C.Os. and Men employed in the present area will be relieved by the 31st Divn. on the 18th inst., and will be sent back to their Units under Divl. arrangements. They will be rationed by their Units from 19th inst. inclusive.

7. AMMUNITION. Divl. Ammunition Dump for the provision of Ammunition, Grenades, etc., required for training purposes, will be established at TINCQUES by 20th inst. Application to draw upon this Dump will be made to Divl. H.Q. (A & Q).

8. SALVAGE. Salvage Dumps will be established in Brigade Areas near the Billets of the Divisional Train Company in each case. O.C. Salvage Coy. will arrange to attach 1 N.C.O. & 10 men to each Coy. of the Divl. Train for accommodation and rations from the 20th inst. They will report to O.C.Train Companies at 10 a.m. on that (date.

9. POLICE. M.M.P. will be attached to Inf. Bde. H.Qs. for duty, accommodation and rations from the 20th inst. as shown below:-

    167th. Inf. Bde.   1 Sgt. and 6 Corporals.
    168th " "   1 " " 3 "
    169th " "   1 " " 3 "

The party for 167 Inf. Bde. will remain in their present accommodation. They will report to the Staff Captain in each case for orders at 6 p.m. on the 19th inst.

    ANZIN,

10. VETERINARY. The Mobile Veterinary Section will remain at G.7.b.

11. ORDNANCE. The Stores and Shops of the I.A.D.O.S. will remain at ST. CATHERINE. A branch Issuing Depot will be opened on the 19th inst. at CHELERS for 169th Inf. Bde. Group.

12. "BOW-BELLS". The "Bow-Bells" will close at ECURIE after the performance on the 18th inst., and will re-open in the new Area at a place and date to be notified later.

13. CANTEEN. The Divl. Canteen will close at ECURIE on the 18th inst. and will re-open at ECOIVRES, with a branch at TINCQUES, on the 20th inst. Free Tea Canteens and Soup Kitchens will remain open in this Area until the relief has been completed.

    (14. Cinema)

14. **CINEMA.**

The Divl. Cinematograph will close at ECURIE after the last performance on the 18th, and will reopen at TINCQUES on a date to be notified later.

15. **LEAVE ARRANGEMENTS.**

Troops in the ECOIVRES and forward areas will entrain at MONT ST. ELOI in accordance with the instructions contained in XIII Corps Routine Order No. 1220.

Troops in the CHELERS-MONCHY BRETON Area will entrain either at AUBIGNY 1.20 a.m., TINCQUES 1.40 a.m., or LIGNY ST. FLOCHEL 2.06 a.m. on the day of embarkation. They must be paid before leaving their Units.

16. **AREA & TRENCH STORES.**

All Area and Trench Stores will be handed over, and Army Form W.3405 forwarded to this Office as soon as possible after relief.

All Soyer Stoves which were handed over by 31st Divn, will be handed back.

Chaff Cutters and Soyer Stoves which were issued by the D.A.D.O.S. will not be handed over.

Lieut.-Colonel,
A.A.& Q.M.G., 56th Divn.

15th December, 1917.

- DISTRIBUTION -

G.O.C.		TOWN MAJORS:-
167th Inf. Bde.	Div. Sig. Coy.	ST. CATHERINE
168th "	Div. Employment Coy.	ANZIN
169th "	Gas Officer.	ST. AUBIN
C.R.A.	Salvage Officer.	MAROEUIL
C.R.E.	Officer i/c "Bow-Bells".	BRAY
1/5th Cheshire Regt.	Officer i/c Baths & Laundry.	ECOIVRES
193 M.G.Coy.	Lt. SPICER, 1/5th Cheshire Regt.	TINCQUES.
C.C. Train.	N.C.O. i/c Divl.Canteen.	
A.D.M.S.	S.C.F. (C of E).	War
D.M.G.O.	S.C.F. (Non C of E).	Diary.
A.P.M.	French Mission.	
D.A.D.O.S.	Div. Supply Col.	
Camp Commandt.	31st Division.	
"G".	AREA COMMANDANTS:-	
D.A.D.V.S.	ROCLINCOURT	
XIII Corps 2 "Q"	PONT DU JOUR	
XIII Corps L.R.O.	BAILLEUL	
	NINE ELMS	
	ECURIE	
	VALLEY	
	MADAGASCAR. MAGNICOURT.	

APPENDIX "A".

EMBUSSING TABLE.

Serial No.	Date.	Units to Embuss.	Point where head of Bus Convoy will rest.	Time at which Units will be drawn up at place of Embussment ready to embuss.	Destination.
	Dec.				
1.	17th.	2nd London Regt.	AUBREY CAMP on LENS-ARRAS Road, facing S.W.	8.45 a.m.	MAGNICOURT EN COMTE.
2.	"	5th Cheshire Regt., less 2 Coys.; 60 All ranks of 2/3rd Fld. Ambce.	-do-	1.45 p.m.	TINQUES.
3.	18th	16th London Regt.	G.12.a.3.5., on BAILLEUL - ARRAS Rd. facing S.W.	1.45 p.m.	FREVILLERS.
4.	"	193 M. G. Coy.	Cross Roads in ROCLINCOURT.	2.45 p.m.	TINQUES.
5.	19th	Divl. H.Q. Divl. R.E. H.Q. Divl. Train H.Q. 247 Employmt Coy.	AUBREY CAMP on LENS - ARRAS Road, facing S.W.	10.45 a.m.	VILLERS CHATEL
6.	19th	169th Bde. H.Q. 5th London Regt.	G.12.a.3.5, on BAILLEUL-ARRAS Road, facing S.W.	12.45 p.m.	BAILLEUL & CHELERS.
7.	19th	9th London Regt. 169th M.G.Coy. 169th T.M.Bty. 2/3rd Field Ambce.	-do-	2.45 p.m.	MONCHY, BRETTON and CHELERS.

APPENDIX "B".

56th: IV. LIGHT RAIL WAY ENTRAINMENT TABLE.

Serial No.	Date	Station of Entrainment.	Time of Entrainment.	Units to Entrain.	Capacity of Train, All ranks.	Destinations of Trains.
1.	13th Dec.	DAYLIGHT RAILHEAD.	1 p.m.	14th London Regt. 193 M.G.Coy.	650	ROCLINCOURT & EC IVRES.
2.	"	"	4 p.m.	13th London Regt. 167 M.G.Coy.	650	ROCLINCOURT & BRAY.
3.	19th	"	12.30 p.m.	12th London Regt. 167th Inf. Bde. H.Q. 168th " " 512 Field Coy. R.E.	750	ROCLINCOURT - MARUEIL - EC IVRES.
4.	19th	"	3.30 p.m.	168 M.G.Coy. 168 T.M.Bty. 167 " " and Stragglers of Serial No. 3.	350	ROCLINCOURT-ST.CATHERINE AFZIN - MARUEIL - EC IVRES.

APPENDIX "C".

56th DIVISION LOCATION TABLE on completion of Relief by 31st DIVISION.

UNIT.	DESTINATION.	Date of Arrival DECEMBER	BILLETS from
Div.H.Q.Group.) Div.H.Q. Div.Arty.H.Q. Div.R.E.H.Q. Div.Train H.Q. 247 Employment Coy.)	VILLERS CHATEL and MINGOVAL.	19th	Camp Commandant.
1/5th Ches.Rgt.(less 2 Coys)	TINCQUES.	17th)	Town Major
103rd (Div) M.G.Coy.	"	18th)	TINCQUES.
167th Inf.Bde.Group.			
H.Q. 167th Inf.Bde.	TRAFALGAR CAMP C.3.d.7.4.	19th.	Area Comdt.VALLEY.
7th Middx.Regt.	AUBREY CAMP.	18th.	" "
8th ")	Forward Area,	(18th.	" "
1st London Regt.)	Transport Lines A.28.c.		
3rd "	WAKEFIELD CAMP.	19th	" "
167th M.G.Co.	AUBREY CAMP (for ROBERTS CAMP)	18th	" "
167th T.M.By.	ANZIN.	19th.	Town Major.ANZIN.
416th Field Co.R.E.	Wagon Lines, VALLEY AREA.	-	-
No.2 Co. Divl.Train.	MADAGASCAR.	-	-
2/1st London Field Ambce.	AUBIGNY.	-	-
168th Inf.Bde.Group.			
H.Q.168th Inf.Bde.	WHITE HO. ST.ELOI.	19th.	Town Major ECOIVRES.
4th London Regt.	VILLAGE CAMP,ECOIVRES.	19th.	T.M.BRAY.
12th "	YORK CAMP, "	19th.	T.M.ECOIVRES.
13th "	BRAY.	18th.	" "
14th "	LANCASTER CAMP,ECOIVRES.	18th.	" "
168th M.G.Co.	ST CATHERINE (for ROBERTS CAMP)	19th	" ST.CATHERINE.
168th T.M.By.	DURHAM CAMP,ECOIVRES.	19th.	" ECOIVRES.
512th Field Co.R.E.	MAROEUIL.	19th	" MAROEUIL.
No.3 Co.Div.Train.	MADAGASCAR.	-	-
2/5 London Field Ambce.	ANZIN.	19th.	" ANZIN.
169th Inf.Bde.Group.			
H.Q. 169th Inf.Bde.	CHELERS.	19th.	" TINCQUES.
2nd London Regt.	MAGNICOURT & HOUVELIN.	17th.	Area Cdt.MAGNICOURT.
5th "	BAILLEUL AU CORNAILLES.	19th.	T.M.TINCQUES.
9th "	MONCHY BRETON.	19th.	Area Cdt.MAGNICOURT.
16th "	FREVILLERS.	18th.	" "
169th M.G.Co.	CHELERS.	19th.	T.M.TINCQUES.
169th T.M.Bty.	"	19th	" "
513th Field Co.R.E.	Wagon Lines VALLEY AREA.		
No.4 Co.Div.Train	ROCOURT.) Between 17th		A.C.MAGNICOURT.
2/3rd London Fld.Ambce.	HOUVELIN.) and 19th.		" "
280th Bde.R.F.A.	G..b.	16th.	-
281st "	FREVIN CAPELLE.	16th.	-
56th D.A.C.	ANZIN ST AUBIN.	16th	-
1/1st Lon:Mob:Vet:Soc:	ANZIN, G.7.b.	-	-

Appendix U

SECRET. A.Q.S.462/1.

The Relief being cancelled Administrative Instructions No. 1 (AQS 462) of 15.12.17 in connection with Relief of 56th Division by 31st Division are cancelled.

16.12.17

Lieut.-Colonel,
A.A.& Q.M.G., 56th Divn.

Addssd. All recipients of Administrative Instructions No. 1.

SECRET. AQX 569/315.

Appendix V wanting. V

BACK AREA ACCOMMODATION.

1. During the next few days the 31st Divn. will be moving into the back area accommodation of the Left Divisional Area. This will necessitate the following moves by Units of this Division into the Right Divisional Back Area.

UNIT.	Move to (Place)	On (Date) December.	Billets from
Transpt. Lines & Qr-Mr. Stores. 168 Inf. Bde.	A.28.c.1.5. G.9.a.5.8.	19th	Area Commandt. VALLEY. Town Major, ST.CATHERINE
Transpt. Lines & Qr-Mr. Stores. 167 Inf. Bde.	ROCLINCOURT, A.29.c. REDCAR CAMP. A.28.c.	21st	Area Commdt. ROCLINCOURT " VALLEY.
169 Inf. Bde.	G.3.d. (Opposite TRAFALGAR CAMP).	"	Town Major, ST.CATHERINE
Hdqrs. & Transpt. Lines 1 Field Coy.RE.	G.3.d.	"	" "
" " 1 "	G.9.d.	"	" "
" " 1 "	G.3.c.2.7.	"	D.A.A.G., 56th Divn.
" " 193 M.G.Coy.	To be notified later.	"	
Transpt. Lines & Qr-Mr. Stores, 1/5th Cheshire Regt.	G.3.c.2.3.	"	D.A.A.G., 56th Divn.
Reserve Sections of M.G.Coys.	AUBREY CAMP.	"	Area Commdt. VALLEY
"Bow-Bells".	Theatre at G.4.c.0.9.	"	" "
Divl. Canteen.	Canteen at G.4.c.0.9.	"	" "
Cinema.	Hall at A.28.c.9.8.	"	" "
Gas School.	To be notified later.	"	" "
Salvage Dump.	"	"	" "
Soda Water Factory.	G.3.c.4.4.	"	" "

In all cases Units of this Division must be clear of their present areas by 10 a.m. on the dates named. Rear Parties must be left behind to hand over the area in a satisfactory state to Units of the 31st Divn.

Locations of Units new Qr.Mr's Stores must be reported to this Office and repeated to Divl. Train.

2. The accommodation in the Right Divl. Back Area is at present insufficient. It will be increased and improved under the direction of the C.R.E. in accordance with a scheme which has been prepared in this Office.

3. (a) The C.R.E. has appointed Lieut. J. E. AITKEN, 416 Field Coy.RE. to supervise the carrying out of the scheme referred to in para. 2. Lieut. AITKEN will coordinate the work and regulate the supply of material.
(b) (i) Material for hutments will be delivered by Lt. AITKEN direct to sites as it becomes available.
(ii) Other material for improvement and repair of existing accommodation will be drawn as allotted by Lt. AITKEN from C.R.E.Dump at ROCLINCOURT by Units Transport.
(c) All labour will be provided by Units concerned, under R.E. supervision to be arranged by Lt. AITKEN as required.

Lt.-Colonel
A.A.& Q.M.G., 56th D{

18th December, 1917.

P.T.O

Copies to:-　　　　　167 Inf. Bde.　(8)
　　　　　　　　　　168　"　　　(8)
　　　　　　　　　　169　"　　　(8)

　　　　　　　　　　1/5th Cheshire Regt.

　　　　　　　　　　　C.R.E. (4)

　　　　　　　　　　193 M. C. Coy.

　　　　　　　　　　　D.M.C.O.

　　　　　　　　　　Divisional Train.

　　　　　　　　　　Gas Officer.

　　　　　　　　　　Salvage Officer.

　　　　　　　　　　　　"C"

　　　　　　　　　　Officer i/c. "Bow-Bells".
　　　　　　　　　　　"　　"　Canteen.

　　　　　　　　XIII Corps "Q") For information.
　　　　　　　　31st Divn. "Q")

　　　　　　　　　　Area Commandant, VALLEY.
　　　　　　　　　　　　"　　　　　　ROCLINCOURT.

　　　　　　　　　　Town Major,　　ST.CATHERINE.

Appendix W

SECRET.

AQS 468.

ADMINISTRATIVE INSTRUCTIONS ISSUED WITH REFERENCE TO 56th DIVISION ORDER No. 144.

These Instructions will take effect from December 22nd, 1917, except where otherwise stated.

1. **TRENCH AMMUNITION.** The Divl. S.A.A. and Grenade Dump is at G.9.Central on ARRAS-LENS Road.

2. **R.E. MATERIAL.** Divl. R.E. Dump remains at ROCLINCOURT, A.29.c.8.2.

3. **BACK AREA ACCOMMODATION.**

In continuation of this Office AQX 560/315 of 18.12.17 areas are allotted as below:-

Unit.	Area.	Billets from
Reserve Battn. Right Inf. Bde.	AUBREY CAMP.	Area Commandt. VALLEY.
" " Left "	ROCLINCOURT.W.	" NINE ELMS.
Leading Bn. Reserve "	WAKEFIELD.	" VALLEY.
Hdqrs. & Reserve Coys. 1/5th Cheshire Regt.	ST. CATHERINE, (from 21st)	Town Major, ST. CATHERINE.
Reserve Section of M.G.Coys. in the Line.	- do -	" "
Transport Lines, 193rd M.G.Coy.	G.8.d.5.2. (from 21st)	" "
Hdqrs. of Divl. Employt. Co., Gas Officer, Salvage Officer.	G.9.b.3.5.	" "

4. **BATHS.** Baths are allotted as below:-

(a) ROCLINCOURT. A.28.d.7.8. Capacity 150 men per hour. Units billeted in VALLEY & ROCLINCOURT Areas.

(b) ST. CATHERINE. Capacity 60 Men per hour. Units billeted in ST. CATHERINE, MADAGASCAR & ANZIN Areas.

(c) MAROEUIL. Units billeted in MAROEUIL & ST. AUBIN Areas.

(d) H.1.a.7.3. (near Right Bde. H.Q.). Capacity 60 Men per hour. Units billeted in Right Bde. Area.

(e) TUNNEL DUMP. B.15.c.40. Capacity - 30 Men per hour. Available on Sunday, Tuesday, Thursday and Saturday mornings for Units billeted in Left Bde. area. They are allotted to 31st Divn. at other times.

MAROEUIL Baths will be stocked with clean underclothing under Divl. arrangements. Units using the other Baths must draw clean underclothing from the Divl. Clean Clothing Store and take it to the Baths, returning soiled underclothing as early as possible.

Application for Bath Allotments to be made to N.C.O. i/c. Baths in all cases.

P.T.O.

5. **SALVAGE.** The Divl. Salvage Dump is at G.9.b.3.5.

6. **GUM BOOTS.** Gum boots will continue to be drawn from, and returned to, the Store at ROCLINCOURT, A.29.c.9.2., which will be in charge of 31st Divn.

7. **DIVISIONAL CANTEEN** will be at G.4.c.0.9. from 21st.
   The "Free Tea" Canteens on the Ridge Track are being taken over by the 31st Divn. and are available for 56th Divn.

8. **SOUP KITCHEN.** at TUNNEL DUMP is being taken over by 31st Divn. and may be used by 56th Divn.

9. **MEDICAL ARRANGEMENTS.** will be as at present.

10. **"BOW-BELLS"** will open at Theatre G.4.c.0.9. on 22nd December.

11. **CINEMA** will open at the Hall at A.28.c.9.8. on 22nd December.

12. **GASSED CLOTHING STORE** and **SOLDER KILNS.** Orders regarding these will be issued later.

[signature]
Lieut.-Colonel,
A.A.& Q.M.G., 56th Division.

20th December, 1917.

- DISTRIBUTION. -

G.O.C.	D.M.G.O.	
167th Inf. Bde. (8)	D.A.D.V.S.	AREA COMMANDANTS:-
168th " (8)	D.A.D.O.S.	
169th " (8)	A.P.M.	ROCLINCOURT.
56th Div. Arty. (4)	Camp	PONT DU JOUR
5th Cheshires. (1)	Commandant.	BAILLEUL
C.R.E. (4)	"G"	NINE ELMS
193 M.G..Coy. (1)	Signals.	ECURIE
Divl. Train. (5)	Employt.Coy.	VALLEY
A.D.M.S. (4)	Gas Officer.	
	Salvage	TOWN MAJORS:-
	Offr. i/c.Baths & Laundry.	
	O.C. "Bow-Bells".	ST. CATHERINE
	O.C. Canteen.	MAROEUIL.
	S.C.F.(C.of E.)	
	" (Non C. of E.)	
	French Mission.	Lt. SPICER.
	31st Divn. "Q".	

167th Inf. Bde.
168th   "
169th   "
56th Divl. Arty.
5th Cheshire Regt.
C.R.E.
A.D.M.S.
Officer i/c, Baths & Laundry.
31st Div. "Q".

Appendix X War Diary A.Q.S.468.

Para. 4 (e) of "Administrative Instructions issued with reference to 56th Div. Order No. 144" (this Office AQS 468 of today) should be amended to read as below:-

(e)   TUNNEL DUMP B.15.c.4.0. - Capacity 30 Men per hour.

Available for the whole day on Sundays, Tuesdays and Thursdays and for the morning only on Saturdays, for Units billeted in left Brigade Area.   These Baths are allotted to 31st Divn. at other times.

20.12.17.

Lieut.-Colonel,
A.A.& Q.M.G., 56th Divn.

Appendix Y

56th DIVISION.
LIGHT RAILWAY ENTRAINMENT TABLE

A.Q.G.468.

Issued with reference to 56th Divl Order No. 144.

ALL MOVES ARE FROM DAYLIGHT RAILHEAD ON 22nd INSTANT.

Serial No.	Time of Entrainment	Units to Entrain	Capacity of Train. All ranks.	Destination of Trains.
1.	10.30 a.m.	1/2nd Bn. London Rgt.	800	St. AUBIN.
2.	3 p.m.	1/8th Bn. Middlesex Rgt.) 167 Inf. Bde. H.Q. (less personnel waiting until completion of relief.)	800	SOLINGHURST. MARQUEIL.
3.	6 p.m.	1/1st Bn. London Rgt. 167 M.G. Coy. 167 L.T.M. Battery Balance of Brigade Hdqrs.	670	SOLINGHURST AND MARQUEIL.

20th December, 1917.

Lieut.-Colonel,
A.A.& Q.M.G., 56th Divn.

DISTRIBUTION:-

167 Inf. Bde. (5 copies).
XIII Corps Light Railway Officer.
51st Divn. "Q".

Appendix *Z* War Diary AQS 5.

LOCATION TABLE.
56th DIVISION.
28.12.17.

Unit	HEADQUARTERS.		TRANSPORT LINES.
Divl. H.Q.	G.3.b.7.3.		—
			Camp:-
167th Inf. Bde. H.Q.			DOVER. A.29.c.1.7.
7th Middx. Regt.	In		REDCAR. A.28.c.5.8.
8th "	the		" "
1st London Regt.	Line.		CALAIS. A.29.c.2.9.
3rd "			REDCAR. A.28.c.5.8.
167th M.G.Coy.			CALAIS. A.29.c.2.9.
167th T.M.Bty.			" "
168th Inf. Bde. H.Q.	LOUEZ		COLLINGWOOD. A.28.c.1.2.
4th London Regt.	ST.AUBIN		" "
12th "	MAROEUIL	In	" "
13th "	WAKEFIELD CAMP	Reserve	PORT- G.9.a.5.7.
14th "	MAROEUIL		LAND. "
168th M.G.Coy.	ANZIN		" "
168th T.M.Bty.	"		" "
169th Inf. Bde. H.Q.			NELSON. G.9.b.3.7.
2nd London Regt.	In		" "
5th "	the		" "
9th "	Line.		" "
16th "			" "
169th M.G.Coy.			" "
169th T.M.Bty.			" "
193rd (Div) M.G.Coy.	G.8.d.5.2.		G.8.d.5.2.
1/5th (E of C) Cheshire R.	ST.CATHERINE.		GROPI. G.3.c.3.0.
56th Divl. Arty.	G.3.b.7.3.		—
280th Bde. R.F.A.	H.1.c.8.0.		G.11.c.
281st "	L.6.a.4.2.		L.6.a.4.2.
D.A.C.	ANZIN.		
C.R.E.	G.3.b.7.3.		
416th Fld.Coy.R.E.	—		EDINBURGH. G.3.c.2.3.
512th "	—		PLYMOUTH. G.9.b.0.0.
513th "	—		HARDY. G.9.a.9.5.
A.D.M.S.	G.3.b.7.3.		—
2/1st London Fld.A.	AUBIGNY.		—
2/2nd "	ST.CATHERINE.		—
2/3rd "	ANZIN.		—
D.A.D.O.S.	ST.CATHERINE.		—
Divl. Train.	G.3.a.6.5.		CHATHAM. G.3.a.0.5.
H.Q. Coy.	G.3.a.1.3.		GREENWICH. G.3.a.1.3.
No. 2 Coy.	A.26.d.7.2.		SHEERNESS. A.26.d.6.2.
No. 3 "	A.26.d.6.2.		" "
No. 4 "	A.26.d.5.2.		" "
247th Employment Coy.	G.3.b.7.3.		—
56th Divl. Supply Col.	TINCQUES.		—
Mobile Veterinary Sec.	ANZIN.		—

REINFORCEMENTS will be despatched as follows:-

(1) For Units in the Line — To Transport Lines.
(2) For other Units, not) — To H.Q. of their
    in the Line.)   Unit.

Dundas
Captain,
D.A.A.G., 56th Division.

UNIT.	Strength. 1.12.17.		Increase.		Decrease.		Strength. 1.1.18.	
	O.	O.R.	O.	O.R.	O.	O.R.	O.	O.R.
Divl. H.Q.	19	94	1	3	1	11	19	86
167th Inf. Bde. H.Q.	3	21	-	-	-	-	3	21
7th Middlesex Regt.	41	760	6	23	2	49	45	734
8th "	35	571	2	196	7	82	30	685
1st London Regt.	43	740	1	41	9	70	35	711
3rd "	37	813	1	17	1	63	37	767
167th M.G.Coy.	10	146	4	37	1	4	13	179
167th T.M.Bty.	4	43	-	3	-	-	4	46
168th Inf. Bde. H.Q.	3	20	-	1	-	-	3	21
4th London Regt.	32	622	4	120	1	35	35	707
12th "	28	754	6	49	1	52	33	751
13th "	36	850	5	48	2	51	39	847
14th "	42	949	9	84	2	133	49	900
168th M.G.Coy.	9	170	-	9	-	11	9	168
168th T.M.Bty.	3	46	-	-	-	-	3	46
169th Inf. Bde. H.Q.	3	20	-	-	-	-	3	20
2nd London Regt.	32	529	4	162	-	35	36	656
5th "	40	730	1	9	7	54	34	685
9th "	31	789	7	11	4	64	34	736
16th "	30	592	5	130	6	34	29	688
169th M.G.Coy.	11	167	1	17	1	11	11	173
169th T.M.Bty.	4	46	1	-	3	24	2	22
5th Cheshire Regt.	39	972	-	118	3	103	36	987
193rd M.G.Coy.	10	132	2	38	-	2	12	168
H.Q. R.A.	5	19	-	-	1	2	4	17
280th Bde. R.F.A.	29	781	9	7	6	41	32	747
281st "	27	810	6	5	3	62	30	753
D.A.C.	14	580	-	8	-	28	14	560
H.Q. R.E.	2	10	-	-	1	-	1	10
416th (Edin) Fld.Coy.RE.	9	208	-	3	-	3	9	208
512th (Lond) "	7	195	-	13	1	6	6	202
513th (") "	8	207	-	4	1	9	7	202
Divl. Signal Coy.	10	269	-	6	1	4	9	271
Divl. Train.	21	364	3	6	4	10	20	360
Medical Units.	26	517	5	11	7	8	24	520
Mobile Veterinary Sec.	1	25	-	-	-	7	1	18
247th Employment Coy.	-	284	1	3	-	5	1	282

56th Division. Casualties for month of December, 1917.

Dec.	UNIT.	OFFICERS. Killed.	Wounded.	Missing.	O.Rs. K.	W.	M.	Remarks.
1st.	1st Londons.	-	-	-	3	19	2	
	3rd "	-	-	-	-	15	-	Accidentally.
	4th "	-	-	-	-	6	-	
	12th "	-	-	-	1	6	2	
	13th "	-	-	-	-	1	-	
	168th M.G.Coy.	-	-	-	2	4	-	
	5th Londons.	-	-	-	2	5	-	
	169th M.G.Coy	-	-	-	3	8	-	
	5th Cheshires.	-	-	-	-	1	-	
	280th Bde. RFA.	-	-	-	3	13	-	
	281st "	-	-	-	1	1	-	
	513th (London) Fld.Coy.	-	-	-	2	3	4	
	56th Div. Signal Coy.	-	-	-	-	-	-	
2nd	1st Londons.	-	2/Lt.L.N.THOMPSON.	-	2	3	-	
	3rd "	-	2/Lt.G.W.CHARLESWORTH.	-	8	9	-	
	12th "	-	-	-	-	1	-	
	13th "	-	-	-	-	-	-	
	14th "	-	-	-	-	-	-	
	5th "	-	2/Lt.J.F.MAGINN. (18th Londons).	-	3	18	1	
	169th T.M.Bty.	-	-	-	2	1	-	
	7th Middx.	-	-	-	1	4ø	-	ø Includes 1 at duty.
	5th Cheshires.	-	-	-	-	2ø	-	ø At duty.
	513th (London) Fld. Coy.	-	-	-	1	1	-	
3rd	280th Bde. RFA.	-	-	-	2	-	-	
	512th (London) Fld.Coy.	-	-	-	-	1	-	
4th	2/3rd London Fld. Ambce.	-	-	-	1	-	-	
6th	280th Bde. RFA.	-	-	-	-	3	-	
8th	7th Middx.	-	-	-	-	-	-	
	4th Londons.	-	-	-	1	1	-	Accidentally.
9th	13th Londons.	-	-	-	1	1	-	
10th	7th Middx.	-	-	-	-	3	-	

(1)

P.T.O.

		OFFICERS.			O. Rs.			Remarks.
Dec.	UNIT.	Killed.	Wounded.	Missing.	K.	W.	M.	
11th	7th Middx.	-	-	-	1	2	-	
	4th Londons.	-	-	-	-	-	-	Accidentally, by/ revolver.
12th	7th Middx.	-	-	-	-	2	-	On patrol.
	4th Londons.	-	-	-	-	1	-	Accidentally.
	"	-	-	-	-	1	-	
	416 (Edin) Fld. Coy	-	-	-	-	1	-	
13th	3rd Londons.	-	-	-	1	1	-	Accidentally.
	9th "	-	-	-	-	2	-	
	280th Bde. RFA.	-	-	-	1	1	-	
14th	5th Londons.	-	-	-	1	1	-	
	281st Bde. RFA.	-	-	-	3	-	-	
15th	16th Londons.	-	-	-	-	2	-	
	5th Cheshires.	-	-	-	-	2	-	
16th	7th Middx.	-	-	-	1	1	-	
	14th Londons.	-	-	-	-	2	-	
	16th "	-	-	-	2	1	-	
	169th M.G.Coy.	-	-	-	-	1	-	
17th	3rd Londons.	-	-	-	1	1	-	
	167th T.M.Bty.	-	-	-	-	1	-	
18th	8th Middx.	-	-	-	-	1	-	
	3rd Londons.	-	-	-	-	1	-	
19th	1st Londons.	-	-	-	-	1	-	
	5th "	-	-	-	-	2	-	
20th	1st Londons.	Major L.L.PARGITER ∅ Capt. H.A.EILOART,MC ∅ Capt. H.W.GOODWAY. ∅ Lieut.J.H.W.WYATT. ∅ Capt. J.H.BARRY, DSO.,MC. ∅✱ Rev. R.A.P. COLBOURNE. ∅✱	-	-	4∅	-∅	-	Wounded (Gas). ✱ Medical Offr.attached. ✱ C.F. attached.
21st	13th Londons.	-	-	-	-	2	-	
	280th Bde. RFA.	-	-	-	-	2	-	
	1st Londons.	-	-	-	-	5	-	
	4th Londons.	-	-	-	-	1	-	
	9th "	-	-	-	1	1	-	
22nd	4th Londons.	-	-	-	1	-	-	

(Contd.)

(Contd.)

			OFFICERS.		O.Rs.			
Dec.	UNIT.	Killed.	Wounded.	Missing.	K.	W.	M.	Remarks.
23rd	2nd Londons.	-	-	-	1	-	-	
	9th "	-	-	-	-	3	-	
	169th T.M. Bty.	-	-	-	1	1	-	
	2/3rd London Fld. Ambce.	-	-	-	1	1	-	
25th	12th Londons.	-	-	-	-	1	-	
26th	4th Londons.	2/Lt. E.L.STUCKEY (17th Ldns)	-	-	-	1	-	
	12th "	-	2/Lt. (A/Capt.)S.G.BEER,MC.	-	-	-	-	
	14th "	-	-	-	1	1	-	
28th	14th Londons.	-	-	-	1	-	-	
	16th "	-	2/Lt. T.J.M.VAN DER LINDE⌀	-	-	-	-	⌀ 9th Londons attached.

Secret.

War Diary

Administrative Branch

56th Division.

Period 1st to 31st January 1918

Volume XXIV

WAR DIARY
or
INTELLIGENCE SUMMARY

Army Form C. 2118.

Vol XXIV Page 1

Place	Date	Hour	Summary of Events and Information	Remarks and references to Appendices
VICTORY CAMP RUCLINCOURT	1.1.18		Administrative Instruction No 1 (Appendix A) and No 2 (Appendix B) issued in connection with relief of 56 Div by 62nd Div. Following relief carried out:- 5th & 16th London from Reffuel & Barorie to line in relief of 9th and London, to Red Line and Support respectively.	
	2.1.18		Administrative Instruction No 3 (Appendix C) and No 4 (Appendix D) in connection with above relief.	
	3.1.18		Following Inter Brigade Relief carried out, 185th Inf Bde to Reserve to line in relief of 1/6th Inf Bde to ~~~ Divl Reserve. Dispositions:- 185th Inf Bde :- 4 London Rifles & 13th London left front, 14 London Support, 12th London Reserve	
	4.1.18		Following relief carried out 1st London 88 Middx to line in relief, 3rd London & 7th Middx to Reserve and support respectively.	
	5.1.18		Units of 62nd Divn commenced to move into the forward area. 1/6th Inf Bde less 2 Batts moved back to the FREVILLERS Area. Administrative Instruction No 5 issued (Appendix E)	
	6.1.18		185 Inf Bde relieved in the line by the 187th Inf Bde of 62nd Divn. 185 Inf Bde moved back to the MAROEUIL Area in Reserve	
	7.1.18		Arrangements for Scheme "A" issued, for Entrainment of Division whilst in G.H.Q Reserve (Appendix F)	

Army Form C. 2118.

WAR DIARY
or
INTELLIGENCE SUMMARY
(Erase heading not required.)

Page 2.

Place	Date	Hour	Summary of Events and Information	Remarks and references to Appendices
VICTORY CAMP	7/1/18 (contd)		Scheme 'C' issued with reference to move of Division by Tactical Trains from Reserve Area to ECURIE (Appendix 6).	
ROELINCOURT	8.1.18		168th Inf Bde (less 1 Batn.) moved back into the MONCHY-BRETON Area. 167th Inf Bde returned in the line by the 185th Inf Bde and moved to MAROEUIL Area in Div. Reserve.	
VILLERS-CHATEL	9.1.18		167th Inf Bde (less 1½ Bns) moved back to CHELERS Area. G.O.C. 62nd Div took over Command of Right Div. front of XIII Corps. 56th Div in howr'n Corps Reserve Area as G.H.Q Reserve, excepting 1 Brden & each Brigade, 2 Fd Coys and 1 Co. 5/Cheshire Regt and Div Artillery who remain in forward Area. H Q of Div moved to VILLERS-CHATEL	
	10.1.18		Gk Londons from forward area returned 186½ Inf Brigade in back Area	
	11.1.18		During the thaw, a warning message issued to all concerned in preparation for the taking of air precaution action at midnight 11th-12th.	
	12.1.18		Extracts from List of New Year's Honours Gazette issued. (Appendix H) and Location report (Appendix 1)	
	13.1.18		No change	

Army Form C. 2118.

Page 3

WAR DIARY
or
INTELLIGENCE SUMMARY

(Erase heading not required.)

Place	Date	Hour	Summary of Events and Information	Remarks and references to Appendices
VILLERS -CHATEL	14.1.18		"Resume normal traffic" issued in connection with Rest precautions.	
	15.1.18.		The Headquarters 1) to 280th and 281st Bde. moved back.	
	16.1.18		Rest precautions issued at 6am. Following moves carried out; the three Battns in the forward area, 3rd, 12th and 2nd London relieved by the 1st, 11th and 5th Londons respectively and proceeded to reserve area.	
	17.1.18		No change	
	18.1.18		Location table issued (Appendix K).	
	19.1.18			
	20.1.18		no change	
	21.1.18			
	22.1.18			
	23.1.18.		No change	
	24.1.18		Resume normal Traffic issued 6am. Following reliefs 1st Battn working in forward area carried out. 8th Middx relieved 1st London, 4 Londons relieved 14th Londons, 16th Ldn. relieved 5th Ldn. Battn then relieved proceeded to villages in Reserve Area. Vacated by Relieving Units.	
	25.1.18.		Location Report issued (Appendix L).	

Army Form C. 2118.

WAR DIARY
or
INTELLIGENCE SUMMARY
(Erase heading not required.)

Page 4

Instructions regarding War Diaries and Intelligence Summaries are contained in F. S. Regs., Part II. and the Staff Manual respectively. Title Pages will be prepared in manuscript.

Place	Date	Hour	Summary of Events and Information	Remarks and references to Appendices
VILLERS CHATEL	26.1.18 27.1.18		No change.	
	28.1.18.		Reorganisation of Divn into Bdes of 9 Bns commenced. 3", 9" + 12" Londons read draft to Training Bns.	
	29.1.18		Reorganisation continues. Instructions Nos 1 + 2 have been issued by Divn in this connection — vide attached Appendices "M" + "N".	
	30.1.18		Reorganisation completed. Three T.F. of 3 Bns. that have left the Divn remain with the Divn + are attached to respective Inf. Bdes.	
	31.1.18		Arrangements being made for the renewal of gunnery instruction within the Army Aprenticeship Scheme. Orders issued that about 50 men under instruction in the Size Area. Murphey has commenced.	

John Sulter

Lieut Colonel
AA+QMG 1/5 Division

56th DIVISION
AQS 476
Appendix A — War Diary

ADMINISTRATIVE INSTRUCTIONS No. 1.

in connection with Relief by 62nd Division.

1. **ADMINISTRATION.**

   (a) The Divl. Area is divided into sub-areas which are administered by Area Commandants. The portions of the Area forward of the Eastern Boundaries of BAILLEUL AREA and PONT DU JOUR AREA are administered by the Left and Right Line Brigades respectively.

   (b) Map (Appendix "A") attached (to one copy only) shows Divl. Area Boundaries and the Sub-Area Boundaries.

   (c) Area Commandants' Offices are located as follows:-

Area	Officer	Location
MAROEUIL AREA	Lt.Col. H. A. FIELDING.	F.27.d.7.2.
ST. AUBIN "	2/Lt. J. C. HICKMAN.	L.10.b.3.6.
MADAGASCAR "	Lt.Col. W. G. FLEMING.	L.6.a.3.3.
ANZIN "	Lt. R.S.F. WELLS.	G.7.b.8.9.
ST.CATHERINE "	Major H.A.N.FYERS, M.V.O.	G.9.c.9.0.
VALLEY "	Capt. J. VERTH.	G.4.a.1.7.
ROCLINCOURT "	Capt. T. HAWKINS.	A.28.d.Central G.6.d.8.7.
BAILLEUL "	Major W. JOYCE.	G.6.d.8.7.
PONT DU JOUR "	Major E.G. KENNING.	G.6.d.8.7.

   The ST. AUBIN & MADAGASCAR AREAS are being amalgamated.

2. **ACCOMMODATION.**

   (a) Appendix "B" attached shows available accommodation in the Area
   (b) Divl. Location Table attached. (Appendix "C").

3. **LIGHT RAILWAYS.**

   (a) (i) Office of Divl. Tramway Officer is at Office of XIII Corps Traffic Officer at ROCLINCOURT, A.29.d.2.5.
   (ii) Units requiring truckage send indents to Divl. Tramway Officer by 3.00 p.m. the day previous to that on which truckage is required. These indents state:-
   Name of Unit.
   Place, Date, and Time at which Trucks are required.
   Nature and Amount of Material to be transported.
   Destination of Trucks.
   (iii) Applications for trains for Reliefs, etc., should be made to:-
   Capt. GRAVES, XIII Corps Lt. Rly. Officer, XIII Corps H.

   (b) ROUTES. Shown on attached Map. (Appendix "A").

   All lines are worked by Tractor with the exception of the TYNE & OPPY Branches which run from B.23.a.0.7. to B.24.a.7.0. and B.18.a.Central respectively. These two branches are worked by man power.

   Forward of DAYLIGHT RAILHEAD (B.19.b.7.2.) and Cutting in B.26.b. the Light Railway cannot be used in daylight.
   A line is under construction as follows:-
   H.1.Central - H.8.b.3.3. - H.9.b.8.5. - GAVRELLE.

(c) **PASSENGER SERVICE.** The following is the Passenger Service on the Light Railways:-

ECOIVRES.	8.00		17.45
MAROEUIL.	8.20		18.02
ARTILLERY CORNER. (L.12.a.0.7.)	8.43		18.28
MILL ST. (G.8.a.0.3.)	8.50		18.35
DISTILLERY. (G.15.a.8.3.)	9.00	15.30	18.45
ST. CATHERINE JUNC.			
CHANTECLER.		15.58	
CUTTING.		16.10	
ROCLINCOURT. Arr.	9.25		19.10
Dep.	9.30		21.30
ASHFORD JUNC.			
CHANTECLER.	10.05		
ST. CATHERINE JUNC.			
DISTILLERY.	10.30		21.35
MILL ST.	10.38		22.04
ARTILLERY CORNER.	10.45		22.12
MAROEUIL.	11.10		22.40
ECOIVRES.	11.30		23.00

(d) **RATION TRAINS.**

    4.30 p.m. from ROCLINCOURT running to WILLERVAL and also to BAILLEUL, ARLEUX.
    3.30 p.m. from CHANTECLER JUNC. (G.6.d.) to BAILLEUL & TYNE & OPPY Branches.

4. **WATER.**

(a) One Officer of the Division is appointed Divisional Water Service Officer.

(b) There are two main pipe lines serving the Area:-
  (i) From ANZIN to ECURIE, and thence over the RIDGE to B.17.c.
  (ii) From ST. NICHOLAS to CHANTECLER AREA.

(c) Water Points in the Divisional Area:-

B.19.b.9.3.	Bottle Filler.	A.28.c.4.7.	Stand pipe.
H.1.d.4.3.	Well.	A.28.c.1.6.	Water Trough.
H.2.a.7.1.	Stand pipe & bottle filler.	A.26.d.8.0.	Stand pipe.
H.1.a.3.1.	Horse Trough (at present closed).	A.28.d.7.7.	(Stand pipe - (Bottle Filler.
B.19.d.2.5.	Bottle Filler.		
B.15.c.6.0.	"	G.3.b.8.1.	Stand pipe.
B.16.a.2.2.	"	G.5.b.2.9.	Stand pipe.
B.17.d.2.2.	"		

A Well has been bored and is nearing completion at H.5.a.2.7.

/AMMUNITION SUPPLY.

(Contd.)

5. **AMMUNITION SUPPLY.**

   (a) DIVL. A.R.P. at DUMP SPUR, G.11.b.8.3.
   Delivery to the A.R.P. by Light Railway.

   (b) DIVL. S.A.A. & GRENADE DUMP at DUMP SPUR, G.11.b.8.3.
   Delivery to the Dump by Light Railway or Lorries from XIII Corps Dump at MAROEUIL.

   (c) (i) Left Bde. Dump. CRUCIFIX JUNC., BAILLEUL.
   Delivery by Light Railway or by Road, from Divl. Dump.
   The Evening Ration Train passes the Dump and arrangements can conveniently be made to have ammunition put on this Train and sent forward to Battn. H.Q., etc.
   (ii) Right Brigade Dump. POINT DU JOUR, H.9.a.7.7.
   Delivery to Dump by road from Divl. Ammn. Dump. The GAVRELLE Light Railway Line (under construction) will pass near the Dump.

6. **R. E. MATERIAL SUPPLY.**

   (a) Main Divl. R.E. Dump. ROCLINCOURT, A.29.c.8.2.
   Delivery by Light Railway from XIII Corps Dump, MAROEUIL.
   This is a C.R.E. Dump and material can only be drawn with C.R.E. Authority.

   (b) Left Sector Dump. CUTTING DUMP, H.27.a.3.7.
   Delivery to Dump by Light Railway from Main Divl. Dump under R.E. arrangements.

   (c) Right Sector Dump. TONIC DUMP, H.29.d.7.6.
   Delivery to Dump by Road under R.E. arrangements.

   (d) SAPPER & TONIC DUMPS are treated as Brigade Dumps. Material can be drawn either with Brigade or R.E. authority.

   (e) The system of supply at present in use is:-

   (i) Brigades indent on Affiliated Field Companies.
   (ii) Field Companies notify where material can be drawn, and are responsible for keeping CUTTING & TONIC DUMPS supplied.

7. **SUPPLIES.**

   (a) SUPPLY RAILHEAD. ECURIE STN. A.20.Central.

   (i) Pack Train arrives about 8.00 a.m.

   (ii) Rations are drawn by Train Transport to Refilling Points and delivered to Units' Q.M.Stores by Train Transport.

   (iii) Coal Dump is at ST. CATHERINE.
   Coal delivered to Dump by Light Railway and drawn from Dump by First Line Transport.

   (b) RATIONS, WATER & COOKING in the Forward Areas.

   (1) Right Bde. Sector.

   Rations go up by Road by dark. Route followed is as follows:-
   ST.NICHOLAS-POINT DU JOUR-the GAVRELLE road as far as "Battn. H.Q. Line" B.30.a.2.1.

   WATER. Two 100 gall. Water Tanks are situated on the GAVRELLE road at B.H.Q. Line, B.30.a.2.1., and are filled nightly by Water Carts.

   COOKING. Food for the Line Battns. is cooked in cookhouses in the vicinity of Battn. H.Qs.

   P.T.O.

(ii) **Left Brigade Sector.**

Rations
For Bde. H.Q. & Units in vicinity of TUNNEL DUMP:- By Light Railway train leaving ROCLINCOURT at 4.30 p.m. Rations dumped at TUNNEL DUMP STN. The train then goes on to WILLERVAL.

For Line & Support Battns. By Light Railway Train leaving CHANTECLER JUNC. at 3.30 p.m. This is drawn by tractor as far as OPPY-TYNE JUNC., B.23.a.0.7. Trucks are pushed on from there. The tractor starts back from OPPY-TYNE JUNC. two hours after arriving there. Trucks should be pushed back to the Junction by then.

WATER. There are Water Points well forward in the trenches

COOKING. There are Cook-houses in the vicinity of Line Battn. H.Qs.

(iii) **General.**

Light Railway Trains can be stopped at any point "en route". Personnel going up with Rations should know at what point rations are to be dumped. On the regular Ration train 4 trucks are reserved for each Battn. using the train each day. Indents for additional trucks for "Relief Days", etc., should be made to Divl. Tramways Officer, ROCLINCOURT, the previous afternoon.

8. **BATHS.**

(a) Operated by 56th Divn.
   (i) ROCLINCOURT. 150 per hour.
   (ii) CHANTECLER BATHS. 60 "
      (H.1.a.7.3.)
   (iii) MAROEUIL. 100 "
   (iv) TUNNEL DUMP BATHS. 30 "
      (B.15.c.5.0.)
   (v) ST. CATHERINE. 80 "

(b) Operated by T.M. ANZIN - Baths at ANZIN. (Coal for Units of 56th Divn. bathing is supplied by 56th Divn.)

9. **CLEAN LINEN.**

(a) Divl. Clean Linen Store is situated at ST. CATHERINE.
(b) Dirty linen is washed at XIII Corps Laundry, MAROEUIL.
(c) Divl. Foden Thresh Disinfector is located at XIII Corps Laundry, MAROEUIL.

10. **SOCK DRYING ROOMS.** One in each Brigade Transport Lines.

11. **GUM BOOT STORE.** Units draw direct from Corps Gum Boot Store and Drying Room, ROCLINCOURT, A.29.c.9.3. This is run by 31st Divn.

12. **GASSED CLOTHING STORE.**

(1) Issues will be made from the following Stores on certificate signed by Os.C. Units concerned for men whose clothing has become tainted by contact with Yellow Cross Gas.

/TUNNEL DUMP.

(Contd.)

(a) TUNNEL DUMP at B.15.c.3.2.

100 Complete sets of S.D. and underclothing i/c. Divn. on left of 56th Divn. Can be used by 56th Divn. in emergency.

(b) The Gun Pits at A.D.S. H.4.9.5.4.

100 complete sets of S.D. and underclothing i/c. a R.A.M.C. Officer.

(c) At each Battery Gun Position

50 complete sets of S.D. and underclothing for the Battery concerned

(d) Divisional Reserve.

(2). Tainted Clothing is sent to XIII Corps Gassed Clothing Disinfecting Plant at ECURIE DISTILLERY, A.28.a.4.4. All such clothing will be clearly marked TAINTED WITH GAS.

(3). At (1) (a) and (b) 50 suits of Service Dress are maintained for issue to men whose clothes have got wet through on patrols. Suits are issued on C.O's certificate.

13. CANTEENS & RECREATION.

(a) Divl. Canteen. G.3.b.9.2.
(b) Divl. Theatre. G.3.b.9.3. Capacity 400.
(c) Divl. Cinema. A.29.c.9.9. " 350.
(d) XIII Corps Officers Club. A.29.c.3.9.
(e) Also Y.M.C.A. and Church Army Huts.
(f) DECHET Recreation Huts have been promised by XIII Corps as follows:-
    One for MAROEUIL   ) Y.M.C.A. have promised to run catering
    One for AUBREY CAMP)   in both Huts.
(g) Large Hut for Theatre at MAROEUIL has been promised by Corps
(h) 31st Divn. allow this Divn. to use their "Free Tea" Canteens at bottom of Ridge Track and at Daylight Railhead.

14. CHURCH. There is a C. of E. Church opposite VICTORY CAMP, G.3.b.9.2

15. SOUP KITCHENS. Operated in the Forward Areas under Bde. Arrangements. At TUNNEL DUMP there is a Soup Kitchen run by 31st Dv & available for use by 56th Divn.

16. D.A.D.O.S. STORE. Established at ST. CATHERINE.

17. SALVAGE.

(a) Divl. Salvage Dump is located at G.9.b.2.8.
(b) Units send Salvage direct to this Dump. Salvage from Forward Area is sent back by returning ration limbers in Right Bde. Sector.
    In the Left Bde. Sector it is sent down by returning Ration Train to CHANTECLER, and is then met by limbers and taken to the Dump.

12. SOLDER. (a) A Solder Kiln is established at ST. CATHERINE, G.15.a.8.
            (b) A kiln is being built at G.3.b.9.5.

19. MEDICAL. (a) A.D.S. (Left Sector) CUTTING, B.27.a.4.8.
             (b) A.D.S. (Right Sector) GUNPITS, H.4.c.5.4.
    (A new A.D.S. is being constructed at POINT DU JOUR, H.9.a.9.9.)
             (c) M.B.S. ST. CATHERINE, G.15.a.2.5.

20. AREA EMPLOY. List of Area Employ found by 56th Divn to be relieved by 62nd Divn. attached. (Appendix "D").

P.T.O.

21. **LEAVE ARRANGEMENTS.**

(a) Leave Train leaves MONT ST. ELOI STATION 1.32 a.m. on day previous to embarkation.
Light Railway train leaves ROCLINCOURT 9.30 a.m. in connection with this train.

22. **REINFORCEMENTS & DETAILS.**

(a) Details Railhead MONT ST. ELOI.

(b) XIII Corps Reinforcement Camp is at FLORINGHEM.
Reinforcements are sent from there to ECOIVRES when they spend the night at the Reinforcement Rest Camp. They proceed next day by Light Railway to ROCLINCOURT STATION, where Guides are sent to meet them at 9.30 a.m.

23. **CEMETERIES & BURIALS.** The following system is at present in force:

(a) Bodies are brought down to ROCLINCOURT MILITARY CEMETERY, (A.29.c.4.5.) and on arrival placed in the mortuary.
Funerals take place in ROCLINCOURT Cemetery normally between 2 and 3 p.m., and are not permitted after 4 p.m.
Burials are arranged by Divl. Burials Officer.

(b) The following Cemeteries are also situated in the Area. They should only be used in very exceptional circumstances.
ALBUERA.   B.21.a.8.7.   CHANTECLER.   H.1.a.8.1.
OUSE VALLEY. B.17.c.7.0.   NAVAL TRENCH.   B.30.d.6.5.
(Closed).

24. **TRAFFIC.**

(a) Limits of Daylight Traffic:-

(i) ARRAS-GAVRELLE Road.- PONT DU JOUR, H.9.a.9.9.
(ii) ARRAS-BAILLEUL Road - MAISON DE LA COTE, B.20.d.7.2.
(iii) CONCRETE ROAD. DAYLIGHT RAILHEAD B19 d.5.7.

(b) The Concrete Road (RIDGE TRACK) starts from A.29.b.3.1., and is completed as far as B.20.a. wide enough for single traffic. It is only open for Infantry marching, and Staff Cars. Vehicles are only permitted to use the road if in possession of a written authority from XIII Corps H.Q.
Rations etc., for Units living near this track must therefore be sent up by Light Railway.

1st January, 1918.

Lt.-Colonel,
A.A.& Q.M.G., 56th Division.

APPENDIX "B".

ACCOMMODATION.

Unit.	Place.	Location.	Remarks.
Divl. H.Q. Group.	VICTORY CAMP.	G.3.b.7.3.	
C.R.A.	"	"	
C.R.E.	"	"	
A.D.M.S.	"	"	
Employment Company.	COCKPIT.		
1 Battn. Camp.	AUBREY CAMP.	G.4.a.0.5.	
"	WAKEFIELD CAMP.	G.4.a.1.6.	
"	ROCLINCOURT W. CAMP.	A.28.b.1.1.	
1 Battn. (less 2 Coys)	ROUNDHAY CAMP.	H.1.c.4.5.	
1 Coy. Billet.	ROCLINCOURT.	A.28.d.5.7.	
1 Battn. (less 3½ Coys.))			
D.A.D.O.S.)			
Reserve Secs.M.G.Coys.)	ST. CATHERINE.		
1 Field Ambulance.)			
1 Field Coy. R.E.	EDINBURGH CAMP.	G.3.d.5.7.	(Includes H.Q. and
"	PLYMOUTH CAMP.	G.9.b.2.0.	(Transport Lines.
"	HARDY CAMP.	G.9.a.9.5.	"
H.Q., Infantry Bde.	TRAFALGAR CAMP.	G.3.d.7.4.	
Heavy & Medium T.M.B's.	CUPOLA CAMP.	G.6.c.Central.	6 Offrs. 100 O.Rs.

TRANSPORT LINES.

1 Infantry Bde.	NELSON CAMP.	G.9.b.3.7.	
	(DOVER CAMP.	A.29.c.1.7.	Bde.H.Q.Lines.
	(CALAIS CAMP.	A.29.c.2.9.	1 Bn. 1 M.G.C. &
	(REDCAR CAMP.	A.28.c.5.8.	3 Bns. (1 T.M.B.
"	(COLLINGWOOD.	A.28.c.1.2.	Bde.HQ & 2 Bn.Line
	(PORTLAND.	G.9.a.5.7.	2 Bns.& 1 M.G.C. (& T.M.B.
Divl. Train H.Q.	CHATHAM CAMP.	G.3.a.0.5.	
1 Coy.	GREENWICH.	G.3.a.1.3.	
2 "	SHEERNESS.	A.26.d.6.3.	
3 "	"	-	
4 "	"	-	

BACK AREA.

2 Battns.	MAROEUIL.	
1 "	ST. AUBIN.	
Bde. H.Q.	LOUEZ.	
1 M.G.Coy.	ANZIN.	
1 T.M.Bty.	"	
D.A.C.	"	
1 Mob. Vet. Sec.	"	
1 Field Ambce.	"	
1 "	AUBIGNY.	

LOCATION TABLE.   APPENDIX "C".
56th DIVISION.

	Headquarters.	Transport Lines.

Divl. H.Q.	G.b.3.7.3.	—
		Camp:-
167th Inf. Bde. H.Q.		DOVER. A.29.c.1.7.
7th Middx. Regt.	In	REDCAR. A.28.c.5.8.
8th "	the	"
1st London Regt.	Line.	CALAIS. A.29.c.2.9.
3rd "		REDCAR. A.28.c.5.8.
167th M.G.Coy.		CALAIS. A.29.c.2.9.
167th T.M.Bty.		"
168th Inf. Bde. H.Q.	LOUEZ.	COLLINGWOOD. A.28.c.1.2.
4th London Regt.	ST. AUBIN.	"
12th "	MAROEUIL. In	"
13th "	WAKEFIELD CAMP. Reserve.	PORTLAND. G.9.a.5.7.
14th "	MAROEUIL.	"
168th M.G.Coy.	ANZIN.	"
168th T.M.Bty.	"	"
169th Inf. Bde. H.Q.		NELSON. G.9.b.3.7..
2nd London Regt.		"
5th "	In	"
9th "	the	"
16th "	Line.	"
169th M.G.Coy.		"
169th T.M.Bty.		"
193rd (Div) M.G.Coy.	G.3.d.5.2.	G.8.d.5.2.
Reserve Secs.M.G.Coys.	ST.CATHERINE.	
(Rgt.		
1/5th (E of C) Cheshire	"	GROPI. G.9.c.5.5.
56th Divl. Arty.	G.3.b.7.3.	—
280th Bde. R.F.A.	H.1.c.8.0.)	G.11.Central.
281st "	L.6.a.4.2.)	
D.A.C.	ANZIN.	
Heavy & Medium T.M.B's.	(CUPOLA CAMP,	
	(G.6.c.Central.	
C.R.E.	G.3.b.7.3.	
416 Field Coy.R.E.	"	EDINBURGH. G.3.d.5.7.
512 "	"	PLYMOUTH. G.9.b.0.0.
513 "	"	HARDY. G.9.a.9.5.
A.D.M.S.	G.3.b.7.3.	—
2/1st London Fld.A.	AUBIGNY.	—
2/2nd "	ST.CATHERINE.	—
2/3rd "	ANZIN.	—
D.A.D.O.S.	ST.CATHERINE.	—
Divl. Train.	G.3.a.0.5.	CHATHAM. G.3.a.0.5.
H.Q. Coy.	G.3.a.1.3.	GREENWICH. G.3.a.1.3.
No. 2 Coy.	A.26.d.7.2.	SHEERNESS. A.20.d.6.2.
No. 3 "	A.26.d.6.2.	"
No. 4 "	A.26.d.5.2.	"
247th Employment Coy.	G.3.b.7.3.	—
56th Divl. Supply Col.	TINCQUES.	—
Mobile Veterinary Sec.	ANZIN.	—

REINFORCEMENTS will be despatched as follows:-
(1) For Units in the Line — To Transport Lines.
(2) For other Units, not in) — To H.Q. of their Unit.
the Line.)

Appendix "D"

LIST of AREA EMPLOY furnished by
56th DIVISION to be relieved by 62nd DIVISION at 11am. 7.1.'18.

Serial No.	Post.	Offrs.	N.C.Os.	Men.	Nature of Work.	Where Reliefs to report.	By whom rationed.
1.	A.C.MADAGASCAR.	1.	1.	3.	Clerk,Billet Wardens	A.C.MADAGASCAR.	A.C.MADAGASCAR.
2.	– POINT du JOUR.	1.	1.	7.	do.	G.6.d.8.7.	A.C.POINT du JOUR.
3.	– ROCLINCOURT.	1.	1.	6.	do.	do.	– ROCLINCOURT.
4.	T.M.St.AUBIN.	1.	1.	4.	do.	T.M.ST.AUBIN.	T.M.ST.AUBIN.
5.	Div.Water Service.	1.	6.	29.	Water Wardens.	56th Div.Water Service Officer c/o A.C.ECURIE.	Under arrangements made by D.W.S.O.
6.	Div.Burial Officer.	1.	2.	4.	Burial duties.	56th Div.Burial Officer.	Under arrangements made by D.B.O.
7.	Tramway Offr. ROCLINCOURT.	1.	2.	3.	On Tramway.	ROCLINCOURT Station.	No.7 A.T.Coy.
8.	No.7A Tramway Co.R.E. ROCLINCOURT.	1.	1.	26.	Tramway maintenance.	do.	do.
9.	Musketry Ranges:- MAROEUIL. ROCLINCOURT.	1. 1.	1. 1.	2. 2.	Wardens. do.	T.M.MAROEUIL. A.C.ROCLINCOURT.	T.M.MAROEUIL. A.C.ROCLINCOURT.
10.	R.E.Dump,ROCLINCOURT.	1.	1.	28.	Loading & unloading Party.	R.E.Dump, ROCLINCOURT.	C.R.E.
11.	XIIIth Corps AMMN. DUMP G.9.d.	1.	2.	14.	Staff i/c Dump.	At Dump.	Offr. i/c Dump.
12.	Div.Ammn.Dump G.9.d.c.8.	1.	1.	3.	Holding Party.	At Dump.	O.C.Employment Co.
13.	Coal Dump St.CATHERINES.	1.	1.	3.	Guard.	BLUE ST. ST.CATHERINE.	T.M.ST.CATHERINE.
14.	R.R.O. PERNES.	2.	1.	1.		R.R.O. PERNES.	

Serial No.	Post.	Offs. N.C.Os. Men.	Nature of Work.	Where Reliefs to Report.	By whom rationed.
15.	XIIIth Corps S.C.	- - 1.	Thatcher at Corps Straw Depot.	XIIIth Corps S.C. MAROEUIL.	XIIIth Corps S.C.
16.	83rd H.A.G. (G.5.b.4.6.)	- - 1.	Bricklayer on Gun Emplacements.	83rd H.A.G. (G.5.b.4.6.)	83rd H.A.G.
17.	R.E.PARK, MAROEUIL.	- - 5.	Tinsmiths making Stoves.	R.E.Park, MAROEUIL.	O.C., R.E. Park.
18.	148 A.T.Co. MAROEUIL.	- - 3.	Sappers supervising Chinese labour.	148 A.T.Co. "	148 A.T.Co.
19.	M.& R.Camp, FLORINGHEM.	- - 3.	Sappers erecting Buildings.	M. & R. Camp.	M. & R. Camp.
20.	Div. S.A.A. & Grenade Dump, G.11.b.9.3.	1. 2. 3.	Guard.	Offr. i/c Dump, G.11.b.9.3.	O i/c Dump.
21.	Traffic Control.	To be arranged between A.P.Ms. of 56th and 62nd Divisions.			
22.	Baths at TUNNEL DUMP,	1. - 2.			
23.	CHANTECLER.	1. - 3.			
24.	ROUINCOURT.	1. - 3.	To be arranged between Baths Officers of 56th and 62nd Divisions.		
25.	ST.CATHERINES.	1. - 5.			
26.	ANZIN.	1. - 7.			
27.	MAROEUIL.	1. - 4.			
28.	Corps Roads Officer, B.15.c.7.9.	1. - 10.	Sappers superintending repair of Forward Roads.	Corps Roads Offr. B.15.c.7.0.	O.R.E.
29.	Rest Camp ST.POL.	1 W.O.	Light duty.	Rest Camp, ST.POL.	At Camp.
30.	XIIIth Corps Troops Supply Column.	- - 2.	(Div.Train) Loaders.	XIIIth Corps S.C. MAROEUIL.	XIIIth Corps S.C.
31.	Reinforcement Camp, ECOIVRES.	1. 1. 9.	Div.Disbursing Offr. Staff. 5 Cooks, 5 Clerks, 3 Carpenters or handymen.	At Camp.	O.C.Camp.

Serial No.	Post.	Offs.	N.C.Os.	Mrn.	Nature of Work.	Where Reliefs to Report.	By whom rationed.
32.	No.33, Ordnance Workshops.	–	1	5.	Employed in Workshop.	No.33 Ordnance Workshop A.26.b.central.	At workshop.

SECRET. B   War Diary
                                                               AQS. 476.
                        56th DIVISION   Appendix B

                 ADMINISTRATIVE INSTRUCTIONS No. 2,

                  Issued with reference to 56th Div.
                           Order No.147.
----

1. The attached Table shows the Camps and Billeting Areas which are to be occupied on each day during the period of the Relief, by Battns. of 56th and 62nd Divisions. The positions are those to be occupied on completion of the moves ordered for the particular day.

2. Battalions are described as shown below:-

   "A" Battn. is that moving into or out of the Right Line position.
   "B"   "   "   "   "   "   "   " " " Left   "   "
   "C"   "   "   "   "   "   "   " " " Support position.
   "D"   "   "   "   "   "   "   " " " Reserve   "

   Names of the various Battns. will be reported to this Office by Infantry Brigades as early as possible.

3. Whilst in the MAROEUIL - ST. AUBIN - OTTAWA Staging Area -

   Bde. H.Qrs. will be accommodated at   LOUEZ.
   M.G.Coy.   "   "   ANZIN.
   T.M.Bty.   "   "   ANZIN.

4. Locations of individual Units in the FREVILLERS .. CHELERS and MONCHY-BRETON Areas will be notified from this Office as early as possible.

5. Application for Billets is to be made as under:-

   MAROEUIL.   Town Major, MAROEUIL.
                             Office -   MAROEUIL.
   ST. AUBIN & LOUEZ.   Town Major, ST. AUBIN.
                             Office -   ST. AUBIN.
   ANZIN.   Town Major, ANZIN.
                             Office -   ANZIN.
   OTTAWA CAMP.   Town Major, ST. ELOI.
                             Office -   ST. ELOI.
   Attd. TUNNELLING COYS.   O's. C.   TUNNELLING COYS.
   STEWART CAMP.   A.C.   NINE ELMS.
                             Office -   A.28,b,7,2.
   TRAFALGAR CAMP.   A.C.   VALLEY.
                             Office -   G.4.a.1.7.
   AUBREY CAMP.   - do -   - do -
   WAKEFIELD CAMP.   - do -   - do -

                                              Lt.-Colonel,
1st. January, 1918.   A.A.& Q.M.G., 56th Divn.

                            - P.T.O. -

- DISTRIBUTION -

    167th Inf. Bde.
    168th   "
    169th   "
    62nd Divn. "Q".
           "G"
    O.C. Train.
     A.D.M.S.
    D.A.D.V.S.
      A.P.M.
    Xlll Corps "Q".
    31st Divn. "Q".

    Area Commdts.
       and
    Town Majors
     concerned.

    176th Tunnelling Coy.
    185th   "   ".

Date Jan.	FREVILLERS AREA	CHELERS AREA	MONCHY-BRETON AREA	MAROEUIL	MAROEUIL	ST.AUBIN	OTTAWA CAMP — ST.ELOI	Attd. Tunng. Coys.	STEWART CAMP — TRAFAL-GAR OP.	AUBRY CAMP	RED LINE	R'LGHT.W. CAMP — WAKEFIELD CAMP	Left Bde. Sup-port.	Left Bde. Line left	Left Bde. Line right	Right Bde. Sup-port.	Right Bde. Line left	Right Bde. Line right
5.	A.D. / 169	A.B. ½C. / 136	A.B.C. / 185	A. / 187	B. / 187	C. / 169	C. / 187	½C. / 186	D. / 185	D. / 186	D. / 169	D. / 167	D. / 168	C. / 167	B. / 167	A. / 167	C. / 168	B. / 168	A. / 168
6.	A.B. / 169	A.B. ½C. / 186	A.B.C. / 185	A. / 168	B. / 168	D. / 168	C. / 168	½C. / 186	D. / 185	D. / 186	D. / 169	D. / 167	D. / 187	C. / 167	B. / 167	A. / 167	C. / 187	B. / 187	A. / 187
7.	A.B. / 169	A.B. ½C. / 136	A.B.C. / 168	A. / 185	B. / 185	D. / 185	C. / 185	½C. / 186	D. / 163	D. / 186	D. / 169	D. / 167	D. / 187	C. / 167	B. / 167	A. / 167	C. / 187	B. / 187	A. / 137
8.	A.B. / 169	A.B. ½C. / 186	A.B.C. / 163	A. / 167	B. / 167	D. / 167	C. / 167	½C. / 186	D. / 163	D. / 186	D. / 169	D. / 185	D. / 187	C. / 185	B. / 185	A. / 185	C. / 187	B. / 187	A. / 137
9.	A.B. / 169	A.B. ½C. / 187	A.B.C. / 163	A. / 186	B. / 186	D. / 186	C. / 136	½C. / 187	D. / 163	D. / 167	D. / 169	D. / 185	D. / 187	C. / 185	B. / 185	A. / 185	C. / 187	B. / 187	A. / 137
10.	A.B.D A.½C. / 147	A.B. ½C. / 147	A.B.C. / 168	A. / 186	B. / 186	D. / 186	C. / (Returned to CANADIANS)	½C. / 167	D. / 163	D. / 167	C. / 136	D. / 135	D. / 137	C. / 135	B. / 135	A. / 135	C. / 137	B. / 137	A. / 137

C   War Diary
Appendix C
AQS/476.

ADMINISTRATIVE INSTRUCTIONS No. 3,

Issued with Reference to 56th Divn. Order No. 147.

Time Table of Moves by Light Railway on 6th and 8th January, 1918.

January 6th.

Serial No.	Departure Station.	Time.	Units.	Capacity of Train. All Ranks.	Destination	Time of Arr.
1.	MAROEUIL. ST. AUBIN.	a.m. 7.15	"A" Bn. 187 Bde. H.Q. 187 Bde.	600	CHANTECLER.	a.m. 8.30
2.	MAROEUIL. ANZIN.	7.45	"B" Bn. 187 Bde. 137 T.M.B.	550	"	9.00
3.	OTTAWA (LAUREL JUNC.)	10.30	"C" Bn. 187 Bde.	500	"	11.45
4.	CHANTECLER.	p.m. 2.00	"A" Bn. 168 Bde.	550	MAROEUIL.	
5.	"	2.30	"B" Bn. 168 Bde.	550	"	
6.	"	4.30	"C" Bn. 168 Bde. H.Q. 168 Bde. 168 T.M.B.	650	ANZIN. ST. AUBIN. OTTAWA.	

January 8th.

Serial No.	Departure Station.	Time.	Units.	Capacity of Train. All Ranks.	Destination	Time of Arr.
1.	MAROEUIL. ST. AUBIN.	a.m. 7.00	"A" Bn. 185 Bde. H.Q. 185 Bde.	680	DAYLIGHT RAILHEAD.	a.m. 8.30
2.	MAROEUIL. ANZIN.	7.30	"B" Bn. 185 Bde. 185 T.M.B.	630	"	9.00
3.	OTTAWA.	10.00	"C" Bn. 185 Bde.	530	"	11.30
4.	DAYLIGHT R'HEAD	2 p.m.	"A" Bn. 167 Bde.	450	MAROEUIL.	
5.	"	2.30	"B" Bn. 167 Bde.	400	"	
6.	"	4.30	"C" Bn. 167 Bde. H.Q. 167 Bde. 167 T.M.B.	600	ANZIN. ST. AUBIN. OTTAWA.	

Lt.-Colonel,
A.A.& Q.M.G., 56th Division.

2nd January, 1918.

— DISTRIBUTION —

167th Inf. Bde.   62nd Divn. "Q".   C.L.R.O.
168th   "   XIII Corps "Q".   "G"
                 Div. Tramway Officer.

War Diary
Appendix D
AQS 476.

ADMINISTRATIVE INSTRUCTIONS No. 4,
in connection with Relief of 56th Divn. by 62nd Divn.
Issued with reference to 56th Div. Order,
No. 147.

---

1. LOCATIONS.   A Location Table is attached showing Locations of Units on completion of their Relief.

2. 1st LINE TRANSPORT.

   (a)   1st Line Transports of Units will move on the same day as the remainder of their Unit.
   (b)   Transport Lines in the present Divisional Area must be handed over to Units of 62nd Divn. on the days on which Units of this Divn. move either into the MAROEUIL Staging Area or into a "Wiring Unit" Camp.
   (c)   Locations of Transport Lines for "Wiring Units" are as follows:

   For Bn. with H.Q. in TRAFALGAR.   ST. CATHERINE.
   "   AUBREY.   "
   "   STEWART.   BRAY.
   For Bn. attd. to Tunnelling Coys. G.10.b.5.9. & A.26.d.94.
   For Field Coy. with H.Q. in AUBREY.   ST. CATHERINE.
   "   ROBERTS.   ECOIVRES.

3. WORK IN PROGRESS.   Details of Hutting Schemes and other work in progress in the Back Area will be handed over by Formations & Units to Relieving Formations & Units.

4. AREA & TRENCH STORES.   All Trench Stores, Ammunition, supplies in Supporting Points, etc., will be handed over. A.F.W3405 receipted by both incoming and outgoing Units will be forwarded to 56th Div. "Q" within 3 days after relief
   Water & Petrol tins, less those carried on water carts, and all Soyer Stoves except those on the establishment of F.A's. will be handed over.
   167 & 168 Inf. Bdes. will each hand in 1500 pairs of socks and their Sock Wringers, to the 56th Div. Linen Store the day before relief.
   The White Overall Suits for patrols (vide G.R.O.3030) will be handed in to the D.A.D.O.S. 56th Div. at the first opportunity after relief.
   Gum Boots and Inner Soles will be handed in to the Store at ROCLINCOURT and receipts obtained. (Vide D.R.O.2211).
   All Area & Billet Stores will be handed over to incoming Units, receipts obtained and countersigned by Area Commandants and Town Majors.

5. CAMPS & BILLETS.   Particular attention is to be paid to handing over all Camps, Billets, Trenches and Horse Lines in a clean and sanitary condition. Certificates to that effect must be obtained from Area Commandants or Advance Parties of incoming Units. Where necessary Rear Parties must be left behind to hand over.

6. CHAFF CUTTERS.   The following Units will hand in their Chaff Cutters to the D.A.D.O.S. by Noon 8th instant.
   3rd London Rgt. 13th London Rgt. 16th London Rgt. 193 M.G.Coy.
   Divl. Signal Coy. D.A.D.O.S.
   Total - 6.
   The D.A.D.O.S. will hand over the above Chaff Cutters to 62nd Div. on their arrival in the Area.
   The following Units will take their Chaff Cutters to the New Area:
   8th Middx. 4th London Rgt. 14th London Rgt. 9th London Rgt. 1st Londons.
   169 M.G.Coy. Divl. H.Q.
   Total - 7.

P.T.O.

7. **ORDNANCE.**

   The D.A.D.O.S. Store will be open at TINQUES (C28.d.9.3.) on the 8th instant.

   Units of 56th Divn. remaining in the 31st and 62nd Divn Areas will submit their indents to the D.A.D.O.S. 56th Div. as usual. Stores will be delivered direct to Qr.Mrs. Stores of these Units by the D.A.D.O.S.

8. **VETERINARY.** The Mobile Veterinary Section will be established at TINQUES after the 9th inst.

9. **BATHS.**

   (a) Baths in the new Area will be ready for use by Units on their arrival, as shown below:

Place.	For Troops at
TINQUES.	Tinques, Tincquette, Bailleul, Chelers, Bethencourt, Villers-Brulin, Marquay.
MAGNICOURT.	Orlencourt, la Thieuloye, Monchy-Breton, Rocourt, Houvelin, La Comte, Frevillers, Magnicourt.
CAUCOURT.	Caucourt, Gauchin, Hermin, Viller Chatel, Cambligneul.

   (b) Units remaining in the Forward Area will use the Baths run by the 31st or 62nd Div. according to the Area in which they are billeted. Clean Clothing will be obtained from the Div. Linen Stores of those Divisions.

   (c) O.C. Train will arrange for coal up to 1 ton a week to be delivered at each Bath House, so that the Baths may be ready for use when required.

   (d) The Divl. Clean Clothing Store will open at TINQUES on 9th inst. Units in the Reserve Area will draw underclothing from there direct, making their own transport arrangements. The Baths will not be stocked with underclothing.

   (e) Bath allotments will be arranged by Units direct with the N.C.O. i/c. of each Bath House.

10. **SALVAGE.** Salvage Dumps will be established in Brigade Areas near the Billets of the Divl. Train in each case. O.C. Salvage Coy. will arrange to attach 1 N.C.O. and 10 men to each Coy. of the Divl. Train for accommodation and rations from the 10th instant. They will report to O.C. Train Companies at 10 a.m. on that date.

                                    Lieut.-Colonel,
                                    A.A.& Q.M.G., 56th Division.

3rd January, 1918.

- Distribution -

			Area Commdts.
G.O.C.	A.P.M.	N.C.O. i/c. Div. Canteen.	BETHONSART.
167 Inf. Bde.	D.A.D.O.S.	S.C.F. (C of E)	MAGNICOURT.
168 "	Camp Cmdt.	" (Non C of E)	LA COMTE.
169 "	Div.Sig.Coy.	Lt.SPICER,1/5th Cheshires.	ROCLINCOURT.
C.R.A.	Div.Emp.Coy.	French Mission.	VALLEY.
C.R.E.	D.A.D.V.S.	56 D.S.C.	MADAGASCAR.
5th Cheshires.	"C".	31st Div. "Q".	Town Majors:-
193 M.G.Coy.	Gas Officer.	62nd " "	AUBIGNY. TINQUES.
Train.	Salvage "		CAMBLIGNEUL.
A.D.M.S.	O. i/c."Bow-Bells".		CAUCOURT. MAROEUIL.
D.M.G.O.	" Baths & Laundry.		ST.AUBIN. ANZIN.ST.CATH ERINE.

56th DIVISION LOCATION TABLE on Completion of Relief by 62nd Divn.

AQS 476.

Bn.Ltr. in Admin. Instns. No. 2.	Unit.	Destination.	Date of Arrival	Billets from
	Divl. H.Q.	VILLERS CHATEL.	9th	A.C.BETHONSART.
	Divl. Arty. H.Q.	VICTORY CAMP.	"	
	Divl. R.E., H.Q.	ECURIE WOOD.	"	A.C.ECURIE.
	Divl. Train H.Q.	SAVY.	"	T.H.AUBIGNY.
	1/5th Cheshire R.	BAILLEUL AUX CORNAILLES.	"	T.H.TINCQUES.
	193 (Div) M.G.Coy.	CAMBLIGNEUL.	8th	T.M.CAMBLIGNEUL.
	247th Employ.Coy.	HINGOVAL.	9th	A.C.BETHONSART.
	Mob. Vet. Sec.	TINQUES.	-	T.M.TINQUES.

167th Inf. Bde. Group.

	Unit.	Destination.	Date of Arrival	Billets from
	H.Q. 167 Inf. Bde.	CHELERS.	9th	T.M.TINCQUES.
C.	7th Middx.(less 2)	"	"	"
B.	8th " (Coys)	TINCQUES.	"	"
A.	1st London Regt.	VILLERS-BRULIN.	"	A.C.BETHONSART.
D.	3rd "	AUBREY CAMP.	"	A.C.VALLEY AREA.
	167 M.G.Coy.	TINCQUETTE.	10th	T.M.TINCQUES.
	167 T.M.Bty.	BAILLEUL AUX CORNAILLES.	9th	"
	416 Fld.Coy.R.E.	TINCQUES.	"	"
	No.2 Coy.Div.Train.	TINCQUETTE.	"	"
	2/1st Fld.Ambce.	AUBIGNY.	-	T.M.AUBIGNY.

168th Inf. Bde. Group.

	Unit.	Destination.	Date of Arrival	Billets from
	H.Q. 168 Inf. Bde.	ORLENCOURT.	7th	A.C.MAGNICOURT.
A.	4th London Rgt.	MONCHY-BRETON.	"	"
D.	12th "	STEWART CAMP.	"	A.C.NINE ELMS.
B.	13th "	MAGNICOURT.	"	A.C.MAGNICOURT.
C.	14th "	LA THIEULOYE.	"	A.C. LA COMTE.
	168 M.G.Coy.	BAJUS.	8th	"
	168 T.M.Bty.	"	7th	"
	512 Fld. Coy.R.E.	AUBREY CAMP.	8th	A.C.VALLEY AREA.
	No. 3 Coy.Train.	ROCOURT.	7th	A.C.MAGNICOURT.
	2/2nd Fld.Ambce.	HOUVELIN.	5th & 7th.	"

169th Inf. Bde. Group.

	Unit.	Destination.	Date of Arrival	Billets from
	H.Q. 169 Inf. Bde.	FREVILLERS.	5th	A.C.MAGNICOURT.
C.	2nd London Rgt.	TRAFALGAR CAMP.	6th	A.C.VALLEY AREA.
B.	5th "	FREVILLERS.	5th	A.C.MAGNICOURT.
D.	9th "	CAMBLIGNEUL.	10th	T.M.CAMBLIGNEUL.
A.	16th "	CAUCOURT.	5th	T.M.CAUCOURT.
	169 M.G.Coy.	LA COMTE.	"	A.C.LA COMTE.
	169 T.M.Bty.	CAMBLIGNEUL.	"	T.M.CAMBLIGNEUL.
	513 Fld. Coy.R.E.	ROBERTS CAMP.	6th	A.C.ECURIE.
	2/3rd Fld. Ambce.	HERMIN.	8th	T.M.CAUCOURT.
1 Sec.2/3rd	"	BETHENCOURT.	"	T.M.TINCQUES.
	No.4 Coy.(Div)Trn.	HERMIN.	5th	T.M.CAUCOURT.

	Unit.	Destination.	Date of Arrival	Billets from
	D.A.D.O.S.	TINCQUES.	8th	T.M.TINCQUES.
	Div. Clothing Store.	"	"	"

	Unit.	Destination.		
	280th Bde. R.F.A.	G.H.Central.		
	281st "	"		
	56th D.A.C.	ANZIN ST.AUBIN.		

Appendix E

ADMINISTRATIVE INSTRUCTIONS No. 5
in connection with relief of 59th Divn. by 62nd Division.
Issued with reference to 56th Div. Order No. 147.

1. **MOVES BY TACTICAL TRAIN.** Arrangements are being made for personnel to move from PARD UP Area to the new Area by Tactical Train.
    The arrangements are not yet complete but will be notified as soon as possible.
    All transport will march.

2. **SUPPLIES AND FUEL.** Supplies and Fuel in the Reserve Area will be drawn from Refilling Points by Units' first line transport, commencing on the day after a Units' arrival in the Reserve Area. A Supply Grouping Table (Appendix "A") is attached.

3. **ACCOMMODATION M.G.COYS.** Staging Billets for M.G.Coys., and rear parties of Infantry Bdes., on the night after they are relieved have been arranged as shown below:-

Unit.	Night	Place.	Billets from.
128th M.G.Coy.	7/8th	FRAMET CAMP	Town Major PONT ST. LOI
153rd M.G.Coy.	7/8th	" "	" "
167th M.G.Coy.	9/10th	" "	" "

    Light Railway truckage for conveyance of these units from the Line to their Staging Billets will be arranged by Infantry Bdes. and Div. M.G.O. direct with Div. Tramways Officer..

4. **AMMUNITION.** An initial supply of S.A.A., Grenades etc., for practice purposes will be delivered to Bde. Headquarters on the day after their arrival in the New Area.
    Further supplies should be demanded from Div. Headquarters (A & Q).

5. **THE BOW BELLS** will close in the present area after the performance on the 8th inst: and will reopen in the new area at a place and date to be notified later.

6. **THE CINEMA** will close in the present area after the last performance on the 8th inst: and will reopen at TINQUES on a date to be notified later.

7. **THE DIVISIONAL CANTEEN** will be established on the 8th inst: at TINQUES with a branch at VILLERS CHATEL. Orders for Soda Water will be taken at both branches.

8. **SURPLUS BAGGAGE** must be cleared from the Dump at BEAUMOTSART within two days of arrival in the new area. of the Unit to which it belongs.

                                                    Lieut-Colonel,
5th January, 1918.   A.A. & Q.M.G., 56th Division.

-Distribution-

G.O.C.		Camp Cdt.	O i/c "Bow Bells". Canteen
167 Inf. Bde.	125 M.G.Coy.	Sig. Coy.	O " Baths Laundry.
168 Inf. Bde.	Train	Employt. Coy.	S.C.F. (C. of E.)
169 Inf. Bde.	A.D.M.S.	D.A.D.V.S.	S.C.F. (Non C. of E.)
C.R.A.	D.I.C.O.	"G"	Lt. SPIERS
C.R.E.	A.P.M.	Gas Officer	French Mission
5th Ches. R.	D.A.D.O.S.	Salvage O.	56 D.S.C. 61st Div. "Q"
62nd Div. "Q"	A.C. BEAUMETSART, AGNICOURT, LA COMTE
Town Majors, AUBIGNY, TINQUES, CAMBLICHEUL, CAUCOURT, MAROEUIL, ST. AUBIN
" " PONT St. LOI. Div. Tramways Officer.

APPENDIX "A".

SUPPLY GROUPING TABLE TO TAKE EFFECT AS UNITS ARRIVE IN VILLERS-CHATEL, MONCHY-BRETON DIVL. AREA.

RAILHEAD - TINCQUES.

167th Brigade Group, No. 2.	168th Brigade Group, No. 3.	169th Brigade Group, No. 4.
Refilling Point. TINCQUES–CHELERS ROAD. 9 a.m. Near CHELERS.	Refilling Point. MONCHY-BRETON – ROCOURT ROAD. 9 a.m. Near ROCOURT.	Refilling Point. HERMIN VILLAGE SQUARE. 9 a.m.
167th Bde. Hdqrs.	168th Bde. Hdqrs.	169th Bde. Hdqrs.
167th T.M.B.	168th Bde. T.M.B.	169th Bde. T.M.B.
167th Bde. M.G.Coy. (Arrives 10th)	168th Bde. M.G.Coy. (Arrives 8th).	169th Bde. M.G.Coy.
1/1st London Regt.	1/4th London Regt.	1/5th London Regt. (Arrives 10th)
Half 1/7th Middx. Regt.	1/13th "	1/9th "
1/8th Middx. Regt.	1/14th "	1/16th "
No. 2 Coy. Train.	No. 3 Coy. Train	No. 4 Coy. Train.
416th Field Coy. R.E.	2/2nd London Field Ambce.	2/3rd London Field Ambce.
Divl. Hdqrs.		
Train Hdqrs.		
Signal Coy. R.E.		
193rd (Div) M.G.Coy. (Arrives 8th) ∅		
247th Employment Coy.		
1/5th Cheshire Regt. (less 1 Coy).		
1/1st London M.V.S.		
D.A.D.O.S.		
Above Units to commence drawing with their First Line Transport from above Refilling Point on 10th inst.	Above Units to commence drawing with their First Line Transport from above Refilling Point on the 8th inst.	Above Units to commence drawing with their First Line Transport from above Refilling Point on 6th inst.

O's. C. A.S.C. Companies will supply Baggage Wagons for delivery of Supplies from Refilling Points to those Units who have no First Line Transport.

∅ . O.C. Train will issue special instructions to this Unit.

F

War Diary
Appendix F

SECRET.   56th Division No. G.3/807.

SCHEME A.

Movement of 56th Division by Strategical Trains.

1. Herewith copy of arrangements for entrainment and detrainment for 56th Division in case a move is ordered whilst it is in G.H.Q. Reserve.

2. This scheme will become operative on receipt of a telegram from Divisional Headquarters worded as follows :-

    "Move AAA Scheme 'A' AAA Time of first train AAA
    SAVY _____ AAA AUBIGNY _____ AAA
    TINQUES _____ AAA Acknowledge.

3. Acknowledge.

B. Pakenham
Lieut-Colonel.
General Staff,
56th Division.

7: 1: 1918.

Copies to :-
  167th Infantry Brigade.
  168th Infantry Brigade.
  169th Infantry Brigade.
  1/5th Cheshire Regt.
  C.R.A.
  C.R.E.
  193rd (Div.) M.G. Coy.
  56th Div. M.G. Officer.
  56th Div. Signal Coy.
  56th Div. Gas Officer.
  A.D.M.S.
  "Q".
  A.P.M.
  D.A.D.O.S.
  D.A.D.V.S.
  56th Div. Train.
  56th Div. Supply Col.
  56th Div. Amm. Sub-Park.
  A.D.C.
Camp Commandant.
  French Mission.
  XIII Corps "G".
  XIII Corps "Q".
  War Diary.
  File.

SCHEME "A".   A.Q.S. 482

Arrangements for the Entrainment and Detrainment of the 56th Division in case a move by rail is ordered whilst in G.H.Q.Reserve.

Issued with reference to 56th Division Order No. 148.

1. STATIONS OF ENTRAINMENT.
Units will entrain at stations as under, under the orders of the Brigadier Generals Commanding Brigade Groups and Divisional Artillery and of Divl. H.Q. in the case of Units of Divl. Troops not affiliated (to Inf. Bdes.

At SAVY
167th Brigade Group.
Divisional Train Headquarters.
193rd Machine Gun Coy.
247th (Div.) Employment Coy.
Mobile Veterinary Section.
280th Bde. R.F.A. (less "D" Bty) and portion of DAC

At TINQUES
168th Bde. Group.
1/5th (E. of C.) Bn. Cheshire Regt.
Headquarters D.A.C. No. 1 Coy. Divisional Train.
Divisional Artillery Headquarters.
D/280th Battery R.F.A.
Heavy and Medium T.M.Batteries.

At AUBIGNY
169th Brigade Group.
Divisional Headquarters.
Divisional R.E. Headquarters.
Headquarters and No. 1 Section Divl. Signal Coy.
281st Bde. R.F.A. and portion of D.A.C.

2. Times of entrainment
The order of entrainment is shown in Table "D". Trains from each station will leave at 3 hour intervals.
All Transport will arrive at Stations of Entrainment 3 hours and personnel 1½ hours before the time of departure of the train in which they are to travel.

3. LOADING PARTY.
Each Infantry Brigade will detail a Company from their last train load as a loading party for all trains, except those conveying units of Divisional Artillery, which leave their respective entraining stations. These Companies, with their cookers and rations, will report to the R.T.O., at the entraining station 4 hours before the first train is due to leave. They will travel by the last train of their Brigade Group.

4. UNLOADING PARTY.
Similarly each Infantry Brigade will detail a Company from their first train load as unloading party for all trains arriving at their respective detraining stations, except those conveying Units of Divisional Artillery. They will report to the R.T.O., immediately on arrival at the station of detrainment. They will be rationed by their own unit and will rejoin their unit after the last train of their Brigade Group has been unloaded.

5. Divisional Artillery will make their own arrangements for loading and unloading parties. 1 Company of 5th Cheshire Regt. travelling with part of the SAA Section D.A.C., will assist in loading and unloading that train.

6 FIELD COMPANIES.
   Each Field Coy. R.E., will detail 1 Officer and 60 O.R., to assist the permanent loading and unloading parties at Stations of Entrainment and Detrainment in dealing with their own transport. These parties will report to the Officers referred to in para. 7, 3 hours before the departure of the trains by which the Field Coys. travel, and to the Officers referred to in para. 8 on arrival.

7 ENTRAINMENT OFFICERS.
   Each Infantry Brigade will detail two Officers, not below the rank of Captain, to report to the R.T.O., of their respective entraining station 4 hours before the first train is due to leave, to assist him in the general supervision of the entrainment of the Division (less Artillery). The Officers will work in 2 reliefs and will travel by the last train of their Brigade Group. The C.R.A. will make corresponding arrangements for Officers to assist in the entrainment of (the Divl. Arty.

8. DETRAINMENT OFFICERS.
   Similarly each Infantry Brigade will detail 2 Officers to proceed by the first train, and report for the same purpose to the R.T.O., at the Station of Detrainment. Similar arrangements will be made by the C.R.A. for supervising the detraining of the Divisional Artillery.

9. O.C., Signal Coy. will detail a Motor Cyclist orderly for duty at each station of entrainment and detrainment. They will report to the Officers mentioned in paras 7 and 8.

10. A.D.M.S., will detail an Ambulance Car to be on duty at AUBIGNY Station during the period of the entrainment; and another Car to be on duty at a detraining station, which will be notified later, during the period of detrainment.

11. ENTRAINMENT AND DETRAINMENT OFFICERS.
    While Entrainment and Detrainment Officers are on duty they should wear the blue Brigade armband as a distinguishing badge.

12. DIVISIONAL STAFF.
    An Officer from Division Headquarters will visit stations of entrainment and detrainment at frequent intervals.

13. POLICE.
    For the Control of Traffic on the road approaches to each of the Entraining Stations the A.P.M., will detail 6 policemen to report to the Officers referred to in para. 7, four hours before the first train is due to leave. These policemen will travel by the last train and will rejoin Div. H.Q. from the station of detrainment.
    For the Control of Traffic on the roads leading from each of the detraining stations the A.P.M. will also detail 6 policemen to proceed by the first train from each station with orders to report to the Officers referred to in para. 8 on arrival. On completion of detrainment these policemen will rejoin Div. H.Q. The A.P.M. will provide the necessary Rations for these 36 policemen.

14. BAGGAGE and SUPPLY WAGONS.
    Baggage and Supply Wagons will entrain with the Units for which they are carrying.
    Baggage Wagons will join Units on receipt of orders to entrain.
    Supply Wagons will join Units before they entrain, as arranged in para 18.

15. ENTRAINMENT.

(a) A Senior Officer from each Unit must be sent to report to the R.T.O. at Stations of Entrainment to receive detailed instructions, in sufficient time to permit of them being made known to all concerned before the arrival of the Unit at the Station.

(b) Units must provide a horse holder for each horse, also drag ropes for use as breast lines in the trucks. The Railway Authorities provide lashings for vehicles.

(c) No fused bombs or grenades are to be carried on any train.

(d) No lights will be lit in any train after dark. The fires of cookers will be drawn before entrainment.

16. MOTOR CARS etc.

All Motor Cars, Motor Ambulances and Motor Cycles will proceed by road on the days on which the Units to which they belong entrain.

17. SURPLUS BAGGAGE.

In the event of lorries being available for moving surplus baggage arrangements will be notified at the time.

If lorries are not available surplus baggage will be dumped by Units at the Divisional Dump, BETHONSART, directly orders are received to entrain.

O.C. Divl. Employment Company will hold a guard of 1 N.C.O. and 2 men with 7 days rations ready to take over this dump on its formation.

Units in the 31st and 62nd Divl. Area will dump their surplus baggage at their Q.M. Stores and leave a guard of 1 N.C.O. and 2 men with 7 days rations.

18. SUPPLIES.

Rations for consumption on the day of entrainment will be delivered in the normal manner, early on the day of entrainment minus 1.

Rations for consumption on the day of entrainment plus 1 will be sent to Units by Supply Wagon early on the day of entrainment minus 1, and the loaded Supply Wagons will proceed to, and remain with, Units until the completion of the move.

Rations for consumption on the day of entrainment plus 2, will be delivered as follows:-

(i) For Units entraining before 12 noon, by Supply Column at Refilling Points in the new area, thence by Supply Wagon on day of entrainment, plus 1.

(ii) For Units entraining after 12 noon, by Supply Column lorries direct to Entraining Stations, where they should be taken over by representatives of Units by 12 Noon on the day of Entrainment, and loaded by Units direct into their Railway Trains and not into Supply Wagons. Although in reality for consumption on day of entrainment plus 2, these rations should be consumed on day of entrainment plus 1, and the supplies already loaded on the supply wagons for consumption on day of entrainment plus 1 should be consumed on the day of entrainment plus 2.

7th January, 1918.

Lieut.-Colonel,
A.A.& Q.M.G., 56th Division.

TABLE "D" 1.

AUBIGNY.	SAVY.	TINQUES.	SERIAL NUMBER.	Date.	Time of departure.
1			(5630,5631a,5635,5636, (5637		
	1		(5610,5611a,5615,5616, (5617.		
		1	5620,5621a,5625,5626, 5627.		
2			5631.		
	2		5611.		
		2	5621.		
3			5632.		
	3		5612.		
		3	5622.		
4			5633.		
	4		5613.		
		4	5623,5604b.		
5			5634.		
	5		5614.		
		5	5624,5604c.		
6			5601,5605,5603.		
	6		5606,5608,5609,5675,5690.		
		6	5604.		
7			5632a,5678,5683.		
	7		5612a,5681,5676.		
		7	5622a,5677, 5682.		
8			5633a,5634a,5688.		
	8		5613a,5614a,5686.		
		8	5623a, 5624a,5687.		
9			5651,5672a.		
	9		5641,5671a.		
		9	5602,5670,5675a.		
10			5650,5672.		
	10		5640,5671.		
		10	5673a,5691,5692,5693,5694.		
11			5652,5672b.		
	11		5642,5671b.		
		11	5673b,5604a.		
12			5653,5672c.		
	12		5643,5671c.		
		12	5644,5671d.		
13			5654,5672d.		

In the event of the Division entraining less Artillery, Hdqrs. Divl. Arty. (5602) will entrain with Divl. Hdqrs.(5601) and Hdqrs. Divl. Engineers (5603) will travel by the 6th train from SAVY in addition to those already allotted to that train.

The Company of the 5th Cheshires (5604a) will travel by the second train from TINQUES in addition to 5621.

TABLE "D" 2.

		Serial No.	Description.
Entraining Station.	AUBIGNY	5601	Divl. H.Q.
	TINQUES	5602	H.Q. Divl. R.A.
	AUBIGNY	5603	" " R.E. (5604c.
		5604	1/5th Cheshires less 5604a, 5604b,
	TINQUES	5604a	1 Coy. 1 Cooker & team 1/5th Ches.
		5604b	2 G.S.W. & teams, 1/5th Cheshires.
		5604c	2 " " " "
	AUBIGNY	5605	H.Q. & No. 1 Sec. Divl. Signals.
	AUBIGNY	5606	----
		5607	247 Employment Coy. (& 5609).
	SAVY	5608	193 M.G.Coy.
		5609	247 Employment Coy. (& 5607).

167th Inf. Bde. Group.	5610	Bde. H.Q.
	5611	"A" Bn.(VILLERS BRULIN) less 11a.
Entraining Station -	5611a.	1 Coy., 1 cooker & team "A" Bn.
	5612	"B" Bn.(TINQUES) less 12a.
SAVY.	5612a	1 Coy., 1 cooker & team "B" Bn.
	5613	"C" Bn. (CHELERS) less 13a.
	5613a	1 Coy., 1 cooker & team "C" Bn.
	5614	"D" Bn. (AUBREY CAMP) less 14a.
	5614a	1 Coy. 1 cooker & team "D" Bn.
	5615	Bde. Signal Sec.
	5616	Bde. M.G.C.
	5617	Bde. T.M.B..
	5676	No. 2 Coy. Divl. Train.
	5681	416 Fld. Coy. R.E.
	5686	2/1st London Fld. Ambce.

168th Inf. Bde. Group.	5620	Bde. H.Q.
	5621	"A" Bn.(MONCHY-BRETON) less 21a.
Entraining Station -	5621a	1 Coy. 1 cooker & team "A" Bn.
	5622	"B" Bn.(MAGNICOURT) less 22a.
TINQUES.	5622a	1 Coy. 1 cooker & team "B" Bn.
	5623	"C" Bn. (LA THIEULOYE) less 23a.
	5623a	1 Coy. 1 Cooker & team. "C" Bn.
	5624	"D" Bn.(STEWART CAMP) less 24a.
	5624a	1 Coy. 1 cooker & team "D" Bn.
	5625	Bde. Signal Section.
	5626	Bde. M.G.C.
	5627	Bde. T.M.B.
	5677	No. 3 Coy. Divl. Train.
	5682	512th Fld. Coy. R.E.
	5687	2/2nd London Fld. Ambce.

169th Inf. Bde. Group.	5630	Bde. H.Q.
	5631	"A" Bn.(CAUCOURT) less 31a.
Entraining Station -	5631a	1 Coy. 1 cooker & team, "A" Bn.
	5632	"B" Bn. (FREVILLERS) less 32a.
AUBIGNY.	5632a	1 Coy. 1 cooker & team "B" Bn.
⌀	5633	"D" Bn.(CAMBLIGNEUL) less 33a.
	5633a	1 Coy. 1 cooker & team "D" Bn.
	5634	"C" Bn. (TRAFALGAR CAMP) less 34a.
	5634a	1 Coy. 1 cooker & team "C" Bn.
	5635	Bde. Signal Section.
	5636	Bde. M.G.C.
	5637	Bde. T.M.B.
	5678	No. 4 Coy. Divl. Train.
	5683	513th Fld. Coy. R.E.
	5688	2/3rd London Fld. Ambce.

⌀ "D" Bn. is in the Red Line until 10th inst.

T A B L E "D".

UNIT		Serial No.	Description
280th (London) Brigade, R.F.A.		5640	Bde. Headquarters.
		5641	93rd Battery.
Entraining Station SAVY		5642	"A" "
		5643	"C" "
" TINQUES		5644	"D" "
281st (London) Brigade R.F.A.		5650	Bde. Headquarters.
		5651	109th Battery.
Entraining Station AUBIGNY.		5652	"A" "
		5653	"B" "
		5654	"D" "
DIVL. AMMN. COL.	(Entraining Stn.		
	" TINQUES.	5670	H.Q. Divisional Ammn. Column.
	" SAVY.	5671	No. 1 Sec. less 5671a,5671b,5671c,5671d.
		5671a	1 G.S. Wgn & 4 Lmbd Ammn Wgns & Teams of
		5671b	- do -
		5671c	- do - (5671.
	" TINQUES.	5671d	- do -
		5672	No. 2 Sec. less 5672a,5672b,5672c,5672d.
		5672a	1 G.S. Wgn. 4 Lmbd Ammn Wgns & Teams of
	" AUBIGNY.	5672b	- do -
		5672c	- do - (5672.
		5672d	- do -
	" TINQUES.	5673a	½ S.A.A. Section D.A.C.
		5673b	- do -
DIVISIONAL TRAIN.	" SAVY.	5675	H.Q. Divisional Train.
	TINQUES.	5675a	No. 1 Company,
	SAVY.	5676	No. 2 Company.
	TINQUES.	5677	No. 3 "
	AUBIGNY.	5678	No. 4 "
DIVISIONAL ENGINEERS.	" SAVY.	5681	416th (Edinburgh) Field Coy. R.E.
	TINQUES.	5682	512th (London) " "
	AUBIGNY.	5683	513th (") " "
MEDICAL UNITS.	" SAVY.	5686	2/1st London Field Ambulance.
	TINQUES.	5687	2/2nd " "
	AUBIGNY.	5688	2/3rd " "
VETERINARY UNIT.	" SAVY.	5690	1/1st London Mobile Veterinary Sec.
TRENCH MORTAR BATTERIES.	" TINQUES.	5691	"V" Trench Mortar Bty. (Heavy).
		5692	"X" " " (Medium).
		5693	"Y" " " " "
		5694	"Z" " " " "

War Diary
AQS/482.
Appendix G

SCHEME "C".

Move of 56th Division by Tactical Trains from Reserve Area to ECURIE.

1. **ENTRAINING STATIONS.**

   Units will entrain as follows, under the orders of Brigade Group Commanders and C.R.A., and of Divl. H.Q. in the case of Units of Divl. Troops not affiliated to Infantry Brigades.

   AUBIGNY.

   First Train. Personnel only. 169th Inf. Bde. less M.G.C. and T.M.B.
   Second Train. (Omnibus). Part transport of 169th Inf. Bde. only.
   (See Appendix Y).

   SAVY.

   First Train. Personnel only. 167th Inf. Bde. less M.G.C. & T.M.B.
   Second Train. " " 167, 168, 169 T.M.B. (with handcarts).
   193 M.G.C., 5th Cheshires, 416 Field Coy.R.E., 2/2nd and 2/3rd London Fld. Ambces.
   Divl. H.Q.
   H.Q. Divl. Engineers.
   H.Q. and No. 1 Sec. Divl. Signal Coy - X.Y.Z. and V.T.M. Batts.
   Third Train. (Omnibus). Part Transport of 167th Inf. Bde. only.
   (See Appendix Y)

   TINQUES.
   First Train.(Personnel only) 168th Inf.Bde.less M.G.C.,T.M.B.
   Second Train (Omnibus) Part.Transpt. 168 Bde. only.(See Appendix Y)
   DETRAINING STATION - ECURIE.

2. **ENTRAINMENT & DETRAINMENT.**

   167th, 168th and 169th Bde. Group Commanders will each detail Officers to supervise the entrainment at SAVY, TINQUES, and AUBIGNY respectively. The detrainment at ECURIE will be supervised under Divisional arrangements.

3. **BAGGAGE.**

   All surplus baggage and stores will be placed in Unit dumps under a guard of 2 men for each Dump. This guard will be told off and 7 days rations held ready for them directly Units arrive in the Reserve Area. The position of Unit dumps will be reported to Div H.Q. directly a Unit has reconnoitred its billeting area. At least one blanket per man must be carried on the baggage wagons.

4. **NUCLEUS PERSONNEL.**

   The personnel mentioned in SS.135, Sect. XXX, will not proceed with their Units, but will concentrate at TINQUES after the departure of the last tactical train, and will there come under command of the Senior Officer. They will include a proportion of cooks and be provided by their Units with a sufficient number of Camp kettles; also rations for the following day if these are in possession of the Unit. Further orders regarding the move from TINQUES to PERNES will be sent from Divl. H.Q. to the Senior Officer of the Party, c/o. Town Major, TINQUES.

7th January, 1918.

Lt. Lieut.-Colonel,
A.A.& Q.M.G., 56th Div.

APPENDIX "Y".

COMPOSITION OF OMNIBUS TRAIN.

UNIT.	Personnel. Offrs.	O.R.	Horses.	G.S. Limbered.	2 wheeled carts.
Riding Horses & Transport of Bde. H.Q.	-	14	9	1	-
" " Signal Section.	-	14	9	1	1
L.G. Detachment,Transport 4 L. G.S. Wagons per Battn.	-	32	32	16	-
Pack animals, 6 per Battn.	-	24	24	-	-
Medical Personnel and 1 Maltese Cart per Battn.	4	8	4	-	4
One Motorcart. per Battn	-	16	8	-	4
ϕ M.G. Company,and 2 L. G.S. Wagons per section.	10	200	34	8	1
Riders. 5 for Battn. 7 M.G.C.	-	28	27	-	-
	14	336	147	26	10

62 Axles.

ϕ Finds loading and unloading party of 100 men.

Appendix H   War diary

EXTRACTS FROM LIST OF NEW YEAR'S HONOURS GAZETTE.

PROMOTIONS.
Brevet Colonel.	Brig.-General G. G. LOCH, C.M.G.,	Royal Scots.
Brevet Lt.-Col.	T/Lt.Col. H. W. GORDON, D.S.O.,	R.E.
Brevet Major.	Captain W. T. BROOKS, M.C.,	D.C.L.I.
Pay of Next Higher Rank.	Qr.Mr. & Hon. Lieut. G. BROWN.	London Rgt.

DISTINGUISHED SERVICE ORDER.
Brig.General E. S. d'e COKE, C.M.G. — K.O.S.B.
Colonel G. A. MOORE, C.M.G. — A.M.S.
Bt.Lt.-Col. H. W. GRUBB. — Border Regt.
Major F. J. LEMON. — W. Yorks Regt.
T/Lt.Col. A. G. GALLOWAY. — A.S.C.
Lt.Col. E. W. GRIFFITH. — R.F.A.
Lt.Col. S.W.L. ASCHWANDEN. — "
Major G. L. DYMOTT. — "
Major E. R. C. WARRENS. — "
Major G. T. KINGSFORD. — R.E.
Major J. T. PARK. — "
T/Major F. G. P. GEDGE. — "

Qr. Mr. & Hon. Major J. T. H. HUDSON. — Middlesex Regt.

A/Lt.Col. R. H. HUSEY, M.C. — London Regt.
A/Lt.Col. E. D. JACKSON. — "
Captain H. A. EILOART, M.C. — "
QR.MR. & Hon. Major T. C. IBBS. — "
"   "   "   "   W. E. WEBB. — "

Captain J. L. WILLCOCKS, M.C. — Black Watch.

A/Lt.Col. C. S. BREBNER. — R.A.M.C.

MILITARY CROSS.
T/Captain R. VERNET. — General List.
Captain E. R. BROADBENT. — Hussars.
Capt. R. T. LEE. — R.F.A.
Capt. H. V. HUMMEL.
Lieut. J. R. C. JORGENSEN. — D.A.C.
A/Major G. C. KENNARD. — R.E.
A/Capt. A. LEVY. — Middlesex Regt.
A/Lt.Col. R. E. F. SHAW. — London Regt.
Capt. J. C. ANDREWS. — "
A/Capt. F. C. BISHOP. — "
Captain R. S. PRICE. — "
A/Capt. T. G. McCARTHY. — "
Captain J. NICHOLS. — "
A/Capt. A. H. JOLLIFFE. — Cheshire Regt.
Captain G. S. SMITH. — M.G. Corps.
Lieut. H. USHER. — "
Lieut. A. WILSON. — "
Rev. J. K. F. BICKERSTETH. — Army Chaplains' Dept.
Rev. D. C. LUSK. — "

MERITORIOUS SERVICE MEDAL.
930031	A/RSM.	F. T. G. BENNETT.	R.A.
930030	BSM.	F. BISHOP.	R.F.A.
925123	BQMS.	C. G. WEBSTER.	"
200100	A/Sgt Maj.	H. HESTER.	London Regt.
510031	Rgtl.Q.M.Sgt.	J. GIBSON.	"
240524	CSM.	E. JAMES.	Cheshire Regt.
71400	CQMS.	F. G. POOK.	M.G. Corps.
510549	Sergt.	J. H. ROBERTS.	London Regt.
390652	A/Cpl.	H. T. PENNY.	"
S/22109.	A/Staff Q.M.Sgt.	A. J. COOK.	A.S.C.
T4/038863	C.Q.M.S.	A. L. CLARKE.	"
512426	Sgt.	E. BOURTON.	R.A.M.C.
02468	T/Condr.	J. ANDERSON.	A.O.C.
716	A/Squad Sgt.Maj.	A. C. BRIDGES.	M.M.P.

List of Officers, N.C.Os. and Men Mentioned in Dispatches will be published later.

Appendix I War Diary

LOCATIONS

56th DIVISION.
AQS/5.
12th January, 1918.

Divl. H.Q.	VILLERS-CHATEL.
S.S.O.	SAVY.
D.A.D.O.S.	TINCQUES.
Divl. Artillery.) 280th Bde. RFA.) 281st " ") D. A. C.)	Detached from Division.
C. R. E.	A.28.b.5.3.
416th Field Coy.	TINCQUES.
512th " "	AUBREY CAMP.
513th " "	ROBERTS CAMP.
167th Inf. Bde. H.Q.	CHELERS.
1/7th Middx. Regt.	"
1/8th " "	TINCQUES.
1/1st London Regt.	VILLERS-BRULIN.
1/3rd " "	AUBREY CAMP.
167th M.G.Coy.	TINCQUETTE.
167th T.M.Bty.	BAILLEUL AUX CORNAILLES.
168th Inf. Bde. H.Q.	ORLENCOURT.
1/4th London Regt.	MONCHY-BRETON.
1/12th " "	STEWART CAMP.
1/13th " "	MAGNICOURT.
1/14th " "	LA THIEULOYE.
168th M.G.Coy.	BAJUS.
168th T.M.Bty.	" "
169th Inf. Bde. H.Q.	FREVILLERS.
1/2nd London Regt.	TRAFALGAR CAMP.
1/5th " "	FREVILLERS.
1/9th " "	CAMBLIGNEUL.
1/16th " "	CAUCOURT.
169th M.G.Coy.	LA COMTE.
169th T.M.Bty.	CAMBLIGNEUL.
Divl. Train H.Q.	SAVY
Headquarters Coy.	Detached from Division.
No. 2 Coy.	TINCQUETTE.
No. 3 Coy.	ROCOURT.
No. 4 Coy.	HERMIN.
No. 56 Supply Column.	TINCQUES.
Pioneer Bn. (1/5th Cheshire Regt.)	BAILLEUL AUX CORNAILLES.
193rd (Div) M.G.Coy.	CAMBLIGNEUL.
A. D. M. S.	MINGOVAL.
2/1st London Fld. Ambce.	AUBIGNY.
2/2nd "	HOUVELIN.
2/3rd "	HERMIN.
Mobile Veterinary Section.	TINCQUES.

Captain,
D.A.A.G., 56th Division.

Appendix K.   War Diary
AQS/5.

LOCATIONS.

56th DIVISION   19th January, 1918.

Divl. H.Q.	VILLERS-CHATEL.
S.S.O.	SAVY.
D.A.D.O.S.	TINCQUES.
Divl. Arty. H.Q.	BERLES.
280th. Bde. R.F.A. H.Q. & Wagon Lines.	DETHENCOURT. CAPELLE FERMONT. BERLES. FREVIN CAPELLE. GAUCHIN-LEGAL.
281st. Bde. R.F.A. H.Q. & Wagon Lines	CAUCOURT. SAVY. GAUCHIN-LEGAL.
D.A.C.	A.26.b.5.3.
C.R.E. H.Q.	
416th Field Coy.	AUBREY CAMP.
512th " "	ROBERTS CAMP.
513th " "	
167th Inf. Bde. H.Q.	CHELERS.
1/7th Middlesex Regt.	TINCQUES.
1/8th "	AUBREY CAMP.
1/1st London Regt.	VILLERS-BRULIN.
1/3rd "	TINCQUETTE.
167th M.G. Coy.	BAILLEUL AUX CORNAILLES.
167th T.M. Bty.	
168th Inf. Bde. H.Q.	ORLENCOURT.
1/4th London Regt.	MONCHY-BRETON.
1/12th " "	LA THIEULOYE.
1/13th " "	MAGNICOURT.
1/14th " "	SEWART CAMP.
168th M.G. Coy.	MARQUAY.
168th T.M. Bty.	
169th Inf. Bde. H.Q.	FREVILLERS.
1/2nd London Regt.	TRAFALGAR CAMP.
1/5th " "	CAMBLIGNEUL.
1/9th " "	CAUCOURT & HERMIN.
1/16th London Regt.	LA COMTE.
169th M.G. Coy.	CAMBLIGNEUL.
169th T.M. Bty.	
56th Divl. Train. H.Q.	SAVY.
Headquarters Company.	TINCQUETTE
No. 2 Coy.	
No. 3 "	ROCOURT.
No. 4 "	HERMIN.
No. 56 Supply Coln.	TINCQUES.
Pioneer Battn. (1/5th Cheshire Regt.)	BAILLEUL AUX CORNAILLES.
192nd (Div) Machine Gun Coy.	CAMBLIGNEUL.
A.D.M.S.	MINGOVAL.
2/1st London Fld. Ambce.	AUDIGNY.
2/2nd " " "	HOUVELIN.
2/3rd " " "	HERMIN.
Mobile Veterinary Section.	VANMELICOURT.

Captain
for D.A.A.G. 56th.Divn.

Appendix L

SECRET.   LOCATIONS.   A.Q.S. 5.

56th DIVISION.   25th January, 1918.

Divl. Headquarters.	VILLERS CHATEL.
S.S.O.	SAVY.
D.A.D.O.S.	TINCQUES.

Divl. Artillery H.Q. — BERLES.
- 280th Bde. R.F.A., H.Q. — BETHENCOURT.
-     "   Wagon Lines — CAPELLE FERMONT. BERLES. FREVIN CAPELLE
- 281st Bde. R.F.A., H.Q. — GAUCHIN LEGAL
-     "   Wagon Lines — GAUGOURT. SAVY

Attached.
- 46th A.F.A. Bde. and 1 Battery — ACQ
- 155th A.F.A. Bde. — VALHOUT

56th D.A.C. — GAUCHIN LEGAL.

C.R.E., Headquarters. — A.26.b.5.3
- 413th Field Coy. — "
- 512th Field Coy. — ROBERTS CAMP.
- 513th Field Coy. — AUDREY CAMP.

167th Inf. Bde. Headquarters. — CHELERS.
- 1/7th Middlesex Regt. — "
- 1/8th Middlesex Regt. — AUDREY CAMP.
- 1/1st London Regt. — TINCQUES.
- 1/3rd London Regt. — VILLERS-BRULIN.
- 167th M.G.Coy. — TINCQUETTE.
- 167th T.M.Battery — BAILLEUL AUX CORNAILLES

168th Inf. Bde. Headquarters. — ORLENCOURT.
- 1/4th London Regt. — STEWART CAMP.
- 1/12th   "   " — LA THIEULOYE
- 1/13th   "   " — MAGNICOURT.
- 1/14th   "   " — MONCHY-BRETON.
- 168th M.G.Coy. — MARQUAY.
- 168th T.M.Battery — "

169th Inf. Bde. Headquarters. — FREVILLERS.
- 1/2nd London Regt. — "
- 1/5th   "   " — CAUCOURT & HERMIN.
- 1/9th   "   " — CAMBLIGNEUL.
- 1/16th   "   " — TRAFALGAR CAMP.
- 169th M.G.Coy. — LA COMTE
- 169th T.M.Battery — CAMBLIGNEUL.

56th Divl. Train Headquarters. — SAVY
- Headquarter Coy. — "
- No. 2 Company — TINCQUETTE
- No. 3 Company — ROCOURT
- No. 4 Company — HERMIN

No. 56 Supply Column. — TINCQUES.
Pioneer Battn. (1/5th Cheshire Regt.) — BAILLEUL AUX CORNAILLES
193rd (Div.) Machine Gun Coy. — CAMBLIGNEUL.
A.D.M.S. — MINGOVAL.
- 2/1st London Field Ambce. — AUBIGNY.
- 2/2nd   "   " — HOUVELIN
- 2/3rd   "   " — HERMIN

Mobile Veterinary Section — VANDELICOURT.

[signature]
Captain,
for D.A.A.G., 56th Division.

Appendix M

SECRET. AQS/488.

Subject:- **REORGANISATION.**

56th Div. Instructions No. 1.

Issued with reference to 56th Div. G148/1, dated 22.1.18.

The following procedure will be observed in the reorganisation of the 56th Division. Unless otherwise stated, no definite action will be taken until orders to do so are issued. Battalions concerned must however at once make careful arrangements to ensure that no delay or confusion takes place when definite orders for the reorganisation to begin are issued.

1. **General Principles.**

   (a) A nucleus only of the 3 Battns selected will proceed to 58th Divn. The strength of this nucleus will be notified later, but it will probably be - 13 Officers and 270 O.Rs.

   (b) The surplus of these 3 Battns. will be available for transfer either within the LONDON REGT. or within their Corps (as defined by A.B.250 of 1916) as circumstances require.

   (c) In selecting the nucleus care should be taken that as far as possible it is composed of personnel who have served in the same Platoon or Company.

   (d) The Battn. H.Qs. of the Battns. about to be amalgamated will be included in the Nucleus. The Nucleus will not leave the Divl. Area until all surplus personnel has been posted to other Units.

   (e) The Transport Personnel detailed to accompany animals in accordance with 56th Div. AQS.488, dated 24.1.18, will be that authorised in War Establishment plus one man to two riding horses.
   The Transport Officer must be in possession of an accurate Nominal Roll of such personnel, stating to what Battns they will be ultimately posted.

   (f) No R.A.M.C. or A.O.C. Personnel will proceed with the Nucleus of Battns. Orders as regards the disposal of such Personnel will be issued later.

2. **Issue of Instructions, etc.**

   (a) Detailed instructions for the posting of Surplus Personnel will be issued later.

   (b) As soon as the Strength of the Nucleus is notified the following action will be taken by the 3 Battns concerned:

   (i) Render in quintuplicate a full Nominal Roll of all Officers W.Os., N.C.Os. and Men selected to compose the Nucleus. Officers and O.Rs. (a) On leave (b) Attending Schools of Instruction and Courses may be included in the Nucleus but it is not advisable unless C.Os. specially desire it to include Officers and O.Rs. in hospital. The fact that certain personnel is on leave, etc., must be stated in the Roll together with the approximate date of return, (if known).

P. T. O.

(ii) Render a Strength Return on Proforma "A" attached (in triplicate) made up to the time of despatch.

Both (i) and (ii) above must reach this Office (through the usual channels) by special D.R.L.S. as early as possible, but not later than 24 hours after the Strength of the Nucleus is notified to the Unit.

(c) Battns. concerned should be prepared, if called upon to do so, to render at short notice a full Nominal Roll of all Officers and O.Rs. on their Effective Strengths, stating any special qualifications possessed by them.

(d) On receipt of this letter all Officers and O.Rs. on the Strength of the 3 Battns to be amalgamated but at present serving away from it, and not on the Strength of another Unit or Formation, will at once be ordered to rejoin their Battns. With the exception of those on leave, attending Courses of Instruction, or in the case of Officers, Staff Learners authorised by G.H.Q. Battns. concerned will at once notify this Office of the names of all such personnel at present serving with, but not on the Strength of, Units or Formations outside this Division, giving full particulars of employments, etc.

3. **1st Line T.F. Battns.**

(a) The Battns. of 1st Line T.F. Regts. which are not being amalgamated will be completed to Establishment by the posting of personnel surplus to 1st Line Units which are being amalgamated or 2nd Line Units to be disbanded.

(b) The C.Os. and Seconds in Command of amalgamated Battns. will be selected by the Military Secretary under the orders of the C.-in-C.

(c) In the case of 1st Line T.F. Units to be amalgamated with their second lines the Q.M. of the 1st line will in all cases be appointed Q.M. of the amalgamated Battn.

4. **Nomenclature.**

The Battn. formed by, say, the amalgamation of the 1/3rd and 2/3rd London Regt. will in future be known as the 3rd Battn. London Regt.

5. **Moves.**

The moves of the Nucleus of the Battns. to be amalgamated will be notified later.

6. **Leave & Courses.**

(a) Leave will not be stopped during the reorganisation.

(b) Immediately orders are issued for the reorganisation to begin Brigades will forward to this Office a Nominal Roll in triplicate of all Officers and O.Rs. of the Battns. to be amalgamated who are on leave or Courses in the U.K., stating in each case the destination, date of return, and Unit to which the Officer or O.R. has been posted. Similar rolls will be rendered by Brigades to this Office daily by 2 p.m. stating all additional names with the necessary particulars.

(e) 169th Inf. Bde.

(c) 169th Inf. Bde. will detail 1 Captain and 1 Sergeant to proceed to BOULOGNE to assist the Base Commandant in despatching men to their correct Units. They will report at Base H.Q. on arrival for instructions. The date on which they will proceed will be notified later. On completion of this duty they will rejoin their Units. 169th Infantry Brigade will notify this Office as early as possible of the names of the Officer and N.C.O. selected. They will not be detailed from the 1/9th London Regt., (Q.V.R.).

7. Disposal of Funds.

On receipt of this letter Os.C. Battns. detailed for amalgamation will take immediate steps to effect a settlement of all outstanding accounts in respect of Officers' and Sergeants' Mess, Canteen, and other funds. They will cause a Balance Sheet to be prepared.

The balance of all such funds will be held in charge by the Divisional Commander pending further instructions to be issued from G.H.Q.

The date on which Battns. concerned will hand over such funds will be notified later.

8. The Divisional Commander realises the heavy strain that will be placed on Brigades and Battalions by the reorganisation, but he draws attention to the necessity of keeping a careful trace of all personnel, particularly those on Courses, Leave, etc., and also to the great need of accuracy in rendering nominal rolls and strengths.

Captain,
25th January, 1918.   for A.A.& Q.M.G., 56th Division.

- Distribution -

167th Inf. Bde.
168th   "
169th   "
"G".
D.M.G.O. (for information).

PROFORMA "A".

LONDON REGIMENT

	O.	O.Rs.
No. actually present with the Battn., less Nucleus.		
No. on Leave to U.K.		
∅ No. on Leave to places in FRANCE.		
No. on Courses in U.K.		
∅ No. on Courses in FRANCE.		
∅ No. in F. A.		
∅ No. Detached but not on the Strength of other Units or Formations.		
Nucleus.		
EFFECTIVE STRENGTH.		
ESTABLISHMENT BY W.E.	43	964

NO OFFICER OR O.R. SELECTED TO COMPOSE THE NUCLEUS WILL BE INCLUDED IN THESE FIGURES.

∅   Nominal Rolls of all such personnel must be attached hereto, giving full particulars in each case, and where known the date of return.

Made up to

Made up to .... a.m. / p.m. .... 1918.

Lieut.-Colonel,
Commanding ...... London Regt.

SECRET. 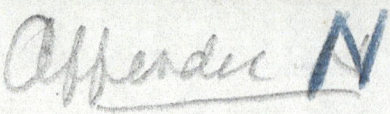 AQS 408.

SUBJECT: REORGANISATION.

56th DIVISION INSTRUCTIONS No.2.

1. With reference to para.2 (a) of AQS 408 dated 25.1.18, postings of all Personnel will be carried out by Officers Commanding Battalions to be amalgamated in accordance with Table "A" attached.

2. The strength of the Nucleus will be 12 Officers and 200 O.Rs.

3. Strict attention must be paid to the following instructions with regard to the posting of Officers and O.Rs.

(a) A Nominal Roll showing the proposed postings of Officers will reach this office as early as possible tomorrow 28th inst. If the proposed postings are approved the fact will be wired to Brigades at once.

(b) N.C.Os. of and below the rank of Sergeant are to be included in the Nucleus and posted to other Units so far as available in the proportion of 2 Sgts. 3 Cpls. and 3 L/Cpls. in every 50 O.Rs. and one Lance Sergeant in addition in every 100 O.Rs.

(c) Regimental Signallers to the extent laid down in Table "A" will be posted in accordance with that Table. The remainder will be disposed of in accordance with the following paragraph. (para. D)

(d) All personnel -(on Courses, Detached, Specialists &c. (Men on leave, will be included proportionately in the postings ordered in Table "A".

(e) Orders for the disposal of W.Os. and N.C.Os. above the rank of Sgt. not already provided for in Table "A" will be issued later.

(f) Transport Personnel will not be included in the Nucleus or in the parties posted to other Units. They will remain attached to their present Brigades and will await further orders as to disposal.

NOTE. Every endeavour should be made to, as far as possible, post Officers N.C.Os. and men who have previously served together to the same Unit.

4. All postings ordered herein will at once be detailed. Personnel posted to other Units will not be despatched to join those Units until orders to do so are issued by this office.

5. In addition to the Nominal Roll and Return called for in para. 2 (b) of AQS 408 dated 25.1.18, the following Returns will be rendered to this office as early as possible but not later than 1st. D.R. 31st inst.

(a) Nominal Rolls in quadruplicate of all Officers and O.Rs. selected for posting to other Units in accordance with these instructions. A separate Roll will be rendered for each Unit to which postings are made.
1 Copy of this Roll will be retained by the Unit for them to hand to the Senior Officer in charge of each party when it proceeds to join its new unit.
These Rolls will show any special qualifications possessed

by Officers and O.Rs. so as to facilitate their employment in their new Units. If any Officers or O.Rs. shown on the Nominal Roll are not actually present with the Unit their whereabouts will be stated against their name, such as "on leave" "at ......Corps R. and R. Camp" &c.

These Nominal Rolls will be made out in the following form

Old Regtl. No.	Old Battn.	Name and Rank.	New Regtl. No.	New Battn.	Any special qualifications.	Remarks.

(see para. 8 below re the allotting of new numbers.)

(b) As soon as all postings ordered herein have been completed and the parties despatched, a wire will be sent to this office stating number and rank of any surplus still remaining available. This wire will show (i) number actually with the Unit, (ii) number detached from the Unit. In the case of (ii) a Nominal Roll of such personnel giving full particulars will be sent by Special D.R.L.S. to this office.

6. In order to localise as far as possible inconvenience caused by this reorganisation personnel who have rejoined from the following employments (or who for any reason still remain in them) will be posted to other Units in the same Brigade of this Division and will again take up their detached duties under Brigade arrangements on a date to be notified later.

Permanent Staff XIII Corps R. and R. Camp.
Traffic Control Police attached to A.P.M. 53th Division.
N.C.Os. and Men attached to the D.A.D.O.S. 53th Division.
N.C.Os. and Men attached to 53th Div. Train.
N.C.Os. and Men attached to Camp Commandant H.Q. 53th Division.

"T.U" personnel attached to 247th Div. Employment Co. as set forth on the Nominal Rolls forwarded under this Office AQS 408 dated 26.1.18 will be similarly dealt with.

7. (a) R.A.M.C. personnel attached to Battalions selected for amalgamation will be disposed of under orders to be issued direct to Brigades by the A.D.M.S. He will forward a copy of his instructions to this office.

(b) A.O.C. personnel attached to such battalions will remain with the D.A.D.O.S. 53th Division.

8. All personnel posted from one Battalion to another will be allotted new numbers. To assist in carrying out the work an Orderly Room Sergt. is being sent to the Division by the D.A.G. with the necessary blocks of numbers. The New numbers allotted will be notified to Battalions as early as possible for inclusion in the Rolls referred to in para. 5 (a) above. All such personnel will have their new numbers and names of their new Battalions entered in their A.Bs. 64 and other documents. New Identity Discs not being available the old ones will be remarked under Brigade arrangements.

In the case of personnel detached from their present Units and posted to other Units "on paper" the C.O. of the Unit to which such personnel is posted will be responsible for notifying the formation or unit to which the Officers or O.Rs. are attached of the new numbers allotted and of the name of the Battalion to which they have been posted. Battalions concerned will obtain a certificate from that formation or unit stating that the necessary corrections have been made in the mans A.B.64 and other documents and that the identity disc has been altered accordingly.

9. The Nominal Rolls referred to in para. 6 (b) of AQS 408 dated 25.1.18 will be forwarded to this office immediately C.Os. have detailed the postings and daily additions/ as instructed therein until further orders. forwarded

139th Infantry Brigade will arrange for the Officer and N.C.O. detailed to assist the Base Commandant, BOULOGNE to be ready to proceed at very short notice

10. All postings made in accordance with this letter will be carried out under authority G.H.Q. (3rd Echelon) letter S/7074 dated 25.1.18.

A. Dundas
Captain,
for A.A. & Q.M.G., 56th Division.

27.1.18.

Copies to :-

137th Inf. Bde.	A.D.M.S.
138th Inf. Bde.	56th Div. Train.
139th Inf. Bde.	D.A.D.O.S.
"G".	A.P.M.

TABLE "A".

POSTINGS to be carried out by 56th DIVISION.

(Under the provisions of G.H.Q. (3rd Echelon) Letter S/7074, dated 25.1.1918.)

Post from:-	Offrs.	O.Rs.	To include Regtl. Signrs.	Post to:-	Divn.	Corps.	Army.	Remarks.
1/3rd London Regt.	12	200		2/3rd London Regt.	58th	III	Fifth	2/3rd Becomes 3rd London Rgt.
1/3rd "	11	250		1/1st "	56th	XIII	First	
1/3rd "	11	250	8	1/2nd "	56th	XIII	First	
1/3rd "	2	50		1/4th "	56th	XIII	First	
1/9th "	12	200		2/9th "	58th	III	Fifth	2/9th becomes 9th London R.
1/9th "	5	150		1/13th "	56th	XIII	First	
1/9th "	12	250	7	1/16th "	56th	XIII	First	
1/9th "	5	150		1/4th "	56th	XIII	First	
1/12th "	12	200		2/12th "	58th	III	Fifth	2/12th becomes 12th Lond n R.
1/12th "	8	300		1/5th "	56th	XIII	First	Corps Trans to their R.S...
1/12th "	7	230		1/23rd "	47th	V	Third.	Corps Transfor.

UNIT.	Strength. 1.1.18. O.	O.R.	Increase. O.	O.R.	Decrease. O.	O.R.	Strength. 1.2.18. O.	O.R.
Divl. H.Q.	19	86	1	-	2	2	18	84
167th Inf. Bde. H.Q.	3	21	-	-	-	-	3	21
7th Middlesex Rgt.	45	734	7	132	4	35	48	831
8th "	30	685	20	208	1	20	49	873
1st London Rgt.	35	711	20	300	2	13	53	998
3rd "	37	767	R E O R G A N I S E D.					
167th M.G.Coy.	13	179	-	1	1	4	12	176
167th T.M.Bty.	4	46	-	-	-	-	4	46
168th Inf. Bde. H.Q.	3	21	-	-	-	-	3	21
4th London Regt.	35	707	9	198	3	21	41	884
12th "	33	751	R E O R G A N I S E D.					
13th "	39	847	6	158	3	32	42	973
14th "	49	900		62	3	59	46	903
168th M.G.Coy.	9	168	1	18	-	15	10	171
168th T.M.Bty.	3	46	1	2	-	2	4	46
169th Inf. Bde. H.Q.	3	20	-	1	-	-	3	21
2nd London Regt.	36	656	13	364	1	13	48	1007
5th "	34	685	14	320	2	34	46	971
9th "	34	736	R E O R G A N I S E D.					
16th "	29	688	14	402	3	80	40	1010
169th M.G.Coy.	11	173	-	9	1	7	10	175
169th T.M.Bty.	2	22	2	23	-	-	4	45
5th Cheshire Regt.	36	987	5	32	1	13	40	1006
193rd M.G.Coy.	12	168	-	11	-	3	12	176
H.Q. R.A.	4	17	-	-	-	-	4	17
280th Bde. R.F.A.	32	747	7	53	1	19	38	781
281st " "	30	753	1	72	6	16	25	809
D.A.C.	14	560	-	35	-	12	14	583
H.Q. R.E.	1	10	1	-	-	-	2	10
416th (Edin) Fld Coy.	9	208	-	1	2	5	7	204
512th (Ldn) "	6	202	-	7	-	6	6	203
513th (") "	7	202	2	10	-	6	9	206
Div. Signal Company.	9	271	2	6	-	5	11	272
Divl. Train.	20	360	-	-	3	46	17	314
Medical Units.	24	520	2	9	-	8	26	519
Mob. Vet. Sec.	1	18	-	3	-	-	1	21
247th Employment Coy.	1	282	-	34	-	15	1	301

56th Division.

CASUALTIES for the month of JANUARY, 1918.

Date.	UNIT.	OFFICERS. Killed.	Wounded.	Missing.	O.Rs. K.	W.	M.	Remarks.
2nd	7th Middlesex Regt.	-	-	-	-	3	-	
4th	512th Field Coy. R.E.	-	-	-	-	1	-	At duty.
5th	168th M.G. Coy.	-	-	-	1	1	-	
	13th London Regt.	-	-	-	1	1	-	
8th	X/56th T.M.Bty.	-	-	-	-	1	-	
12th	513th (London) Field Coy. RE.	-	2/Lt. W. S. HARVEY.	-	-	-	-	
14th	5th London Regt.	-	(Capt. W.C.VONBERG 1.12.17.)	-	-	-	-	
	169th T.M.Bty.	-	(Capt. P. BROMLEY 21.12.17) ø	-	-	-	-	ø Gas.
		-	Capt. A.J.WHITTLE 30.11.17)	-	-	-	-	
15th	1/5th Cheshire Regt.	-	2/Lt. C. H. LANG 3.12.17 } ø	-	-	-	-	ø Gas.
			F.E.DAVENPORT " "	-	-	-	-	
24th	3rd London Regt.	-	-	-	-	2	-	Accidentally, bomb explosion.
"	2nd London Regt.	-	-	-	-	1	-	Accidentally Bayonet wound.

Vol 25

Secret

War Diary

Administrative Branch

56th Division

Period :- 1st to 28th Feby: 1918.

Volume XXV

Army Form C. 2118.

WAR DIARY
or
INTELLIGENCE SUMMARY

(Erase heading not required.)

Page 1

Place	Date	Hour	Summary of Events and Information	Remarks and references to Appendices
VILLERS-CHATEL	Feb 1		Location Table arrived attached hereto (Appendix "A")	
	2		Amendments to Schemes "A" & "C" (re movement of Div. in G.H.Q. Reserve by rail or plus motors) published to set pride for Reorganisation of 1 Bdes into 3 Bns each. Copies attached – Appendix "B".	
	3		Staff moved to forward Area to Conner with 56 Div as to details of their relief by 56 Div	
	4		—	
	5		Admin. Instruction No 1 in Connection with relief of 62nd Div. issued attached hereto "Appendix C".	
	6		Arrangements for Entraining of the 56 Div. (Less Arty) in case of a move by bus is ordered from I Army Area whilst in R.H.Q. Reserve. Issued today attached "Appendix D".	

WAR DIARY or INTELLIGENCE SUMMARY

Army Form C. 2118.

Page 2

Place	Date	Hour	Summary of Events and Information	Remarks and references to Appendices
VILLERS-CHATEL	(A:)		"Administrative Instructions No 2" in connection with Relief of 62nd Div. issued. (attached hereto – Appendix "E") by Bde. HQ. moving out of forward area.	
	Feb 8		Administrative Instructions No 3" in connection with Relief of 62nd Div. issued & attached hereto. Appendix "F" Croton Table "Appendix G" attached showing traters of units on completion of Relief of 62nd Div.	
	Feb 9		168 Inf Bde. move forward area.	
	Feb 10		—	
ROCLINCOURT	AT Feb 11		Completion of Relief of 62nd Div. (less Divisional) Band HQ close VILLERS-CHATEL 11.00 a.m. & open VICTORY CAMP, ROCLINCOURT same hour.	
	Feb 12		Sund. Front reorganised & now 3 Bdes. in the line as follows :- 3 Bde. in line, 3 Bde. Support, 3 Bde. Reserve. Centre Sector – 167 Bde – 1st London in line, 7th Middx Support.	
	Feb 13		Following relief last night. 8th Middx Reserve.	

WAR DIARY or INTELLIGENCE SUMMARY

Army Form C. 2118.

Page 3

Place	Date	Hour	Summary of Events and Information	Remarks and references to Appendices
ROCLINCOURT	Feb 14		Relief carried out last night, 169 Bde - Right Sector - 2nd Londons to line relieving 16th Londons & Reserve.	
	Feb 15		Relief carried out last night, 168 Bde Left Sector 16th Londons to line relieving 4th Londons. 13th Londons from Reserve to Support. Centre Sector - 167 Bde - 1st London Rin & Reserve Line & 5th Middx to line relieving 8th Middx Reserve to Support.	
	Feb 16		Orders received to commence reorganization of Brigade on 3 Bn. basis. Right Sector - 169 Bde - 2nd Londons line to Reserve & line 16th Londons support, 5th Londons Reserve.	
	Feb 18		Left Sector 168 Bty Bde 13th Londons to line & Reserve. Support 14th Londons & Reserve.	
	Feb 19		Ploughing commenced in Div. Area. It is intended to place about fifty acres under cultivation in the present (Forward) Div Area.	

WAR DIARY or INTELLIGENCE SUMMARY

Army Form C. 2118.
Page 4.

Place	Date	Hour	Summary of Events and Information	Remarks and references to Appendices
ROCLINCOURT	Jan 31		Centre Sector – 16 Bde – 8th Middx & Lines 1st London & Support. 7th Middx Reserve. Poor Positions (received from them today returned to them a 1 month earlier. Quantities over 100 Ws.	
	Feb 1		Right Sector – 169 Bde – 16th London & Line, 5 London & Support 2nd London Reserve. Great difficulty in getting the experiences & taking times which from the Tea Bar. Comms re	
	Feb 2		Left Sector – 168 Bde – 4th London & Line – 10th London & Support – 13th London & Reserve.	
	Feb 3		Commander in Chief visits Div. HQ in the morning.	
	Feb 4		Centre Sector – 167 Bde – 1st London & Line – 7th Middx & Support – 8th Middx & Reserve.	
	Feb 5/26		No change	
	Feb 27		Left Sector 168 Bde – 4th London & Line – 13th London & Support – 4th London & Reserve	

Army Form C. 2118.

WAR DIARY
or
INTELLIGENCE SUMMARY
(Erase heading not required.)

Page 5.

Place	Date	Hour	Summary of Events and Information	Remarks and references to Appendices
ROCLINCOURT	Feb 27		Right Sector - 169 Bde - 2" Londons to Line - 16 Londons to Support - 5" Londons to Reserve.	
	Feb 28		no change.	

W. Sutton Lieut:-Col:
A.A. & Q.M.G. 56th Division.

Appendix "A" War Diary

SECRET.   LOCATIONS.   A.Q.S.5.

56th DIVISION.   1st. FEBRUARY, 1918.

 Divl. H.Q.   VILLERS CHATEL.

 S.S.O.   SAVY.

 D.A.D.O.S.   TINCQUES.

Divl. Artillery H.Q.   BERLES.
 280th Bde. R.F.A., H.Q.   BETHENCOURT.
   "   Wagon Lines.)   CAPELLE FERMONT. BERLES.
)   FREVIN CAPELLE.
 281st Bde. R.F.A., H.Q.   GAUCHIN-LEGAL.
   "   Wagon Lines.   CAUCOURT. SAVY.
 Attached.
 48th A.F.A. Bde., & 1 Battery.   ACQ.
 155th "   "   "   VALHOUN.

 56th D.A.C.   GAUCHIN-LEGAL.

C.R.E., H.Q.   A.26.b.5.3.
 413th Field Coy.   "
 512th "   "   ROBERTS CAMP.
 513th "   "   AUBREY CAMP.

167th Inf. Bde. H.Q.   CHELERS.
 1/7th Middlesex Regt.   "
 1/8th "   AUBREY CAMP.
 1/1st London Regt.   TINCQUES.
 167th M.G.Coy.   TINCQUETTE.
 167th T.M.Bty.   BAILLEUL AUX CORNAILLES.

168th Inf. Bde. H.Q.   ORLENCOURT.
 1/4th London Regt.   MAGNICOURT.
 1/13th "   STEWART CAMP.
 1/14th "   MONCHY BRETON.
 168th M.G.Coy.   MARQUAY.
 168th T.M.Bty.   "

169th Inf. Bde. H.Q.   FREVILLERS.
 1/2nd London Regt.   TRAFALGAR CAMP.
 1/5th "   CAUCOURT & HERMIN.
 1/16th "   FREVILLERS.
 169th M.G.Coy.   LA COMTE.
 169th T.M.Bty.   CAMBLIGNEUL.

56th Div. Train H.Q.   SAVY.
 Headquarters Coy.   "
 No. 2 Coy.,   TINCQUETTE.
 No. 3 Coy.,   ROCOURT.
 No. 4 Coy.,   HERMIN.

No. 56 Supply Column.   TINCQUES.

Pioneer Battn. (1/5th Cheshire Regt.)   BAILLEUL AUX CORNAILLES.

193rd (Div.) Machine Gun Coy.   CAMBLIGNEUL.

A.D.M.S.   MINGOVAL.
 2/1st London Field Ambulance.   AUBIGNY.
 2/2nd "   "   "   HOUVELIN.
 2/3rd "   "   "   HERMIN.

Mobile Veterinary Section.   VANDELICOURT.

                     Captain,
                for D.A.A.G., 56th Division.

SECRET.   Appendix "B"   War Diary

AQS.482.

Arrangements for the Entrainment and Detrainment
of the 56th Division in case a move by Rail is ordered
whilst in G.H.Q. Reserve.

Issued with reference to 56th Div. Order No.148.

Reference AQS.482 dated 7.1.18.

SCHEME "A". The following amendments will be made:-

Para. 5. Delete the sentence "1 Company of 5th Cheshire Regt."
"travelling............"
"............ that train."

The attached Entraining Tables will be substituted
for Table "D.1." and the First Page of Table "D.2."

SCHEME "C". The following amendment will be made:-

Para. 1. SAPK. Delete 416th Field Company, R.E.

For Appendix "Y" substitute attached.

A.C. Dundas Captain,
for A.A.& Q.M.G., 56th Divn.

2nd February, 1918.

Copies to:-
167th Inf. Bde.
168th   "
169th   "
1/5th Cheshire Regt.
C.R.A.
C.R.E.
193rd (Div.) Machine Gun Coy.
56th Div. M.G. Officer.
56th Div. Signal Company.
56th Div. Gas Officer.
A.D.M.S.
"Q"
A.P.M.
D.A.D.O.S.

D.A.D.V.S.
56th Div. Train.
56th Div. Supply Col.
56th Div. Ammn. Sub-Park.
A.D.C.
Camp Commandant.
French Mission.
XIII Corps "G".
 "   "   "Q".
War Diary.
File.

APPENDIX "Y".

COMPOSITION OF OMNIBUS TRAIN.

UNIT.	Personnel. Offrs.	O.R.	Horses.	G.S. Limbered.	2 wheeled carts.
Riding Horses & Transport of Bde. H.Q.	-	14	9	1	-
" " Signal Section.	-	14	9	1	1
L.G. Detachment Transport 5 L.G.S. Wagons & 1 Grenade L.G.S. Wagon per Battn.	-	32	30	15	-
Pack Animals, 6 per Battn.	-	24	18	-	-
Medical Personnel & 1 Maltese Cart per Battn.	4	8	3	-	3
1 Water Cart per Battn. and 1 M.G.C.	-	16	8	-	4
∮ M.G.Coy. and 2 L.G.S. Wagons per section.	10	200	34	8	1
Riders, 6 per Battn. 7 M.G.C.	-	28	31	-	-
	14	336	142	25	9

59 Axles.

∮ Finds loading & unloading party of 100 men.

TABLE "D" 2.

		Serial No.	Description.
Entraining Station.	(AUBIGNY	5601	Divl. H.Q.
	(TINQUES	5602	H.Q. Divl. R.A.
	(AUBIGNY	5603	" " R.E. (5604c.
	(TINQUES	(5604	1/5th Cheshires less 5604a,5604b,
		(5604a	1 Coy. 1 Cooker & team 1/5th Ches.
		(5604b	2 G.S.W. & teams, 1/5th Cheshires.
		(5604c	2 " " " " "
	(AUBIGNY	5605	H.Q. & No. 1 Sec. Div. Signals.
		5606	-----
	(SAVY	(5607	247 Employment Coy. (& 5609).
		(5608	193 M.G.Coy.
		(5609	247 Employment Coy. (& 5607).

167th Inf. Bde. Group.	5610.	Bde. H.Q.
Entraining Station S A V Y.	5611	"A" Bn. (TINQUES) less 5611a.
	5611a	1 Coy. 1 cooker & team "A" Bn.
	5612	"B" Bn. (CHELERS) less 5612a.
	5613a	1 Coy. 1 cooker & team "C" Bn.
	5613	"C" Bn. (AUBREY CAMP) Less 5613a.
	5612a	1 Coy. 1 cooker & team "B" Bn.
	5615	Bde. Signal Sec.
	5616	Bde. M.G.C.
	5617	Bde. T.M.B.
	5676	No. 2 Coy. Div. Train.
	5681	416 Field Coy., R.E.
	5686	2/1st London Field Ambce.

168th Inf. Bde. Group.	5620	Bde. H.Q.
Entraining Station T I N Q U E S.	5621	"A" Bn. (MONCHY BRETON) less 5621a.
	5621a	1 Coy. 1 cooker & team "A" Bn.
	5623	"B" Bn. (MAGNICOURT) less 5623a.
	5623a	1 Coy. 1 cooker & team "B" Bn.
	5624	"C" Bn. (STEWART CAMP) less 5624a.
	5624a	1 Coy. 1 cooker & team "C" Bn.
	5625	Bde. Signal Sec.
	5626	Bde. M.G.C.
	5627	Bde. T.M.B.
	5677	No. 3 Coy. Div. Train.
	5682	512 Field Coy. R.E.
	5687	2/2nd London Field Ambce.

169th Inf. Bde. Group.	5630	Bde. H.Q.
Entraining Station A U B I G N Y.	5631	"A" Bn. (CAUCOURT) less 5631a.
	5631a	1 Coy. 1 cooker & team "A" Bn.
	5632	"B" Bn. (FREVILLERS) less 5632a.
	5634a	1 Coy. 1 cooker & team "C" Bn.
	5634	"C" Bn. (TRAFALGAR CAMP) less 5634a.
	5632a	1 Coy. 1 cooker & team "B" Bn.
	5635	Bde. Signal Sec.
	5636	Bde. M.G.C.
	5637	Bde. T.M.B.
	5678	No. 4 Coy. Div. Train.
	5683	513 Field Coy., R.E.
	5688	2/3rd London Field Ambce.

The three surplus Battn. Transports will move by march route under orders of Div. H.Q.

TABLE "D" 1.

AUBIGNY.	SAVY.	TINQUES.	Serial Number.	Date.	Time of Departure
1			(5630, 5631a, 5635, 5636, (5637.		
	1		(5610, 5611a, 5615, 5616, (5617.		
		1	(5620, 5621a, 5625, 5626, (5627.		
2			5631		
	2		5611.		
		2	5621.		
3			5632.		
	3		5612.		
		3	5623, 5604b.		
4			5634.		
	4		5613.		
		4	5624, 5604c.		
5			5601, 5605, 5603.		
	5		5607, 5608, 5609, 5675.		
		5	5604.		
6			5634a, 5673, 5683.		
	6		5613a, 5676, 5681.		
		6	5604a, 5677, 5682.		
7			5632a, 5688.		
	7		5612a, 5686, 5690.		
		7	5623a, 5624a, 5687.		
8			5651, 5672a.		
	8		5641, 5671a.		
		8	5602, 5670, 5675a.		
9			5650, 5672.		
	9		5640, 5671.		
		9	5673a.		
10			5652, 5672b.		
	10		5642, 5671b.		
		10	(5673b, 5691, 5692, 5693, (5694.		
11			5653, 5672c.		
	11		5643, 5671 c.		
		11	5644, 5671d.		
12			5654, 5672d.		

In the event of a Division entraining less Artillery, Hdqrs. Divl. Arty. (5602) will entrain with Divl. Hdqrs. (5601) and Hdqrs. Divl. Engineers (5603) will travel by 5th Train from SAVY in addition to those already allotted to that train.

Appendix "C" War Diary

ADMINISTRATIVE INSTRUCTIONS.
No. 1.
AQS/495.

In connection with 56th Division Order 149.

1. **STAGING.** On moving from present Area Infantry Bde. Groups (less Field Coys. R.E., Field Ambulances, Train Coys., and Battns. now in Forward Area) will be accommodated as follows in Maroeuil Area.

Feb. 7th.	169th Inf. Bde.	Bde. H.Q.	ST. AUBIN.	Billets from Town Majors.
		"A" Bn.	"	
		"B" Bn.	MAROEUIL.	
		M.G.C.& T.M.B.	ANZIN.	
9th.	168th "	Bde. H.Q.	ST. AUBIN.	
		"A" Bn.	MAROEUIL.	
		"B" Bn.	"	
		M.G.C.& T.M.B.	ANZIN	
11th.	167th "	Bde. H.Q.	ST. AUBIN.	
		"A" Bn.	MAROEUIL.	
		"B" Bn.	"	
		"C" Bn.	ST. AUBIN.	
		M.G.C.& T.M.B.	ANZIN	

2. **ACCOMMODATION.**
   Accommodation in Forward Area, with the exception of Transport Lines, will be taken over from the Brigades relieved by arrangement between Brigades.
   Transport Lines will be taken over as follows on the dates stated.

Date	Unit	Lines	From
7th.	169th Inf. Bde.	NELSON LINES,	from 187th Bde.
9th.	168th "	COLLINGWOOD & PORTLAND. "	186th "
11th.	167th "	REDCAR DOVER & CALAIS. "	185th "
10th.	1/5th Cheshire R.	GROPI LINES.	
	M.V.S.	ANZIN.	Under arrangements between D.A.D.V.S.

   The following Camps and Lines will be taken over by the C.R.E. under arrangement with C.R.E. 62nd Divn.
   PORTSMOUTH CAMP. EDINBURGH, PLYMOUTH & HARDY LINES.

3. **ADVANCE PARTIES.** not in excess of 13 per Bde. will be sent forward by ordinary Train Service under Bde. arrangements the day before Units move.

4. **WORK BATTALIONS.**
   Accommodation now occupied by Battns. of this Divn in forward area will be handed over to relieving Units of 62nd Divn, TRAFALGAR CAMP and Company Accommodation on 8th inst.
   STEWART CAMP by 3 p.m. 10th inst.
   AUBREY CAMP " 5 p.m. "
   1 Battn. 167th Inf. Bde. from AUBREY CAMP will be accommodated on 10th and 11th inst. at ST. AUBIN.

5. Paillasses, Lamps F.S., as detailed in AQX98/492 of 20.1.18, and all practice ammunition will be handed over to incoming Units and receipts obtained.

6. **SURPLUS TRANSPORT.**
   Brigades will arrange for drivers, horses and harness of cookers and water carts of Surplus Transports to report to O.C. Div. Train the day before Brigades move. They will carry rations for the day following that on which they report to Div. Train. They will be returned to Brigades the day after arrival in forward area. Remainder of Surplus Transport will move with Brigades.

P.T.O.

7. CHAFF CUTTERS except those on the establishment of the Div. Arty. and Div. Train will be handed over to relieving Units of 62nd Divn. or to Area Commandants. Receipts will be obtained and forwarded to Div. H.Q. Units will take over the Chaff Cutters of the 62nd Div. in the Forward Area.

8. SURPLUS BAGGAGE will be deposited at the Div. Dump, Billet No. 11, TINQUES.

9. GUM BOOTS THIGH will be drawn from the Corps Boot Store, ROCLINCOURT. They will not be taken over in the Trenches.

10. AREA & TRENCH STORES. All Trench Stores, Ammunition, Supplies in Supporting Points, etc., will be carefully taken over and copies of the receipts given by Units will be forwarded to Div. H.Q. within 24 hours of taking over. A.F.W.3405 will not be compiled and forwarded by Bdes. Special attention will be paid to taking over Water and Petrol tins and the checking of L.T.M. ammunition.

11. BATHS, GASSED CLOTHING, STORES, Ammunition Supply, Ordnance, M.V.S., R.E. Material Supply, Supplies, Clean Linen, Bde. Sock Drying Rooms; Salvage. The arrangements for these services will be as before. (See AQX 476).

12. DIVISIONAL CANTEEN.   G.3.b.9.2.
    DIVISIONAL THEATRE.   G.3.b.9.3.
    DIVISIONAL CINEMA.   A.29.c.9.9.

    ORDNANCE.   ST. CATHERINE.

    SOLDER.   Tins for Solder, and Waste Paper will be returned to
    WASTE PAPER. the Div. Dumps, ST. CATHERINE, (opposite Div. Ordnance).

13. The importance of leaving all Billets and Standings in a clean and Sanitary Condition should be impressed on all Ranks. Certificates of Cleanliness will be obtained by rear parties from Area Commandants.

14. SUPPLIES & FUEL. Separate instructions will be issued.

5th February, 1918.

A.C.Dundas
Captain
for ..., & D.A.G., 56th Division.

SECRET.　　　　　　　Appendix D War Diary　　　　　AQS. 482.

ARRANGEMENTS FOR EMBUSSING OF THE 56th DIVISION (LESS ARTY.) IN CASE A MOVE BY 'BUS IS ORDERED FROM FIRST ARMY AREA WHILST IN G.H.Q. RESERVE

1.　　　The Division will be prepared to move:-

  (1)　　Over a period of Three Days:-

   First Day.　　Transport only.
   Second Day.　 "A" Group.
   Third Day.　　"C" & "B" Groups.

　　　　　　　　　- or -

  (2)　　On one day, groups moving at two hours interval in the order A.C.B. and Transport following as soon as possible.

　　　The following General Instructions will hold good whichever method is adopted, except that arrangements for vehicles will be made with XIII Corps and not O.C. Aux 'Bus Park, FREVENT, should the move be within the First Army Area.

2.　　　On receipt of orders to move:-

  (a)　　Immediately on receipt of orders to move by bus an Officer of the Divl. Staff, with the Embussing Strengths of All Units, will get in touch with O.C. Aux. Omnibus Park, FREVENT. He will ascertain from O.C. Park the number and type of vehicles for each Embussing Point, and the times of Embussing and will notify B.Gs by wire.

  (b)　　A wire will be sent to XIII Corps "Q" asking for 14 Lorries to move Machine Guns and Stokes Mortars.

3.　　EMBUSSING POINTS.　　Units will embus at the following points, under Orders of the Brig.-General Commanding Brigade Groups :-

E.28.

Bus Point C.4.d.0.5. - U.26.d.0.0.　(Map Sheets 51c. & 36b.

"A" Group.　　"A" Battn. 167th Inf. Bde.
　　　　　　　 "B"　"　　"　　"　　"
　　　　　　　167th Machine Gun Coy.
　　　　　　　167th Trench Mortar Bty.
　　　　　　　167th Bde. H.Q.
　　　　　　　416th Field Coy. R.E.
　　　　　　　2/1st London Field Ambce.
　　　　　　　"C" Battn. 167th Inf. Bde.
　　　　　　　1/5th Cheshire Regt.

Troops will be drawn up on the North side of the road facing WEST, head of Column at U.26.d.0.0.

E.30.

Bus Point D.9.a.2.0. - D.7.a.0.7. (Map Sheet 51c.)

"B" Group.　　"A" Battn. 169th Inf. Bde.
　　　　　　　 "B"　"　　"　　"　　"
　　　　　　　169th M.G. Coy.
　　　　　　　169th T.M. Bty.
　　　　　　　169th Bde. H.Q.
　　　　　　　513th Field Coy. R.E.
　　　　　　　2/3rd London Field Ambce.
　　　　　　　"C" Battn. 169th Inf. Bde.
　　　　　　　193rd M.G. Coy.
　　　　　　　H.Q. Div. Engineers.
　　　　　　　Divl. H.Q.
　　　　　　　Employment Coy.

Troops will be drawn up on the north side of the road facing WEST, head of Column at D.7.a.0.7.

E.29.

Bus Point N.18.c.7.0. - N.22.c.9.4. (Map Sheet 36b.)

"C" Group.   "A" Battn. 168th Inf. Bde.
           "B" "   "   "   "
168th M.G.Coy.
168th T.M.Bty.
168th Bde. H.Q.
512th Field Coy. R.E.
2/2nd London Field Ambce.
"C" Battn. 168th Inf. Bde.

Troops will be drawn up on the north-west side of the road facing SOUTH-WEST, head of Column at N.22.c.9.4.

4. **TIMES OF EMBUSSING.** The order of Embussing is given in para. 3
The times at which Groups will be ready to embus will be notified to B.G.C. Groups who will be responsible for issuing the necessary march orders to all concerned so that each Group is ready to embus half an hour before the column is due to start.

5. **EMBUSSING OFFICERS.** Each Bde. will detail an Officer not below the rank of Captain who will proceed to the head of each Embussing Column directly orders to move are received and will there await the arrival of O.C. Bus Column. He will take with him a state showing the embussing strengths of all parties of his Group. He will ascertain from O.C. Bus Column the number of busses and lorries that will be provided and will arrange for the Troops to be distributed in 6 Groups for every 80 yards of road space, each Group consisting of 25 All Ranks for each Bus or 20 all Ranks for each seated lorry. He will travel on the last lorry.

6. **DEBUSSING OFFICERS.** Similarly each Bde. will detail an Officer to supervise the Debussing. This Officer will travel on the first lorry of each Group.

7. O.C. Signal Coy. will detail a Motor Cyclist for duty at each Embussing and Debussing Point. They will report to the Officers mentioned in para. 3 and 4.

8. A.D.M.S. will arrange for an Ambulance Car to be on duty at each Embussing and Debussing points.

9. **EMBUSSING & DEBUSSING OFFICERS.** Whilst Embussing and Debussing Officers are on duty they will wear the Blue Armband as a distinguishing badge.

10. **Div. Staff.** An Officer from Div. H.Q. will visit each Embussing Point whilst Embussing is in progress.

11. **Police.** For the control of traffic at each of the Embussing Points the A.P.M. will detail 4 Mounted Policemen to report to the Officers referred to in para. 3 at each bus point one hour before embussing is due to begin.

12. **TRANSPORT.** Transport will move in 3 groups as shown in para. 3, and in addition Train H.Q. Transport & M.V.S. will move with Group "B", and each Train Coy. with the Group to which it is affiliated.

13. **MOTOR CARS, etc.** All Motor Cars, Motor Ambulances and Motor Cycles will proceed on the days on which the Units to which they belong

14. **BAGGAGE WAGONS.** Baggage Wagons will join Units directly orders to embus are received. After being loaded they will march under orders of O.C. Train.

15. **SURPLUS BAGGAGE.** In the event of lorries being available for moving surplus baggage arrangements will be notified at the time. If lorries are not available surplus baggage will be dumped at the Div. Dump, No. 10 TINCQUES, directly orders to embus are received. If there is not sufficient time to take baggage to TINCQUES it will be left in Unit Dumps, each Unit providing a guard of not more than 2 O.R. per Dump.

16. **BAGGAGE & ADVANCE PARTIES LORRIES.** 45 Lorries from No. 8 G.H.Q. MT. Reserve Coy. will be provided for Baggage and Billeting Parties. 15 will report at each Bde. H.Q. as soon as possible after notice to embus has been received. They will be allotted by B.G.C. Groups as follows, and ordered to report to H.Q. of the Units concerned They will move off as soon as they are ready, and will travel independently of the Column conveying the Troops.

    Reporting to 167th Inf. Bde. H.Q., CHELERS:-
    167th Bde.   10.
    Billeting party.   1.
    C.R.E.   1.
    Div. H.Q.   3.

    Reporting to 168th Inf. Bde. H.Q., ORLENCOURT:-
    168th Inf. Bde.   10.
    Billeting Party.   1.
    5th Cheshires.   3.
    Train.   1.

    Reporting to 169th Bde. H.Q., FREVILLERS:-
    169th Bde.   10.
    Billeting Party.   1.
    Div. H.Q.   4.

    (N.B. In case of a move within the Army these lorries will be detailed by XIII Corps.)

17. **LEWIS & MACHINE GUNS, STOKES T.M's.** Lewis Guns and magazines will be taken with the men on the lorries. Two lorries will report at each Bde. H.Q. and 193 M.G.C. for moving Machine Guns and Belts. Two lorries will report at each Bde. H.Q. for moving the handcarts and Stokes Mortars of each L.T.M.B.

18. **SUPPLIES.** The unexpended portion of the current day's ration will be carried on the man, and if available rations for the following day will be taken. Cooking utensils will be taken on the lorries, as travelling kitchens may not be available for three days.

II.

Arrangements for the three battalions, three Field Companies, three Companies Pioneer Battn. and 350 Officers and O.Rs. attached to Tunnelling Companies in the Forward Area to join the Division in case a Move is ordered whilst in G.H.Q. Reserve.

(a) **If 48 hours notice is given.**

Dismounted Personnel of above Units will be moved back to Reserve Div. Area by lorries and will rejoin their Brigade Groups. They will assemble at Embussing Point in Forward Area in the following order. Transport will move by road:-

```
H.Q. Div. Engineers.
416 Field Company.
512    "      "
513    "      "
"C" Battn. 167th Bde.
"C"   "    168th  "
"C"   "    169th  "
Tunnellers.
```

(b) **If there is not sufficient time for Units to return to Billets in the Reserve Area.**

Dismounted Personnel of the above Units will assemble as quickly as possible; move to the bus point mentioned below and move off by first available lorries and join their groups at the embussing points in reserve area. Transport will join the groups either in billets in Reserve Area, or on the march.

In the above two cases the embussing point will be on the ARRAS - SOUCHEZ Road, head of the Column MADAGASCAR CROSS ROADS facing North. The C.R.E. will be responsible for detailing an Embussing Officer and for supervising the assembling and embussing of Units.

In connection with the above see G.R.O.3159.

[signature]
Captain,
6th February, 1918. for A.A.& Q.M.G., 56th Division.

SECRET.   AQS.482. *War Diary*

Reference AQS.482, 6/2/18.

Para 12, for "in para 1" read "in para 3".

                                                    A D Dundas
                                                            Captain,
7/2/18.   for A.A. & Q.M.G. 56th Divn.

SECRET. Appendix "E" War Diary
AQS.495

ADMINISTRATIVE INSTRUCTIONS No. 2,

In connection with 56th Div Order 149.

(1)

1. **SUPPLIES.** Moves of Train Companies will take place as follows:-

No. 4 Coy. to Forward Area on 7th Feb.1918.) Exchanging with their
"   3 "   "   "   " 9th   "   ) opposite numbers of
"   2 "   "   "   " 11th   "   ) 62nd Div. Train.

For Supply arrangements see Appendix attached.
Supply Wagons will march empty (with the exception of the 168th 169th and 193rd Machine Gun Companies, 5th Cheshires and M.V.S., which will march full) and will re-fill and deliver on the afternoon of arrival in the new Area.
With reference to para. 6, Administrative Instructions No. 1, issued in connection with 56th Div. Order No. 149, Train Companies will arrange direct with the Headquarters of their respective Bdes. for the cookers and water carts to report to them, and move with the Train Companies. These vehicles are at present parked in No. 1 Company's lines, SAVY. Officers Commanding Train Companies will arrange direct with their respective Brigades regarding the distribution of the surplus 2nd Line Transport.

(2) Brigade Supply Officers, on arrival in the new area, will take over the re-filling points, with their contents, similarly handing over re-filling points in the Back Area to Brigade Supply Officers of the 62nd Division.

(3) Railhead for the 56th Divn. (less Artillery) will change to ECURIE on the 11th inst.
Railhead for the 62nd Divn. (less Artillery) will change to TINCQUES on the 11th inst.

(4) Train Headquarters will close at SAVY at 11 a.m. on the 11th inst. and will open at CHATHAM CAMP at 12 noon the same day.

2. **MEDICAL.** A.D.M.S. will move to VICTORY CAMP on the 11th inst.

2/2nd London Field Ambce. will take over A.D.S. and forward posts of Div. Front. H.Q. at ANZIN.
2/3rd London Field Ambce. will relieve W.Riding Field Ambce. at ST. CATHERINE and MAROEUIL. H.Q. ST. CATHERINE.

3. **AMENDMENTS TO ADMINISTRATIVE INSTRUCTIONS No. 1.**

Para. 1. M.G.Coys. will arrive in MAROEUIL Area the day before their respective Brigade Groups.

Para. 4. 1 Battn. 167th Inf. Bde. from AUBREY CAMP will be accommodated on the 10th and 11th inst. at WAKEFIELD CAMP with 1 Company at ST. AUBIN

4. **ORDNANCE.** The D.A.D.O.S. will move to ST. CATHERINE 11th inst.

5. **CANTEEN.** An Advanced Divl. Canteen will be opened at H.I.B. on the 11th inst.

6. Arrangements for standard gauge trains, and for the transport of baggage have been notified to all concerned.

7th February, 1918.

A.Dundas Captain,
for A.A. & Q.M.G., 56th Divn.

REFILLING POINTS.

Feb.	167th Inf. Bde. Group.	168th Inf. Bde. Group.	169th Inf. Bde. Group.	Div. Troops (less Arty.)	Remarks.
6th	TINQUES.	ROCOURT.	HERMIN. M.G.C. refill Hermin, with rations for 7th and march full.	SAVY.	
7th	TINQUES.	ROCOURT.	MADAGASCAR CORNER.	SAVY.	
8th	TINQUES.	ROCOURT. M.G.C. refill Rocourt, with rations for 9th and march full.	MADAGASCAR CORNER.	SAVY.	193 M.G.C. refill Rocourt with rations for 9th and march full, afterwards join No. 2 Coy., Madagascar Corner.
9th	TINQUES.	MADAGASCAR CORNER.	MADAGASCAR CORNER.	SAVY.	
10th	TINQUES.	MADAGASCAR CORNER.	MADAGASCAR CORNER.	SAVY.	5th Cheshires refill Tinques for their H.Qrs. with rations for 11th and march full. Afterwards join No. 2 Coy. MADAGASCAR CORNER.
11th	MADAGASCAR CORNER.	MADAGASCAR CORNER.	MADAGASCAR CORNER.	MADAGASCAR CORNER. No. 2 Coy.	

Appendix "F" War Diary

SECRET.

56th DIVISION   AQS 495.

ADMINISTRATIVE INSTRUCTIONS No. 3,

in connection with Relief of 62nd Division.

----

1. **ADMINISTRATION.**

    (a) The Divl. Area is divided into sub-areas which are administered by Area Commandants. The portions of the Area forward of the Eastern Boundaries of BAILLEUL AREA and PONT DU JOUR AREA are administered by the Brigades in the Line.

    (b) Area Commandants' Offices are located as follows:-

MAROEUIL AREA.		F.27.d.7.2.
ST. AUBIN AREA.		L.10.b.3.6.
ANZIN AREA.		G.7.b.8.9.
ST. CATHERINE AREA.		G.9.c.9.0.
ROCLINCOURT AREA.	G.6.d.8.7.	A.28.d.Central.
BAILLEUL AREA.		G.6.d.8.7.
PONT DU JOUR AREA.		G.6.d.8.7.

2. **LIGHT RAILWAYS.**

    (a) (i) Office of Divl. Tramway Officer is at Office of XIII Corps Traffic Officer at ROCLINCOURT, A.29.d.2.5.

    (ii) Units requiring truckage will send indents to Divl. Tramway Officer by 3.00 p.m. the day previous to that on which truckage is required. These indents state:-
    Name of Unit.
    Place, date, and time at which trucks are required.
    Nature and amount of material to be transported.
    Destination of Trucks.

    (iii) Applications for trains for Reliefs should be made to:- Capt. GRAVES, XIII Corps Lt. Rly. Officer, XIII Corps H.Q.

    (b) ROUTES. All lines are worked by tractor with the exception of the TYNE & OPPY Branches which run from B.23.a.0.7. to B.24.a.7.0. and B.18.a.Central respectively, and the GAVRELLE line forward of H.5.c.2.8. These branches are worked by man power.
    Forward of DAYLIGHT RAILHEAD (B.19.b.7.2.) and Cutting in B.26.b. the Light Railway cannot be used in daylight.

    (c) RATION TRAINS. 5 p.m. from ROCLINCOURT running to WILLERVAL and also to BAILLEUL, ARLEUX.
    4.30 p.m. from CHANTECLER JUNC. (G.6.d.) to BAILLEUL & TYNE & OPPY Branches.
    4.30 p.m. from CHANTECLER JUNC. to GAVRELLE.
    The times of departure vary according to the daylight.

3. **AMMUNITION SUPPLY.**

    (a) DIVL. A.R.P. at DUMP SPUR, G.11.b.8.3.
    Delivery to A.R.P. by Light Railway.

    (b) DIVL. S.A.A. & GRENADE DUMP at DUMP SPUR, G.11.b.8.3.
    Delivery to the Dump by Light Railway or Lorries from XIII Corps Dump at MAROEUIL.

    P.T.O.

(Ammunition Supply. (Contd.)

    (c) (i) Left Bde. Dump. CRUCIFIX JUNCTION, BAILLEUL.
Delivery by Light Rly. or by road from Divl. Dump.
The evening ration train passes the Dump and
arrangements can conveniently be made to have
ammunition put on this train and sent forward to
Battn. H.Q. etc.

       (ii) Right Bde. Dump. POINT DU JOUR, H.9.a.7.7.
Delivery to Dump by road from Divl. Ammn. Dump.
The GAVRELLE Light Rly. Line passes near the Dump.

4. R.E. MATERIAL SUPPLY.

    (a) Main Divl. R.E. Dump. ROCLINCOURT, A.29.c.8.2.
Delivery by Light Rly. from XIII Corps Dump, MAROEUIL.
This is a C.R.E. Dump and material can only be drawn with
C.R.E. authority.

    (b) Left Sector Dump. CUTTING DUMP, B.27.a.3.7.
Delivery to Dump by Light Rly. from Main Divl. Dump under
R.E. arrangements.

    (c) Right Sector Dump. TONIC DUMP, B.29.d.7.6.
Delivery to Dump by road under R.E. arrangements.

    (d) CUTTING & TONIC DUMPS are treated as Brigade Dumps. Material
can be drawn either with Brigade or R.E. authority.

    (e) The system of supply at present in use is:-
       (i) Brigades indent on Affiliated Field Companies.
      (ii) Field Companies notify where material can be drawn,
and are responsible for keeping CUTTING & TONIC
DUMPS supplied.

5. BATHS.

    (a) Operated by 56th Divn. (i) ROCLINCOURT. 150 per hour.
                           (ii) CHANTECLER BATHS. 60 "
                                  (H.1.a.7.3.)
                             (iii) MAROEUIL. 100 "
                             (iv) ST. CATHERINE. 80 "

    (b) " T.M. ANZIN. Baths at ANZIN. (Coal for Units of
56th Divn. bathing is supplied by 56th
Divn.)

    (c) " 31st Divn. TUNNEL DUMP BATHS (B.15.c.5.0) 30 per
hour.

6. CLEAN LINEN
    (a) Divl. Clean Linen Store is situated at ST. CATHERINE.
    (b) Dirty Linen is washed at XIII Corps Laundry, MAROEUIL.
    (c) Divl. Foden Thresh Disinfector is located at XIII Corps
Laundry, MAROEUIL.

7. SOCK DRYING ROOMS. One in each Brigade Transport Lines.

8. GASSED CLOTHING STORE.
   (i) Issues will be made from the following Stores on certificate
signed by Os.C. Units concerned for men whose clothing has
become tainted by contact with Yellow Cross Gas.

/Tunnel Dump.

(Contd.)

    (a) <u>TUNNEL DUMP</u> at B.15.c.3.2.

        100 Complete sets of S.D. and underclothing i/c. Divn. on left of 56th Divn. Can be used by 56th Divn. in emergency.

    (b) The <u>GUN PITS at A.D.S.</u> H.4.c.5.4.

        100 complete sets of S.D. and underclothing i/c. a R.A.M.C. Officer.

    (c) <u>At each Battery Gun Position.</u>

        50 complete sets of S.D. and underclothing for the Battery concerned.

    (d) <u>Divisional Reserve.</u> At Ordnance Stores, ST. CATHERINE.

(2) Tainted clothing is sent to XIII Corps Gassed Clothing Disinfecting Plant at ECURIE DISTILLERY, A.28.a.4.4. All such Clothing will be clearly marked TAINTED WITH GAS.

(3) At (1) (a) and (b) 50 suits of Service Dress are maintained for issue to men whose clothes have got wet through on patrols. Suits are issued on C.O's certificate.

9. <u>EMPTY BOTTLES.</u>

Ref. C.R.O.1395. Empty Bottles, other than those required for Soda Water, will be returned to the Divl. Tin Dump, ST. CATHERINE, (opposite Ordnance).

10. <u>MEDICAL.</u>

    (a) A.D.S. (Left Sector) CUTTING, B.27.a.4.8.
    (b) A.D.S. (Right Sector) GUNPITS. H.4.c.5.4.
        A new A.D.S. is being constructed at POINT DU JOUR, H.9.a.9.9.)
    (c) M.D.S. ST. CATHERINE, G.15.a.2.5.

11. <u>CEMETERIES & BURIALS.</u>

    (a) Bodies are brought down to ROCLINCOURT MILITARY CEMETERY (A.29.c.4.5.) and on arrival placed in the mortuary.
        Funerals take place in ROCLINCOURT Cemetery normally between 2 and 3 p.m., and are not permitted after 4 p.m.
        Burials are arranged by Divl. Burials Officer.
    (b) The following Cemeteries are also situated in the Area. They should only be used in very exceptional circumstances.
        ALBUERA. B.21.a.6.7.   CHANTECLER. H.1.a.8.1.
        OUSE VALLEY. B.17.c.7.0.   NAVAL TRENCH. B.30.d.6.5.
                                            (Closed).

12. <u>TRAFFIC.</u> (a) Limits of Daylight Traffic:-
        (i) ARRAS-GAVRELLE Road - PONT DU JOUR, H.9.a.9.9.
        (ii) ARRAS-BAILLEUL Road - MAISON DE LA COTE, B.20.d.7.2.
        (iii) CONCRETE ROAD. - DAYLIGHT RAILHEAD, B.19.d.5.7.
        (b) The Concrete Road (RIDGE TRACK) starts from A.29.b.3.1., and is completed as far as B.20.a. wide enough for single traffic. It is only open for Infantry marching and Staff Cars. Vehicles are only permitted to use the road if in possession of a written authority from XIII Corps H.Q.
        Rations, etc., for Units living near this track must therefore be sent up by Light Railway.

                                                      A.C.Dundas
                                                            Captain,
<u>8th February, 1918.</u>   for A.A.& Q.M.G., 56th Division

Appendix "G" War Diary

56th DIVISION.

LOCATIONS of UNITS on completion of RELIEF of 62nd DIVISION.

UNIT.	HEADQUARTERS.	LOCATION.	TRANSPORT. DATE of ARRIVAL.
Divnl. H.Q.	G.3.b.7.3.	—	—
167th Inf.Bde.H.Q.) 7th Middx.Regt.) 8th Middx.Regt.) 1st London Regt.) 167th M.G.Co.) 167th T.M.By.)	In the Line and WAKEFIELD CAMP.	Camp:— DOVER. A.29.c.1.7. REDCAR. A.28.c.5.8. " " " CALAIS. A.29.c.2.9. " " " " " "	) 11th.)))))
168th Inf.Bde.H.Q.) 4th London Regt.) 13th " ") 14th " ") 168th M.G.Co.) 168th T.M.By.)	In the Line and ROCLINCOURT ? CAMP.	COLLINGWOOD.A.28.c.1.2. " " " PORTLAND. G.9.a.5.7. " " " COLLINGWOOD.A.28.c.1.2. " " "	) 9th.)))))
169th Inf.Bde.H.Q.) 2nd London Regt.) 5th London Regt.) 16th London Regt) 169th M.G.Co.) 169th T.M.By.)	In the Line and ST.AUBIN.	NELSON. G.9.b.3.7. " " " " " " " " " " " " " " "	) 7th.)))))
193rd M.G.Co.	G.8.d.5.2.	G.8.d.5.2.	8th.
1/5th (E of C) Cheshire Regt.	ST.CATHERINE.	GROPI. G.3.c.3.0.	10th.
56th Divl.Arty.H.Q. 280th Bde.R.F.A. 281st " " D.A.C.	G.3.b.7.3. Line. " " ANZIN.	G.3.b.7.3. G.11.c. " " " ANZIN.	11th.) 17th.) 17th.
C.R.E. 416th Fld.Co.R.E. 512th " " " 513th " " "	G.3.b.7.3. " " "	EDINBURGH. G.3.c.2.3. PLYMOUTH. G.9.b.0.0. HARDY. G.9.a.9.5.	11th. 11th. 9th.
A.D.M.S. 2/1st Lon.F.A. 2/2nd " " 2/3rd " "	G.3.b.7.3. AUBIGNY. ANZIN. ST.CATHERINE.	AUBIGNY. ANZIN. ST.CATHERINE.	No change. 11th. 10th.
D.A.D.O.S.	ST.CATHERINE.		
Divnl. Train. H.Q.Coy. No.2 Co. No.3 Co. No.4 Co.	G.3.a.3.3. G.3.a.1.3. A.26.d.7.2. A.28.d.6.2. A.26.d.5.2.	CHATHAM. G.3.a.0.5. GREENWICH. G.3.a.1.3. SHEERNESS. A.20.d.6.2. " " " " " "	11th. 17th. 11th. 9th. 7th.
347th Employment Co. 56th Divl.Supply Col. Mobile Vet.Sec. Div.Gas Offr. Div.Salvage Offr.)	G.3.b.7.3. TINQUES. ANZIN. G.9.b.3.9.	ANZIN.	11th.

REINFORCEMENTS will be despatched to TRANSPORT LINES.

Captain,
D.A.A.G., 56th Division.

7.2.18.

56th Division.

CASUALTIES for the month of February, 1918.

Date.	UNIT.	OFFICERS. Killed.	OFFICERS. Wounded.	OFFICERS. Missing.	O.Rs. K.	O.Rs. W.	O.Rs. M.	Remarks.
1st.	7th Middlesex Regt.	-	-	-	-	2	-	⎫ All wounded by Grenade
½	8th Middlesex Regt.	-	-	-	1	1	-	⎬ Explosion, accidentally.
	1st London Regt.	-	-	-	-	5	-	⎭
	2nd London Regt.	-	-	-	-	1	-	
5th.	167th T.M. Battery.	-	-	-	-	1	-	Accidentally self-inflicted.
9th.	5th London Regt.	-	2/Lt.E.T.F.R. CHILMAN.	-	-	-	-	
13th.	4th London Regt.	-	-	-	-	1	-	Accidentally by bayonet.
14th.	1st London Regt.	-	-	-	-	-	-	
Additional								
10th.	169th T.M. Battery.	-	-	-	1	1	-	Accidentally by bayonet.
17th.	193rd M.G.Company.	-	-	-	1	-	-	
18th.	13th London Regt.	-	-	-	-	1	-	Accidentally by explosion in fire.
19th.	7th Middlesex Regt.	-	-	-	-	1	-	∅ Includes 1 Accidentally,
	13th London Regt.	2/Lt.W.H.PEARCE.19.2.18.	-	-	-	2∅	-	cleaning rifle.
	C/Forward.	1	1		2	16		

- 2 -

Date.	UNIT.	Officers Killed.	Officers Wounded.	Officers Missing.	O.Rs. K.	O.Rs. W.	O.Rs. M.	Remarks.
	B/Forward.	1	1	-	2	16	-	
20th.	7th Middlesex Regt.	-	-	-	1	6	-	Includes 2 at duty.
	13th London Regt.	-	-	-	-	3	-	
	5th "	-	-	-	-	1	1x	x Wounded & missing. Did not return from patrol.
21st.	7th Middlesex Regt.	-	-	-	1	1	-	
	13th London Regt.	-	-	-	-	2	-	
	56th D.A.C.	-	-	-	1	1	-	
22nd.	13th London Regt.	-	-	-	-	2	-	
	281st Bde. R.F.A.	-	-	-	1	1	-	Accidently by discharge of rifle.
	56th D.A.C.	-	-	-	1	-	-	Died of wounds.
	512th Fld.Coy. R.E.	-	-	-	-	7	-	Includes 2 at Duty.
23RD.	167th M.G. Company.	-	-	-	-	1	-	
	512th Fld.Coy. R.E.	-	-	-	-	1	-	At.Duty.
24th.	8th Middlesex Regt.	-	-	-	-	1	-	
	281st Bde. R.F.A.	-	-	-	-	1	-	
25th.	8th Middlesex Regt.	-	-	-	-	1	-	Accidentally by discharge of rifle.
26th.	1st. Londons Regt.	-	-	-	1	1	-	
	16th London Regt.	-	-	-	-	2	-	
	5th London Regt.	-	-	-	-	1	-	
27th.	4th London Regt.	-	-	-	-	2	-	
	16th "	-	-	-	1	2	-	
28th.	280th Bde. R.F.A.	-	-	-	-	-	-	Lt. F.K.HEADINGTON,M.C.27.2.18.
	1st London Regt.	-	-	-	-	2	-	
	14th London Regt.	-	-	-	-	3	-	Includes 1 accidentally by rifle.

UNITS	Strength 1.2.18. O.	Strength 1.2.18. O.R.	INCREASE O.	INCREASE O.R.	DECREASE O.	DECREASE O.R.	Strength 1.3.18. O.	Strength 1.3.18. O.R.
Divisional H.Qtrs.	18	84	2	4	1	4	19	84
167th Infantry Bde.HQ.	3	21	-	-	-	-	3	21
1/7th Middlesex Rgt.	48	831	8	162	3	46	53	947
1/8th Middlesex Rgt.	49	873	8	155	3	42	54	986
1/1st London Rgt.	53	998	2	37	4	61	51	984
167th M.G.Company	12	176	RE-ORGANISED.				-	-
167th T.M. Battery	4	46	-	-	-	-	4	46
168th Infantry Bde.HQ.	3	21	-	-	-	-	3	21
1/4th London Regt.	41	884	6	96	2	67	45	913
1/13th London Regt.	42	973	3	101	2	66	43	1008
1/14th London Regt.	46	903	-	90	4	65	42	928
168th M.G.Company	10	171	RE-ORGANISED.				-	-
168th T.M. Battery.	4	46	-	-	-	-	4	46
169th Infantry Bde.HQ.	3	21	-	-	-	-	3	21
1/2nd London Regt.	48	1007	4	15	1	37	51	985
1/5th London Regt.	46	971	3	46	3	82	46	935
1/16th London Regt.	40	1010	6	107	-	133	46	984
169th M.G.Company	10	175	RE-ORGANISED.				-	-
169th T.M.Battery.	4	45	-	1	1	-	3	46
1/5th Cheshire Regt.	40	1006	-	9	1	130	39	885
193rd M.G.Company.	12	176	RE-ORGANISED.					
Hd. Qtrs. R.A.	4	17	-	-	-	-	4	17
280th Bde.R.F.A.	38	781	2	14	6	18	34	777
281st Bde.R.F.A.	25	809	4	6	5	35	24	780
D.A.C.	14	583	-	4	2	6	12	581
Hd. Qtrs. R.E.	2	10	-	-	-	-	2	10
416th (E'boro8)Fd.Coy R.E.	7	204	-	5	-	3	7	206
512th (L'don) — " —	6	203	-	2	-	9	6	196
513th (L'don) — " —	9	206	-	7	-	5	9	208
Divl. Signal Coy.	11	272	1	10	1	6	11	276
Divl. Train.	17	314	-	44	-	7	17	351
Medical Units.	26	519	-	28	6	5	20	542
Mobile Vet'y Section.	1	21	-	-	-	-	1	21
247th Employment Coy.	1	301	-	12	-	4	1	309
56th Battn. M.G.C.	-	-	-	-	-	-	44	771

Administration
56th Division

A & Q

56th Division

MARCH 1918

Admini trati

Army Form C. 21

Volume XXVI
Page 1

WAR DIARY
or
INTELLIGENCE SUMMARY

(Erase heading not required.)

Place	Date	Hour	Summary of Events and Information	Remarks and references to Appendices
ROCLINCOURT	March 1		Division situated as shown in attached beaten table. (App^x A) 4 Machine Gun Companies organised into 5/6th Battalion M. G. C. under Lt. Col. C. S. JERVIS DSO	
	2			
	3		Centre Brigade moves. 1st London Regt. from Reserve to Support, 7th Middx Regt. from line to Reserve, 8th Middx Support to line	
	4			
	5		Left Brigade moves. 4th London Regt from Reserve to Support, 13th London Regt Support to line, 14th London Regt line to Reserve	
	6		Right Brigade moves. 2nd London Regt from line to Support, 3rd London Regt Reserve to line, 16th London Regt Support to line	
	7			
	8		Centre Brigade moves 1st London Regt from Support to line, 7th Middx Reserve to Support, 8th Middx Regt line to Support	
	9			
	10			
	11		Left Brigade moves. 4th London Regt Support to line, 13th London Regt line to Reserve, 14th London Regt Reserve to Support	
	11		Right Brigade moves, 2nd London Regt Support to Reserve, 5th London Regt line to Support, 16th London Regt Reserve to line	
	12		2nd London Regt from Reserve at ST AUBIN to close Reserve at CHANTICLER accommodated in tents and Bessoneau shelters. In case of enemy attack taking place Wagon and Transport accommodation in case of withdrawal recommended in MAROEUIL and FREVENT CARELLE huts	
	13		Centre Brigade Moves. 1st London from line to Reserve, 7th Middx Support to line 8th Middx Reserve to Support (See App^x B)	
	14		2nd London Regt moved back to Reserve at ST AUBIN from close Reserve at CHANTICLER	
	15			
	16			
	17		Left Brigade Moves 4th London Regt from line to Reserve, 13th London Regt Reserve to Support, 14th London Regt Support to line	
	18		Right Brigade moves 1st London Regt Reserve to line, 5th London Regt Support to Reserve, 16th London Regt line to Support	
	19		1096 lbs of golden millet out of total mint-fines collected since 21st February	

Army Form C. 2118.

Volume XXVI
Page 2

WAR DIARY or INTELLIGENCE SUMMARY.

(Erase heading not required.)

Instructions regarding War Diaries and Intelligence Summaries are contained in F. S. Regs., Part II. and the Staff Manual respectively. Title pages will be prepared in manuscript.

Place	Date	Hour	Summary of Events and Information	Remarks and references to Appendices
ROCLINCOURT	March 19		Orders for Division to be relieved by 62nd (WEST RIDING) Division received. Division to go to rest at VILLERS CHATEL	
	20		Administrative instructions for relief issued. See APPX C	
	21		Reorganisation of line. Centre Brigade 167th withdrawn into Divisional Reserve, line held by two Brigades, 168th Bde on Left 169th Bde on Right each with 2 Battns in line and 1 Battn in Support. Reserve Brigade located:- HQrs and 1 Battn ST AUBIN, 1 Battn WANEFIELD Camp (ROCLINCOURT) 1 Battn GREENLING Trench Mortar Battery ANZIN	
	21		Relief by 62nd Division cancelled	
	22		Warning order for relief by 2nd CANADIAN Division received	
	23		Above warning order cancelled	
	23		Reserve Brigade Head Quarters and Battalion brought forward to TRAFALGAR Camp and AUBREY Camp All leave cancelled. Ammunition Refilling Point moved back from G.11.D to L.5.D owing to heavy bombardment of MONCHY LE PREUX	
	24		Masses Left sector, 14th London Regt from Brigade Support to line 14th London Regt from Reserve to Bde Support 13th London Regt in line — no change	
	25		Masses Right Sector, 2nd London Regt from line to Bde Support, 16 London Regt from Bde Support to line 5 London Regt in line — no change	
	26			
	27			
	28			
	29		Rear HQrs established at AGNIEZ. The enemy attacked along the whole Divisional Front but was kept fairly outnumbered & opposed by overwhelming ordnance the line remained intact until ordered to withdraw to the Main line of resistance where two attacks of the enemy were completely repulsed until our Artillery. Casualties 50 approx D. Ammunition expended in the Division front by Divisional Artillery AX 3000 rounds BX 3000 rounds. Division was later relieved by the 4th Canadian Division	RFC

Army Form C. 2118.

Volume XXVI
Page 3

WAR DIARY
or
INTELLIGENCE SUMMARY.
(Erase heading not required.)

Place	Date	Hour	Summary of Events and Information	Remarks and references to Appendices
ACQ	March 30 31		Division relieved by 4th Canadian Division & reliefs as shown in attached location table A4+C	

M Dundas Myr Lieut.-Col.
A.A. & Q.M.G. 56th Division.

SECRET.   Appendix 'A'   AQS. 5.

LOCATIONS.

56th DIVISION.   **1st MARCH, 1918.**

Divnl. H. Qtrs.	VICTORY CAMP. G.3.b.7.3½
S.S.C.	G.3.a.2.5.
D.A.D.O.S.	ST. CATHERINE.
Divl. Artillery H.Qtrs.	VICTORY CAMP.
280th Bde. R.F.A. H.Q.	H.1.c.8.0.
" " Wagon Lines.	G.11.c.
281st Bde. " H.Q.	B.21.a.0.2.
" " Wagon Lines.	G.11.c.
56th D.A.C.	ANZIN.
C.R.E. H.Q.	VICTORY CAMP.
413th Field Coy.	EDINBURGH, G.3.d.5.7.
512th " "	PLYMOUTH, G.9.d.0.5.
513th " "	HARDY. G.9.a.9.5.
167th Inf. Bde. H.Qtrs.	LINE CENTRE.
7th Middlesex Regt.	LINE.
8th Middlesex Regt.	SUPPORT.
1st London Regt.	WAKEFIELD CAMP.
167th T.M.Bty.	LINE.
168th Inf. Bde. H.Qtrs.	LINE LEFT.
4th London Regt.	ROCLINCOURT, W.
13th London Regt.	SUPPORT.
14th London Regt.	LINE.
168th T.M.Bty.	LINE.
169th Inf. Bde. H.Qtrs.	LINE RIGHT.
2nd London Regt.	LINE.
5th London Regt.	ST. AUBIN.
16th London Regt.	SUPPORT.
169th T.M.Bty.	LINE.
56th Divl. Train H.Qtrs.	G.3.a.2.5.
Headquarters Company.	GREENWICH, G.3.a.1.3.
No. 2 Coy.	A.26.d.7.2.
" 3 Coy.	A.26.d.6.2.
" 4 Coy.	A.26.d.5.2.
No. 56th Supply Column.	ACQ.
Pioneer Battn.(1/5th Cheshires)	ST. CATHERINE.
56th M.G. Battn.	TRAFALGAR CAMP. G.3.d.central.
A.D.M.S.	VICTORY CAMP.
2/1st London Field Amblce.	AUBIGNY.
2/2nd " "	CHANTECLER. H.1.c.5.8.
2/3rd " "	ST. CATHERINE.
Mobile Veterinary Section.	ANZIN.

A.E.Dundas Capt.
for Major General.
Commanding 56th Division.

SECRET.

AQS/5.

LOCATIONS.

56th DIVISION. 8th MARCH, 1918.

Divl. Hd.Qtrs.	VICTORY CAMP. G.3.b.7.3.
S.S.O.	G.3.a.2.5.
D.A.D.O.S.	ST. CATHERINE.
Divl. Artillery Hd.Qtrs.	VICTORY CAMP.
280th Bde. R.F.A. H.Q.	H.1.c.8.0.
" " " Wagon Lines	G.11.c.
281st Bde. R.F.A. H.Q.	B.21.a.0.2.
" " " Wagon Lines	G.11.c.
56th D.A.C.	ANZIN.
C.R.E. Hd.Qtrs.	VICTORY CAMP.
413th Field Coy.	EDINBURGH, G.3.d.5.7.
512th " "	PLYMOUTH, G.9.d.0.5.
513th " "	HARDY, G.9.a.9.5.
167th Inf. Bde. Hd.Qtrs.	LINE CENTRE.
7th Middlesex Regt.	SUPPORT. Line
8th " " "	~~WAKEFIELD CAMP.~~ Support
1st London Regt.	~~LINE.~~ Wakefield Camp
167th T.M.Battery.	LINE.
168th Inf. Bde. Hd.Qtrs.	LINE LEFT.
4th London Regt.	SUPPORT. Line
13th London Regt.	LINE. Roclincourt W
14th " "	ROCLINCOURT, W. Support
168th T.M.Battery.	LINE.
169th Inf. Bde. Hd.Qtrs.	LINE RIGHT.
2nd. London Regt.	~~SUPPORT.~~ St Aubin
5th. " "	~~LINE.~~ Support
16th. " "	~~ST. AUBIN.~~ Line
169th T.M.Battery.	LINE.
56th Div. Train Hd.Qtrs.	G.3.a.2.5.
Headquarters Company.	GREENWICH, G.3.a.1.5.
No. 2 Coy.	A.26.d.7.2.
" 3 "	A.26.d.6.2.
" 4 "	A.26.d.5.2.
No. 56th ~~Supply Column~~ M T Company	~~ACQ.~~ Maroeuil
Pioneer Battn.(1/5th Cheshires)	ST. CATHERINE.
56th M.G. Battalion.	TRAFALGAR CAMP, G.3.d.central.
A.D.M.S.	~~VICTORY CAMP.~~ MILL HOUSE ANZIN
2/1st London Field Amblce.	MAROEUIL.
2/2nd " " "	CHANTECLER. H.1.c.5.6.
2/3rd " " "	ST. CATHERINE.
Mobile Veterinary Section.	ANZIN.

Alexander Capt
c/o Major General,
Commanding 56th Division.

SECRET. AGS/5.

LOCATIONS.

56th DIVISION.   **15th MARCH, 1918.**

Divl. H.Qtrs.	VICTORY CAMP. G.3.b.7.3.
G.S.O.	G.3.a.8.5.
D.A.D.O.S.	ST. CATHERINE.
Divl. Artillery H.Qtrs.	VICTORY CAMP.
280th Bde.R.F.A. H.Qtrs.	H.1.c.8.0.
" " " Wagon Lines.	G.11.c.
281st Bde.R.F.A. H.Qtrs.	B.21.a.0.2.
" " " Wagon Lines.	G.11.c.
56th D.A.C.	ANZIN.
C.R.E. H.Qtrs.	VICTORY CAMP.
413th Field Coy.	EDINBURGH, G.3.d.5.7.
512th " "	PLYMOUTH, G.9.d.0.5.
513th " "	HARDY, G.9.a.9.5.
167th Inf. Bde. H.Qtrs.	LINE CENTRE.
7th Middlesex Regt.	LINE.
8th " "	SUPPORT.
1st London Regt.	WAKEFIELD CAMP.
167th T.M. Battery.	LINE.
168th Inf. Bde. H.Qtrs.	LINE LEFT.
4th London Regt.	LINE.
13th " "	ROCLINCOURT, W.
14th " "	SUPPORT.
168th T.M. Battery.	LINE.
169th Inf. Bde. H.Qtrs.	LINE RIGHT.
2nd London Regt.	ST. AUBIN.
5th " "	SUPPORT.
16th " "	LINE.
169th T.M. Battery.	LINE.
56th Divl. Train H.Qtrs.	G.3.a.2.5.
Headquarters Company.	GREENWICH, G.3.a.1.3.
No. 2 Company.	A.26.d.7.3.
" 3 "	A.26.d.6.2.
" 4 "	A.26.d.5.2.
No. 56th ~~Supply Column.~~ M T company	MAROEUIL.
Pioneer Battn.(1/5th Cheshires)	ST. CATHERINE.
56th M.G. Battalion.	TRAFALGAR CAMP, G.3.d.central.
A.D.M.S.	MILL HOUSE, ANZIN.
2/1st London Field Ambulance.	MAROEUIL.
2/2nd " " "	CHANTECLER, H.1.c.5.8.
2/3rd " " "	ST. CATHERINE.
Mobile Veterinary Section.	ANZIN.

A.C.Dundas Major
for Major General,
Commanding 56th Division.

War Diary.

SECRET.

AQS/537.

111th Corps "Q".

APPX B

Your No. GS.270/89/4 of 12.3.18.

The proposed locations of wagon and transport lines and refilling points in the various situations are as follows :-

1. **Withdrawal to RED or BROWN LINES.**

(a) First Line Transport of Inf.Bdes., M.G.Battn., Pioneer Battn., and R.E. - G.2. and G.9.c. (including present Div.Train standings).
(b) Wagons Lines of Artillery Bdes. ANZIN G.8.a and c.(present D.A.C. standings.)
(c) D.A.C.   L.2.d. and L.3.c.
(d) A.R.P.   G.11. until expended, then Artillery Corner.
(e) Div. Train. ((a)L.2.central (whilst RAILHEAD is at ECURIE.)
                ((b)E.9.c. and E.8.a. (Railhead FREVIN CAPELLE).
(f) Supply Refilling Point.- (a) Road in L.2.central.
                             (b) (1) North & South Road in E.9.c.
                                 (2) Farm at E.8.b.95.
                                 (3) North & South Road in E.8.a.

2. **Withdrawal to GREEN LINE, CHANTECLER SWITCH, or ROCLINCOURT - LA TARGETTE LINE.**

(a) First Line Transports -   E.24.b. and d.
(b) Wagon Lines of Artillery Bdes. - L.2.central.
(c) D.A.C.   E.7.d. and c.
(d) A.R.P.   Artillery Corner until expended. Then L.4.c.
(e) Div. Train.   E.9.c. and E.8.a.
(f) Supply Refilling Points.   (1) North & South Road in E.9.c.
                               (2) Farm at E.8.b.95.
                               (3) North & South Road in E.8.a.

3. **Withdrawal to ST. AUBIN - BERTHONVAL LINE.**

Horse lines and Refilling Points of "A" Division would be in Brigade Group Areas.

(sd) F.R. Dudgeon.

Major General,
Commanding 56th Division.

14.3.18.

SECRET.   AQS.554.   App. C

ADMINISTRATIVE INSTRUCTIONS NO. 1. IN CONNECTION
WITH RELIEF OF 56TH DIVN. BY 62ND DIVN.
Issued with reference to 56th Divn. No. G.3/02 of
19th instant.

1. **WORK IN PROGRESS.** Formations and Units will hand over to relieving Formations and Units all details of work in progress in Back Areas.

2. **TRENCH AND AREA STORES.** All trench and area stores and trench ammunition will be handed over, and one copy of the Units' receipted list will be forwarded by all Units in the Division, through the usual channels so as to reach Div. "Q" within 24 hours of relief. Consolidated returns need not be forwarded by Formations. Separate lists will be prepared for trench stores, trench ammunition, Special Brigade reserves of S.A.A. and tools, and area stores.
Area stores will be considered as being all stores, except water tins, handed over west of Brigade Headquarters in the line.
All water tins (2 gall. petrol and water tin pattern) on charge of Formations and Units as trench stores will be handed over on the establishment shown in Div. Defence Scheme Appendix Va.
Attention is drawn to D.R.O. 2363, regarding the handing over of rations.
Gum Boots will be handed in to the Corps Gum Boot Store, ROCLINCOURT. They are not to be handed over to relieving Units.
The attention of Units should be drawn by Formations to the amounts of stores and ammunition already reported as having been placed in their areas, and it should be seen that the amounts handed over agree with these.

3. **TRANSPORT LINES.**
 (a) Infantry Brigade Transport lines will be handed over as below :-
  REDCAR.   )
  CALAIS.   ) by 167th Inf. Bde. to 187th Inf. Bde. on 23rd instant.
  DOVER.   )
  NELSON.   by 169th   "   to 185th   "   " 24th   "
  COLLINGWOOD) by 168th   "   to 186th   "   " 25th   "
  PORTLAND.   )

 (b) Div. M.G. Battalion Transport lines will be handed over as below :-
  "A" Company at CALAIS CAMP   on 23rd instant.
  "C"   "   " NELSON CAMP   " 23rd   "
  "B"   "   " COLLINGWOOD CAMP   " 24th   "
  "D"   "   " LONE FARM   " 25th   "

 (c) 1/5th Cheshire Battalion Transport lines at GROPI CAMP will be handed over on 25th instant.

4. **COMPANIES OF DIV. TRAIN** will move on the dates shown below :-

  No. 2 Company on 23rd instant.
   " 4   "   " 24th   "
   " 3   "   " 25th   "
  Billots are allotted as shown in para. 12.

5. **FIELD AMBULANCES.** will move on dates to be arranged by A.D.M.S., to the billets shown in para. 12. Dates of moves will be notified to this office and to O.C., Divisional Train.

P.T.O.

6. Arrangements for Bus moves and lorries for blankets and baggage, will be notified later.

7. **LIGHT RAILWAY** trains for Units moving to ANZIN and ST.AUBIN on 23rd and 24th. Will be arranged in this office. Infantry Brigades concerned will report to this office 48 hours in advance the places and times at which trains are required and the numbers to be conveyed.

8. **AREA EMPLOY.** 62nd Division are relieving all personnel employed in this Area, on the 23rd instant. This personnel will be sent to the Transport lines of their Units under Divisional arrangements. Those belonging to 167th Infantry Brigade will be sent to 169th Infantry Brigade Transport lines and will move to the Reserve Area under the orders of the 169th Infantry Bde.

9. **CAMPS AND BILLETS.** Particular attention is to be paid to handing over all Camps, Billets, Trenches and Horse Standings in a clean and sanitary condition. Certificates to that effect must be obtained from Area Commandants or Advance Parties of incoming Units. Where necessary rear parties must be left behind to hand over.

10. **GASSED CLOTHING.** Gassed Clothing at Div. Gas Clothing Store, Ordnance, Brigade Changing Rooms, and all on charge of the A.D.M.S. and Div.Artillery will be handed over in situ.

11. **BRIGADE SOCK ROOMS.** All socks and sock wringers on charge of Infantry Brigades for Brigade Sock Rooms will be handed in to the Div. Linen Store, ST. CATHERINE, not less than 24 hours before each Brigade leaves the forward area.

12. **ACCOMMODATION.**

(a) Area allotted for Brigade in Div. Reserve; to be used as Staging area during the Relief period :-

Inf. Bde. Hd.Qtrs.	ST. AUBIN.	Billets from T.M. ST.AUBIN.
Trench Mortar Battery.	ANZIN.	" " " ANZIN.
1 Battalion.	ST. AUBIN.	" " " ST.AUBIN.
1 "	ROCLINCOURT WEST CAMP.	" " A.C. ST.CATHERINE.
1 "	WAKEFIELD CAMP.	" " " "

(b) M.G.Coys. Staging Area. AUBREY CAMP. " " " "
(c) Areas allotted in Reserved Divisional Area.

Divl. Hd.Qtrs.)	VILLERS CHATEL	Billets from Camp Commandant.
" Train Hd.Qtrs)	MINGOVAL.	" " " "
Employment Coy.	CAMBLIGNEUL.	" " A.C. MINGOVAL.
1/5th Cheshire Regt.	CAMBLIGNEUL.	" " " "
56th Div.M.G.Battn.	LA COMTE.	" " " LA COMTE.
Mobile Vet. Section.	VANDELICOURT.	" " " BERLES.

167th Inf. Bde. Group.

Troops.   167th Inf. Bde., No. 2 Coy. Div. Train, 2/1st and 2/3rd London Field Ambulances, R.E. School.

VILLAGES.	CAUCOURT.)	
	HERMIN.)	Billets from A.C. GAUCHIN - LEGAL.
	BAJUS.	" " A.C. LA COMTE.
	HOUVELIN)	
	ROCOURT.)	
	MAGNICOURT.)	" " A.C. MAGNICOURT.
	FREVILLERS.)	

Restrictions.   Inf.Bde. Hd.Qtrs.   to be at   FREVILLERS.
                Train Coy.   "   "   "
                Field Ambulances.   "   "   HOUVELIN & HERMIN.

12. ACCOMMODATION (contd.)

168th Infantry Brigade Group.

Troops. 168th Inf. Bde., No. 3 Coy. Div. Train, 2/2nd London Field Ambulance

VILLAGES.

VILLERS-BRULIN.	⎫
BETHONSART.	⎬ Billets from A.C. MINGOVAL.
GUESTREVILLE.	⎭
HERLIN LE VERT.	" " " MAGNICOURT.
CHELERS.	⎫
TINCQUES.	⎬ " " " TINCQUES.
BETHENCOURT.	⎭

Restrictions.
Inf. Bde. Hd. Qtrs. to be at CHELERS.
Train Coy. "   "   "
Field Ambulance. "   " BETHENCOURT.

169th Infantry Brigade Group.

Troops. 169th Inf. Bde., No. 4 Coy. Div. Train.

VILLAGES.

HOMCHY BRETON.	⎫
ORLENCOURT.	⎬ Billets from A.C. MAGNICOURT.
LA THIEULOYE.	⎭
MARQUAY.	" " " LA COMTE.
BAILLEUL-AUX-CORNAILLES.	⎫
TINCQUETTE.	⎬ " " " TINCQUES.

Restrictions.
Inf. Bde. Hd. Qtrs. to be at ORLENCOURT.
Train Coy. "   "   " TINCQUETTE.

13. **BATHS.** The baths at TINCQUES will be run by the Div. Baths Officer. The A.D.M.S. will detail one water cart (complete turnout) to report to the Div. Baths Officer, TINCQUES on 24th inst. for filling the baths. This watercart will be accommodated and the personnel and horses rationed by the Div. Baths Officer.
The 167th Inf. Brigade will be responsible for running the baths at CAUCOURT and FREVILLERS. The 169th Inf. Brigade for those at ROCOURT AND MAGNICOURT.
Units will bathe at the most convenient baths, bookings being arranged direct with the N.C.O. in charge.

14. **CLEAN CLOTHING.** The Divl. Linen Store will be at TINCQUES. Brigades will stock the Baths for which they are responsible, with clothing from this store. No issues will be made to Units from the Divl. Linen Store.

15. **CANTEEN.** The Divl. Canteen will open at TINCQUES on 26th instant. A retail branch will be established at VILLERS CHATEL.

16. **SOLDER.** Tins for solder will be sent to the Div. Dump behind billet No. 67, TINCQUES.

17. **WASTE PAPER.** The Divl. Waste Paper Dump will be at billet No. 74, TINCQUES.

P.T.O.

18. ORDNANCE. The Ordnance Stores will open at TINQUES on 26th inst.

19. SALVAGE. The Divl. Salvage Officer will attach a section of the Div. Salvage Company to each Company of the Divisional Train whilst the Division is out of the line.

20. AMMUNITION. The Divl. Ammunition Dump will be established opposite billet No. 8, TINQUES. Indents for ammunition for training purposes will be submitted to Div. "Q".

21. LOCATIONS.
  Div. Baths Officer. Billet No. 10, TINQUES.
  " Salvage " " " " "
 Offr. i/c Div. Ammun. Dump. " No. 8, "
  Div. Gardens Officer. HINGOVAL.

22. PAY. There will be no Railhead Disbursing Officer in the Reserve Area. Leave parties and other details must be paid before leaving their Units.

20th March, 1918.

Lieut.-Colonel,
A.A. & Q.M.G., 56th Division.

DISTRIBUTION.

G.O.C.
167th Infantry Bde.
168th " "
169th " "
Div. M.G.Cdr.
1/5th Cheshire Rgt.
C.R.E.
Div. Artillery.
Divl. Train.
A.D.M.S.

A.P.M.
D.A.D.O.S.
Camp Comdt.
Signal Coy., R.E.
Employment Coy.
D.A.D.V.S.
"G"
S.C.F. (C. of E.)
" (Non C. of E.)
French Mission.

62nd Division "Q".
31st " "
A.C. St. CATHERINE.
" HINGOVAL.
" LA COMTE.
" BERLES.
" GAUCHIN-LEGAL.
" MAGNICOURT.
" TINQUES.
T.M. ST. AUBIN.
" ANZIN.

SECRET.   AQS/5.

LOCATIONS.

56TH DIVISION.   30TH MARCH, 1918.

Divl. Headquarters.	ACQ.
S.S.O.	AGNIERES.
D.A.D.O.S.	AGNIERES.
Divl. Artillery Hd.Qtrs.	ACQ.
280th Bde. R.F.A. Hd.Qtrs.	
" " " Wagon Lines.	G.1.b. G.2.A. & B.
281st Bde. R.F.A. Hd.Qtrs.	
" " " Wagon Lines.	G.1.b. G.2.A. & B.
56th D.A.C.	
C.R.E. Hd.Qtrs.	ACQ.
416th Field Coy.	ANZIN.
512th " "	"
513th " "	"
167th Inf. Bde. Hd.Qtrs.	VILLERS-AUX-BOIS.
7th Middlesex Regt.	"
8th " "	"
1st London Regt.	CAMBLAIN L'ABBE.
3rd London Regt.(Transport.)	VILLERS-AUX-BOIS.
167th T.M. Battery.	"
168th Infantry Bde. Hd.Qtrs.	MONT ST. ELOI.
4th London Regt.	YORK CAMP, ECOIVRES.
13th " "	VILLAGE CAMP. "
14th " " *Lancaster*	LE PENDU CAMP, MONT ST.ELOI.
168th T.M. Battery.	YORK CAMP. ECOIVRES.
169th Inf. Bde. Hd.Qtrs.	ECOIVRES.
2nd London Regt.	FRASER CAMP. BOIS DE AJN.
5th " "	LE PENDU CAMP.
16th " "	OTTAWA CAMP. " "
169th T.M. Battery.	MONT ST. ELOI.
56th Divl. Train Hd.Qtrs.	AGNIERES.
Headquarters Company.	CAPELLE FREMONT.
No. 2 Company.	"
" 3 "	"
" 4 "	"
No. 56th M.T. Company.	TINCQUES.
Pioneer Battn. (1/5th Cheshires).	ST. CATHERINE. *Estree Cauchie*
56th M.G. Battalion.	ST. AUBIN.
A.D.M.S.	AGNIERES.
2/1st London Field Ambulance.	VILLERS-AUX-BOIS.
2/2nd " " "	LES QUATRE VENTS.
2/3rd " " "	AUBIGNY.
Mobile Veterinary Section.	ANZIN. *Agnieres*

A. Dundas Major
for Major General,
Commanding 56th Division.

56th DIVISION.

CASUALTIES for the month of MARCH, 1918.

Date.	UNIT.	OFFICERS Killed.	OFFICERS Wounded.	OFFICERS Missing.	O.Rs. K.	O.Rs. W.	O.Rs. M.	REMARKS.
1ST.	7th Middlesex Regt.	-	-	-	-	1	-	
	13th London Regt.	-	-	-	-	1	-	Accidentally by discharge of rifle.
4th.	13th London Regt.	-	2/Lt. F.W.ELLIS.3/3/18.	-	1	1	-	
	14th London Regt.	-	-	-	1	-	-	
	2nd. London Regt.	-	-	-	1	3	-	Died of Wounds.
5th.	168th T.M.Battery.	-	-	-	1	-	-	⎫
	4th London Regt.	-	-	-	-	2	-	⎬ All attached to
	13th London Regt.	-	-	-	1	1	-	⎬ 168th T.M.Battery.
	14th London Regt.	-	-	-	1	-	-	⎬
	56th M.G.Battn.	-	-	-	1	-	-	⎭
	13th London Regt.	-	-	-	-	8	-	Gassed.
6th.	14th London Regt.	-	-	-	1	1	-	
	5th Cheshire Regt.	-	-	-	1	-	-	
8th.	2nd London Regt.	-	-	-	1	1	-	
	5th London Regt.	-	2/Lt. W.F.HARRINGTON.7/3/18.	-	-	1	-	
9th.	13th London Regt.	-	-	-	1	2	-	
	513th (Ldn) Fld.Coy.R.E.	1	-	-	1	1	-	
	2/2nd Ldn. Field Amb.	-	-	-	-	1	-	
	Carried forward.	1	1	-	8	24	-	

Date.	UNIT.	OFFICERS.			O. Rs.			REMARKS.
		Killed.	Wounded	Missing.	K.	W.	M.	
	Brought forward.	1	1	-	8	24	-	
10th.	1st London Regt.	-	-	-	-	3	-	
	7th Middlesex Regt.	-	-	-	1	1	-	Attd. 167th T.M.B. — At duty.
	13th London Regt.	-	-	-	1	3	-	
	5th " "	-	-	-	2	1	-	
	56th Bn. M.G.C.	-	-	-	-	3	-	Gassed.
11th.	13th London Regt.	-	-	-	-	1	-	
	5th Cheshire Regt.	-	-	-	-	4	-	
	2/2nd Ldn. Fld. Ambce.	-	-	-	-	2	-	Gassed.
	2/3rd " " "	-	-	-	-	6	-	Gassed.
	56th Bn. M.G.C.	-	-	-	-	7	-	Gassed.
12th.	4th London Regt.	-	-	-	-	1	-	
	16th " "	-	-	-	-	6	-	
	5th Cheshire Regt.	-	-	-	-	1	-	
	56th Bn. M.G.C.	-	-	-	-	1	-	Gassed.
	512th (Ldn)Fld.Coy.R.E.	-	-	-	-	2	-	
	513th (Ldn) " "	-	-	-	-	6	-	Gassed.
	14th London Rgt.attd.D.H.Q.	-	-	-	1	-	-	
13th.	7th Midsx.Rgt.att.Bde.H.Q.	-	-	-	-	1	-	
	1st London Regt.	-	-	-	-	2	-	Includes 1 accidently by Revolver.
	4th " "	-	-	-	-	1	-	
	13th Londons att.168th TMB.	-	-	-	-	2	-	Accidentally by explosion in fire.
	56th Bn. M.G.C.	-	-	-	1	1	-	Gassed.
	2/2nd London Field Ambce.	-	-	-	-	1	-	
Additional.								
3rd.	13th London Regt.	-	-	-	-	21	-	Gassed.
	Carried forward.	1	1	-	13	101	-	

Date.	UNIT.	OFFICERS. Killed.	OFFICERS. Wounded.	OFFICERS. Missing.	O.Rs. K.	O.Rs. W.	O.Rs. M.	REMARKS.
	Brought forward.	1	1	-	13	101	-	
14th.	14th London Regt.	-	-	-	-	2	-	
"	16th " "	-	-	-	-	3	-	
"	56th Bn. M.G.C.	-	-	-	-	2	-	
"	2/2nd Ldn. Fld. Ambce.	-	-	-	-	1	-	Gassed.
15th.	1st London Regt.	-	-	-	1	1	-	
"	14th " "	-	-	-	-	1	-	
"	2nd " "	-	-	-	-	1	-	
"	5th " "	-	-	-	-	1	-	Self-inflicted by rifle.
"	512th Fld. Coy. R.E.	-	-	-	-	1	-	
16th.	8th Middlesex Regt.	-	-	-	-	4	-	
"	4th London Regt.	-	-	-	-	1	-	
"	14th " "	-	-	-	-	1	-	X Gassed.
"	16th " "	-	Capt. F.E. WHITBY, 23/2/18.X	-	2	29X	-	X Gassed.
"	56th Bn. M.G.C.	-	Lieut. B. HEYWOOD, 15/3/18.X	-	-	-	-	Gassed.
"	512th (Ldn) Fld.Coy.R.E.	-	-	-	-	1	-	
15th	8th Middlesex Regt.	-	Lieut. A.E. MUZZELL.15/3/18.X	-	-	56X	-	X Gassed.
16/17th.	1st.London Regt.	-	-	-	-	80@	-	@ Includes 79 O.Rs.Gassed.
"	4th " "	-	-	-	-	2X	-	X Gassed.
"	4th Ldn.Rgt. attd.168th T.M.B.	-	-	-	3	4	-	
3rd.	13th London Regt.	-	-	-	-	2X	-	X Gassed.
16/17th.	13th Ldn.Rgt."attd.168th T.M.B.	-	-	-	-	1X	-	" "
"	14th " "	-	-	-	-	5X	-	" "
"	168th T.M. Battery.	-	-	-	-	1X	-	" "
"	56th Bn. M.G.C.	-	-	-	-	2X	-	" "
10th.	5th London Regt.	-	-	-	-	5X	-	" "
11th.	" " "	-	2/Lt. K.W. JONES. X	-	-	56X	-	" "
12th	" " "	-	Lt. W.C. OWEN.(12th Ldns) X	-	-	38X	-	" "
		-		-	-	33X	-	X "
		-		-	-	4X	-	X "
	Carried forward.	1	6	-	19	437	-	

Date.	UNIT.	OFFICERS.			O.Rs.			REMARKS.
		Killed.	Wounded.	Missing.	K.	W.	M.	
	Brought forward.	1	6	-	19	437	-	
13th.	5th London Regt.	-	-	-	-	10X	-	X Gassed.
14th.	"	-	-	-	-	6X	-	" "
15th.	"	-	-	-	-	4X	-	" "
16/17th	"	-	-	-	-	12@	-	@ Includes 2 O.Rs.at duty.
4th.	1/5th Cheshire Regt.	-	-	-	-	1X	-	X Gassed.
7th.	"	-	-	-	-	2X	-	" "
8th.	"	-	-	-	-	1X	-	" "
16/17th	416th (Edin)Fld.Coy.R.E.	-	-	-	-	2o	-	o Includes 1 O.R. gassed.
"	512th (Ldn) " "	-	-	-	-	3X	-	X Gassed.
"	513th (Ldn) " "	-	-	-	-	4X	-	" "
"	" " "	-	-	-	-	2∅	-	∅ Includes 1 O.R. Gassed.
17/18th.	7th Middlesex Regt.	-	-	-	-	11X	-	X Gassed.
16th	1st London Regt.	-	-	-	3	14	-	
4th	"	-	{ Lieut. O.D.GARRATT,M.C.,16/3/18.X { 2/Lt. E.A.RATCLIFF,(1st.Ldns)16/3/18.X { " G.W.FISHER. (9th Ldns) 16/3/18.X }	-	-	36X	-	X Gassed.
"	13th "	-	-	-	-	3X	-	X Gassed.
17th	"	-	-	-	-	32X	-	" "
16th	14th "	-	-	-	-	31@	-	@ Includes 28 O.Rs.gassed.
17th	168th T.M. Battery.	-	-	-	-	1X	-	X Gassed.
16th	5th London Regt.	-	-	-	-	1X	-	" "
11th	16th "	-	-	-	-	2X	-	" "
12th	"	-	-	-	-	1X	-	" "
13th	"	-	-	-	-	11X	-	" "
14th	"	-	-	-	-	1X	-	" "
15th	"	-	-	-	-	1X	-	" "
16th	169th T.M.Battery.	-	-	-	-	2X	-	" "
17/18th	5th Cheshire Regt.	-	-	-	-	9X	-	" "
	Carried forward.	1	9	-	22	641	-	

Date.	UNIT.	OFFICERS.			O. Rs.			REMARKS.
		Killed.	Wounded.	Missing.	K.	W.	M.	
	Brought forward.	1	9	-	22	641	-	
16th.	56th Bn. M.G.C.	-	-	-	-	21@	-	X Gassed. @ Includes 20 O.Rs gassed.
17th	"	-	2/Lt. J.B. KAY.16/3/18.X.	-	-	9X	-	X Gassed.
16/17th	X/56th T.M.Battery.	-	-	-	-	7X ∅	-	" ∅ Includes 5 at duty.
17/18th	512th(Ldn) Fld. Coy. R.E.	-	-	-	-	6X	-	X Gassed.
"	513th "	-	-	-	-	2X	-	"
"	2/2nd Ldn. Fld. Ambce.	-	-	-	-	-	-	
17/18th	1/8th Middlesex Rgt.	-	Capt. L.A. HIGSON,(11th Mdsx)18/3/18.X.	-	-	40X@	-	X Gassed. @ Includes 1 at duty.
"	Mdsx.Rgt.attd.167th T.M.B.	-	2/Lt. C.J.C. SMALL.(11th Msx)17/3/18X.	-	-	-	-	
16th	4th London Regt.	-	-	-	-	1X	-	X Gassed.
17th	14th "	-	-	-	-	54X	-	"
"	5th "	-	-	-	-	9X	-	"
17/18th	5th Cheshire Regt.	-	-	-	-	12X	-	"
"	56th Bn. M.G.C.	-	-	-	-	5X	-	"
18/19th	"	-	-	-	-	6X	-	"
		-	-	-	-	1	-	
17th.	7th Middlesex Regt.	-	-	-	-	5X	-	X Gassed.
"	8th Mdsx.Rgt.att.167th TMB.	-	-	-	-	1X	-	"
18th.	8th Middlesex Regt.	-	2/Lt. E.J. McDONNELL.(11th Msx)18/3/18.X.	-	-	-	-	"
19/20th.	"	-	-	-	-	26@	-	@ Includes 25 O.Rs gassed.
16th.	4th London Regt.	-	-	-	-	3X	-	X Gassed.
19th.	13th "	-	-	-	-	8X	-	"
16th.	14th "	-	-	-	-	10X	-	"
18th.	5th "	-	-	-	-	3X	-	"
18.2.18.	16th "	-	2/Lt. E.W. THOMPSON.18/2/18.X.	-	-	-	-	"
20.2.18.	"	-	2/Lt. R.A. BASSHAM. 20/2/18.X.	-	-	-	-	"
14th.	"	-	-	-	-	4X	-	"
	Carried forward.	1	15	-	22	874	-	

Date.	UNIT.	OFFICERS			O. Rs.			REMARKS.
		Killed.	Wounded.	Missing.	K.	W.	M.	
	Brought forward.	1	15		22	874		
15th.	16th London Regt.					2X		X Gassed.
16th.	" "					6X		"
17th.	" "					5X		"
18th.	" "					19X		"
19th.	" "					4X		"
19/20th.	1/5th Cheshire Regt.		Lt. H.V. STRONG(6th Devons) 16/3/18. X.			5		Includes 1 at duty.
16th.	56th Bn. M.G.C.					1X		X Gassed.
17th.	" "					2X		"
19/20th.	" "		2/Lt. S.F.TOY,19/3/18.X.			4X		
15/16th	X/56th M.T.M.Battery.							
20th.	8th Middlesex Regt.					10X		X Gassed.
17th.	4th London Regt.					5X		"
20th.	13th "					1X		"
16th.	14th "					1X		"
17th.	" "					2X		"
20/21st.	2nd "		2/Lt. J.ROBERTS.20/3/18.X.			3		
20th.	56th Bn. M.G.C.					9X		"
16/17th.	281st Bde.R.F.A.					5X		"
19/20th.	" "					1X		"
20/21st.	513th (Ldn)Fld.Coy.R.E.					1X		"
20th.	7th Middlesex Regt.					1X		X Gassed.
21st.	8th "					2X		"
20th.	14th.London Regt.					14X		
21/22nd.	" "	2/Lt. L.R.FRASER.21/3/18.						
"	5th Cheshire Regt.					2X		"
16/17th	X/56th M.T.M.Bty.					1X		"
21/22nd.	512th (Ldn)Fld.Coy.R.E.					2X		"
	Carried forward.	2	18		22	981		

Date.	UNIT.	OFFICERS. Killed.	OFFICERS. Wounded.	OFFICERS. Missing.	O.Rs. K.	O.Rs. W.	O.Rs. M.	REMARKS.
	Brought forward.	2	18	-	22	981	-	
21/22nd.	513th (Ldn)Fd.Co.R.E.	-	-	-	-	1X	-	X Gassed.
19th.	56th Bn. M.G.C.	-	-	-	-	8X	-	"
20th.	" "	-	-	-	-	8X	-	"
21st.	" "	-	-	-	-	3X	-	"
22/23rd.	4th London Regt.	-	Lieut. A. BATH, 22/3/18.X.	-	-	7X	-	X Gassed.
16th.	14th " "	-	-	-	-	1X	-	"
22/23rd.	2nd " "	-	-	-	1Ø	3X	-(	Ø Died of Wounds X Includes 1 Gassed.
"	5th " "	-	-	-	-	1X	-	X Gassed.
13th.	16th " "	-	-	-	1	1X	-	"
14th.	" " "	-	-	-	-	2X	-	"
17th.	" " "	-	-	-	-	1X	-	"
19th.	" " "	-	-	-	-	12X	-	"
20th.	" " "	-	-	-	-	4X	-	"
21st.	" " "	-	-	-	-	9X	-	"
22/23rd.	280th Bde.RFA.	-	-	-	-	13X	-	"
17/18th.	512th (Ldn)Fld.Coy.R.E.	-	-	-	-	3X	-	"
22/23rd.	513th (Ldn)	-	2/Lt. A.V.KIDMAN,22/3/18.X.	-	-	4X	-	"
23rd.	7th Middlesex Regt.	-	-	-	-	1X	-	X Gassed.
16th.	4th London Regt.	-	-	-	-	2X	-	"
23/24th.	13th " "	-	-	-	3	7	-	
"	14th " "	-	2/Lt.B.A.STARLING,23/3/18.	-	-	5	-	
"	2nd " "	-	-	-	1	5	-	
"	5th " "	-	-	-	3	4@	-	@ Includes l.at duty.
20th.	16th " "	-	-	-	-	1X	-	X Gassed.
22nd.	169th T.M.Battery.	-	-	-	-	34X	-	"
23/24th.	5th Cheshire Regt.	-	-	-	-	1	-	At duty.
"	56th Bn. M.G.C.	-	-	-	-	4	-	
	Carried forward.	3	20	-	31	1127	-	

Date	UNIT	Officers Killed	Officers Wounded	Officers Missing	O.Rs. K	O.Rs. W	O.Rs. M	REMARKS
	Brought forward.	3	20	-	31	1127	-	
22/23rd.	281st Bde. R.F.A.	-	-	-	-	3X	-	X Gassed.
"	X/56th T.M.Bty.	-	-	-	-	2X	-	"
23/24th.	512th (Ldn)Fld.Coy.RE.	-	-	-	-	5X	-	"
"	416th (EDin) "	(Major J.G.GOODFELLOW. 23/3/18.)						
23rd.	7th Middlesex Regt.	-	-	-	-	3X	-	X Gassed.
19th.	8th "	-	-	-	-	5X	-	"
24/25th.	4th London Regt.	-	2/Lieut.C.H.BOARD. 25/3/18.	-	-	2	-	
"	13th "	-	Capt. N.J. INNS. 24/3/18.	-	-	1∅	-	∅ Accidentally by dis--charge of rifle.
"	5th Cheshire Regt.	-	2/Lt. A.L.MORISON.(9th-Ldns)24/3/18.	-	1	-	-	
22nd.	56th Bn. M.G.C.	-	-	-	1	1X	-	X Gassed.
24/25th.	2/1st London Fld.Amb.	-	-	-	1	3∅	-	∅ Includes 2 O.Rs.gassed
"	ASC.MT.attd.2/1st Fd.Amb.	-	-	-	1	2	-	
"	2/2nd "	-	-	-	1	-	-	
20th.	8th Middlesex Regt.	-	Lt. J.D.G.LOUGH.20/3/18.X. Lt. V.A. DITCHAM.20/3/18.X.	-	-	70X	-	X Gassed.
22nd.	" "	-	-	-	2	1@ 13∅	-	1@ Self-Inflicted. POST (∅ Garrison of GAVRELLE)
25/26th.	2nd London Regt.	-	-	-	-	-	-	
"	5th "	-	-	-	-	5	10	After hostile patrol bombed 1 of our posts.
22nd.	56th Bn. M.G.C.	-	-	-	-	1X	-	X Gassed.
25/26th.	280th Bde.R.F.A.	-	-	-	-	1X	-	"
24th.	14th Ldns.att.168th TMB.	-	-	-	-	1X	-	"
26/27th.	1st London Regmt.	-	-	-	-	1X	-	X Gassed.
16th.	7th Middlesex Regt.	-	-	-	-	1X	-	"
26/27th.	4th London Regt.	-	-	-	-	1X	-	"
"	5th "	-	-	-	-	1	-	
	Carried forward.	4	25	-	36	1236	14	

Date.	UNIT.	OFFICERS. Killed.	OFFICERS. Wounded.	OFFICERS. Missing.	O.Rs. K.	O.Rs. W.	O.Rs. M.	REMARKS.
	Brought forward.	4	25		36	1236	14	
25/26th	16th London Regt.					x		ø Accid't'y whilst cleaning rifle.
26/27th	"					12ø		(x.includes 11 ORs.gassed.
25th	56th Bn. M.G.C.				1	1		
26/27th	2/2nd Ldn.Fld.Ambce.				1	2X		X Gassed.
	"					1X		"
27th	281st Bde. R.F.A.		Lieut. S.S.WRIGHT (gassed)			1		
	416th (Edin)Fd.Co.R.E.					2		
	513th (Ldn)							
28th	7th Middlesex Regt.				6	20		
8th	"	2/Lt.W.B.GREEN,27/3/18.			2	7		
	"	" H.J.BARKER,(5th Mdsx)ø						
	1st London Regt.	(2/Lt. A.E.STRAW.				9	1	ø Died of Wounds.
		(Capt. M.K.MATTHEWS,(1st C.of L.Yeo)				7X		X Gassed.
	4th London Regt.	2/Lt.H.T.HANNAY. 2/Lt.(A/Capt)A.M.DUTHIE,D.S.O.			15	44ø	167x	(øincludes 1 gassed.
		R.E.CAMPKIN. Lt. H.M.LORDEN.	2/Lt.(A/Capt)E.E.SPICER.					(x " 12 ORs.wounded. and missing.
			" H.V.COOMBES.(21st Londns)					
	R.A.M.C. att.4th Ldns		" H.O. MORRIS.X					X Wounded & Missing.
	168th T.M.Battery.		" Capt. J.G.M.MOLONY.					
	13th London Regt.		Lt.G.W.DENNING,(4th Ldn)			5	4	
	14th "				3	11	11x	x Includes 1 believed killed.
	2nd London Regt.		2/Lt. W. EDIS,(17th Ldns.)		13	30	4	
	" "		" C.P.S.BRADLEY,(17th Ldns)		17	57		
	" "		Lt.E.J.Y.SIMMONS,(3rd Ldns)X					X AT DUTY.
5th	" Lt.(A/Capt)E.W.ROSE.		2/Lt. H.L.RENWICK. 2/Lt.(A/Capt)J.S.CALDER, M.G.		11	29ø	436	ø Includes 2 at duty.
			2/Lt.(A/Capt)T.E.BURROUGHS,X.					X AT DUTY.
	Carried forward.	9	36	7	104	1474	637	

Date.	UNIT.	Married.	OFFICERS.			O. Rs.			REMARKS.
			Killed.	Wounded.	Missing.	K.	W.	M.	
	Brought forward.		9	36	7	104	1474	637	
28th.	5th London Regt.				Lt.(A/Capt)W.J.GRACE(10th Ldns)				
"	"				2/Lt. R.F.L.HEWLETT.				
"	"				H.G.HIGHAM.				
"	"				" S.C.GOULD(21st Lns)				
"	"				" P.ADAMS " "				
"	"				" W.R.B.KETTLE.				
"	"				" F.S.SILLS.				
"	"				" R.C.THOMPSON.				
"	"				" T.C.KITE-POWELL.				
"	"				" G.M.NEWLAND(9th Lns)				
"	"				" C.S.TRESILIAN(5th Msx)				
RAMC. attd.5th Ldns.					Lieut. E.N.P.MARTLAND	17	32	165	± 6 includes 17 O.Rs. wounded and missing
16th London Regt.					C.H.RAVEN(9th Lns)				
M.O.R.C.USA.; attd.16th Lns.					F.L.CHAMBERLIN.(21st Ldns)				
169th T.M. Battery					Lieut. R.B. RHETT.	11	24@		(@ Includes 1 at duty and 1 gassed.
5th Cheshire Regt.					Lieut. W.E.S.JOTCHAM.(19th Lns) 1		20		
X/56th T.M.Battery.			Lt. W.B.FALCONER(4th Cam.Hdrs) 1		2	9		(X)At duty.
56th Bn. M.G.C.		Lt.G.V.SPURWAY,MC	Lt. A.WILSON,M.C(X) 2/Lt. W.J.BATTING.		9	25	53		
2/Lt. J.F.COLLINS. 2/Lt. H.L.BROMLEY.									
E.R. ASHWORTH.									
416th (Bdln)Fld.Coy.R.E.						1	1		
512th (Ldn) " "							5		Gassed.
2/1st London Fld.Ambce.						1	2	1	
2/2nd " "		Major J.S. WALLACE.					1		
2/3rd " "							8		
Carried forward.		13	41		25	144	1565	904	

Date	UNIT	OFFICERS Killed	OFFICERS Wounded	Missing	O.Rs K	O.Rs W	O.Rs M	REMARKS
	Brought forward.	13	41	25	144	1565	904	
29th.	1st London Regt.		2/Lt. C.V.EVITT.(A.S.C)@		6	16	2	@ At duty.
	8th Middlesex Regt.				2	6		
	13th London Regt.				2	5		
	14th "				5	7		
	5th Cheshire Regt.		Lt.(A/Capt)E.S.HERON.28/3/18.		4	6		
	280th Bde. R.F.A.		Major G.C.T.BRADY.28.3.18.		3	10		
	281st "		Capt. G.B. WOLFE. — do —		7	19		
	56th D.A.C.				1	2		
	416th (E)Fld.Coy.R.E.	Capt.F.W.ANDERSON.28/3/18. Lieut. J. LAIRD.28/3/18.				2x		x Includes 1 gassed
	512th "					3x		x Gassed.
30th.	7th Middlesex Regt.					13X		X Includes 2 gassed.
	8th Mdsx.Rgt.attd.168th T.M.B.					1		"
	13th Ldns. attd. 168th T.M.B.					1		Accidentally.
	168th T.M. Battery.					1		"
	1/5th Cheshire Regt.					1		
	280th Bde. R.F.A.					1		
	281st "					2		
	TOTALS FOR MARCH.	15	45	25	172	1661	906	

UNIT.	STRENGTH. 1.3.18.		INCREASE.		DECREASE.		STRENGTH. 1.4.18.	
	O.	O.R.	O.	O.R.	O.	O.R.	O.	O.R.
56th Divl. Headquarters.	19	84	–	–	1	–	18	84
167th Inf. Bde. Hd.Qtrs.	3	21	1	–	1	–	3	21
1/7th Middlesex Regt.	53	947	–	160	1	169	52	938
1/8th " "	54	986	–	380	9	428	45	938
1/1st London Regt.	51	984	2	33	3	148	50	869
167th T.M. Battery.	4	46	–	–	–	–	4	46
168th Inf. Bde. Hd.Qtrs.	3	21	–	–	–	–	3	21
1/4th London Regt.	45	913	–	276	14	415	31	774
1/13th " "	43	1008	–	224	6	221	37	1011
1/14th " "	42	928	–	288	7	287	35	929
168th T.M. Battery.	4	46	–	–	1	6	3	40
169th Inf. Bde. Hd.Qtrs.	3	21	–	–	–	–	3	21
1/2nd London Regt.	51	985	–	108	9	178	42	915
1/5th " "	46	935	2	591	18	655	30	871
1/16th " "	46	984	1	462	12	488	35	958
169th T.M. Battery.	3	46	–	–	1	12	2	34
1/5th Cheshire Regt.	39	885	–	70	1	159	38	796
56th Bn. M.G.C.	44	771	16	365	14	250	46	886
Hd.Qtrs. Royal Arty.	4	17	–	1	–	–	4	18
280th Bde. R.F.A.	34	777	3	4	5	23	32	758
281st " "	24	780	4	6	3	25	25	761
D.A.C.	12	581	1	2	2	10	11	573
Hd.Qtrs. Royal Engrs.	2	10	–	–	–	–	2	10
416th (Edin)Fld. Coy.R.E.	7	206	–	2	4	20	3	188
512th (Ldns) " "	6	196	–	13	1	34	5	175
513th (") " "	9	208	–	6	–	28	9	186
56th Divl. Signal Coy.	11	276	–	2	–	3	11	275
Divl. Train.	17	351	4	18	–	2	21	367
Medical Units.	20	542	3	4	4	44	19	502
Mobile Veterinary Section.	1	21	–	–	–	–	1	21
247th Employment Coy.	1	309	–	–	–	7	1	302

HQ A & Q 46 Div
Feb
Vol XII

A. & Q.

56th DIVISION

APRIL 1918.

Army Form C. 2118.

Vol. XXVII
Page 1

WAR DIARY
or
INTELLIGENCE SUMMARY.
(Erase heading not required.)

Instructions regarding War Diaries and Intelligence Summaries are contained in F.S. Regs., Part II. and the Staff Manual respectively. Title pages will be prepared in manuscript.

Place	Date 1918	Hour	Summary of Events and Information	Remarks and references to Appendices
ACQ	APRIL 1		Orders received that the Division would move shortly, order cancelled later.	
	2			
	3		H.Q. Div. Arty. moved to BERLES. 5(L) M.G. Bn. moved to CHATEAU de la HAIE.	
	4			
	5		8th MIDDLESEX REST moved to CHATEAU de la HAIE, 416, 517, 513 Field Coys moved to ESTREE CAUCHIE. Division situated as per attached location table, Appendix "A". Warning order received to relieve 1st Canadian Division stating strength.	
	6		Moves carried out in accordance with formation order No. 159.	
	7		Moves carried out in accordance with formation order No. 160.	
	8		Division situated as per attached location table, Appendix "B".	
WARLUS	9			
	10		Hqrs 169 Inf Bde moved to BERNEVILLE.	
	11			
	12			
	13		168 Inf Bde relieved 167 Inf Bde in the front line. 168 Bde disposed as follows. 11th London Regt Right Front Line Bn. 4th London Regt Left Front line Bn. (167 Inf Bde) Reserve Bn to Bde in line. 13th London Regt Support Bn. 7th Middx Regt followed 8th Middlesex Regt. Ronville Caves. when relieved 167 Inf Bde became Support Bde disposed as follows: 1st London Regt. Ronville Caves. 169 Inf Bde relieved the 167 Inf Bde in support, Division situated as per attached location table Appendix "C".	
	14			
	15			
	16			
	17			
	18			
	19		169 Inf Bde relieved 168 Inf Bde in the front line. 169 Bde disposed as follows. 2nd London Regt Left Front line Bn. 16th London Regt Right Front line Bn. 5th London Regt Support Bn. (168 Bde) Reserve Bn to Bde in line when relieved 168 Inf Bde became Support as follows 4th London Regt. Ronville Caves. 11th London Regt. Ronville Caves. 13th London Regt. Ronville Caves. 167 Inf Bde relieved 168 Inf Bde in Support, 167 Inf Bde disposed as follows. 8th Middx Regt	
	20			

Army Form C. 2118.

Page 2.

WAR DIARY
or
INTELLIGENCE SUMMARY.
(Erase heading not required.)

Instructions regarding War Diaries and Intelligence Summaries are contained in F.S. Regs., Part II. and the Staff Manual respectively. Title pages will be prepared in manuscript.

Place	Date 1918 APRIL	Hour	Summary of Events and Information	Remarks and references to Appendices
WARLUS	20		Reserve Bn to Bde in line. 7th Middx Regt to become Reserve Bde. disposed as follows:- Bde Hqrs Berneuille.	
	21			
	22		Reserve Bde. disposed as follows:- 4th & 13th London Regt. Dainville. 14th London Regt & 16th London Regt. Ronville Caves.	
	23			
	24			
	25		The Division extended to its left taking over the front held by the 15th Division, moves carried out in accordance with Order No. 16 M.	
	26			
	27			
	28			
	29		168 Inf Bde relieved 167 Inf Bde in the Right of Divisional front disposed as follows: 4th London Regt Right Bn. 13th London Regt Right Pn. 14th London Regt & Support Bn. on Relief 168 Bde disposed as follows:- Bde Hqrs & 16th London Regt. Berneuille. 2nd London Regt. 5th London Regt. Dainville. Division located & pin attached location Table, Appendix C.	
	30			

(signature) Major
Lieut.-Col:
A.A. & Q.M.G. 56th Division.

Appendix "A"   *War Diary*

S E C R E T.   AQS/5.

LOCATIONS.

56TH DIVISION.   5TH APRIL, 1918.

Divl. Headquarters.	ACQ.
S.S.O.	AGNIERES.
D.A.D.O.S.	AGNIERES.
Divl. Artillery Hd.Qtrs.	BERLES.
280th Bde. R.F.A. Hd.Qtrs.	
" " " Wagon Lines.	G.1.b. G.2.A.
281st " " Hd.Qtrs.	
" " " Wagon Lines.	G.2.A. & B.
56th D.A.C.	ANZIN.
C.R.E. Hd.Qtrs.	ACQ.
416th Field Company.	ESTREE CAUCHIE.
512th " "	" "
513th " "	" "
167th Inf. Bde. Hd.Qtrs.	VILLERS-AUX-BOIS.
7th Middlesex Regt.	"
8th " "	CHATEAU de la HAIE.
1st London Regiment.	CAMBLAIN L'ABBE.
3rd " " Transport.	VILLERS-AUX-BOIS.
167th T.M. Battery.	"
168th Inf. Bde. Hd.Qtrs.	MONT ST. ELOI.
4th London Regiment.	VILLERS-AUX-BOIS.
13th " "	VILLAGE CAMP, ECOIVRES.
14th " "	LANCASTER CAMP, MONT ST.ELOI.
168th T.M. Battery.	MONT ST.ELOI.
169th Inf. Bde. Hd.Qtrs.	ECOIVRES.
2nd London Regiment.	FRASER CAMP, BOIS DES ALLEUX.
5th " "	LE PENDU CAMP, " " "
16th " "	OTTAWA CAMP, " " "
169th T.M. Battery.	MONT ST.ELOI.
56th Divl. Train Hd.Qtrs.	AGNIERES.
Headquarters Company.	CAPELLE FERMONT.
No. 2 Company.	ESTREE CAUCHIE.
" 3 "	CAPELLE FERMONT.
" 4 "	ESTREE CAUCHIE.
No. 56th M.T. Company.	TINQUETTE.
Pioneer Battn. (1/5th Cheshires)	ESTREE CAUCHIE.
56th M.G. Battalion.	CHATEAU de la HAIE.
A.D.M.S.	AGNIERES.
2/1st London Field Ambulance.	VILLERS-AUX-BOIS.
2/2nd " " "	ESTREE CAUCHIE.
2/3rd " " "	AUBIGNY.
Mobile Veterinary Section.	AGNIERES.

A C Dundas Major
for Major General,
Commanding 56th Division.

SECRET Appendix "B" War Diary

LOCATIONS.

56th Division. For 8th April, 1918.

	Headquarters.	Transport Lines.
Divisional Headquarters.	WARLUS.	
C. R. A.	"	
C. R. E.	BERNEVILLE.	
A. D. M. S.	"	
D. A. D. V. S.	"	
D. A. D. O. S.	Near HABARCQ.	
167th Inf. Bde. Head Qrs.	G.29.c.6.8 St. SAUVEUR CAVES	
7th Middlesex Regt.		
8th " "		WANQUETIN.
1st London Regt.		
167th T.M.Battery		
168th Inf. Bde. Head Qrs.	G.28.d.0.3 RONVILLE CAVES	
4th London Regt.		
13th " "		BERNEVILLE.
14th " "		
168th T.M.Battery		
169th Inf. Bde. Head Qrs.	DAINVILLE	
2nd London Regt.		
5th " "		BERNEVILLE.
16th " "		
169th T.M.Battery		
56th Bn. M.G.Corps	WARLUS.	
1/5th (E. of C.) Bn. Cheshire R	RONVILLE CAVES.	DAINVILLE.
416th Field Coy. R.E.	CHATEAU AGNY.	L.35.c.2.7
512th " " "	RONVILLE CAVES	Q.6.d.7.8
513th " " "	AGNEZ LES DUISANS	K.12.d.2.8
Divl. Train Head Qrs.	BERNEVILLE	BERNEVILLE.
No. 1 Company	HABARCQ	HABARCQ
No. 2 Company	WANQUETIN	WANQUETIN
No. 3 Company	HABARCQ	HABARCQ
No. 4 Company	WANQUETIN	WANQUETIN
2/3rd London Field Amboo.	ACHICOURT A.D.S.	
2/1st " " "	DAINVILLE M.D.S.	
2/2nd " " "	AGNEZ LES DUISANS	
247th Div. Employment Coy.	WARLUS.	

A.C.Dundas
Major,
D.A.A.G., 56th Division.

Appendix 'C' War Diary

SECRET. | LOCATION TABLE. | AQS/5.

56th DIVISION.   For 10.p.m. 14.4.18.

Serial No.	UNIT.	Present Position of Hd.Qtrs.	Present Position of Transport Lines.
1.	Divisional Headquarters.	WARLUS.	WARLUS.
2.	167th Inf. Bde. Hd.Qtrs.	BERNEVILLE.	)
3.	7th Middlesex Regt.	DAINVILLE.	)
4.	8th " "	BERNEVILLE.	) WANQUETIN.
5.	1st London Regt.	DAINVILLE.	)
6.	167th T.M. Battery.	BERNEVILLE.	)
7.	168th Inf. Bde. Hd.Qtrs.	RONVILLE CAVES, G.28.d.1.3.	)
8.	4th London Regt.	N.1.a.2.6.	)
9.	13th " "	M.5.b.5.7.	) BERNEVILLE.
10.	14th " "	N.7.a.2.8.	)
11.	168th T.M. Battery.	G.29.c.89.	)
12.	169th Inf. Bde. Hd.Qtrs.	RONVILLE CAVES) G.28.d.1.3.	)
13.	2nd London Regt.	RONVILLE CAVES.	)
14.	5th " "	M.10.a.3.2.	) BERNEVILLE.
15.	16th " "	RONVILLE CAVES.	)
16.	169th T.M. Battery.	" "	)
17.	1/5th Cheshire Regt.	" "	) WANQUETIN.
18.	416th Field Company R.E.	CHATEAU? AGNY.	L.35.c.2.7.) DAINVILLE.)
19.	512th " " "	RONVILLE CAVES.	Q.6.d.7.8.) BERNEVILLE.)
20.	513th " " "	" "	L.22.a.2.0.) WANQUETIN.)
21.	2/1st Ldn. Fld. Ambulance.	K.28.d.52.	WANQUETIN.
22.	2/2nd. " " "	WARLUS.	WARLUS.
23.	2/3rd " " "	ACHICOURT.	WANQUETIN.
24.	56th Div. Artillery H.Q.	WARLUS.	WARLUS.
25.	280th Bde. R.F.A.	M.8.b.75.42.	BERNEVILLE.
26.	281st " " "	G.28.d.1.3.	DAINVILLE.
27.	56th Div. Ammn. Column.	SIMENCOURT.	SIMENCOURT.
28.	56th Bn. M.G.C.	WARLUS.	WARLUS.
29.	56th Divl. Train.	WANQUETIN.	WANQUETIN.
30.	No. 1. Company.	SIMENCOURT.	SIMENCOURT.
31.	" 2. "	WANQUETIN.	WANQUETIN.
32.	" 3. "	"	"
33.	" 4. "	"	"
34.	247th Employment Coy.	WARLUS.	
35.	Mobile Veterinary Section.	WANQUETIN.	WANQUETIN.
36.	D.A.D.O.S.	MONTENESCOURT.	
37.	D.A.D.V.S.	WARLUS.	
38.	A.D.M.S.	"	
39.	C.R.E.	BERNEVILLE.	

G.P. Lowden Capt
for Major,
D.A.A.G., 56th Division.

Appendix 'C'   War Diary

LOCATIONS.   AQS/5.

56th DIVISION.   For 29th April, 1918.

	Headquarters.	Transport Lines.
Divisional Headquarters.	WARLUS.	WARLUS.
C.R.A.	"	"
C.R.E.	BERNEVILLE.	-
A.D.M.S.	WARLUS.	-
D.A.D.V.S.	"	-
D.A.D.O.S.	MONTENESCOURT.	-
167th Infantry Brigade.	G.29.d.0570.	DAINVILLE.
7th Middlesex Regt.	H.25.b.25.25.	WANQUETIN.
8th " "	H.31.b.3.8.	"
1st London Regt.	G.30.c.10.25.	"
167th T.M. Battery.	H.25.d.25.80.	DAINVILLE.
168th Infantry Brigade.	G.27.b.8.3.	BERNEVILLE.
4th London Regt.	N.1.a.6.3.	"
13th " "	N.7.a.2.8.	"
14th " "	M.5.b.5.7.	"
168th T.M. Battery.	G.29.c.8.9.	"
169th Infantry Brigade.	BERNEVILLE.	BERNEVILLE.
2nd London Regt.	DAINVILLE.	"
5th " "	"	"
16th " "	BERNEVILLE.	"
169th T.M. Battery.	G.27.b.94.40.	"
56th Battn. M.G.Corps.	WARLUS.	MONTENESCOURT.
1/5th Cheshire Regt. (Pioneers)	RONVILLE CAVES.	WANQUETIN.
416th Field Company R.E.	St.SAUVEUR CAVES.	DAINVILLE.
512th " " "	G.28.a.7.6.	BERNEVILLE.
513th " " "	G.27.b.15.90.	WAGNONLIEU.
2/1st London Field Ambulance.	K.28.d.5.3.	WANQUETIN.
2/2nd " " "	L.1.c.45.	AGNEZ-LES-DUISANS.
2/3rd " " "	ACHICOURT.	WANQUETIN.
280th Brigade R.F.A.	M.8.b.75.42.	BERNEVILLE.
281st " "	G.34.b.2.9.	SIMENCOURT.
56th Divl. Ammunition Column.	SIMENCOURT.	"
277th A.F.A. Brigade.	G.33.c.27.	BERNEVILLE.
70th Brigade R.F.A.	G.28.b.2086.	"
71st " "	G.22.d.10.90.	"
277th Brigade Ammunition Column.	HABARCQ.	HABARCQ.
Divisional Train Headquarters.	WANQUETIN.	WANQUETIN.
No. 1 Company.	SIMENCOURT.	SIMENCOURT.
" 2 "	WANQUETIN.	WANQUETIN.
" 3 "	"	"
" 4 "	"	"
Mobile Veterinary Section.	MONTENESCOURT.	MONTENESCOURT.
247th Employment Company.	WARLUS.	-
56th M.T. Company.	TILLOY-LES-HERMAVILLE.	-

A.Dundas
Major,
D.A.A.G., 56th Division.

SECRET.   56th DIVISION AQS/607.

ADMINISTRATIVE INSTRUCTIONS No. 1. IN CONNECTION WITH THE POSSIBLE TRANSFER OF THE DIVISION (LESS ARTILLERY) TO ANOTHER CORPS BY BUS.

1.   In the event of the Division being relieved in the line it will probably be transferred by Bus to another Corps.

2. (a) One of the two following embussing situations will arise :-
SITUATION "A". Troops will embus from their present positions, Units now in the line marching straight to the busses after being relieved
or
SITUATION "B". The Division will concentrate in a back area after relief and will embus from the Concentration Area.

(b) An embussing Table for each of the above situations is attached.
(c) In the event of the Division being relieved as a preliminary to a Bus move, Officers responsible for arranging reliefs should ensure that they are arranged so as to fit in with the embussing table, for whichever situation is in force.

3.   As soon as it is apparent that the Division is about to be transferred elsewhere by Bus, a wire worded as follows will be sent out to all concerned.
"Bus move Situation A (or B)" - on receipt of this wire the following action will be taken :-
 (a) By all units. Wire Embussing strength (all ranks) to this office, through the usual channels; and in the case of Divisional Troops repeat the wire to their Bus group Commander.
 (b) By Divisional Train. Return Baggage Wagons to Units.
 (c) By all Units. Load all transport and park it ready to move at 1 hours notice.
 (d) By Infantry Brigades. Report to this office name; unit and address of Officer appointed to command Brigade Group Horse Transport Column Also names of Officers appointed Brigade Group Embussing and Debussing Officers.
 (e) By Infantry Brigades. Collect Billetting parties of their Bus group and notify this office where a lorry should be sent to pick them up.
 (f) By all concerned. Take action in accordance with the subsequent paragraphs of these instructions.

4.   A Zero-hour for each convoy will be notified from this office. All troops will arrive at the embussing Point at Zero-30 minutes. For Situation "A" units of Divisional troops will move to embussing points under orders of the O.C. Divisional Troops units concerned. On the arrival at the embussing point they will come under the orders of the Brigade Bus Group Commander, to whom they will report.
For Situation "B" all units of Brigade Bus Groups will move to embussing points under the orders of the Brigade Bus Group Commander.

5. Embussing arrangements.
Each Infantry Brigade will detail an Officer not below the rank of Captain who will proceed to the head of each embussing point at Zero-1 hour with 1 guide for each unit of the group and will there await the arrival of O.C. Bus Convoy. He will take with him a state showing the embussing strength of each unit in his convoy. He will ascertain from O.C. Bus Convoy the number and distribution of busses and seated lorries in the convoy. Each Bus holds 25 all ranks and each seated lorry 20 all ranks. He will allot the required number of busses and lorries

to each unit and will then despatch the guides to meet units, with instructions to load them to that portion of road space on which their section of busses and lorries is drawn up. Guides must know the distribution of busses and seated lorries in their section of the convoy. O.C. Units will form up their units clear of the road, on the right hand side if possible and facing towards the head of the convoy; the troops being equally distributed in 6 groups for every 80 yards of road space, each group consisting of 25 for each bus and 20 for each seated lorry. All vehicles will be loaded simultaneously as soon as the vehicles and the troops are in position. The Embussing Officer will travel on the last Bus. Similarly each Infantry Brigade will detail an Officer to supervise the Debussing. This Officer will travel on the leading vehicle of the convoy. Embussing and Debussing Officers will wear the Blue Arm band whilst on duty, as a distinguishing badge.

6. Communication and Medical Arrangements.
O.C. Signal Company will detail a Motor Cyclist and A.D.M.S. will detail an Ambulance car to be on duty at each Embussing and Debussing Point. They will report to Embussing and Debussing Officers at Zero-1 hour.

7. Traffic Control.
For the control of traffic at each of the Embussing Points the A.P.M. will detail 4 M.M.P. to report to the embussing Officer at each embussing point at Zero-1 hour.

8. Machine and Lewis Guns.
Machine Guns and belts, and Lewis Guns and Magazines will be taken with the men on the Busses.

9. Billetting Parties.
One lorry will be allotted to each Infantry Brigade for conveyance of billetting parties of their Brigade Bus Group.

10. Additional M.T. Transport.
Lorries will be provided under Divisional arrangements for transport of Blankets, and Stokes Trench Mortars and Handcarts.

11. Packs.
Packs of Infantry, Pioneer and M.G. Battalions and R.E. Units will be left in four dumps (one for each Infantry Brigade and one for the Divl. Troops Units) in this Area. These dumps will be cleared and stored under Corps arrangements. Locations of Infantry Brigade Dumps will be reported to this office. The Divl. Troops Dump will be at No. 1 Camp, WARLUS. Divisional arrangements will be made for guarding these dumps.

12. Horse Transport and Bicycles.
Horse transport and bicycles will move in columns constituted similarly to the Brigade Bus groups. Each Infantry Brigade will detail a Senior Officer to command the Brigade Group Transport Column. Orders for the move of Transport Columns will be sent to these Officers direct by this office.
Train Headquarters, Transport and Mobile Veterinary Section will move with "A" Infantry Brigade Transport Group. Train Companies will move with the Infantry Brigade Groups to which they are affiliated.

13. Supplies.
The unexpended portion of the current day's ration will be carried on the man, and, if time permits and length of journey necessitates, the following day's rations will also be carried on the man.
In the event of the Bus Party overtaking the Horse Transport party and arriving at their destination before the Horse Transport Party,

Supplies which would ordinarily be refilled and delivered to Units by Horse Transport will be delivered by to Units by M.T., in detail, under the direction of Supply Officers.

The Horse Transport Party will be rationed for day of departure, and, if time permits, for day of departure + 1, and will carry those rations.

Rations of the Horse Transport Party for consumption on the day of departure + 1 (if necessary), day of departure + 2, and any following days while still on the march, will be delivered on route, in detail, by M.T. under the direction of Supply Officers.

If Horse Transport Party reaches its destination before Bus Party, supplies for both Bus Party and H.T. Party will be picked up from Refilling Points in new Area in the normal manner.

For the present the Meat Ration of units likely to have to move by bus at short notice will include a high percentage of preserved meat.

14. Motor Transport.

All Motor cars, Motor Ambulances, and motor cycles will move on the days on which the units, to which they belong, embus.

14th April, 1918.

Lieut.-Colonel,
A.A. & Q.M.G., 56th Division.

DISTRIBUTION.
....

167th Inf. Bde.	D.M.G.C.	D.A.D.V.S.
168th " "	Divl. Train.	Camp Comdt.
169th " "	A.D.M.S.	Div.Employ.Coy.
Divl. Artillery.	Div. Signals.	"G"
5th Cheshire Regt.	A.P.M.	XVII Corps "Q".
C.R.E.	D.A.D.O.S.	56th M.T.Company.

EXTRACTS from Notes on ADMINISTRATIVE ARRANGEMENTS during
RECENT OPERATIONS, from a DIVISIONAL point of view.

1. Supplies :
   (a) Railhead:
   Railhead was changed frequently, and often at the last moment. On one occasion supplies were drawn from 3 different centres on the same day. On some occasions Supplies were drawn from Reserve Stores or R.S.Os.

   (b) Refilling Points :
   Early in the operations it was decided to do away with Refilling Points, and deliver direct to Units Q.M.Stores. This was done, partly owing to the difficulty in choosing suitable places during moving operations, and consequent congestion on the roads, and partly to save units extra trouble. This system worked very well in practice. To ensure it doing so, attention must be paid to the following points :-
   1. Units must know where the Train is located.
   2. The Train must know where Units' Q.M.Stores are. Brigades therefore, must be certain that any changes of locations are notified to train at once.
   3. Quartermasters must give their indents for rations to the Train representative who brings their rations.

   In the case of the Artillery who were detached, and whose Wagon Lines were constantly moving, arrangements were made for representatives from all Batteries to attend daily at the Train to guide wagons back. If the Train moved, information was left to enable the guides to find it, and the C.R.A. was informed.
   Considerable difficulty was experienced by units whose rations for consumption the following day were delivered to their Q. M. Stores and the Units' Transport had to move the same day, after delivery.
   It was not possible to allow Supply wagons to remain with Units, as the Train was probably moving also, and the wagons were required for loading supplies which had been drawn from Railhead by M.T.
   This fact was taken into consideration, and as far as possible Supply wagons allowed to remain with Units, but it must be recognised that units will have to make arrangements to carry the rations on their cookers and limbers under such circumstances.

   (c) Supply of Rations forward to Troops in the Line.
   It is realised that the difficulty in keeping touch between Battalions in the Line, and their Transport Lines, is great. Brigades must arrange to do this, which can best be done by a plentiful supply of runners: the tendency was to arrange for rations to be taken too far forward in the first place.
   "Rendezvous" should be made well behind the line, and arrangements made to send runners down to these spots at the times fixed for rations to be there, so that the limbers can be guided to the actual spot where the Battalion is to be found. If units move they must endeavour to inform their Rear Echelon.
   Quartermasters or Transport Officers should make a point of seeing their Battalions every night, so that they can assert in any requirements they may have.

Ammunition:
   There was a certain amount of misunderstanding about the system of Supply of ammunition during open warfare.
   The supply should always be forwarded through the following

P.T.O. / channels.

channels :-
  (a) The D.A.C. which is refilled under arrangements made by the Division.
  (b) Brigade Limbers (detached from the D.A.C.) refilled from the D.A.C.
  (c) Forward fighting limbers and pack ponies of units whose duty is to keep in touch with their Battalion.

In moving warfare dumps should not be formed. A mounted orderly from No. 3 Section of the D.A.C. was attached to each Staff Captain to enable him to keep in touch with the S.A.A. Section.

It is the duty of Staff Captains to keep up the supply of ammunition, and it should not be necessary to apply to the Division at all, except in difficulties.

There was no shortage of ammunition during the operations.

Transport.

The actual composition of forward Echelons of units should be decided by Brigade Commanders, but it should be borne in mind that, as regards Cookers, although it is most essential that the men forward should be given hot food whenever possible, it is not advisable to send more Cookers forward than is actually necessary. If Cookers are lost, men will suffer when units come out of the line, until it is possible to replace them.

There should always be an Officer in charge of the Forward Echelon of units.

Ordnance.

It is inevitable that the normal supply of Ordnance Stores cannot be maintained during active operations.

(a) As regards stores required for fighting, such as Vickers, Lewis guns, Lewis Gun Drums, etc. units should wire their immediate requirements through their Brigades to D.A.D.O.S. The indents supporting them can be sent subsequently. This was not always done during recent operations, and complaints were received in this office that such and such a unit was short of Lewis Gun drums, when no demands for their replacements had been submitted. It is essential that Staff Captains should see that demands for such articles are submitted with as little delay as possible.

(b) The chief shortages that appear to have been felt were rifle oil, flannelette and socks.

In future, arrangements will be made to carry a small supply of these.

The point to be borne in mind is that units should endeavour to demand only what is urgently required, but that such demands should be put in at once.

Surplus stores.

It will have to be recognised that in moving warfare, units will have nothing but their baggage wagons for moving stores.

Units will carefully consider what stores to dump. Care must be taken to see that nothing that is required for fighting is left behind. Officers' kits should be reduced to a minimum.

SECRET.

No. G3/518 AQS/582.
Date 6.5.18
GENERAL STAFF, 56th DIVISION.

167th Inf. Bde.   S.A.A. Section,   D.A.C.   A.D.M.S.
168th "   "   C. R. E.   Divl. Signals.
169th "   "   D.M.G.C.   "G".
Divl. Artillery. Divl. Train.

    Issued for information in continuation of this office AQS. 582 of 3.4.18, 609 of 16.4.18, and 609/1 of 17.4.18.

6.5.18.

Lieut. Colonel,
A.A. & Q.M.G., 56th Division.

A.A. & Q.M.G.,
56th
DIVISION.
No. AQS/582.
Date.........

XVII Corps Q.1222/265.

15th Division.
51st Division.
56th Division.
CORPS HEAVY ARTILLERY
17th Cyclist Battalion.

1. The following notes and suggestions collected from Divisions which took part in the open warfare on the Somme during March and April, are forwarded for your information.

2. It is most important to impress on all ranks the normal channel of supply for rations and ammunition. Owing to the artificial conditions of trench warfare, many officers appear to be quite ignorant of the normal system.

3. Supplies:

If the Divisional Artillery is detached from the Division, care must be taken to send off its Train wagons and Supply lorries at once. A car should always be sent with this detachment.

The question of intercommunication between the various Supply Echelons requires careful arrangement. All changes of position of units must be notified to the transport lines and all movements of the latter to the Train.

Pack transport was never used.

The importance of providing hot meals for troops cannot be over-rated.

S.S.O. must remain in close touch with Advanced "Q", and he should have 2 cyclist orderlies from the Train.

Brigade Supply Officers should remain at the Transport lines with the Quartermasters.

A small reserve of rations and medical comforts should be carried to meet demands for rations for stragglers and to avoid delay in providing medical comforts to Field Ambulances.

4. Mechanical Transport:

If extra transport is not available, the Supply lorries will probably be placed at the disposal of Divisions.

A M.T. Officer should remain with Advanced "Q".

Ammunition lorries will be retained under Corps control.

Divisions must not expect any further assistance with lorries, as all ammunition lorries will be working to the fullest extent on Ammunition supply. The delivery of supplies and ammunition was frequently jeopardised by officers commandeering returning empty lorries for unauthorised work. All lorry drivers are being warned that they must not accept orders of this nature, and all officers attempting to misuse M.T. in this way will be severely dealt with.

5. Ammunition - S.A.A. etc.

The normal channel for S.A.A. supply, pack animals, Battalion limbers, Brigade Reserve limbers, D.A.C., M.T. Company, is not generally known.

A small reserve of Very Lights, Flares, Rifle Grenades, and S.O.S. signals should be carried, in lieu of some of the hand grenades.

Advanced "Q" must keep in close touch with the S.A.A. Section of the D.A.C.

It may be advisable to divide the S.A.A. Section into two echelons - an advanced section close to Advanced "Q" and main echelon about 2 miles behind, with mounted Orderlies at Advanced "Q".

P.T.O./ Brigades -

Brigades must be kept constantly informed of the position of S.A.A. Section.

The wagon containing reserve of demolition explosives should be with S.A.A. Section D.A.C., otherwise, if the Divl. Artillery is detached, the R.E. have no reserves of explosives.

6. **Ammunition – Artillery.**

Ammunition Refilling Points will be fixed by Corps "Q".

In moving warfare it was not found possible to supply more than about 180 rounds per gun for 18-prs and 120 rounds per gun for 4.5" Howitzers, per day.

The great importance of close touch being kept between the various echelons was emphasized.

Large dumps at the guns should not and cannot be made.

Ammunition lorries will be pooled under Corps control.

7. **Divisional Headquarters.**

All Divisions agree that Divisional Headquarters should be in two Echelons – the A.A.& Q.M.G., and D.A.Q.M.G. being with the Advanced Echelon.

The S.S.O., Headquarters Train and representatives of Brigades with mounted orderlies, should be with Advanced "Q".

Reserve rations should be held in view of the large numbers of officers who are given meals at such times.

It was found that 1 lorry was sufficient to move Advanced Headquarters, and 1 lorry for Rear Headquarters.

8. **Stragglers:**

The numbers of stragglers to be dealt with may be very large. The majority are genuine cases of men who have lost their units and only require rest and food. Rations for these men must be arranged, and if possible, hot meals provided.

It is an advantage to combine the Walking Wounded Collecting post and the Straggler Collecting Post, as it facilitates the feeding arrangements and re-arming, if necessary.

These posts should be behind the heavily shelled area, as the men should have a night's rest before being returned to their units.

Looting must be firmly suppressed, even the most minor cases.

Officers not taken into action can be usefully employed at Straggler Collecting posts.

9. **Medical :**

It is suggested that Field Ambulances should be divided into 3 echelons – 2 advanced echelons and 1 rear echelon with the heavy transport.

One advanced echelon functions while the second advanced echelon is moving back and preparing to function as soon as the first closes down. The rear echelon should be kept well back.

10. **Ordnance:**

Care must be taken to see that men's boots are kept in good condition and that horses are kept shod up. The supply of Ordnance Stores from the Base is bound to be dislocated during mobile warfare.

Spare shoes must be carried for all animals.

Heavy casualties may be expected in :-
- Bicycles.
- Vickers guns, belts and boxes.
- Lewis guns and magazines.
- Very pistols.
- Waterproof sheets.
- Socks.

and care must be taken that these stores are not abandoned

P.T.O. / unnecessarily.

unnecessarily.

It was found convenient for D.A.D.O.S. to deliver Vickers guns, Lewis Guns, belts and magazines, to the main echelon D.A.C. Units must get rid of surplus baggage and stores now or else be prepared to abandon them in the event of mobile warfare.

11. <u>Liaison and Communication</u>:

The most important lesson of the operations was the difficulty of maintaining communications.

Units have become so used to an elaborate telephone system that they were entirely at sea when telephones no longer existed.

The maintenance of liaison between the various echelons of the Staff, supply, ammunition, and transport, requires very careful arrangement and fullest use must be made of Runners, cyclists and mounted Orderlies.

Close liaison with the R.A. is especially important, particularly with A.F.A. Brigades.

F. F. H. Hobbs.

Brigadier-General,

D.A. & Q.M.G., XVII Corps.

4th May 1918.

Copies to:
"G"   S.M.T.O.
R.A.   D.A.D.L.
C.R.E.   Camp Commandant.
"A"
D.D.M.S.
A.P.M.

S E C R E T. 56th Division AQS/582.

"Q" NOTES ON OPERATIONS DURING THE PERIOD MARCH 22ND - APRIL 1ST
OBTAINED FROM A DIVISION IN THE LINE DURING THE PERIOD.

AMMUNITION SUPPLY.

(a) Artillery Ammunition.

(i) The present organisation of D.A.Cs is not satisfactory. The old Division into a G.S. wagon echelon, and an ammunition wagon echelon, had to be reverted to, and it is recommended that this organisation be re-introduced, both for Artillery ammunition and S.A.A.

(ii) The system of Forward dumps of Artillery ammunition, instead of distribution in depth led to shortages at several junctures.

(iii) The frequent changes of Railheads often made it very difficult for D.A.Cs to know where they could draw.

(iv) It is considered essential in warfare demanding much movement that the Officer Commanding D.A.C. has a motor cyclist orderly attached to him from the M.T.Company. Whether he be drawing from them or no, he can then keep in touch with the situation at various Railheads and dumps and save a great deal of unnecessary journeying of his wagons.

S.A.A.

(i) The Division of First Line Transport into "A" and "B" Echelons is considered essential, the "A" Echelon being the Brigade Ammunition Reserve plus such vehicles as the Brigades may consider advisable.

The system of working is not however understood.

"A" Echelon, which is essentially tactical transport, must be moved and receive its orders from the Brigade. It is the link between the battalion, and the S.A.A. Section of the D.A.C., and the Officer Commanding "A" must be thoroughly conversant with the system of ammunition supply. Officer Commanding D.A.C. is responsible for keeping in touch with Brigade Reserves Orderlies sent from D.A.C. to "A" Echelon must have plenty of energy and initiative so that proper touch may be maintained, which was not always the case. There was a tendancy on the part of Brigades to forget Brigade Reserve and ask for ammunition which all the time was available near by.

(ii) DUMPS.

Large dumps of S.A.A. cannot be made without considerable warning and this practice entails much extra effort on the part of the D.A.C., so they cannot be expected except at positions where <u>protracted</u> resistance is looked for.

(iii) In addition to Mobile Brigade S.A.A. Reserves a similar reserve must be formed for the Machine Gun Battalion.

(iv) The necessity for the inclusion of Very Lights, Flares, Rifle Grenades, and S.O.S. Rockets, in the Brigade Mobile Reserve was again demonstrated, and it is recommended that a definite establishment of these be laid down for each battalion transport. At present they should be included at the discretion of Brigadiers; this will have to be done at the expense of S.A.A.

(v) Expenditure of S.A.A. was enormous. One Battalion fired 270,000 rounds in one morning.

SUPPLIES.

(i) Attached artillery must bring their lorries with them for attachment to Divisional M.T. Company.

(ii) Difficulty was experienced in keeping in touch with Artillery Brigade Wagon Lines, especially A.F.A. Brigades, which were constantly moving, and caused a certain amount of trouble on two occasions. Careful arrangements must be made to overcome this.

SUPPLIES (contd.)

(iii) Trouble was experienced on several occasions in getting rations to the Front Line, owing to enemy machine gun fire and no communication trenches. Limbered Wagons must deliver to ration carrying parties. Dumping and expecting carrying parties to draw is unsatisfactory, on account of uncertainty of movements; similarly the Train should not deliver too early in the day, or First Line Transport may have to carry.

(iv) Pack transport was never used, as roads or tracks fit for limbers were always available.

PROVOST DUTIES.

(a) Straggling.

In a withdrawal of the size of the present one, straggling is liable to be intensified and strong battle posts are essential. Mounted men must be employed, as men can so easily go across country.

(b) Traffic.

Traffic Control was, on the whole, well carried out. It is suggested, however, that Divisions are allotted areas for such control. In several instances there were Traffic personnel of several Divisions in one village and none in the next.

Overland tracks should be made more use of by all light transport and artillery. Many of these tracks which had existed in the battle area last year had ceased to exist during the winter. Every area should have a properly thought out system of tracks, marked, and looked after.

ORDNANCE.

Heavy casualties in following articles :-
- Bicycles.
- Lewis Guns.
- Vickers Guns.
- Magazines.
- Belts & Boxes.
- Waterproof Sheets.
- Very Pistols.

REMOUNTS.

The more open nature of warfare and frequent moving of Artillery leads to higher animal casualties than in a more closely fought battle.

MISCELLANEOUS.

(a) The outstanding difficulty was intercommunication between the various echelons of supply. A forward Echelon frequently moved without notifying the fact to the rear echelon responsible for supplying it with ammunition or rations as the case might be. At least two mounted orderlies from every rear echelon of supply should be with its corresponding forward echelon and vice versa. Whenever one echelon moves one of the orderlies should be sent to the corresponding echelon to notify the new location.

(b) To facilitate communication with wagon lines these should be established by Artillery Brigades in one area, with the Brigade HdQtr. Wagon line at a central spot, which might be marked by a Brigade flag. Orderlies should be sent by each Battery to Brigade Hd.Qtrs. Wagon lines and a mounted orderly to the C.R.A.

(c) On occasions great difficulty was experienced in sending rations from Refilling Point to Artillery Wagon lines. One representative per Artillery Brigade should be sent daily at 10 a.m. to Div. Artillery H.Qtrs. to find out Refilling Points and guide Supplies to Wagon lines.

MISCELLANEOUS. (contd.)

(d) Moves of "B" Echelons First line Transport (Infantry Brigades, Div.M.G.Batt., Pioneer Battn., and R.E.) and of Div. Train will be controlled by Div. Headquarters. Mounted orderlies from "B" Echelons and from Div. Train must be at Div. Headquarters.

(e) RATIONS were delivered by Div. Train to "B" Echelon First Line Transports. The Train also had to deliver rations to gun teams at Battery positions.
   65% of preserved meat and biscuits was found to be a satisfactory proportion.

(f) Barbed wire and pickets were the only R.E. material used, and 6 L.G.S. Wagon loads per Infantry Brigade per diem sufficed.

(g) BLANKETS AND PACKS were an encumbrance and were soon all lost. They should be left far behind.

(h) The Sub-Park was often short circuited and D.A.Cs drew direct from Railhead.

Lieut.-Colonel,
A.A. & Q.M.G. 56th Division.

3rd April, 1918.

DISTRIBUTION.

G. O. C.

167th Inf. Bde.	D.M.G.Batt.	Div. Artillery.	A.P.M.
168th " "	C.R.E.	"G"	D.A.D.O.S.
169th " "	Div. Train.	"Q"	D.A.D.V.S.
1/5th Cheshire Rgt.	A.D.M.S.	56th M.T.Coy.	Sig.Coy.R.E.

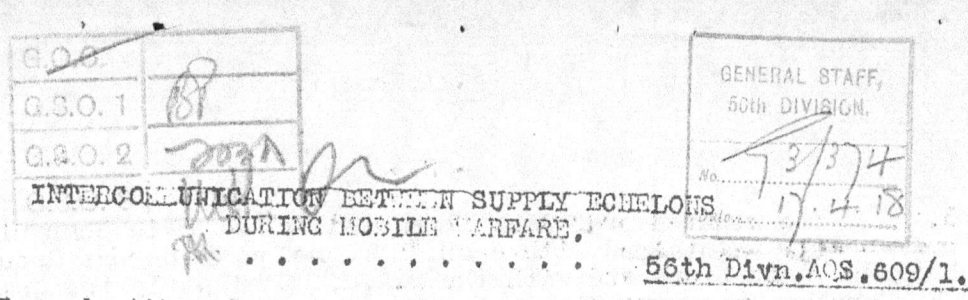

INTERCOMMUNICATION BETWEEN SUPPLY ECHELONS DURING MOBILE WARFARE.

56th Divn. AQS.609/1.

Issued with reference to the following :-

56th Divn. AQS/582. ("Q" notes on operations during the period March 22nd - April 1st).
56th Divn. AQS/609. (Organisation of First Line Transport for Mobile Warfare).

1. It is anticipated that during the present type of mobile warfare the selection before a move of a "meeting point for Train Wagons", which is the existing system according to Field Service Regulations, of arranging inter-communication between Supply Echelons, would not be practicable, as all moves would be liable to be influenced by hostile action to such an extent as to make it probable that "destinations" and "meeting points" would have to be changed after the original orders for the move had been issued.

Permanent intercommunication between the various Supply Echelons by frequent interchange of orderlies would therefore be necessary, in order to ensure that the rear supply echelons always knew the location of the forward Echelons.

2. In the event of any move of transport lines from present positions being rendered necessary by the commencement of a state of mobile warfare, moves of "B" Echelons 1st Line Transport of all units (except Artillery) would be controlled by Divisional Headquarters "A" & "Q"; and it is the intention to arrange the moves so that at the conclusion of the initial move these "B" Echelons should be grouped as shown below :-

167th Inf. Bde. Group.	168th Inf. Bde. Group.	169th Inf. Bde. Group.
167th Inf. Brigade.	168th Inf. Brigade.	169th Infantry Brigade.
416th Fld. Coy. R.E.	512th Fld. Coy. R.E.	513th Fld. Coy. R.E.
2/1st Ldn.Fld. Ambce.	2/2nd Ldn. Fld. Ambce.	2/3rd Ldn. Fld. Ambce.

Divisional Headquarters Group.

Divl. Hd.Qtrs.   Divl. M.G.Bn.
"   Arty H.Q.   1/5th Cheshire Rgt.
"   R.E. H.Q.   Divl. Employ.Coy.

Units of Divisional Troops will join their "B" Echelon Transport groups under orders, which will be issued from this office, to Commanders of Units of Divisional Troops when the necessity arises.

3. On completion of this initial move, the Senior Transport Officer with each group of transport will assume command of all units in his group. He will at once send 2 mounted orderlies to Divisional Headquarters, ("A" & "Q") to report his name and location, and to remain at Divisional Headquarters. Any further orders affecting "B" Echelon Transport Groups will be sent from Divisional Headquarters ("A" & "Q") to the Officers Commanding Groups.

4. O.C. Train will arrange for Train Companies to supply "B" Echelon Transport groups as below :-

No. 2 Coy. Train to supply 167th Inf. Bde. Group.
No. 3   "   "   "   " 168th "   "   "
No. 4   "   "   "   " 169th "   "   " & Divl.H.Q. Group.

5. ~~permanently maintained~~ Two mounted orderlies from affiliated Train Companies will be with each "B" Echelon Transport Group, each Artillery Brigade Wagon Lines and with the D.A.C. Similarly the Commanders of each "B" Echelon Transport Group, Artillery Brigade Wagon lines, and D.A.C. will each send two mounted orderlies to remain with their affiliated Train Companies.

Orderlies will be exchanged every time either Echelon moves. All the above orderlies will be established on receipt of a wire from this office worded "Establish Supply orderlies".

6. With reference to para. 2 it should be noted that "B" Echelon Transport Groups will not necessarily be constituted as shewn therein for an ordinary move out of the line or for a lateral move (by bus or otherwise) on transfer to another part of the line.

7. In the event of any unit of Divisional Troops becoming detached from its normal group (see para. 2), that unit should at once send an orderly to its affiliated Train Company to notify its location.

17thhApril, 1918.

Lieut. Colonel,
A.A. & Q.M.G., 56th Division.

- DISTRIBUTION -

167th Inf. Bde.	Divl. M.G.Bn.	A.P.M.
168th " "	C.R.E.	D.A.D.V.S.
169th " "	Divl. Train.	Divl. Employ. Coy.
Divl. Artillery.	A.D.M.S.	56th M.T. Company.
1/5th Cheshire Rgt.	Camp Comdt.	"G".

ORGANISATION OF FIRST LINE TRANSPORT FOR MOBILE WARFARE.

56th DIVISION AQS/609.

167th Inf. Bde.   O.C. D.M.G.Bn.
168th   "   "   1/5th Cheshire Regt.
169th   "   "   C.R.E.
O.C. S.A.A. Section, D.A.C.
56th Divl. Artillery)
"G"   ) for information.
O.C. Divl. Train.   )

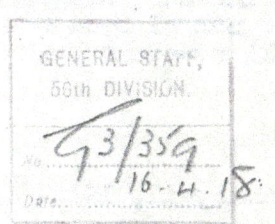

1. The G.O.C. wishes 1st Line Transports to be organised forthwith into "A" and "B" Echelons. During active operations "A" Echelons will be controlled by Brig.-Generals Commanding Infantry Brigades, O.C. 56th Bn. M.G.Corps, C.R.E. and O.C. 1/5th Cheshire Regt. respectively. "B" Echelons will be controlled by Divisional Headquarters ("A" & "Q").

2. In connection with the above the following suggestions are put forward for consideration by Brig. Generals Commanding Infantry Brigades. O.C. M.G. Battn. C.R.E. and O.C. 1/5th Cheshire Regt.

   (a) "A" Echelons should consist solely of vehicles required for supplying the fighting troops with S.A.A., Grenades, etc.
   (b) In each Infantry Brigade and unit of Divisional Troops it should be controlled by an Officer.
   In Infantry Brigades this will probably be the Brigade Bombing Officer. This Officer will be responsible for keeping his echelons filled from the D.A.C. and for meeting the requirements of Battalions, or Companies in the case of Divisional Troops.
   (c) "A" Echelons will have to be located as near to the Firing line as possible, immunity from hostile fire not being essential. Convoys from this echelon will have to proceed to the firing line during daylight under fire. "B" Echelons will deal with rations and R.E. Material at a location further in rear where those supplies can be received and dealt with under conditions of comparative quiet. Convoys from "B" Echelon will proceed to the firing line under cover of darkness.
   (d) "A" and "B" Echelons will therefore probably be widely separated. Both Echelons will however have to send convoys to the firing line. This points to the conclusion that there should be two sets of Transport Officers to lead convoys to the firing line, one Set at "A" Echelon and one Set at "B" Echelon.
   (e) Grenades would be detonated at "A" Echelon.

3. Brig.-Generals Commanding Infantry Brigades, O.C. Div.M.G.Bn., C.R.E. and O.C. 1/5th Cheshire Regt. will please submit their views on the points raised in para. 2, by 1st E.R.19th instant; and will in particular state the number and nature of vehicles they propose to retain with "A" Echelon.

4. Brig.-Generals Commanding Infantry Brigades, O.C. Div.M.G.Bn., C.R.E. and O.C. 1/5th Cheshire Regt. will inform O.C. S.A.A. Section, D.A.C. direct, and repeat to this office, the present location of their "A" Echelon and the name of the Officer appointed to command it. O.C. S.A.A. Section, D.A.C. and "A" Echelons, 1st Line Transport will from then onwards arrange for permanent inter-communication by orderlies. If at any time it appears that for any reason the present "stationary warfare" system of supplying S.A.A. etc. from Dumps is not feasible, notification to that effect will be sent from this office

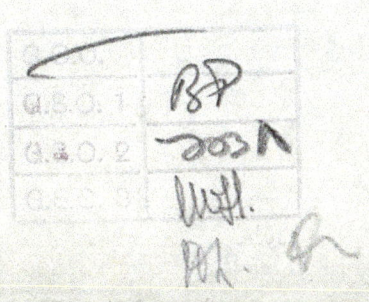

- 2 -

to Infantry Brigades etc, and to O.C. S.A.A. Section, D.A.C. and the normal system of supply from S.A.A. Section to "A" Echelons will re-commence.

16th April, 1918.

[signature]
Lieut. Colonel,
A.A. & Q.M.G., 56th Division.

SECRET.

/AQS/582.

167th Inf. Bde.	C. R. E.	A.D.M.S.
168th " "	1/5th Cheshire Rgt.	D.A.D.O.S.
169th " "	D.M.G.C.	"Q".
Divl. Artillery.	Divl. Train.	Camp Comdt.
S.A.A. Section, D.A.C.		

GENERAL STAFF,
56th DIVISION.
No. G3/531
Date 9.5.18

Forwarded for information in continuation of this office AQS.582 of 3.4.18, AQS.609 of 16.4.18, and AQS. 609/1 of 17.4.18.
 As regards para. 1.(b), it is understood that the Division who compiled these notes was working under abnormal conditions as regards supplies. It is not proposed to adopt the suggested arrangements for Supply in this Division; and the paragraph should be disregarded.

G.O.C.	
G.S.O.1	
G.S.O.2	
G.S.O.3	

8.5.18.

Lieut. Colonel,
A.A. & Q.M.G., 56th Division.

EMBUSSING TABLE - SITUATION "A". Reference 1/100,000 Map. Sheet LENS 11

Serial Letter of Convoy.	Bus Group Commander.	TROOPS.	Concentration Area for Embussing	Embussing Point	Head of Bus Convoy to be at	Bus Convoy to face.
"A"	Brig-General Commanding Reserve Inf. Brigade.	M.G.Battn. (less 3 Coys) Reserve Inf. Bde. 512th Field Coy. R.E. Divl. Head Quarters. H.Q. and No. 1 Section Divl. Signal Coy. Divl. R.E. Head Qrs. 2/1st London Fd. Ambce.	Present Locations.	BERNEVILLE— AGNEZ LES DUISANS Road	WARLUS CEMETERY	AGNEZ LES DUISANS.
"B"	Brig-General Commanding Inf. Bde. in Support.	Support Inf. Bde. 1 Coy. M.G.Battn. 1/5th Cheshire Regt. 2/2nd London Fd. Ambce.	Present Locations.	—do—	—do—	—do—
"C"	Brig-General Commanding Inf. Bde. in the line.	2 Coys. M.G.Battn. Inf. Bde. in the line 413th Field Coy. R.E. 513th Field Coy. R.E. 2/3rd London Fd. Ambce. Divl. Employment Coy.	BERNEVILLE— DAINVILLE— WARLUS Area.	—do—	—do—	—do—

Units will be allotted busses from the head of the convoy in the order in which they are named in Column 3

EMBUSSING TABLE - SITUATION B.   Refce. 1/100000 Map Sheet LENS II.

Serial letter of Convoy	Bus Group Commander.	Troops.	Concentration Area for Embussing.	Embussing Point.	Head of Bus Convoy to be at	Bus Convoy to face.
A.	Brig.-General Comdg. Inf. Bde. in Reserve.	M.G. Battn. Reserve Inf. Bde. 513th Fld. Coy. R.E. Divl. Hd.Qtrs. H.Q. & No. 1 Sec. Div. Sig. Coy. Div. R.E. Hd.Qtrs. 2/1st London Fld. Ambulance.	SIMENCOURT - WARLUS - WANQUETIN - FOSSEUX Area.	SIMENCOURT-WANQUETIN Road.	Road Junction 500 yds. N.W. of WANQUETIN.	WANQUETIN.
B.	Brig.-General Comdg. Inf. Bde. in Support.	Inf. Bde. in support. 1/5th Cheshire Rgt. 512th Fld. Coy. R.E. 2/2nd London Fld. Ambce.	AGNEZ LES DUISANS - GOUVES - MONTENESCOURT Area.	WARBARCQ-ETRUN Road.	Road Junction ½ mile west of E. of ETRUN.	ETRUN.
C.	Brig.-General Comdg. Inf. Bde. in the line.	Inf. Bde. in Line. 416th Fld. Coy. R.E. 2/3rd Ldn. Fld. Ambulance. Div. Employ. Coy. (Div. Employ.Coy. at WARLUS).	DAINVILLE - BERNEVILLE Area.	BERNEVILLE - AGNEZ LES DUISANS Road.	AGNEZ LES DUISANS - WARLUS CEMETERY.	AGNE Z LES DUISANS.

Units will be alighted busses from the head of the convoy in the order in which they are named in Column 3.

INTERCOMMUNICATION BETWEEN SUPPLY ECHELONS
DURING MOBILE WARFARE.

56th Divn.AQS.609/1.

Issued with reference to the following :-

56th Divn. AQS/582. ("Q" notes on operations during the period
March 22nd - April 1st).
56th Divn. AQS/609. (Organisation of First Line Transport for
Mobile Warfare).

1.   It is anticipated that during the present type of mobile warfare the selection before a move of a "meeting point for Train Wagons", which is the existing system according to Field Service Regulations, of arranging inter-communication between Supply Echelons, would not be practicable, as all moves would be liable to be influenced by hostile action to such an extent as to make it probable that "destinations" and "meeting points" would have to be changed after the original orders for the move had been issued.

Permanent intercommunication between the various Supply Echelons by frequent interchange of orderlies would therefore be necessary, in order to ensure that the rear supply echelons always knew the location of the forward Echelons.

2.   In the event of any move of transport lines from present positions being rendered necessary by the commencement of a state of mobile warfare, moves of "B" Echelons 1st Line Transport of all units (except Artillery) would be controlled by Divisional Headquarters "A" & "Q"; and it is the intention to arrange the moves so that at the conclusion of the initial move these "B" Echelons should be grouped as shown below :-

167th Inf.Bde. Group.	168th Inf.Bde. Group.	169th Inf.Bde.Group.
167th Inf. Brigade.	168th Inf. Brigade.	169th Infantry Brigade.
416th Fld. Coy. R.E.	512th Fld. Coy. R.E.	513th Fld. Coy. R.E.
2/1st Ldn.Fld. Ambce.	2/2nd Ldn. Fld. Ambce.	2/3rd Ldn. Fld. Ambce.

Divisional Headquarters Group.

Divl. Hd.Qtrs.   Divl. M.G.Bn.
 "   Arty H.Q.   1/5th Cheshire Rgt.
 "   R.E. H.Q.   Divl. Employ.Coy.

Units of Divisional Troops will join their "B" Echelon Transport groups under orders, which will be issued from this office, to Commanders of Units of Divisional Troops when the necessity arises.

3.   On completion of this initial move, the Senior Transport Officer with each group of transport will assume command of all units in his group. He will at once send 2 mounted orderlies to Divisional Headquarters, ("A" & "Q") to report his name and location, and to remain at Divisional Headquarters. Any further orders affecting "B" Echelon Transport Groups will be sent from Divisional Headquarters ("A" & "Q") to the Officers Commanding Groups.

4.   O.C. Train will arrange for Train Companies to supply "B" Echelon Transport groups as below :-
No. 2 Coy. Train to supply 167th Inf. Bde. Group.
No. 3   "   "   "   "   168th "   "   "   & Divl.H.Q. Group.
No. 4   "   "   "   "   169th "   "   "

5.   Two mounted orderlies from affiliated Train Companies will be permanently maintained with each "B" Echelon Transport Group, each Artillery Brigade Wagon Lines and with the D.A.C. Similarly the Commanders of each "B" Echelon Transport Group, Artillery Brigade Wagon lines, and D.A.C. will each send two mounted orderlies to remain with their affiliated Train Companies.

Orderlies will be exchanged every time either Echelon moves. All the above orderlies will be established on receipt of a wire from this office worded " Establish Supply orderlies".

6.   With reference to para. 2 it should be noted that "B" Echelon Transport Groups will not necessarily be constituted as shewn therein for an ordinary move out of the line or for a lateral move (by bus or otherwise) on transfer to another part of the line.

7.   In the event of any unit of Divisional Troops becoming detached from its normal group (see para. 2), that unit should at once send an orderly to its affiliated Train Company to notify its location.

17thhApril, 1918.

Lieut. Colonel,
A.A. & Q.M.G., 56th Division.

- DISTRIBUTION -

167th Inf. Bde.
168th   "   "
169th   "   "
Divl. Artillery.
1/5th Cheshire Rgt.

Divl. M.G.Bn.
C.R.E.
Divl. Train.
A.D.M.S.
Camp Comdt.

A.P.M.
D.A.D.V.S.
Divl. Employ. Coy.
56th M.T. Company.
"G".

AMENDMENTS TO ADMINISTRATIVE INSTRUCTIONS
NO. 1. DATED 22.4.18.
(Issued with reference to 56th Division Warning Order No. 163).

War Diary

56th Div.AQS/615.

Para. 4 (a) in lines 2 and 7 for "Reserve" read "168th"
Delete sentence "These posts will be relieved by Infantry
Brigades as they move into Reserve."

Para. 5 will be amended to read
    Prisoners of War. During active operations Prisoners of War [from both Sectors]
will be sent to the ARRAS Prison (unless otherwise disposed of by
Intelligence Branch, General Staff) where they will be taken over
by A.P.M., ARRAS.
    In all cases when prisoners are captured, the A.P.M. Division
will be notified by Brigades of the numbers by ranks captured,
stating date and method of disposal.

Lieut. Colonel,
A.A. & Q.M.G., 56th Division.

24.4.18.

Issued to all recipients of 56th Division AQS/615.

SECRET   56th Division AQS/615.

ADMINISTRATIVE INSTRUCTIONS NO. 1. IN THE EVENT OF THE DIVISION RELIEVING THE 15th DIVISION.

Issued with reference to 56th Division Warning order No. 163.

In the event of this Division relieving the 15th Division in the line the following additions and amendments will be made to the administrative arrangements of this Division.

1. No change in Locations of Transport lines, Supplies, Gun Ammunition, Veterinary, Burials, Ordnance, Solder Collection.

2. TRENCH MUNITIONS.
Divisional Trench Munition Dumps at CHESTER CAVE G.29.a.21. and CEMETERY DUMP G.29.b.25. will be drawn upon by the Left Brigade in the line until expended, and will not be maintained thereafter.
The Divisional Trench Munition Dump will remain at L.27.d.5.0.
Brigade Trench Munition Dumps in the new area are located as under :-
Main Brigade Dumps. - G.36.c.37. and G.30.c.70.
Advanced   "   "   - H.31.c.08.
Other Dumps.   - H.31.c.26. - H.32.c.26. - H.31.b.22.
                       H.31.b.47. - G.30.c.71. - G.30.c.33.
                       G.25.d.72. - G.30.b.53.

3. MEDICAL ARRANGEMENTS.
(a) Advanced Bearer Post. G.36.b central (shortly to be moved to G.30.c.74.)
(b) Walking Wounded and Reserve Bearers. Girl's School, FAUBERG. ST SAUVEUR. G.29.c.63.
(c) Reserve Walking Wounded Post. - ECOLE NORMALE, ARRAS.G.21.c.23.
(d) Advanced Dressing Station.   Hospital ST JEAN, ARRAS.
(e) Main Dressing Station, Left Sector. - C.C.S. Site, AGNEZ LE DUISANS.

4. BATTLE STRAGGLER POSTS.
(a) The following Battle Straggler Posts at present furnished by 15th Division will be relieved by the Reserve Infantry Brigade at a date and hour to be notified later :-
BAPAUME ROAD Bridge. G.28.c.87.   1 N.C.O. 6 men.
ARRAS OLD STATION.   G.23.b.31.   1   "   6 "
CAMBRAI ROAD Bridge. G.28.b.97.   1   "   6 "
On being established by the Reserve Infantry Brigade this line of Straggler Posts will come under the orders of the A.P.M. These posts will be relieved by Infantry Brigades as they move into Reserve. They will remain rationed by their own units.
(b) Stragglers of 1st Canadian Division will be handed over at their Right Post at BLANGY Road Level Crossing, G.28.c.83.
(c) Straggler Collecting Station will remain at DAINVILLE as at present. During active operations a N.C.O. from the Transport lines of each "B" Echelon Transport Group will visit this station at frequent intervals to collect Stragglers.

5. PRISONERS OF WAR. During active operations Prisoners of War should be sent by the Left Infantry Brigade to ARRAS Prison where the A.P.M. will take them over.

6. WATER SUPPLY.

The nearest water cart filling points to the Left Brigade front are at RUE DE LA REPUBLIQUE (G.28.b.50) - RUE ST MAURICE (G.21.b.73) and at St NICOLAS (G.16.d.47).

A pipe line runs up St SAUVEUR CAVES with taps at frequent intervals.

7. R.E. STORES.

The Left Infantry Brigade may draw from BULL DOG DUMP at G.28.d.84. on application to the C.R.E.

8. BATHS.

The following Baths will be run under Divisional arrangements. They will be stocked with clean underclothing. Bookings to be arranged with N.C.O. in charge.

    SCHRAMM Barracks, ARRAS. - CANAL BANK, ARRAS. G.16.c.71.
    BERNEVILLE.

The Baths at WARLUS, SIMENCOURT and WANQUETIN will cease to be run under Divisional arrangements.

9. LIGHT RAILWAYS.

"B" and "D" Lines are working as far east as the following stations :-

    Station "B" 304. in H.19.c. on "B" Line.
    Station "D" 4. in H.6.c. on "D" Line.

Demands for trucks will be made to this office by 3 p.m. on the day before they are required. Time and date, starting point, destination, number of trucks required, Stores or personnel for which transport is required are to be stated in the demand.

10. An Officer is being appointed Cave Major ST SAUVEUR CAVES and will work under the orders of this office.

11. SANITARY.

Headquarters No. 5. A. Sanitary Section is at Hospital St JEAN, ARRAS.

12. SALVAGE.

No alteration will be made in the existing arrangements for collection and clearance of Salvage.

                                                            Lieut. Colonel,

22nd April, 1918.   A.A. & Q.M.G., 56th Division.

DISTRIBUTION.

167th Inf. Bde.	A.P.M.	1st Canadian Divn. "Q".
168th " "	S.C.F.(C.of E).	15th Division "Q".
169th " "	S.C.F.(Non C.of E).	Area Comdt. WANQUETIN.
1/5th Cheshire Regt.	D.A.D.O.S.	" " DAINVILLE.
Divl. Artillery.	Camp Comdt.	" " BERNEVILLE.
C.R.E.	Signal Coy. R.E.	" " ACHICOURT.
D.M.G.C.	French Mission.	Cave Major, RONVILLE.
Divl. Train.	247th Employ. Coy.	" " ST SAUVEUR.
A.D.M.S	Divl. Baths Officer.	"G"
D.A.D.V.S.	" Salvage "	XVIIth Corps "Q".

SECRET.   AQS/537.

FORMATION OF DIVISIONAL PROVISIONAL BATTALION.

In view of the possibility of its becoming necessary to organize all available personnel into a Battalion at short notice the following preliminary instructions are issued :-

1. ORGANISATION. This Battalion will be known as the DIVISIONAL PROVISIONAL BATTALION, and will be organised into Battalion Headquarters and three Companies known as 167th, 168th and 169th. Brigade Companies.

2. ASSEMBLY. All concerned will be informed from this Office the date and place of assembly of the Battalion.

3. PERSONNEL.
   1. The nucleus of the Battalion will be provided as shown below :-
   (a) COMMANDER AND 2ND-IN-COMMAND. Infantry Brigades will report to this office the names and Seniority of the two Senior Officers in the Brigade who are left out of action as nucleus personnel. The Commander and 2nd-in-Command will then be appointed from this Office.
   (b) ADJUTANT. Capt. F.P. HOBSON. Divisional Employment Coy.
   (c) QR.MASTER. Capt. R.W. HUNTER.   "   "   "
   (d) Remainder of Battalion Headquarters to be selected by Battalion Commander.
   (e) Each Infantry Brigade will form a Company from the nucleus and other personnel left out of action by units of the Brigade. The name of the Officer appointed to command the Company will be reported to this Office.

   II. Additional personnel will be provided from the following Divisional Employments. They will join the Provisional Battalion under the orders of their Employer on receipt by the latter of a wire from this office ordering his class to join. This additional personnel will be distributed amongst Headquarters and Brigade Coys. at the discretion of the O.C. Provisional Battalion.

	Offrs.	O.Rs.	
CLASS "A".	1	30	to be detailed by Officer i/c Baths.
" "B".	1	40	" " " " Salvage Company.
" "C".			" " by Town Majors and other Area Employ.
" "D".	-	22	" " D.A.D.O.S. from Infantry employed in Shops and Offices.
" "E".	2	20	" " O.C. Employment Coy. from Coy. Headquarters.
" "F".		20	" " Camp Comdt. from servants, Mess Employ, Supernumerary Clerks and Sanitary men at Divisional Headquarters.
" "G".		12	To be detailed by N.C.O. i/c Div. Canteen and Soda Water Factory.
" "H".		28	" " by W.O. i/c Div. Band.
" "I".	1	18	" " Offcr. i/c Bow Bells, and Cinema.

4. INTERIOR ECONOMY.
   (a) Infantry Brigades will arrange for their companies to be provided with sufficient cooks and cooking utensils for the use of the personnel furnished by the Brigade.
   1 Shoemaker and 1 Tailor will be provided by each Brigade.

- 2 -

INTERIOR ECONOMY (contd.)

    (b) Additional Cooks and cooking utensils for the additional personnel when they join, will be provided by O.C. Div. Employ. Coy.

5. RATIONS. All personnel joining the Provisional Battalion will do so with rations for consumption on day of assembly + 1.

    O.C. Train will arrange to deliver rations for consumption on day of assembly + 2, and subsequently, to the Provisional Battalion. Until such time as the Provisional Battalion is able to draw the rations indented for by itself, its rations will be withdrawn from those units which send personnel to the Battalion. Formations, units and employers sending personnel to the Provisional Battalion will inform O.C. Train, and this Office, the numbers being sent.

6. ORDNANCE STORES. (including rifles for unarmed men), will be indented for by the Battalion direct upon the D.A.D.O.S. The D.A.D.O.S. will deliver the Stores to the Battalion.

7.   Other equipment, Transport etc, will be handed over to the Battalion at its place of assembly as shown below :-
    4 Lewis guns by each Infantry Brigade from those held on charge
        for Anti-Aircraft purposes.
    3 Pack Animals (C.T.O.) by C.R.E.
    2 " " " by Pioneer Battalion.
    2 L.G.S. Wagons by C.R.E.
    1 Trestle Wagon by C.R.E.
    1 Water Cart by A.D.M.S.
    S.A.A, Grenades, Tools, etc, from the most convenient echelon as
        ordered by this office.
    8 Stretchers by A.D.M.S.

                                            Lieut.-Colonel,
3rd April, 1918.   A.A. & Q.M.G. 56th Division.

DISTRIBUTION.

167th Inf. Bde.	O.C. Prov. Batt.	A.D.M.S.	Camp Comdt.
168th " "	" Emplyy.Coy.	"G"	Div. Canteen.
169th " "	C.R.E.	Baths Officer.	" Band.
C.R.A.	Cheshires.	Salvage "	Bow Bells.
D.H.Q.C.	Div. Train.	D.A.D.O.S.	

SECRET.   56th Division AQS/582.

"Q" NOTES ON OPERATIONS DURING THE PERIOD MARCH 22ND - APRIL 1ST
OBTAINED FROM   A DIVISION IN THE LINE DURING THE PERIOD.

AMMUNITION SUPPLY.

(a) Artillery Ammunition.
 (i) The present organisation of D.A.Cs is not satisfactory. The old Division into a G.S. wagon echelon, and an ammunition wagon echelon, had to be reverted to, and it is recommended that this organisation be re-introduced, both for Artillery ammunition and S.A.A.
 (ii) The system of Forward dumps of Artillery ammunition, instead of distribution in depth led to shortages at several junctures.
 (iii) The frequent changes of Railheads often made it very difficult for D.A.Cs to know where they could draw.
 (iv) It is considered essential in warfare demanding much movement that the Officer Commanding D.A.C. has a motor cyclist orderly attached to him from the M.T.Company. Whether he be drawing from them or no, he can then keep in touch with the situation at various Railheads and dumps and save a great deal of unnecessary journeying of his wagons.

S.A.A.

(i) The Division of First Line Transport into "A" and "B" Echelons is considered essential, the "A" Echelon being the Brigade Ammunition Reserve plus such vehicles as the Brigades may consider advisable.
 The system of working is not however understood.
 "A" Echelon, which is essentially tactical transport, must be moved and receive its orders from the Brigade. It is the link between the battalion, and the S.A.A. Section of the D.A.C., and the Officer Commanding must be thoroughly conversant with the system of ammunition supply. Officer Commanding D.A.C. is responsible for keeping in touch with Brigade Reserves. Orderlies sent from D.A.C. to "A" Echelon must have plenty of energy and initiative so that proper touch may be maintained, which was not always the case. There was a tendency on the part of Brigades to forget Brigade Reserve and ask for ammunition which all the time was available near by.
 (ii) DUMPS.
   Large dumps of S.A.A. cannot be made without considerable warning and this practice entails much extra effort on the part of the D.A.C., so they cannot be expected except at positions where protracted resistance is looked for.
 (iii) In addition to Mobile Brigade S.A.A. Reserves a similar reserve must be formed for the Machine Gun Battalion.
 (iv) The necessity for the inclusion of Very Lights, Flares, Rifle Grenades, and S.O.S. Rockets, in the Brigade Mobile Reserve was again demonstrated, and it is recommended that a definite establishment of these be laid down for each battalion transport. At present they should be included at the discretion of Brigadiers; this will have to be done at the expense of S.A.A.
 (v) Expenditure of S.A.A. was enormous. One Battalion fired 270,000 rounds in one morning.

SUPPLIES.

 (i) Attached artillery must bring their lorries with them for attachment to Divisional M.T. Company.
 (ii) Difficulty was experienced in keeping in touch with Artillery Brigade Wagon Lines, especially A.F.A. Brigades, which were constantly moving, and caused a certain amount of trouble on two occasions. Careful arrangements must be made to overcome this.

SUPPLIES (contd.)

(iii) Trouble was experienced on several occasions in getting rations to the Front Line, owing to enemy machine gun fire and no communication trenches. Limbered Wagons must deliver to ration carrying parties. Dumping and expecting carrying parties to draw is unsatisfactory, on account of uncertainty of movements; similarly the Train should not deliver too early in the day, or First Line Transport may have to carry.

(iv) Pack transport was never used, as roads or tracks fit for limbers were always available.

PROVOST DUTIES.

(a) Straggling.

In a withdrawal of the size of the present one, straggling is liable to be intensified and strong battle posts are essential. Mounted men must be employed, as men can so easily go across country.

(b) Traffic.

Traffic Control was, on the whole, well carried out. It is suggested, however, that Divisions are allotted areas for such control. In several instances there were Traffic personnel of several Divisions in one village and none in the next.

Overland tracks should be made more use of by all light transport and artillery. Many of these tracks which had existed in the battle area last year had ceased to exist during the winter. Every area should have a properly thought out system of tracks, marked, and looked after.

ORDNANCE.

Heavy casualties in following articles :-
Bicycles.   Lewis Guns.
Vickers Guns.   Magazines.
Belts & Boxes. Waterproof Sheets.
Very Pistols.

REMOUNTS.

The more open nature of warfare and frequent moving of Artillery leads to higher animal casualties than in a more closely fought battle.

MISCELLANEOUS.

(a) The outstanding difficulty was intercommunication between the various echelons of supply. A forward Echelon frequently moved without notifying the fact to the rear echelon responsible for supplying it with ammunition or rations as the case might be. At least two mounted orderlies from every rear echelon of supply should be with its corresponding forward echelon and vice versa. Whenever one echelon moves one of the orderlies should be sent to the corresponding echelon to notify the new location.

(b) To facilitate communication with wagon lines these should be established by Artillery Brigades in one area, with the Brigade HdQtr. Wagon line at a central spot, which might be marked by a Brigade flag. Orderlies should be sent by each Battery to Brigade Hd.Qtrs. Wagon lines and a mounted orderly to the C.R.A.

(c) On occasions great difficulty was experienced in sending rations from Refilling Point to Artillery Wagon lines. One representative per Artillery Brigade should be sent daily at 10 a.m. to Div. Artillery H.Qtrs. to find out Refilling Points and guide Supplies to Wagon lines.

MISCELLANEOUS. (contd.)

(d) Moves of "B" Echelons First line Transport (Infantry Brigades, Div.M.G.Batt., Pioneer Battn., and R.E.) and of Div. Train will be controlled by Div. Headquarters. Mounted orderlies from "B" Echelons and from Div. Train must be at Div. Headquarters.

(e) RATIONS were delivered by Div. Train to "B" Echelon First Line Transports. The Train also had to deliver rations to gun teams at Battery positions.
   65% of preserved meat and biscuits was found to be a satisfactory proportion.

(f) Barbed wire and pickets were the only R.E. material used, and 6 L.G.S. Wagon loads per Infantry Brigade per diem sufficed.

(g) BLANKETS AND PACKS were an encumbrance and were soon all lost. They should be left far behind.

(h) The Sub-Park was often short circuited and D.A.Cs drew direct from Railhead.

[signature]
Lieut.-Colonel,
A.A. & Q.M.G. 56th Division.

3rd April, 1918.

DISTRIBUTION.

G. O. C.

167th Inf. Bde.	D.M.G.Batt.	Div. Artillery.	A.P.M.
168th " "	C.R.E.	"G"	D.A.D.O.S.
169th " "	Div. Train.	"Q"	D.A.D.V.S.
1/5th Cheshire Rgt.	A.D.M.S.	56th M.T.Coy.	Sig.Coy.R.E.

War Diary

56th Divn. AQS/587

AMENDMENT TO ADMINISTRATIVE INSTRUCTIONS NO. 1 OF TO-DAY.
para. 7. ORDNANCE.

D.A.D.O.S. will be established at HABARCQ (and not WANQUETON) from 8th instant with an Advanced Refilling Point at WARLUS.
 The following units will draw from the main store at HABARCQ.
167th Inf. Bde. - All Surplus Transports - Div. M.G.Bn. - 513th Field Coy.RE.Divl. Train - 2/1st London Field Ambulance.
 All other units will draw from the advanced Refilling Point at WARLUS.

6th April, 1918.

A. Dundas Major
for Lieut.-Colonel,
A.A. & Q.M.G., 56th Division.

SECRET.

AQS/587.

ADMINISTRATIVE INSTRUCTIONS NO. 1.
in connection with relief of 1st Canadian Division by 56th Division.

Issued with reference to 56th Divl. Orders No. 159 and 160.

1. ACCOMMODATION. Accommodation is allotted as below for units of Divisional Troops and for Transport Lines.

(i)
		BILLETS FROM.
Divl. Hd.Qtrs.	WARLUS.	Camp Commandant.
C.R.A.	"	" "
C.R.E.	BERNEVILLE.	" "
A.D.M.S.	"	" "
D.A.D.V.S.	"	" "
D.A.D.O.S.	WANQUETIN.	A.C. WANQUETIN.

(ii) TRANSPORTS AND DETAILS will be accommodated as below :-

167th Inf. Bde.	WANQUETIN.	A.C. WANQUETIN.
168th " "	SIMENCOURT.	" " "
169th " "	BERNEVILLE.	A.C. BERNEVILLE.
All Surplus Transports	AGNEZ les DUISANS (temporarily)	Comdt. XVII Corps R. & R. Camp.
56th Bn. M.G.C.	GOUVES (temporarily)	T.M. GOUVES.
1/5th Cheshire Regt.	DAINVILLE.	DAINVILLE.
Field Coys. R.E.	L.31.c.59.	A.C. WANQUETIN.
" "	Q.6.d.78.	" BERNEVILLE.
" "	K.12.d.28.(temporarily)	Comdt. XVII Corps R. & R. Camp.
Hd.Qtrs. Div. Train.	BERNEVILLE.	Camp Comdt.
1 Company.	SIMENCOURT.	A.C. WANQUETIN.
2 Companies.	WANQUETIN.	" "
1 Field Ambulance.	ACHICOURT. (Adv. Dressing Station)	
1 " "	DAINVILLE (Main " ")	
1 " "	AGNEZ les DUISANS.	

Reinforcements and other Details should be despatched to unit's transport lines.

2. AMMUNITION.
(a) DIVL. A.R.P. is at L.27.c.92 on the WARLUS-DAINVILLE Road, and is known as "DAIN" Dump.
In addition Div. Artillery may draw by Horse Transport from XVII Corps Dumps at HORSESHOE L.29.d.66 and LARISSET K.5.b.58.
(b) DIVL. TRENCH MUNITION DUMP is located at Billet No. 22 AGNY. Brigades etc. will draw from there on application to this office. In addition to the above dump, Brigades etc. can draw from XVII Corps "X" Dump at G.20.c.33. on telegraphic authority from this office.
At present both dumps are drawn from by Horse Transport. It is hoped that AGNY Dump will be connected up with the Light Railway in the near future.

P.T.O.

3. BATTLE STRAGGLER POSTS AND PRISONERS OF WAR.

(a) The following are the locations of Battle Straggler Posts.

No. 1.	M.9.c.51.	Sheet 51 B.	1 N.C.O. 6 men.
No. 2.	M.3.c.52.	"	"
No. 3.	G. 33.c.53.	"	"
No. 4.	G.33.a.53.	"	"

These will be manned by the Support Brigade at noon 8th instant; at which hour the Straggler post line will come under the orders of the A.P.M., who will place one N.C.O. of M.M.P. in charge of each group of two posts.

(b) STRAGGLER COLLECTING STATION will be established by A.P.M. in DAINVILLE. The A.P.M. will take over this post on 8th instant with his own personnel. From the 9th and subsequently the personnel (1 N.C.O. 6 men) will be furnished by the Reserve Brigade. They should report to the A.P.M. at 3 p.m. 9th instant at the Town Major's Office, DAINVILLE.

(c) The above personnel will remain rationed by their own units.

(d) Any Stragglers of 15th Division will be handed over to the Straggler post at G. 28.c.87.

(e) Stragglers of other formations will be sent to the CIVIL PRISON at ARRAS.

(f) Prisoners of War will be sent under Brigade escorts to ACHICOURT where they will be taken over by the A.P.M. The exact location of the A.P.M's collecting station in ACHICOURT will be notified later. For the present escorts should apply to one of the Straggler Posts for redirection.

4. BATHS etc.,

Baths will be run by the Divl. Baths Officer at BERNEVILLE, DAINVILLE and WARLUS.

They will be stocked with clean clothing.

The Foden Disinfector will be at the BERNEVILLE Baths. Blankets may be sent there for disinfection by arrangement with Divl. Baths Officer, whose address will be c/o Divl. Train Hd.Qtrs. BERNEVILLE.

5. WATER SUPPLY.

For the present no water will be supplied east of a line running from M.4.a.8.0 - G.34. d and b - G.35.a - G.29.c. d and b. - G.30. a and b. - G.24.d - H.19.c. d. and b.

Water is available at the following places in ARRAS:-
(a) 1 Water cart point in RUE St. MAURICE, near St. JEAN Hospital.
(b) 1 French tap in RUE de MARCHE AU FILLET.
(c) 1 French tap in RUE St. CROIX.
(d) At the Horse troughs opposite PORTSLADE Camp.
(e) 1 French tap at junction of RUE DONORE with RUE St. AUGUSTINE.
(f) 1 Point at junction of RUE St. JACQUES " " " "
(g) 2 Water cart points in RUE JEANE BODEL.
(h) French tap in Square opposite St. JEAN Hospital.
(i) One French tap at junction of RUE de la PAIX with RUE D'AMIENS.
(j) Two French taps at junction of RUE St. CLAIRE " " "

At present there is a large amount of water running to waste but the French have now returned to run the Town Pumping Station CHATEAU D'EAU, G.21.b.6.7., and as the Town Mains are put in order the supply will improve and will be available on the auxiliary main (M.3.b.8.9 to G.23.c.)

Information of bursts should be sent to the British N.C.O. at the CHATEAU D'EAU who is in charge of the party carrying out repairs under Lieut. DUMOND the French Officer in Command of the ARRAS Water Supply.

6. CEMETERIES and BURIALS.

Divisional Burial Officer is located at WARLUS.
The following Cemeteries will be used by this Division:-
(a) FAUBOURG D'AMIENS Cemetery, G.26.b.9.7. Sheet 51 B.
(b) DAINVILLE Communal Cemetery, L.29.d.5.4, Sheet 51 C.

The latter to be used in preference to any other.

The following may also be used, but units must make their own arrangements as no burial details will operate there:-
(a) DUISANS Cemetery, L.1.c.8.7, Sheet 51 C.
(b) WANQUETIN Communal, K.33.a.1.9, Sheet 51 B.
(c) ACHICOURT Road Cemetery, M.3.b.2.9. Sheet 51 B

7. ORDNANCE.

D.A.D.O.S., will be established at WANQUETIN from 8th instant.
Only stores absolutely necessary should now be demanded and Indents should be endorsed 'ESSENTIAL', by Commanding Officers. This is necessary owing to the present congestion of Railways etc.
I.O.M., (LIGHT) for Vehicles, is at SAVY.
The I.O.M., for Guns is at LOUEZ.

8. LIGHT RAILWAYS.

As a result of the recent operations, the Light Railway System in the XVII Corps Area is not as effective as it was. Trucks are earmarked at BERNEVILLE on the B. 6 line at 4 P.M. daily to take rations to the Brigade in the line. Applications for this and other truckage required should reach this office by 5 P.M. daily for the services required on the following day. Demands on C.L.R.O., XVII Corps will then be made by this office. The C.L.R.O., will repeat his reply to the Brigade etc concerned in order to save time.

9. CANTEEN.

Divisional Canteen will open at BERNEVILLE on the 8th instant.

10. SUPPLIES.

RAILHEAD — AGNEZ LES DUISANS

REFILLING POINTS — 167th Bde. Group. WANQUETIN.
168th Bde. Group. WANQUETIN.
169th Bde. Group. GOUVES.

Rations will be delivered by Divisional Train to Units' Qr. Mr. Stores. Fuel will be drawn from Refilling Points by Units' 1st Line Transport.

11. R.E. MATERIAL.

(1) The Divisional R.E. Park has been moved from No. 8 R.E. Park, RONVILLE, to the CHATEAU, AGNY, M.8.a.6.8.
(2) This Park will be small and used mainly as a Workshop and, as there is a considerable amount of material still remaining at the No. 8 R.E. Park, RONVILLE, Units will still draw from this point on indent from C.R.E.

12. RONVILLE CAVES and TUNNELS.

(1) The RONVILLE CAVES and TUNNELS System is being administered by this Division.
(2) The St. SAUVEUR CAVES and TUNNELS System is being administered by the 15th Division.
(3) Captain GILLESPIE, 7/8th K.O.S.B., has been appointed Area Commandant, St. SAUVEUR, by the 15th Division.
(4) The Cave Major of the RONVILLE CAVES and TUNNELS is being appointed by this Division.
(5) The Cave Major will allot accommodation to Units, and Units requiring accommodation in the CAVE SYSTEM, or vacating such accommodation will report to him.
(6) No fires or braziers will be allowed in the CAVES or TUNNELS, except where authorised by the Cave Major.
(7) Any further orders necessary for the administration of the RONVILLE CAVES will be issued when a reconnaissance has been made by the Cave Major, including Water, Cooking arrangements, Anti-Gas Protection, Traffic Control etc.

[signature]
Lieut-Colonel,
A.A. & Q.M.G., 56th Division.

6th April, 1918.

DISTRIBUTION.

G.O.C.	"G"	XVII Corps "Q"	Area Commdt.
167th Inf. Bde.	5th Ches: Regt.	D.A.D.O.S.	WANQUETIN.
168th Inf. Bde.	Div. H.G.Cdr.	Camp Commdt.	DAINVILLE.
169th Inf. Bde.	Divl. Train.	Employt. Coy.	BERNEVILLE.
Divl. Arty.	A.D.M.S.	Baths Officer.	GOUVES.
C.R.E.	D.A.D.V.S.	1st Canadian Div. "Q"	RONVILLE CAVES.
Sig. Coy. R.E.	A.P.M.	15th Div. "Q"	
French Mission.	S.C.F., C. of E.	S.C.F., Non C. of E.	
	XVII Corps M. and R. Camp	R.T.O., AGNEZ LES DUISANS	
	XIII Corps " "		

War Diary

56th Divn. AQS/587

AMENDMENT TO ADMINISTRATIVE INSTRUCTIONS NO. 1 OF TO-DAY.
para. 7. ORDNANCE.

D.A.D.O.S. will be established at HABARCQ (and not VANQUETON) from 8th instant with an Advanced Refilling Point at WARLUS.
The following units will draw from the main store at HABARCQ.
167th Inf. Bde. - All Surplus Transports - Div. M.G. Bn. - 513th Field Coy. R.E. Divl. Train - 2/1st London Field Ambulance.
All other units will draw from the advanced Refilling Point at WARLUS.

6th April, 1918.

A.C. Dundas Major
for Lieut.-Colonel,
A.A. & Q.M.G., 56th Division.

War Diary

SECRET.

AQS/587.

ADMINISTRATIVE INSTRUCTIONS NO. 1.
in connection with relief of 1st Canadian Division by 56th Division.

Issued with reference to 56th Divl. Orders No. 159 and 160.

1. **ACCOMMODATION.** Accommodation is allotted as below for units of Divisional Troops and for Transport Lines.

   (i)
		BILLETS FROM.
Divl. Hd.Qtrs.	WARLUS.	Camp Commandant.
C.R.A.	"	" "
C.R.E.	BERNEVILLE.	" "
A.D.M.S.	"	" "
D.A.D.V.S.	"	" "
D.A.D.O.S.	WANQUETIN.	A.C. WANQUETIN.

   (ii) TRANSPORTS AND DETAILS will be accommodated as below :-

167th Inf. Bde.	WANQUETIN.	A. C. WANQUETIN.
168th " "	SIMENCOURT.	" " "
169th " "	BERNEVILLE.	A.C. BERNEVILLE.
All Surplus Transports	AGNEZ les DUISANS (temporarily)	Comdt. XVII Corps R. & R. Camp.
56th Bn. M.G.C.	GOUVES (temporarily)	T.M. GOUVES.
1/5th Cheshire Regt.	DAINVILLE.	" DAINVILLE.
Field Coys. R.E.	L.31.c.59.	A.C. WANQUETIN.
" "	Q.6.d.78.	" BERNEVILLE.
" "	K.12.d.28.(temporarily)	Comdt. XVII Corps R. & R. Camp.
Hd.Qtrs. Div. Train.	BERNEVILLE.	Camp Comdt.
1 Company.	SIMENCOURT.	A.C. WANQUETIN.
2 Companies.	WANQUETIN.	" "
1 Field Ambulance.	ACHICOURT. (Adv. Dressing Station)	
1 " "	DAINVILLE (Main " ")	
1 " "	AGNEZ les DUISANS.	

   Reinforcements and other Details should be despatched to unit's transport lines.

2. **AMMUNITION.**
   (a) DIVL. A.R.P. is at L.27.c.92 on the WARLUS-DAINVILLE Road, and is known as "DAIN" Dump.
   In addition Div. Artillery may draw by Horse Transport from XVII Corps Dumps at HORSESHOE L.29.d.66 and LARISSET K.5.b.58.
   (b) DIVL. TRENCH MUNITION DUMP is located at Billet No. 22 AGNY. Brigades etc. will draw from there on application to this office.
   In addition to the above dump, Brigades etc. can draw from XVII Corps "X" Dump at G.20.c.33. on telegraphic authority from this office.
   At present both dumps are drawn from by Horse Transport. It is hoped that AGNY Dump will be connected up with the Light Railway in the near future.

P. T. O.

3. BATTLE STRAGGLER POSTS AND PRISONERS OF WAR.

(a) The following are the locations of Battle Straggler Posts.

No. 1.	M.9.c.51.	Sheet 51 B.	1 N.C.O.	6 men.
No. 2.	M.3.c.52.	" "	"	"
No. 3.	G.33.c.53.	" "	"	"
No. 4.	G.33.a.53.	" "	"	"

These will be manned by the Support Brigade at noon 8th instant; at which hour the Straggler post line will come under the orders of the A.P.M., who will place one N.C.O. of H.M.P. in charge of each group of two posts.

(b) STRAGGLER COLLECTING STATION will be established by A.P.M. in DAINVILLE. The A.P.M. will take over this post on 8th instant with his own personnel. From the 9th and subsequently the personnel (1 N.C.O. 6 men) will be furnished by the Reserve Brigade. They should report to the A.P.M. at 3 p.m. 9th instant at the Town Major's Office, DAINVILLE.

(c) The above personnel will remain rationed by their own units.

(d) Any Stragglers of 15th Division will be handed over to the Straggler post at G.28.c.87.

(e) Stragglers of other formations will be sent to the CIVIL PRISON at ARRAS.

(f) Prisoners of War will be sent under Brigade escorts to ACHICOURT where they will be taken over by the A.P.M. The exact location of the A.P.M's collecting station in ACHICOURT will be notified later. For the present escorts should apply to one of the Straggler Posts for redirection.

4. BATHS etc.,

Baths will be run by the Divl. Baths Officer at BERNEVILLE, DAINVILLE and WARLUS.

They will be stocked with clean clothing.

The Foden Disinfector will be at the BERNEVILLE Baths. Blankets may be sent there for disinfection by arrangement with Divl. Baths Officer, whose address will be c/o Divl. Train Hd.Qrs BERNEVILLE.

For the present no water will be supplied east of a line running from M.4.a.8.0 - G.34. d and b - G.35.a - G.29.c. d and b. - G.30. a and b. - G.24.d - H.19.c. d. and b.

Water is available at the following places in ARRAS:-
(a) 1 Water cart point in RUE St. MAURICE, near St. JEAN Hospital.
(b) 1 French tap in RUE de MARCHE AU FILLET.
(c) 1 French tap in RUE St. CROIX.
(d) At the Horse troughs opposite PORTSLADE Camp.
(e) 1 French tap at junction of RUE DONCRE with RUE St. AUGUSTINE.
(f) 1 Point at junction of RUE St. JACQUES " " " "
(g) 2 Water cart points in RUE JEANE BODEL.
(h) French tap in Square opposite St. JEAN Hospital.
(i) One French tap at junction of RUE de la PAIX with RUE D'AMIENS.
(j) Two French taps at junction of RUE St. CLAIRE " " "

At present there is a large amount of water running to waste but the French have now returned to run the Town Pumping Station CHATEAU D'EAU, G.21.b.8.7., and as the Town Mains are put in order the supply will improve and will be available on the auxiliary main (M.3.b.8.9 to G.23.c.)

Information of bursts should be sent to the British N.C.O. at the CHATEAU D'EAU who is in charge of the party carrying out repairs under Lieut. DUMOND the French Officer in Command of the ARRAS Water Supply.

6. CEMETERIES and BURIALS.

Divisional Burial Officer is located at WARLUS.
The following Cemeteries will be used by this Division:-
(a) FAUBOURG D'AMIENS Cemetery, G.28.b.9.7, Sheet 51 B.
(b) DAINVILLE Communal Cemetery, L.29.d.5.4, Sheet 51 C.

The latter to be used in preference to any other.

The following may also be used, but units must make their own arrangements as no burial details will operate there:-
(a) DUISANS Cemetery, L.1.c.8.7, Sheet 51 C.
(b) WANQUETIN Communal, K.33.a.1.9, Sheet 51 B.
(c) ACHICOURT Road Cemetery, M.3.b.2.9. Sheet 51 B

7. ORDNANCE.

D.A.D.O.S., will be established at WANQUETIN from 8th instant.
Only stores absolutely necessary should now be demanded and Indents should be endorsed 'ESSENTIAL', by Commanding Officers. This is necessary owing to the present congestion of Railways etc.
I.O.M., (LIGHT) for Vehicles, is at SAVY.
The I.O.M., for Guns is at LOUEZ.

8. LIGHT RAILWAYS.

As a result of the recent operations, the Light Railway System in the XVII Corps Area is not as effective as it was. Trucks are earmarked at BERNEVILLE on the B. 6 line at 4 P.M. daily to take rations to the Brigade in the line. Applications for this and other truckage required should reach this office by 5 P.M. daily for the services required on the following day. Demands on C.L.R.O., XVII Corps will then be made by this office. The C.L.R.O., will repeat his reply to the Brigade etc concerned in order to save time.

9. CANTEEN.

Divisional Canteen will open at BERNEVILLE on the 8th instant.

10. SUPPLIES.

RAILHEAD - AGNEZ LES DUISANS

REFILLING POINTS- 167th Bde. Group. WANQUETIN.
168th Bde. Group. WANQUETIN.
169th Bde. Group. GOUVES.

Rations will be delivered by Divisional Train to Units' Qr. Mr. Stores. Fuel will be drawn from Refilling Points by Units' 1st Line Transport.

11. R.E.MATERIAL.

(1) The Divisional R.E.Park has been moved from No. 8 R.E.Park, RONVILLE, to the CHATEAU, AGNY, M.8.a.6.8.
(2) This Park will be small and used mainly as a Workshop and, as there is a considerable amount of material still remaining at the No. 8 R.E.Park, RONVILLE, Units will still draw from this point on indent from C.R.E.

12. RONVILLE CAVES and TUNNELS.

(1) The RONVILLE CAVES and TUNNELS System is being administered by this Division.
(2) The St. SAUVEUR CAVES and TUNNELS System is being administered by the 15th Division.
(3) Captain GILLESPIE, 7/8th K.O.S.B., has been appointed Area Commandant, St. SAUVEUR, by the 15th Division.
(4) The Cave Major of the RONVILLE CAVES and TUNNELS is being appointed by this Division.
(5) The Cave Major will allot accommodation to Units, and Units requiring accommodation in the CAVE SYSTEM, or vacating such accommodation will report to him.
(6) No fires or braziers will be allowed in the CAVES or TUNNELS, except where authorised by the Cave Major.
(7) Any further orders necessary for the administration of the RONVILLE CAVES will be issued when a reconnaissance has been made by the Cave Major, including Water, Cooking arrangements, Anti-Gas Protection, Traffic Control etc.

6th April, 1918.

Lieut-Colonel,
A.A. & Q.M.G., 56th Division.

DISTRIBUTION.

G.O.C.	"G"	XVII Corps "Q"	Area Commdt.
167th Inf. Bde.	5th Ches: Regt.	D. A. D. O. S.	WANQUETIN.
168th Inf. Bde.	Div. M.G.Cdr.	Camp Commdt.	DAINVILLE.
169th Inf. Bde.	Divl. Train.	Employt. Coy.	BERNEVILLE.
Divl. Arty.	A. D. M. S.	Baths Officer.	GOUVES.
C. R. E.	D. A. D. V. S.	1st Canadian Div. "Q"	RONVILLE CAVES.
Sig. Coy. R.E.	A. P. M.	15th Div. "Q"	
French Mission.	S.O.F., C. of E.	S.O.F., Non C. of E.	
	XVII Corps M. and R. Camp	R.T.O., AGNEZ LES DUISANS
	XIII Corps " "	

SECRET.   56th Division. AQS/587.

ADMINISTRATIVE INSTRUCTIONS NO. 2
in connection with relief of 1st Canadian Division by 56th Division.

GASSED CLOTHING.

1. A Gassed Clothing changing room with a store for clean clothing attached will be established as below.
    (a) By the Infantry Brigade in the line.
    (b) By the Infantry Brigade in Support. } in their own areas.
    (c) By Divisional Artillery.
    (d) By A.D.M.S. at A.D.S., ACHICOURT.

2. The establishment of suits of Service Dress, S.D. Caps, Puttees, and sets of underclothing to be maintained at each of the above stores is:-

    1 (a) and 1 (b) ... 100.
    1 (c) ... 50.
    1 (d) ... 50.

    The initial issue of all these articles except underclothing will be demanded from the D.A.D.O.S. Underclothing will be demanded from Divl. Baths Officer and drawn from Divisional Linen Store.

3. The locations of the Stores and changing rooms established by Infantry Brigades and Divl. Artillery will be reported to this office.

4. Officers and men whose clothing is badly contaminated with Yellow Cross Gas or has been splashed with the liquid should be sent to the Gassed Clothing changing Room of their Formation, or to the A.D.S. at ACHICOURT, to change their clothing, before being allowed to enter a gas proof dug-out or a billet.

5. Personnel handling gassed clothing will wear Box respirators and Hedging Gloves and a suit of S.D. clothing kept for the purpose. Under no circumstances should gassed clothing be touched with bare hands. Hands should be washed with soap and water after work.

6. Infantry Brigades, Divisional Artillery and A.D.M.S. will send gassed clothing to a Divisional Degassing Room, the location of which will be notified later. Receipts for the numbers of articles handed in should be obtained from the N.C.O. i/c Divl. Degassing Room; and on presentation of these receipts to the D.A.D.O.S. or Divisional Baths Officer (in the case of underclothing) an equivalent number of sets of clean clothing may be drawn. Gassed clothing should be sent to the Divl. Degassing Room securely packed in tarpaulins or in limbers with a tarpaulin or wagon sheet fixed over the top.

7. Personnel belonging to other units in the Division not referred to above will be allowed to change their gassed clothing, when necessary, at any of the changing rooms referred to above.

7th April, 1918.

LIEUT.-COLONEL,
A.A. & Q.M.G. 56th DIVISION.

P.T.O.

DISTRIBUTION.

G. O. C.

"G"

137th Infantry Bde.

138th Infantry Bde.

139th Infantry Bde.

Divl. Artillery.

C. R. E.

Sig. Coy. R.E.

1/5th Ches. Regt.

Div. M.G.Commdr.

Divl. Train.

A. D. M. S.

D. A. D. V. S.

A. P. M.

D. A. D. O. S.

Camp Commdt.

Employt. Coy.

Baths Officer

French Mission.

S.C.F., C. of E.

S.C.F., Non C. of E.

XVIIth Corps "Q"

1st Canadian Division "Q"

UNIT	STRENGTH 1.4.18.		INCREASE.		DECREASE.		STRENGTH. 1.5.18.	
	O.	O.R.	O.	O.R.	O.	O.R.	O.	O.R.
56th Div. Headquarters.	18	84	-	-	1	3	17	81
167th Inf. Bde. H.Q.	3	21	-	-	-	1	3	20
1/7th Middlesex Rgt.	52	938	-	80	11	153	41	865
1/8th " "	45	938	8	49	6	80	47	907
1/1st London Regt.	50	869	5	222	9	124	46	967
167th T.M. Battery.	4	46	-	1	-	1	4	46
168th Inf. Bde. H.Q.	3	21	-	-	-	1	3	20
1/4th London Regt.	31	774	17	288	5	127	43	935
1/13th " "	37	1011	4	82	5	120	36	973
1/14th " "	35	929	15	290	7	162	43	1057
168th T.M. Battery.	3	40	1	8	-	2	4	46
169th Inf. Bde. H.Q.	3	21	1	1	1	1	3	21
1/2nd London Regt.	42	915	3	55	7	89	38	881
1/5th " "	30	871	17	288	8	45	39	1114
1/16th " "	35	958	14	75	7	102	42	931
169th T.M. Battery.	2	34	-	-	-	3	2	31
1/5th Cheshire Regt.	38	796	2	177	2	93	38	880
56th Battn. M.G.Corps.	46	886	4	2	12	74	38	814
Hd.Qtrs. Royal Arty.	4	18	-	1	-	1	4	18
280th Bde. R.F.A.	32	758	9	45	2	18	39	785
281st " "	25	761	2	72	-	51	27	782
D.A.C.	11	573	5	23	-	18	16	578
Hd.Qtrs. Royal Engrs.	2	10	-	-	-	-	2	10
416th(Edin.)Fld.Coy.RE.	3	188	4	50	-	27	7	211
512th(Ldn,) " "	5	175	2	46	1	27	6	194
513th " " "	9	186	1	40	2	19	8	207
56th Divl. Signal Coy.	11	275	-	9	-	8	11	276
Divl. Train.	21	367	2	23	2	8	21	382
Medical Units.	19	502	5	47	1	35	23	514
Mobile Vet. Section.	1	21	-	5	-	2	1	24
247th Employment Coy.	1	302	-	2	-	8	1	296

CASUALTIES — APRIL, 1918.

DATE. APRIL.	UNIT.	OFFICERS. Killed.	Wounded.	Missing.	O.Rs. K.	W.	M.	REMARKS.
2nd.	280th Brigade R.F.A.	—	—	—	—	4	—	
4th.	280th Brigade R.F.A.	—	2/Lt. J.M. WALTON, 3/4/18.	—	—	1	—	
Additional 28/3/18.	280th Brigade R.F.A.	—	—	—	—	1	—	Gassed.
8th.	7th Middlesex Regt.	—	—	—	—	1	—	
	1st London Regt.	—	—	—	—	1	—	
	4th London Regt.	—	—	—	—	1	—	
	56th Div. Signal Coy.	—	—	—	—	1	—	
9th.	7th Middlesex Regt.	—	—	—	—	1	—	
	8th Middlesex Regt.	—	—	—	—	4x	—	x Includes 1 accidentally.
	1st London Regt.	—	—	—	—	6	—	
	13th London Regt.	—	—	—	4	27	—	
	4th London Regt.	—	—	—	1	2	—	
	14th London Regt.	—	—	—	1	1	—	
	56th Bn. M.G.C.	—	—	—	1	1	—	
	416th (Edin.) Fld.Coy. R.E.	—	—	—	—	2	—	
	2/1st Ldn. Fld. Ambce.	—	—	—	4	12	—	
Additional 3rd.	56th Bn. M.G.C.	—	2/Lt. R.A. WILLIAMS. (Gas)	—	—	—	—	
10th.	8th Middlesex Regt.	—	—	—	1x	1	—	x Accidentally by rifle shot.
	13th London Regt.	—	2/Lt. F.W. RUSSELL, 9/4/18.	—	—	1	—	
	16th London Regt.	—	" F. FISHER (9th Ldns) 9/4/18.	—	—	4	—	
	"	—	" E.W.G. MALCOLM (9th Ldns) 9/4/18.	—	—	—	—	
	"	—	" E.F. SIMPSON, 10/4/18.	—	—	—	—	
	1/5th Cheshire Regt.	—	—	—	—	1	—	
	56th Bn. M.G.C.	—	—	—	—	1	—	

(2)

DATE. APRIL.	UNIT.	OFFICERS. Killed.	Wounded.	Missing.	O. Rs. K.	W.	M.	REMARKS.
11th.	8th Middlesex Regt.					2		
	7th Middlesex Regt.					5x		x Includes 1 gassed.
	4th London Regt.					3x		x 1 "
	14th London Regt.					2		At duty.
	2nd London Regt.					3		
	1/5th Cheshire Regt.					2		Accidentally by discharge of rifle.
	281st Bde. R.F.A.					2		
11/12th.	8th Middlesex Regt.		2/Lt. K.L.A.O.HICKS (5th Midlsx) 12/4/18.	2/Lt. H.R. HOLLAND. 12/4/18. @.		2		@. Missing on patrol believed prisoner.
8th.	"					1x		x - Gassed.
9th.	"					8x		"
10th.	"					2x		"
7th.	7th Middlesex Regt.		Capt. E.B.BOWKER.x 7/4/18.			14x		"
9th.	"					3x		"
10th.	"					3x		"
11th.	"					1		
11/12th.	1st London Regt.					19x		"
10th.	4th London Regt.					10x		"
8th.	13th London Regt.				1	4		
11/12th.	"					1x		"
8th.	14th London Regt.					1x		"
11th.	"					1		
11/12th.	"					2x		"
9th.	1/5th Cheshire Regt.					19x		"
8th.	"					20x		"
10th.	"					4x		"
11/12th	281st Brigade R.F.A.					1		x. Gassed.
10th	56th Bn. M.G.C.					2x		"
11th	"		2/Lt. H. EGGLETON.x.11/4/18.					"
13th	7th Middlesex Regt.		Capt. H.K.KING. 12/4/18.		1	2		"
	8th Middlesex Regt.							

(3)

DATE. APRIL.	UNIT.	OFFICERS Killed.	OFFICERS Wounded.	OFFICERS Missing.	O.Rs K.	O.Rs W.	O.Rs M.	REMARKS
13th (contd.)	13th London Regt.	-	-	-	-	1	-	At duty.
	14th London Regt.	-	-	-	-	2	-	
	281st Brigade R.F.A.	-	-	-	-	4	-	
12/13th.	7th Middlesex Regt.	-	-	-	1	1x	-	x Gassed.
	8th Middlesex Regt.	-	-	-	1	1x	-	"
12th	4th London Regt.	-	-	-	-	2x	-	"
8th	13th London Regt.	-	-	-	-	1x	-	"
10th	14th London Regt.	-	-	-	-	1x	-	"
12th	"	-	-	-	-	1x	-	"
13/14th.	16th London Regt.	-	-	-	-	1	-	
"	5th Cheshire Regt.	-	-	-	-	1	-	
9th	280th Brigade R.F.A.	-	-	-	-	1x	-	x Gassed.
3/14th	513th (Ldn)Fld.Coy.R.E.	-	-	-	-	1x	-	
12th	56th Bn. M.G.C.	-	-	-	-	7	-	
15th	13th London Regt.	-	-	-	2	3@	-	@ Includes 1 accident. ally.
12/13th	7th Middlesex Regt.	-	-	-	-	1x	-	x Gassed.
"	8th Middlesex Regt.	-	-	-	-	1x	-	"
"	14th London Regt.	-	-	-	-	1x	-	"
16th	4th London Regt.	-	-	-	-	1	-	
15th	14th London Regt.	-	-	-	-	2	-	
"	7th Middlesex Regt.	-	-	-	-	1x	-	x Gassed.
17th	14th London Regt.	-	-	-	-	3	-	
	169th T.M. Battery.	-	-	-	1	1x	-	x Gassed.
28/3/18.	56th Bn. M.G.C.	-	-	-	-	1x	-	"
15/4/18.	4th London Regt.	-	-	-	-	2x	-	"

2/Lt. A.J. REA. 16/4/18½

Major F.A. PHILLIPS. x
(Montgomeryshire Yeomanry)

(4)

DATE. APRIL.	UNIT.	OFFICERS. Killed.	OFFICERS. Wounded.	OFFICERS. Missing.	O.Rs. K.	O.Rs. W.	O.Rs. M.	REMARKS.
18th	14th London Regt.					1	4	
17th	1st London Regt.						4x	x Gassed.
19th	8th Middlesex Regt.						1	Accidentally, cleaning rifle
	4th London Regt.		2/Lt. E.L. MILLS, 19/4/18.		3	8		
	13th London Regt.					1		
	14th London Regt.		2/Lt. F.A. BAKER, M.M.-x		2	11		x Gassed.
16/3/18.	"							
20th	4th London Regt.		2/Lt. J.L. BACKHOUSE.-@ (20th Londons)		2	16		@ At Duty.
	14th London Regt.				2	19@	2a.	@ Includes 1 accidentally a Believed killed.
	168th T.M. Battery.					1		
	16th London Regt.		2/Lt. F.A. HITCHINGS.(21st Ldns)		1	1		
	56th Bn. M.G.C.				1	1		Gassed.
19th	1st London Regt.							
21st								
20th	4th London Regt.				3	2		
	14th London Regt.				2	2		
	2nd London Regt.					1		At duty.
	5th London Regt.				2	2		
	16th London Regt.				1	2		
	56th Bn. M.G.C.				1	1		
	281st Brigade R.F.A.					1		
20th	7th Middlesex Regt.					1x		x Gassed.
	8th Middlesex Regt.					1x		" "
22nd	7th Middlesex Regt.					1		
	8th Middlesex Regt.				1	5		
	16th London Regt.				1	6		
	2nd London Regt.		2/Lt. F. BOOTH. 22/4/18.		1	2		
13th	56th Bn. M.G.C.		" J. ROBERTSON. (Gas)					
	512th (Ldn) Fld.Coy.R.E.							
20th	X/56th T.M. Battery.					1		

(6.)

DATE APRIL.	UNIT.	OFFICERS Killed.	OFFICERS Wounded.	OFFICERS Missing.	O.Rs. K.	O.Rs. W.	O.Rs. M.	REMARKS.
27th.	7th Middlesex Regt.	-	-	-	1	1	-	
"	1st London Regt.	-	-	-	-	3	-	
"	5th " "	-	-	-	-	2	-	Includes 1 Self-inflicted.
"	16th " "	-	-	-	1	1	-	
20th.	5th " "	-	-	-	-	1	-	Gas.
22nd.	7th Middlesex Regt.	-	-	-	1	2	-	Gas.
28th.	8th Middlesex Regt.	-	-	-	-	2	-	
"	2nd London Regt.	-	-	-	1	4	-	
20th.	5th Cheshire Regt.	-	-	-	1	1	-	Gas.
29th.	1st London Regt.	-	-	-	-	1	-	Gas.
"	14th " "	-	Lt. G.W. PREBBLE. 29/4/18.	-	1	1	-	
30th.	8th Middlesex Regt.	-	-	-	-	2	-	
"	1st London Regt.	-	-	-	-	2	-	
"	5th Cheshire Regt.	-	-	-	-	1	-	Gas.
"	513th (Ldn) Fld.Coy.RE.	-	-	-	1	1	-	
28th	4th London Regt.	-	Lt. L.E. BALLANCE. (11th Ldns)	-	-	-	-	Gas.
"	5th Cheshire Regt.	-	2/Lt. E.A. COVENTRY. X	-	-	-	-	X - Injured.
Additional								
26th	5th Cheshire Regt.	-	-	-	-	1	-	Accidentally cleaning rifle.
TOTALS FOR APRIL.		3	23	2	44	447	4	

(50)

DATE APRIL.	UNIT.	OFFICERS Killed.	OFFICERS Wounded.	OFFICERS Missing.	O.Rs. K.	O.Rs. W.	O.Rs. M.	REMARKS.
23rd.	8th Middlesex Rgt.					1		Accidentally.
	16th London Rgt.					1		
	280th Bde.R.F.A.							
24th.	7th Middlesex Rgt.		2/Lt. E.D. BEARD.23/4/18.			2		
	2nd London Rgt.				1			
	5th London Rgt.					5		Includes 2 at duty.
25th.	56th Divl. Hd.Qtrs.				1a	2b		a 2/2nd Ldn.Fld. Amblce. b R.H.A. & 4th Londons.
23rd.	7th Middlesex Rgt.					1		Gassed.
25th.	"	2/Lt. S.A.DORE.24/4/18. (11th Middlesex Rgt.)	Capt.A.J.ROSE.24/4/18. (10th Middlesex R.)		2	15		
"	13th London Rgt.					2		
"	14th London Rgt.					1		
"	2nd London Rgt.		2/Lt.G.G.SHADBOLT. (20th Ldns)24/4/18.		@	8 1		@ Believed killed.
"	5th Cheshire Rgt.					1		
"	56th Bn. M.G.C.		2/Lt. S.F. WEBB,MC. 24/4/18. (at duty)			2		
"	281st Bde. R.F.A.							
"	515th (Ldn)Fld.Coy.RE.					4x		x Includes 1 at duty.
"	247th Employ. Coy.					1x		x Since returned to duty.
25th.	7th Middlesex Rgt.				2	11		
26th	"					4		
"	1st London Regt.	Lt. A.S. BARTHORPE.25/4/18.			1	3		
"	14th "					2		
"	2nd "							
20th	5th "					1x	1x	X Gassed.
26th	16th "					1	1x	x Missing on patrol.
11th	5th Cheshire Rgt.					1x		x Gassed.
15th	"					1x		"
26th	513th (Ldn) Fld.Coy.RE.				1	3		Includes 2 at duty.

<u>Secret</u>

War Diary

Administrative Branch

56th Division

Vol:- XXVIII

Period - 1st to 31st May, 1918.

WAR DIARY
or
INTELLIGENCE SUMMARY.

Army Form C. 2118.

Volume XXVIII
Page 1

Place	Date 1916 May	Hour	Summary of Events and Information	Remarks and references to Appendices
WARLUS	1			
	2			
	3			
	4		169 Inf Bde relieved 167 Inf Bde in the LEFT SECTOR of the Divisional Front as follows: 14th London Rgt. right front line Bn. 13th London Rgt. left front line Bn. 4th London Rgt. Support Bn. on relief 167 Inf Bde disposed as follows:- became Bde in Div. Reserve. 7th Middx Rgt. Dainville. 8th Middx Rgt. St Sauveur Caves. 1st London Rgt. Ronville Caves. 7th Middx Rgt. Dainville. P.A. NULL KCB assumed Command of the Division. Major General Sir C.	
	5			
	6			
	7			
	8			
	9			
	10			
	11			
	12		Divisional Hqrs moved to the Chateau in Warlus	
	13		167 Inf Bde relieved 168 Inf Bde in the RIGHT SECTOR of the Divisional Front as follows: Middlesex Rgt. right front Bn. 8th Middlesex Rgt. left front Bn. 1st London Rgt. Support Bn. on relief the relieved 168 Inf Bde disposed as follows:- 4th London Rgt employed on work in Grouagl Area Billeted in Barnes. 13th London Rgt. Dainville. 14th London Rgt. Dainville.	
	14			
	15			
	16			
	17			
	18			
	19			
	20			

Army Form C. 2118.

Volume XXVII Page 2

WAR DIARY
or
INTELLIGENCE SUMMARY.
(Erase heading not required.)

Instructions regarding War Diaries and Intelligence Summaries are contained in F. S. Regs., Part II. and the Staff Manual respectively. Title pages will be prepared in manuscript.

Place	Date 1918 MAY	Hour	Summary of Events and Information	Remarks and references to Appendices
WARLUS	21			
	22		168 Inf Bde relieved 169 Inf Bde in the LEFT Sector of the Divisional Front & disposed as follows: 4th London Regt. LEFT Front Line Battn. 13th London Regt RIGHT Front Line Battn. 14th London Regt in Support. on relief 169 Inf Bde disposed as follows: 16th London Regt. Arras 2nd & 5th London Regt. Bavincourt	
	23			
	24			
	25			
	26			
	27			
	28			
	29			
	30		169 Inf Bde relieved 167 Inf Bde in the RIGHT Sector of the Divisional Front as follows: 5th London Regt. Left Front Line Battn. 16th London Regt. Right Front Line Battn. 2nd London Regt Support Battn. on relief 167 Inf Bde disposed as follows: 7th Middlesex Regt. ARRAS. 1st London Regt. & 12th Middlesex Regt. BAVINCOURT.	
	31			

[signature]
Lieut.-Col.
A.A. & Q.M.G. 56th Division.

SECRET.   A. Q. S. 5

LOCATIONS. 56th DIVISION.   13/5/1918.

Divisional Headquarters WARLUS.   Transport WARLUS.
LEFT BRIGADE.   RIGHT BRIGADE.
   Brigade Head Qrs.   G.28.a.9.8   Brigade Head Qrs.   G.27.b.8.3
   Right Line Battn: H.31.b.3.8   Right Line Battn: N. 7.a.2.8
   Left Line Battn: H.25.b.25.25   Left Line Battn: N. 1.a.6.3
   Support   Battn: G.30.c.10.25   Support   Battn: N. 5.b.1.6
T.M.Bty. Left Bde.   H.25.d.25.80   T.M.Bty. Right Bde.   G.27.b.90.35
            Reserve Brigade Head Qrs.   BERNEVILLE.
            1 Battn.   G.21.d.2.5
            2 Battns.   DAINVILLE.
            T.M.Battery   DAINVILLE

UNIT.	Headquarters.	Transport Lines.
167th Infantry Brigade		DAINVILLE
7th Middlesex Regt.		WANQUETIN.
8th Middlesex Regt.		do.
1st London Regt.		do.
167th T.M.Battery		DAINVILLE
168th Infantry Brigade		BERNEVILLE.
4th London Regt.		do.
13th do.		do.
14th do.		do.
168th T.M.Battery		do.
169th Infantry Brigade.		BERNEVILLE.
2nd London Regt.		do.
5th do.		do.
16th do.		do.
169th T.M.Battery		do.
56th Battn: M.G.Corps	WARLUS	BERNEVILLE.
1/5th Cheshire Regt.	G.27.b.7.7	WANQUETIN.
247th (Div) Employment Coy	WARLUS	
C. R. E.	WARLUS	WARLUS
416th Field Coy. R.E.	G.22.d.3.1	L.34.d.3.2
512th Field Coy. R.E.	G.28.a.7.3	BERNEVILLE
513th Field Coy. R.E.	G.27.b.15.90	WAGNONLIEU
A. D. M. S.	WARLUS	WARLUS
2/1st London Field Ambce	K.28.d.5.2	WANQUETIN
2/2nd London Field Ambce	L.1.c.4.5	AGNEZ-LES-DUISANS.
2/3rd London Field Ambce	ACHICOURT	WANQUETIN.
C. R. A.	WARLUS	WARLUS
280th Brigade R.F.A.	M.8.b.75.40	BERNEVILLE
281st Brigade R.F.A.	G.27.b.99.33	SIMENCOURT
277th A.F.A.Brigade	G.28.b.15.87	BERNEVILLE
311th A.F.A.Brigade	G.22.d.2.8	STUART CAMP
56th Div. Ammn. Column	MONTENES COURT	MONTENES COURT
277th Bde. Ammn. Column	HABARCQ	HABARCQ
311th Bde. Ammn. Column	DUISANS	DUISANS
Divisional Train	WANQUETIN	WANQUETIN
No. 1 Company	SIMENCOURT	SIMENCOURT
No. 2 Company	WANQUETIN	WANQUETIN
No. 3 Company	do.	do.
No. 4 Company.	do.	do.

P. T. O.

UNIT.	Headquarters.	Transport Lines.
D.A.D.V.S.	WARLUS	
Mobile Veterinary Section	MONTENES COURT	MONTENES COURT
56th M.T. Company		TILLOY-LES-HERMAVILLE
D.A.D.O.S.	MONTENES COURT.	

A.C.Dundas Major,
D.A.A.G., 56th Division.

UNIT	STRENGTH 1.5.18.		INCREASE.		DECREASE.		STRENGTH 1.6.18.	
	O.	O.R.	O.	O.R.	O.	O.R.	O.	O.R.
Divisional Headquarters.	17	81	1	-	2	3	16	78
247th Employment Company.	1	296	-	45	-	11	1	330
167th Inf. Brigade H.Q.	3	20	-	1	-	-	3	21
1/7th Middlesex Regt.	41	865	4	155	5	157	40	863
1/8th Middlesex Regt.	47	907	4	184	7	163	44	928
1/1st London Regt.	46	967	3	33	9	162	40	838
167th T.M. Battery.	4	46	-	-	-	-	4	46
168th Inf. Brigade H.Q.	3	20	-	1	-	-	3	21
1/4th London Regt.	43	935	7	60	7	108	43	887
1/13th London Regt.	36	973	7	48	4	134	39	887
1/14th London Regt.	43	1057	1	59	5	199	39	917
168th T.M. Battery.	4	46	-	-	-	-	4	46
169th Inf. Brigade H.Q.	3	21	-	-	-	-	3	21
1/2nd London Regt.	38	881	11	78	9	109	40	850
1/5th London Regt.	39	1114	7	58	7	122	39	1050
1/16th London Regt.	42	931	4	77	4	135	42	873
169th T.M. Battery.	2	31	2	14	-	-	4	45
1/5th Cheshire Regt½	38	880	4	67	4	72	38	875
56th Battn. M.G.Corps.	38	814	7	99	-	45	45	868
56th Div. Artillery H.Q.	4	18	-	-	-	-	4	18
280th Brigade R.F.A.	39	785	-	4	7	19	32	770
281st Brigade R.F.A.	27	782	2	21	4	15	25	788
56th D.A.C.	16	578	-	15	-	25	16	568
56th Div. Engineers H.Q.	2	10	-	-	-	-	2	10
416th (Edinboro')Fld.Coy.	7	211	-	4	1	5	6	210
512th (London)Fld.C.R.E.	6	194	-	10	-	3	6	201
513th (London)Fld.C.R.E.	8	207	-	9	1	12	7	204
56th Div. Signal Coy.	11	276	1	25	1	7	11	294
56th Divl. Train.	21	382	-	5	1	4	20	383
Medical Units.	23	514	6	35	4	7	25	542
Mobile Veterinary Section.	1	24	-	-	-	6	1	18

CASUALTIES - MAY, 1918.

DATE MAY.	UNIT	OFFICERS Killed	OFFICERS Wounded	OFFICERS Missing	O. Rs. K.	O. Rs. W.	O. Rs. M.	REMARKS
1st.	8th Middlesex Regt.	-	-	-	-	1	-	
	1st London Regt.	-	-	-	-	2 x	-	x Injured.
	4th " "	-	-	-	-	5	-	Includes 1 accident'y by rifle.
	13th " "	-	-	-	-	4	-	
	5th Cheshire Regt.	-	-	-	-	4	-	
2nd.	8th Middlesex Regt.	-	-	-	1	4 x	-	x At duty.
	14th London Regt.	-	-	-	-	2	-	
	5th " "	-	-	-	-	1 x	-	Accident'y explosion
	513th (Ldn) Fld.Coy.R.E.	-	-	-	-	1	-	(of round S.A.A.)
	2/1st London Fld.Ambce.	-	-	-	-	2 x	-	x Gas.
3rd.	8th Middlesex Regt.	-	-	-	-	1	-	Lewis Gun.
	14th London Regt.	-	-	-	3	5 x	-	Accdt'y by round from.
	4th " "	-	-	-	-	-	-	x Includes 1 accdt'y by discharge of rifle.
	" "	-	-	-	1 x	2 x	-	All accdt'y by discharge of rifle.
	280th Bde. R.F.A.	-	-	-	-	1	-	At duty.
4th.	8th Middlesex Regt.	-	-	-	-	1	-	Injured.
	7th " "	-	-	-	-	1	-	
	13th London Regt.	-	-	-	1	2	-	
	5th Cheshire Regt.	-	-	-	-	2	-	
	416th (Edin')Fld.Coy.RE.	-	-	-	-	1	-	At duty.
	513th (Ldn) " "	-	-	-	-	1	-	
5th	4th London Regt.	-	-	-	-	1	-	2/Lt. J.A.T.DERHAM,5/5/18.
6th.	4th London Regt.	-	-	-	2	4	-	
	14th " "	-	-	-	-	1	-	Accidentally.
	2nd " "	-	-	-	-	2	-	
	5th " "	-	-	-	-	1	-	
	5th Cheshire Regt.	-	-	-	1	1	-	
	56th Battn. M.G.C.	-	-	-	-	2	-	

(2)

DATE. MAY.	UNIT.	OFFICERS. Killed.	OFFICERS. Wounded.	OFFICERS. Missing.	O. RS. K.	O. RS. W.	O. RS. M.	REMARKS.
7th.	4th London Regt.				2	2	-	
	14th " "				-	1	-	
	2nd " "				-	1	-	
	5th " "		Lt.(A/Capt) C.J.SCUDAMORE.6/5/18.		-	-	1	x Injured - Includes 4 at duty.
	5th Cheshire Regt.				5	5	-	x
8th.	1st London Regt.				1	1	-	
	4th " "		2/Lt.A.E.LESTER.MC.(8/5/18)		-	1	-	Failed to return from patrol.
	13th " "				-	-	-	
	5th " "				-	2	-	
	56th.Battn.M.G.C.				-	1	-	
	V/56th T.M.Battery.				-	1	-	
9th.	4th London Regt.				1	2	-	
	5th " "				-	1	-	
	5th Cheshire Regt.				-	1	-	
	56th.D. A. C.				-	1	-	At duty.
	5th 7th Middlesex Regt.				-	2	-	
	7th 5th Cheshire Regt.				2	1	-	Gassed.
10th.	13th London Regt.				-	3	-	
	14th " "				-	1	-	
	5th " "				-	1	-	At duty.
	16th " "				-	1	-	
9th	7th Middlesex Regt.				2	1	-	Gas.
11th.	1st London Regt.				1	1	-	
	13th " "				-	2	-	
	14th " "				-	2	-	
	2nd " "		2/Lt. J.L. HEWITT,(13th Ldns)11/5/18.		1	1	1x	x Failed to return from patrol
	16th " "				-	1	-	
	56th Battn. M.G.C.				2	1	-	

(3)

DATE MAY.	UNIT	OFFICERS Killed	OFFICERS Wounded	OFFICERS Missing	O.Rs. K.	O.Rs. W.	O.Rs. M.	REMARKS
12th	4th London Regt.					1		
	13th " "				2	3		
	14th " "				1	2		
	5th " "					1		
	16th " "					1		Injured.
	5th Cheshire Regt.					5		At duty. All injured.
13th	7th Middlesex Regt.					2		
	8th " "					1		
	14th London Regt.					1		Accidentally.
	16th " "					2		
	5th " "							
	5th Cheshire Regt.					3		Includes 2 injured.
	281st Brigade R.F.A.		Lt. J.T. CAPRON, 12/5/18.			1		Injured – at duty.
	512th (Ldn)Fld.Coy.-R.E.							
27.4.18.	M.O.R.C. attd. 2/1st Fld.Amb.		Lt. J.H. FISCUS. x			2		x Gas.
14th.	8th Middlesex Regt.					2		
	2nd London Regt.				1	6		Includes 2 at duty, 1 injured.
	5th " "					3		Includes 2 at duty & 1 injured.
	16th " "					1		Injured.
	513th (Ldn)Fld.Coy.R.E.					1		
13.5.18.	1st London Regt.							
15th.	7th Middlesex Regt.	2/Lt. J.M. BRODIE,15/5/18.	2/Lt.F.C.W. LAGDEN (5th Mdx) 15/5/18. x		1	1		x Failed to return from patrol.
	8th " "		2/Lt.C.V.EVITT (A.S.C.) 15/5/18. @			2x		@ At Duty.
	5th " "					1		
	16th " "					1		
	2nd London Regt.					1		
	5th " "							
16th.	8th Middlesex Regt.					3		
	2nd London Regt.					2		
	5th " "					5		
	16th " "		2/Lt.J.H.BRYAN.(20th Ldns)16/5/18.		2	10		
	5th Cheshire Regt.					5		

(4)

DATE MAY.	UNIT.	OFFICERS Killed.	OFFICERS Wounded.	OFFICERS Missing.	O. Rs. K.	O. Rs. W.	O. Rs. M.	REMARKS.
17th.	8th Middlesex Regt.					1		
	2nd London Regt.					3		
	2/3rd Ldn.Fld.Ambce.		Major H.E. MACDERMOT.(17/5/18)			1		
	2/1st " "					1		At duty.
	280th Brigade R.F.A.					1		
18th.	8th Middlesex Regt.					2		
	13th London Regt.					1		
	2nd " "					1		
	5th " "					5	2x	x After patrol encounter. At duty. Accid't'y injured.
	5th Cheshire Regt.					1		
	56th Battn. M.G.C.					1		
16th	7th Middlesex Regt.					1		Gas.
19th	8th Middlesex Regt.					2		
	5th London Regt.					1		
	16th " "					2	x	x Gas.
	280th Brigade R.F.A.					1		At duty.
20th	8th Middlesex Regt.					1		
	4th London Regt.		Lt.(A/Capt)E.J.Y.SIMMONS,(3rd Ldns)19/5/18.		1	1		Accident'y by bomb explosion.
	2nd " "					4		
	5th " "					1		Includes 1 gassed.
	16th " "					2		Injured.
	5th Cheshire Regt.					2		
27.3.18.	512th Field Coy.R.E.		Lt. D.S. COUSINS. X			1		X Gassed.
21st.	8th Middlesex Regt.					12x	2	x,Includes 4 at duty.
	1st London Regt.					1		
	14th " "					1		At duty.
	2nd " "					3		
19th	16th " "					1		Gas.
21st	5th Cheshire Regt.					9		

(5)

DATE MAY.	UNIT.	OFFICERS Killed.	OFFICERS Wounded.	OFFICERS Missing.	O.Rs. K.	O.Rs. W.	O.Rs. M.	REMARKS.
22nd.	8th Middlesex Regt.				1	4		Includes 1 at duty.
	1st London Regt.		2/Lt. C.W. ANGRAVE.			5		
21st	16th "				1	1		Gas.
23rd.	7th Middlesex Regt.		2/Lt. G.E. CROSS. 23/5/18 (at duty)			2		Self-inflicted, cleaning rifle
	8th "					1		Includes 1 accidentally.
	2nd London Regt.					4		
	16th "					1		
	169th T.M. Battery.					1		
	280th Brigade R.F.A.					10		
24th.	8th Middlesex Regt.					1		Accidentally.
	1st London Regt.		Lt.(A/Capt) P.A. LE SUEUR. 24/5/18.			1		Includes 1 Gassed.
	13th "					1		
	14th "					2		Injured.
	16th "					2		Gas.
	5th Cheshire Regt.					4		
	56th Battn. M.G.C.							
25th.	1st London Regt.					1		
	4th "					1		
	13th "					3		
	14th "					2		
	56th Battn. M.G.C.					1		
21st	14th London Regt.					1		Gas.
26th.	7th Middlesex Regt.		Lt. H.W. AMIES. 26/5/18.		2	5		
	8th "		2/Lt. A.T. BING.(6th Mdlsx.)26/5/18.			1		
	1st London Regt.					1		x At duty.
	4th "				1	1x		Accidentally.
	2nd "					1		At duty - Accidentally.
	16th "		Lt. A.A.O. MacPHERSON. 25/5/18.			1		
	416th (Edin)Fld.Coy.R.E.							

(6)

DATE	UNIT	OFFICERS. Killed.	OFFICERS. Wounded.	OFFICERS. Missing.	O.Rs. K.	O.Rs. W.	O.Rs. M.	REMARKS.
MAY. 27th.	7th Middlesex Regt.				1	7	-	Includes 1 at duty.
	8th " "				-	3	-	" 1 accidtly.cln'g.rifle
	13th London Regt.		2/Lt. J.L.SULLIVAN.27/5/18.		1	14x	-	x Injured.
	5th " "		Lt.(A/Capt) F.W.HEATH,M.C. 27/5/18.		-	1	-	Gas.
24th.	8th Middlesex Regt.				-	1	-	"
26th.	16th London Regt.				-	1	-	
28th.	1st London Regt.				-	-	-	
	7th Middlesex Regt.				-	-	-	
	8th " "	2/Lt. W.P.HUMPHREY.27/5/18.			-	24	-	Includes 23 O.Rs. Gassed,
	4th London Regt.				1	2	-	
	13th " "		Capt. L.L.GREIG.(@) 27/5/18.		-	4	-	
	14th " "		Lt.(A/Capt)C.L.MILLIGAN.(@) 27/5/18.		1	11x	-	x Includes 9 O.Rs gassed.
	" " "		2/Lt. W.P. ANDREWS.(@) 27/5/18.		-	1	-	(@) Gassed.
	16th "				-	1	-	
	5th Cheshire Regt.				-	1	-	
24th.	7th Middlesex Regt.				-	1	-	Gas.
29th.	7th Middlesex Regt.	2/Lt.D.E.LONG.28/5/18.	Major H.A.EILOART,DSO.MC.28/5/18.		-	24	-	lx x During raid on enemy trenches
	1st London Regt.		Lt. E. FREEDY, MC. 28/5/18.		6	37	-	
Army Chaplains Dept.atta 1st London R.	Rev.R.A.P.COLBORNE.28/5/18.			-	-	-	
	4th London Regt.				-	1	-	
	13th " "				-	2	-	
	14th " "				1	2	-	
	5th Cheshire Regt.				-	1	-	
	56th Battn. M.G.C.				-	1	-	Gas.

(7)

DATE MAY.	UNIT.	OFFICERS. Killed.	OFFICERS. Wounded.	OFFICERS. Missing.	O.RS. K.	O.RS. W.	O.RS. M.	REMARKS.
30th.	7th Middlesex Regt.	-	-	-	-	1	-	Gas.
	8th " "	-	-	-	-	5	-	Includes 1 accidentally.
	1st London Regt.	-	-	-	-	2	-	
	4th " "	-	-	-	1	1	-	
	14th " "	-	-	-	-	1	-	
	2nd " "	-	-	-	1	1	-	
31st.	7th Middlesex Regt.	-	-	-	-	1	-	
	8th " "	-	-	-	-	2	-	
	13th London Regt.	-	-	-	1	2	-	
	5th Cheshire Regt.	-	-	-	-	1	-	Injured.
	280th Brigade R.F.A.	-	-	-	-	1	-	At duty.
	Y/56th T.M.Battery.	-	-	-	-	2	-	
	512th (Ldn)Fld.Coy.R.E.	-	-	-	1	1	-	
	513th (Ldn)Fld.Coy.R.E.	-	-	-	-	1	-	
30th.	8th Middlesex Regt.	-	-	-	-	4	-	Gas.
TOTALS FOR MAY.		4	21	4	38	447	7	

Vol 29

War Diary

of

Administrative Branch

56th Division

June 1918.

Army Form C. 2118.

Volume XXIX
Page 1

WAR DIARY
or
INTELLIGENCE SUMMARY.
(Erase heading not required.)

Instructions regarding War Diaries and Intelligence Summaries are contained in F.S. Regs., Part II and the Staff Manual respectively. Title pages will be prepared in manuscript.

Place	Date 1918 JUNE	Hour	Summary of Events and Information	Remarks and references to Appendices
WARLUS	1			
	2			
	3			
	4			
	5			
	6			
	7			
	8		167 Inf Bde relieved 168 Inf Bde in the LEFT Sector of the Divisional Front, as follows: 7th MIDDLESEX REGT. Left Front Line Bn.. 8th MIDDLESEX REGT. Right Front Line Bn. 1st LONDON REGT. Support Bn., on being relieved 168 Inf Bde disposed as follows: Bde Hqrs. BERNEVILLE. 4th LONDON REGT. and 14th LONDON REGT, DAINVILLE. 13th LONDON REGT. ARRAS. 168 Inf Bde. ARRAS. Hqrs 167	
	9			
	10			
	11			
	12		13th LONDON REGT moved from ARRAS to BERNEVILLE.	
	13			
	14			
	15		1st LONDON REGT relieved 8th MIDDLESEX REGT in the RIGHT Sub-Section of the LEFT DIVNL SECTOR, when relieved 8th MIDDLESEX REGT moved to Support.	
	16			
	17		168 Inf Bde relieved 167 Inf Bde in the RIGHT Sector of the Divisional Front as follows: 1st LONDON REGT, Left Front Line Bn.. 13th LONDON REGT. Right Front Line Bn. 4th LONDON REGT. Support Bn. B DE HQRS. ARRAS. on being relieved 167 Inf Bde disposed as follows: Hqrs and 5th LONDON REGT BERNEVILLE, 2nd LONDON REGT & 16th LONDON REGT. DAINVILLE.	
	18			
	19			
	20			
	21		8th MIDDLESEX REGT relieved 7th MIDDLESEX REGT in the LEFT sub-section of the LEFT DIVNL SECTOR, when relieved 7th MIDDLESEX REGT. moved to Support.	

Army Form C. 2118.

WAR DIARY
or
INTELLIGENCE SUMMARY.

SHEET 11

(Erase heading not required.)

Place	Date	Hour	Summary of Events and Information	Remarks and references to Appendices
ARRAS	22 23 24 25 26		169 Inf Bde relieved 167 Inf Bde in left sector of Divisional front as follows 2nd London Regt in left sub sector 16 London Regt in right subsector 5th London Regt in support. 169 Bde H.Q. Rue Pasteur, Arras. When relieved 167 Inf Bde are held in divisional Reserve and located as follows, 167 Bde H.Q. Berneville, 7th Middlesex Regt in Arras 8th Middlesex Regt and 1st London Regt in Dainville	ht
	30		For the 23rd instant onwards an epidemic in the form of a mild attack of influenza, known as 'three days fever' has been very prevalent in troops of the Division. The average number absent from duty on any particular day was from 550 to 600. Special isolation arrangements were made by the ADMS and tents treated large numbers of the own men & workmen, as the majority of cases the sickness only lasted 5 or 6 days and medium, men ready to return to duty completely recovered in 9 or 10 days	/M

Lieut.-Col:
A.A. & Q.M.G. 56th Division.

UNIT.	STRENGTH. 1/6/18.		INCREASE.		DECREASE.		STRENGTH. 1/7/18.	
	O.	O.R.	O.	O.R.	O.	O.R.	O.	O.R.
Divisional Headquarters.	16	78	1	4	1	1	16	81
247th Employment Company.	1	330	–	15	–	16	1	329
167th Inf. Brigade H.Q.	3	21	–	–	–	–	3	21
1/7th Middlesex Regt.	40	863	2	132	–	75	42	920
1/8th Middlesex Regt.	44	928	–	82	2	102	42	908
1/1st London Regt.	40	838	1	132	3	66	38	904
167th T.M. Battery.	4	46	–	–	–	–	4	46
168th Inf. Brigade H.Q.	3	21	–	–	1	2	2	19
1/4th London Regt.	43	887	4	89	4	67	43	909
1/13th London Regt.	39	887	8	125	6	81	41	931
1/14th London Regt.	39	917	7	134	1	95	45	956
168th T.M. Battery.	4	46	–	–	1	1	3	45
169th Inf. Brigade H.Q.	3	21	–	–	–	–	3	21
1/2nd London Regt.	40	850	3	117	5	68	38	899
1/5th London Regt.	39	1050	2	40	3	93	38	997
1/16th London Regt.	42	873	3	122	5	69	40	926
169th T.M. Battery.	4	45	–	–	–	1	4	44
1/5th Cheshire Regt.	38	875	2	36	–	25	40	886
56th Battn M.G. Corps.	45	868	1	73	1	34	45	907
56th Div. Artillery H.Q.	4	18	–	–	–	–	4	18
280th Bde. R.F.A.	32	770	–	10	–	15	32	765
281st Bde R.F.A.	25	788	2	12	1	10	26	790
56th D.A.C.	16	568	–	7	–	3	16	572
56th Divl Engineers H.Q.	2	10	–	–	–	–	2	10
416th (Edinboro') Fld.Coy.	6	210	1	5	–	5	7	210
512th (London) Fld Coy R.E.	6	201	1	22	–	3	7	220
513th (London) Fld.Coy.R.E.	7	204	–	16	–	6	7	214
56th Divl Signal Coy.	11	294	–	11	–	10	11	295
56th Divl. Train.	20	383	3	4	1	11	22	376
Medical Units.	25	542	2	16	5	10	22	548
Mobile Veterinary Section	1	18	–	–	–	2	1	16

CASUALTIES – JUNE, 1918.

DATE JUNE.	UNIT.	OFFICERS Killed.	OFFICERS Wounded.	OFFICERS Missing.	O.Rs. K.	O.Rs. W.	O.Rs. M.	REMARKS.
1st.	7th Middlesex Regt.	–	–	–	1	–	–	
	8th "	–	–	–	–	–	–	
	4th London Regt.	–	–	–	–	1	–	
	14th "	–	–	–	1	2	–	
	2nd "	–	–	–	–	–	–	
	5th "	–	–	–	2	1	–	Includes 1 Gas.
	16th "	–	–	–	–	2	–	2 injured & 1 at duty.
	5th Cheshire Regt.	–	–	–	1	3	–	
2nd	13th London Regt.	–	2/Lt. C.W. ANDERSON, 1.6.18.	–	2	x20	3	x Includes 1 died of wds.
	14th "	–	–	–	2	3	–	
	16th "	–	–	–	2	2	–	
	2nd "	–	–	–	4	1	–	
	5th "	–	–	–	3	3	–	Includes 2 injured.
	56th Bn. M.G.Corps.	–	–	–	1	1	–	
	281st Brigade R.F.A.	–	–	–	1	1	–	
	56th Div.Sig.Coy.attd.	–	–	–	–	–	–	
	281st Bde. R.F.A.	–	–	–	2	1	–	
	56th D.A.C.	–	–	–	–	–	–	
3rd	8th Middlesex Regt.	–	–	–	1	1	–	Gas.
	4th London Regt.	–	–	–	1	6	–	
	14th "	–	–	–	–	2	–	
	5th "	–	–	–	–	–	–	
	16th "	–	Capt.(A/Lt/Col) P.M. GLASIER, D.S.O. 2.6.18.	–	1	4x	–	x Includes 1 accident'y.
	5th Cheshire Regt.	–	–	–	4x	–	–	x 1 inj'd at duty
	56th Bn. M.G.Corps.	–	–	–	1	1	–	
	281st Bde. R.F.A.	–	–	–	2	2	–	
4th	8th Middlesex Regt.	–	–	–	–	4	–	Includes 1 at duty.
	16th London Regt.	–	–	–	–	1	–	
	5th Cheshire Regt.	–	–	–	–	2	–	At duty, includes 1 inj'd

(2)

DATE JUNE.	UNIT.	OFFICERS Killed.	OFFICERS Wounded.	OFFICERS Missing.	O.Rs. K.	O.Rs. W.	O.Rs. M.	REMARKS.
5th	8th Middlesex Regt.	-	-	-	-	1	-	Injured.
	2nd London Regt.	-	-	-	1	6	-	
	5th London Regt.	-	-	-	-	2	-	Includes 1 at duty & 1 accidentally.
	15th "	-	-	-	-	1	-	Injured.
	5th Cheshire Regt.	-	-	-	-	3	-	Includes 2 at duty.
	56th Bn. M.G.Corps.	-	-	-	-	1	-	Gas
2nd	13th London Regt.	-	-	-	-	1	-	"
6th	8th Middlesex Regt.	-	-	-	-	2	-	1 accident'y wndd.
	4th London Regt.	-	-	-	-	3	-	Includes 1 injured &
	14th "	-	-	-	-	3		(Accidentally by disc'e of rifle. Includes 1 at duty.
	5th London Regt.	-	-	-	-	1	-	At duty.
	16th "	-	-	-	-	1	-	
7th	4th London Regt.	-	-	-	-	1	-	
	8th Middlesex Regt.	-	-	-	-	1	-	
	5th London Regt.	-	-	-	-	1	-	At duty.
	280th Brigade R.F.A.	-	-	-	2	1	-	
	56th Div. Ammn. Column.	-	-	-	-	3	-	
8th	1st London Regt. R.A.M.C. sttd. 8th Middlesex R.	-	Capt. W.F. HALE, Injured X	-	-	2	-	XThrown from horse, Since reptd. Died.
	4th London Regt.	-	2/Lt. A.W. CHIGNEL. 8.6.18.	-	-	4	-	1x x On patrol.
	14th "	-	-	-	-	2	-	
	16th "	-	-	-	-	1	-	
	5th Cheshire Regt.	-	-	-	-	3	-	Injured - 2 at duty.
	512th (Ldn) Fld.Coy. R.E.	-	-	-	-	1	-	

(3)

DATE JUNE.	UNIT.	OFFICERS. Killed	OFFICERS. Wounded.	OFFICERS. Missing.	K.	W.	M.	REMARKS.
9th	5th London Regt.				1			Accidentally.
	16th "				1			
	5th Cheshire Regt.				2			Includes 1 accidentally injured.
	280th Brigade R.F.A.					2		
10th	7th Middlesex Regt.				1			
	5th London Regt.				1			
	56th Bn. M.G.Corps.				1			Gas.
6th	" "				1			Gas.
7th	" "				1			Gas
11th	7th Middlesex Regt.				7			
	8th "				1			
	5th Cheshire Regt.				1			At duty.
12th	1st London Regt.				1			
	4th "				2			
	2nd "				1			
	5th "				1			
	5th Cheshire Regt.				1		2	Injured by fall.
	281st Brigade, R.F.A.				1			At duty.
11th	513th (Ldn) Fld.Coy. R.E.				1			Gas.
13th	7th Middlesex Regt.				1			
	8th "		2		1			
	5th London Regt.		3		11		1x	xAfter raid on enemy trenches.
	16th "		1		2			
14th	7th Middlesex Regt.				1			
	5th London Regt.				1			
	5th Cheshire Regt.				1			Injured at duty.
	56th Bn. M.G.Corps.				1			Gas
	Y/56th T.M.BATTERY.				1			

(4)

DATE JUNE.	UNIT.	OFFICERS. Killed.	OFFICERS. Wounded.	OFFICERS. Missing.	O. RS. K.	O. RS. W.	O. RS. M.	REMARKS.
15th	7th Middlesex Regt.					1		
	3rd " "					1		
	2nd London Regt.					1		
	5th " "					2		
	5th Cheshire Regt.					1		Injured.
16th	5th London Regt.					1		
17th	7th Middlesex Regt.					1		
	8th " "					1		
	14th London "				1	8		
	5th " "					2		
	16th " "				1	4		
	5th Cheshire "					1		
	247th Employment Coy.					1		
	5th London Regt.					1		Injured.
18th	1st London Regt.				1	2		
	8th Middlesex Regt.					1		
	4th London Regt.					1		
	14th " "					1		
	2nd " "					1		
	5th " "					2		
	5th Cheshire Regt.					1		
	2/1st Ldn. Field Amblce.					1		Injured.
17th	1st London Regt.					1		Gas.

(5)

DATE JUNE.	UNIT.	OFFICERS Killed.	OFFICERS Wounded.	OFFICERS Missing.	O.RS. K.	O.RS. W.	O.RS. M.	REMARKS.
19th	7th Middlesex Regt.				1	2		
	4th London Regt.					1		
	14th " "					1		
2nd	Y/56th T.M.Battery.					1		Gas.
16th	13th London Regt.					3		Gas.
20th	7th Middlesex Regt.				1	10		N Gas.
18th	8th " "							
21st	1st London Regt.				1	9		
	7th Middlesex Regt.					4	1x	xDuring raid on enemy trench
	2nd London Regt.					1		-es.
22nd	14th London Regt.					1		At. duty.
	5th Cheshire Regt.					1		
23rd	1st London Regt.				1	1		Injured.
	5th Cheshire Regt.					1		
24th	1st London Regt.					1		
	5th " "					1		
25th	7th Middlesex Regt.				1	1		
	8th " "				1	5		xIncludes 1 injured by
	1st London Regt.					7x		bayonet.)
	4th " "					1		
	13th " "					1		

(5)

DATE JUNE.	UNIT.	OFFICERS Killed.	OFFICERS Wounded.	OFFICERS Missing.	O. RS. K.	O. RS. W.	O. RS. M.	REMARKS.
26th	4th London Regt.					1		Injured.
	13th " "				1	1		
	14th " "					3		
	5th Cheshire Regt.				1	1		At duty.
27th	4th London Regt.						1	Whilst acting as guide to returning patrol.
	16th " "				1	1		Believed self-inflict-ed.
	1st " "					1		Injured.
28th	16th London Regt.				1		1	
29th	2nd London Regt.					1		Injured – Includes 2 at duty.
	5th Cheshire Regt.					3		
30th	2nd London Regt.				1	2		Injured by pick at duty.
	5th Cheshire Regt.					1	1	
TOTALS for JUNE.		2	3		42	267	4	

2/Lt. T.H.MAWBY, 24/6/18.

War Diary

Administrative Branch

56th Division.

Period:— 1st to 31st July, 1918.

Vol: XXX

WAR DIARY
or
INTELLIGENCE SUMMARY.

Army Form C. 2118.

56 Division Q.

VOLUME XXX
Sheet 1

Place	Date July 1917	Hour	Summary of Events and Information	Remarks and references to Appendices
NTR LVS	1st		Three days fair still prevail to a large extent in the Division.	
	2nd			
	3rd			
	4th			
	5th		167 Inf Bde relieved 168 Inf Bde in the RIGHT sector of the Divisional front. 167 Bde HQ. RUE JEANNE D'ARC ARRAS. 168 Bde moved into Divisional Reserve, HQ at BERNEVILLE.	
	6th		Warning order issued for that the Division will be relieved by the 2nd Canadian Division, relief to be completed by 15 inst. The Division when relieved will move into the BERLENCOURT area for training purposes. The Division will be in G.H.Q reserve at 24 hours notice.	
	8th		Administrative Instructions No 1 in connection with relief issued. Copy attached Appendix A	App. A
	10th		Administrative Instructions No 2 in connection with relief issued. Copy attached Appendix B. 56 Div. A.Q. S/1675. Schedule Notes issued Copy attached Appendix C	App. B App. C
	11th		Administrative Instructions No 3 in connection with relief issued.	App. D

Army Form C. 2118.

WAR DIARY
or
INTELLIGENCE SUMMARY.
(Erase heading not required.)

56 Division
Volume XXV
Sheet 4

Instructions regarding War Diaries and Intelligence Summaries are contained in F.S. Regs., Part II. and the Staff Manual respectively. Title pages will be prepared in manuscript.

Place	Date	Hour	Summary of Events and Information	Remarks and references to Appendices
WARLUS	July 12		Location table on completion of relief issued. Copy attached Appendix E	App E
	13		The destination of the Division on relief is altered. The Division will now move to MONCHY-BRETON area and will Open at ROELLECOURT.	
	14		Administrative Instruction No 4 issued. Copy att. App F and G	App F & G
	14		Administrative Instructions No 5 issued, also Lorry Schedule. Copies att. App H v H 2 also Entraining table App H 3.	App H v H 2 App H 3
ROELLECOURT	15		On completion of relief Divisional Headquarters closed at WARLUS at 10 a.m. and reopened at ROELLECOURT at the same hour. Appendix B to 56 Div. G/894 issued. Instructions for move of the Division for Entraining taken whilst in A.H.Q Reserve. Copies att App I	App I
	16		Division ordered to Move to VILLERS-CHATEL area by 18 inst. Administrative Instructions No 1 issued with reference to 56 Div. Warning Order No 183. Copy att. App I 2. Administrative Instructions No 2 issued Copy att. App I 3 Appendix to 56 Div. G/894 of 15-7-15 (App I) issued Copy att App I 4	App I 2 App I 3 App I 4
VILLERS-CHATEL	17		Divisional Headquarters closed at ROELLECOURT at 10 a.m and opened at VILLERS-CHATEL at the same hour Entraining table issued Appendix J Copy att. Location table issued Appendix J.1. copy att	App J App J.1

A.Q.S. 5

Army Form C. 2118.

56 Division Q
Volume XXX Sheet III

WAR DIARY
or
INTELLIGENCE SUMMARY.
(Erase heading not required.)

Place	Date	Hour	Summary of Events and Information	Remarks and references to Appendices
VILLERS - CHATEL	20/7/18		Amendment to 56 Div. G.S./894 of 15.7.18 App "A" (Instructions for move by bus) issued, copy attd App. K.	App. K
	22/7/18		Amendment to 56 Div. G.S./677 issued, copy attd App L.	" L
	22/7/18		Amended lorry table of A.Q.S./677 issued, copy attd App L.1	" L¹
	29/7/18		Order received that the Division will relieve the 1st Canadian Division in the TELEGRAPH HILL sector, relief to be completed by 10.0 a.m 2nd prox. Administrative Instructions No 1 issued, copy attd App M.	" M
	30/7/18		167 Bde moved to DAINVILLE - BERNEVILLE area, 169 Bde moved from DIEVAL area to CAUCOURT area	
	31/7/18		168 Bde moved to Right Bde sector of line from DAINVILLE - BERNEVILLE area. 168 Bde moved to left Bde sector of line from CHATEAU DE LA HAIE area, by light railway. Location table on completion of relief issued, copy attd App N.	App N

Lieut.-Col:
A.A. & Q.M.G. 56th Division.

War Diary
App A.

SECRET.

ADMINISTRATIVE INSTRUCTIONS NO.1.
In connection with relief of the 56th Division by 1st and 2nd Canadian Divisions, issued with reference to 56th Division Warning Order No. 180.

56th Division AQS/675.

1. **Work in progress.** Formations and Units will hand over to relieving Formations and Units all details of work, either projected or in progress, in Back Areas; this particularly applies to Schemes for improvement of Horse Standings and Baths.

2. **Area, Billet and Trench Stores.**
    All trench and Area stores and trench ammunition will be handed over, and one copy of the Units' receipted list will be forwarded by all Units in the Division, through the usual channels so as to reach Divisional Headquarters "Q" within 24 hours of relief. Consolidated returns on A.F. W.3405 need not be forwarded. Separate lists will be prepared for trench stores, trench ammunition, battle equipment ammunition, gas clothing, preserved rations, and area stores.
    Stores on Divisional charge, e.g. washing bowls etc. will not be handed over. In the event of any doubt as to whether stores are on Area or Divisional charge, reference should be made to Divl. Headquarters "Q".

    <u>Petrol Tins.</u> 2000 petrol tins will be handed over as follows.
       167th Inf. Brigade. ... 550.
       169th " " ... 350.
       56th Bn. M.G.Corps. ... 150.
       Divl. Dump. ... 950.

    <u>Preserved Rations</u>
    Preserved Meat and Biscuits held on charge as reserve rations will be handed over as follows:-

	Pres.Meat.tins.	Biscuits.lbs.
167th Infantry Brigade.	490	400
168th " "	1500	1250
169th " "	787	725
56th Battn. M.G. Corps.	481	375

    Attention is drawn to D.R.O. 2363 where it is pointed out that the responsibility for, and onus of proof of, handing over rations rests with the outgoing Unit; and that Unit will be held responsible that the actual quantities shewn on any receipts given or taken, have been actually checked and that they agree with the articles under transfer.

3. **Moves of Divisional Troops.**
    (a) 512th Field Coy. R.E. and No. 3 Coy. Div. Train will move on the 13th inst. under orders of Brig-General Commanding 168th Infantry Brigade.
    (b) 2/2nd London Fld. Ambulance will move independently on the 14th instant.
    (c) 513th Field Coy. R.E., No. 4 Coy. Div. Train and 2/3rd Field Ambulance will move on the 15th instant under the orders of Brig-General Commanding 169th Infantry Brigade.
    (d) 416th Field Coy. R.E., No. 2 Coy. Div. Train and 2/1st Field Ambulance will move on the 15th inst. under the orders of Brig-General Commanding 167th Infantry Brigade.
    (e) A Portion of Divisional Headquarters, Headquarters and No. 1. Section Divl. Signal Coy., Divl. Employment Coy., and Divl. Reception Camp will move on the 15th inst. under the orders of Brig-General Commanding 167th Infantry Brigade.

(2)

3. Moves of Divl. Troops. (contd).

(f). Infantry Brigades concerned will be notified from this office of the numbers from Units named in (c), (d) and (e) who will proceed by bus.

(g) Mobile Veterinary Section will move under the orders of the D.A.D.V.S. who will notify this office and O.C., them of the date of the move.

4. Moves of Transport Columns.

The Transport of Brigade Groups which are moving by Bus on the 15th inst. will move in Brigade Group Columns on that day under the orders of Brigade Group Commanders.

Times and routes will be notified later.

5. Transport Lines.

The 4th Canadian Infantry Brigade will take over the Transport lines of 168th Infantry Brigade and 1/5th Cheshire Regt. on the 13th instant.

The designation of the Brigades which will take over the Transport lines of 167th and 169th Infantry Brigade Transport lines on the 15th instant will be notified later.

Units of Divisional Artillery, Field Coys. R.E., Companies of Divl. Train, and Field Ambulances will hand over their Transport lines to relieving Units.

6. Camps and Billets.

Particular attention is to be paid to handing over all camps, Billets, Trenches and Horse Standings in a clean and sanitary condition. Certificates to that effect must be obtained from Area Commandants and Advance Parties of incoming Units. Where necessary, Rear Parties must be left behind to hand over.

7. Embussing.

Attention is drawn to paras. 4, 5, 6, 7, 10, and 14 of this office letter AQS/607 of 14.4.18, which will be treated as Standing Orders for this Bus Move. The remaining paragraphs of that letter will be in abeyance for this move. Units of Divisional Troops will move to Embussing Points under the orders of Brigade Bus Group Commanders.

Embussing Tables will be issued later.

8. Staging Areas.

Billets in the ARRAS Staging area and in the DAINVILLE - BERNEVILLE Staging Area will be obtained from Area Commandants concerned.

Further instructions will be issued regarding the AVESNES-LES-COMTE Staging Area.

9. Accommodation.

The following areas are allotted in the BERLENCOURT Area :-

Divl. Headquarters.)
Divl. Artillery H.Q.)   LE CAUROY.   Billets from
Divl. Train Hd.Qtrs.)   Camp Commandant.
Divl. Employment Coy.)

1/5 Ches Regt   MAIZIERES   SAC. MAIZIERES.

9. Accommodation. (contd.).

Div. R.E. Hd.Qtrs.	} HOUVIN -	Billets from Area
3 Field Coys. R.E.	} HOUVIGNEUL.	Comdt., LE CAUROY.
2/1st Field Ambulance.		
Divl. Artillery.	{ MAGNICOURT.	
No. 1.Coy. Div. Train.	{ BERLENCOURT.	--- ditto ---
	{ ETREE WAMIN.	
	{ WAMIN.	

167th Inf. Brigade Group.

Troops. 167th Inf. Bde., No. 2 Coy. Div.Train, 2/3rd London Field Ambulance and Div. Rest Station.

Villages.
- MANIN.   Billets from S.A.C., VILLERS-SIR) SIMON.
- GIVENCHY LE NOBLE.   "   "   "   -- do --
- AMBRINES.   "   "   "   MATZIERES.
- BLAVINCOURT.   "   "   "   LIENCOURT.
- BEAUFORT.   "   "   "   -- do --

Restrictions.
    Bde. Hd.Qtrs. to be at MANIN.
    No.2.Coy. Div. Train to be at GIVENCHY. Field Ambce. & D.R.S. to be at GIVENCHY CHATEAU.

168th Inf. Bde. Group.

Troops. 168th Inf.Bde., 56th Bn.M.G.Corps, No.3 Coy.Div. Train, 2/2nd London Field Ambulance.

Villages.
- LIGNEREUIL.   Billets from S.A.C. LIENCOURT.
- DENIER.   "   "   "   "
- LIENCOURT.   "   "   "   "
- GRAND RULLECOURT.   "   "   "   "

Restrictions.
    Bde. Hd.Qtrs. to be at LIGNEREUIL.
    M.G.Battn.   "   "   LIENCOURT.
    Train Coy.   "   "   DENIER.
    Fld. Ambce.   "   "   GRAND RULLECOURT.

169th Inf. Bde. Group.

Troops. 169th Inf. Bde., No.4.Coy. Div. Train, Div. Reception Camp, Mob. Veterinary Section, D.A.D.O.S. Stores.

Villages.
- IZEL LEZ HAMEAU.   Billets from S.A.C., VILLERS) SIR SIMON.
- FARM DUFFINE.   "   "   "   "
- PENIN.   "   "   "   "
- VILLERS SIR SIMON.   "   "   "   "
- ~~GIVENCHY LE NOBLE.~~   "   "   "   "

Restrictions.
    Bde. Hd.Qtrs. to be at IZEL LEZ HAMEAU.
    No.4 Coy.Train   "   "   FARM DUFFINE.
    Reception Camp.   "   "   PENIN.
    D.A.D.O.S.Store   "   "   VILLERS SIR SIMON.

10. Supplies.

    Supply Railhead will change to TINCQUES on the 15th instant. A Supply Group table for the new area will be issued later.

(4)

11. Training Ammunition.

A Divl. Dump of Training Ammunition will be established at BLAVINCOURT by the 14th instant. Authority to draw from this Dump must be obtained from Divisional Headquarters "A" & "Q".

12. Ordnance.

The D.A.D.O.S. will establish his Stores and Workshops at VILLERS-SIR-SIMON, on 14th instant.

13. Police.

M.M.P. will be attached to Infantry Brigades Headquarters for duty, accommodation and rations as shewn below :-

168th Inf. Bde.	1 Sergt. and 4 Corporals	from	13th	inst.
167th " "	1 " and 4 "	"	15th	"
169th " "	1 " and 4 "	"	15th	"
Div. Artillery.	1 " and 4 "	"	16th	"

The Senior N.C.O. will report to Bde. Headquarters for orders at 6 p.m. on the day before the attachment commences.

14. Leave Arrangements.

Leave parties will entrain at TINCQUES at 8.20.a.m. on the day before that of sailing.

They may stay overnight at the Divisional Reception Camp which will be located at PENIN.

8th July, 1918.

A.A. & Q.M.G., Lieut-Colonel, 56th Division.

- DISTRIBUTION -

167th Inf. Bde.	A. P. M.	"G"
168th " "	D. A. D. O. S.	French Mission.
169th " "	Camp Commandant.	1st Canadian Div. "Q".
Divl. Artillery.	Div. M.T. Company.	2nd " "
56th Bn. M.G. Corps.	Div. Signal Coy.	Area Cdt. ARRAS.
1/5th Cheshire Rgt.	247th D.E. Coy.	" " DAINVILLE.
C. R. E.	D. A. D. V. S.	" " BERNEVILLE.
Divl. Train.	S.C.F., (C. of E.)	" " WANQUETIN.
A. D. M. S.	S.C.F. (Non-C. of E)	" " LE CAUROY.

War Diary

<u>S E C R E T .</u>　　　　　　　　　　　　　　　　<u>56th Division AQS/675.</u>

<u>AMENDMENTS TO ADMINISTRATIVE INSTRUCTIONS
NO. 1, DATED 8.7.18.</u>

<u>Para. 9.</u>

Page 2. - Add :-

　　　　　　　　　　　　　　　　　　　　　　　　　Billots from
1/5th Cheshire Regt.　　　MAIZIERES.　　　S.A.C., MAIZIERES.

Page 3. - Delete :-

From 169th Infantry Brigade Group

　　Village.　　...　　GIVENCHY LE NOBLE.

　　　　　　　　　　　　　　　　　　　　　　Lieut-Colonel,
9th July, 1918.　　　　　　　　　　　A.A. & Q.M.G., 56th Division.

War Diary

SECRET.   56th Division AQS/675.

167th Inf. Bde.	A. D. M. S.	247th Employment Coy.
169th " "	C. R. E.	Div. Reception Camp.
56th Bn. M.G.C.	Camp Comdt.	

Reference Administrative Instructions No. 1. dated 8.7.18., para. 3 (f), the following will comprise the bus groups referred to:-

167th Infantry Bde. Group.

	Offs.	O.Rs.	Offs.	O.Rs.
167th Inf. Brigade.	110	2200		
416th Field Coy. R.E.	7	120		
56th Bn. M.G.Corps.	8	142		
2/1st Ldn.Fld. Amblce.	2	150		
			127	2612

169th Infantry Bde. Group.

	Offs.	O.Rs.	Offs.	O.Rs.
169th Inf. Brigade.	114	2426		
513th Fld.Coy. R.E.	7	120		
Divisional H.Q.		30		
247th Employment Coy.	1	237		
2/3rd Ldn.Fld. Amblce.	2	150		
D..., Reception Camp.	8	75		
			132	3038
Grand Totals.			259	5650

9th July, 1918.

Lieut-Colonel,
A.A. & Q.M.G., 56th Division.

S E C R E T.

War Diary

56th Division AQS/675.

AMENDMENTS TO ADMINISTRATIVE INSTRUCTIONS
No. 1, para: 9.

Divisional Artillery Headquarters will be at HOUVIN-HOUVIGNEUL CHATEAU instead of at LE CAUROY. Billets from Area Commandant, LE CAUROY.

No. 2 Coy. Divl. Train will be at DENIER in 168th Infantry Bde. Area instead of at GIVENCHY.

10th July, 1918.

A.A. & Q.M.G.,

Lieut-Colonel,
56th Division.

SECRET. 56th Division AQS/675.

War Diary
App. B

ADMINISTRATIVE INSTRUCTIONS NO. 2.
in connection with relief of the 56th Division.

1. **Area, Billet and Trench Stores.**

   (a) With reference to para. 2. of Administrative Instructions No.1, Tents which have been issued by the D.A.D.O.S. to Area Commandants or Units will be returned to the D.A.D.O.S. by the 14th instant. and all trench shelters Those which are on Area charge will be handed over to Area Commandant.

   (b) Chaffcutters and Soyers Stoves which were originally taken over in this area will be handed over to incoming units.

   (c) Underclothing which is stored in Gas Clothing Stores is on Divisional charge and will be handed in to the Divisional Linen Store by noon 14th instant.
   Jackets, Trousers, puttees, caps, and overcoats are on Area charge and will be handed over to incoming units.

2. **Area Employment.**

   Personnel shown on attached list (Appendix "A" to all concerned) will be relieved as follows:-
   Serial Nos. 1,2,4,5,6,9, and 11, on 12th instant. Officers mentioned in column 2 will send guides to meet reliefs from 2nd Canadian Divn. at office of Area Commandant, DAINVILLE at 12 noon.
   Serial Nos. 7,8,10, on 12th instant, guides to be at Divisional Employment Coy. Orderly Room, WARLUS at 12 noon to meet reliefs from 2nd Canadian Division.
   Serial No. 3. will be relieved by 1st Canadian Division on 13th inst. reliefs reporting at Cave Majors' office.

3. **Transport Lines.**

   The 6th Canadian Infantry Brigade will take over the Transport Lines and Quartermaster's Stores of 169th Infantry Brigade in BERNEVILLE and of 7th Middlesex Regiment in WANQUETIN on the 15th inst.
   The Transport Lines and Quartermaster's Stores of the 8th Middlesex Regiment and 1st London Regiment in WANQUETIN will not be taken over by incoming Units. They will be handed over to the Area Commandant by outgoing Units.

Lieut-Colonel,
A.A. & Q.M.G., 56th Division.

10th July, 1918.

- DISTRIBUTION -

167th Inf. Bde.	A. P. M.	"G".
168th " "	D. A. D. O. S.	French Mission.
169th " "	Camp Commandant.	1st Canadian Div. "Q".
Divl. Artillery.	Div. M.T. Company.	2nd " " "
56th Bn. M.G.Corps.	Div. Signal Coy.	Area Cdt. ARRAS.
1/5th Cheshire Regt.	247th Div. Employ.Coy.	" " DAINVILLE.
C. R. E.	D. A. D. V. S.	" " BERNEVILLE.
Divl. Train.	S.C.F. (C. of E).	" " WANQUETIN.
A. D. M. S.	S.C.F. (Non.C.of E).	" " LE CAUROY.
Offr. i/c S.A.A.Dump.	O.C., No.5.A.Sanitary Sec.	Div. Baths Officer.
Div. Water Service Officer.	Div. Burials Officer.	

AQX 480/213

AREA EMPLOYMENT TO BE RELIEVED UNDER DIVISIONAL ARRANGEMENTS
(Date will be notified)

1 Serial No.	2 By Whom Employed	3 Offrs, NCOs, Men, or Unit.			4 Formation or Unit.	5 Nature of Work.	Where reliefs to report.
		Offrs	NCOs	Men			
1	A.C. Dainville. -Achicourt	-	-	10	247th Divl Employ Coy.	Billet Wardens Sanitary duties etc.	Area Commandant DAINVILLE
2	Cave Major, RONVILLE CAVES.	1 1 1 1	1 1 1 1	11 2 3 6 10	167th Inf Bde 168th " " 169th " " Divl Gas Staff Bde in reserve	Sanitary and Water duties etc. Officer detailed acts as Cave Major. Gas Duties Gas Guards	CAVE MAJOR'S OFFICE RONVILLE CAVES
3	Cave Major, ST. SAUVEUR CAVES.	1 1 1	1 1 2	3 3 3 20	167th Inf Bde. 168th " " 169th " " Bde in reserve	Sanitary & Water duties) etc. Officer detailed) acts as Cave Major.) Gas Guards	CAVE MAJOR'S OFFICE ST. SAUVEUR CAVES.
4	O i/c Divl Amm Dump	1	2	6	56th Divl Arty.	Guards etc	O i/c Horse Shoe Dump L.29.d.Central
5	O i/c Divl S.A.A. Dump	1	1	9	O i/c S.A.A. Dump.	Work on Dump	Divl S.A.A. Dump G.20.c.3.3.
6.	C.R.E.	-	-	15	Detailed by Bde in reserve	Guarding under-mentioned Bridges. No.37. G.28.c.8.7. 38 G.33.c.45.00 39 M.3.c.45.25 40 G.32.b.9.1. 41 L.21.c.5.4	See Previous Column. 413th Fld Coy R.E. 515th Fld Coy R.E.

P.T.O.

1	2	3	4	5	6
Serial No.	By Whom Employed.	Offrs.N.C.Os.Men.or Unit	Formation	Nature of Employ.	Where reliefs to reports
7.	Divl Water Service Officer	1 4 1 5 1 4 1 4 1 2 1 2	247th D.E. Coy. 58th Divl Arty " " " R.A.M.C.Train.l. 58th Divl Arty. " " "	Water Police etc at WARLUS BERNEVILLE SIMENCOURT WARQUETIN DAINVILLE MONTENESCOURT	Divl. Water Service Officer. Warlus.
8.	Divl Baths		To be arranged between Baths Officers.		
9.	Divl. Burials Officers		To be arranged between Burials Officers.		
10.	Traffic Control.		To be arranged between A.P.Ms.		
11.	O.C., No. 5.A. Sanitary Section ARRAS.	1 2.	R.A.M.C. C.R.E.	Driver, horse supplied by R.A.M.C. Drivers, 3.L.D. Horses supplied by C.R.E.	No. 5.A. Sanitary Section.

The Officers shown in Column 2 will be responsible for providing guides to take reliefs to their duties and for returning personnel relieved to their Units without delay.

McInnes   Major.
D.A.A.G. 58th Division.

7/7/18.

S E C R E T.   56th Division AQS/675.

ALL FORMATIONS AND UNITS.

    Reference Administrative Instructions No. 1. dated 8.7.18., the following arrangements for lorries for supplies, personnel, and baggage is given on the attached schedules.

10th July, 1918.
                                            Lieut-Colonel,
                                A.A. & Q.M.G., 56th Division.

SCHEDULE - LORRIES.

DATE. JULY.	UNIT.	Duty.	No. of lorries.	Rendezvous.	Destination.
13th.	Divl. Train.	168th I.Bde. Group. Supplies.	9	AGNEZ Railhead, 8.30.a.m.	DENIER. (AX)
	168th Inf. Bde.	Baggage.	8	BERNEVILLE Baths 9 a.m.	LIGNEREUIL Area.
	1/5th Cheshire Rgt.	"	1	WANQUETIN School 9 a.m.	MIZIERES.
	Div. Grenade Dump.	Ammunition.	1	Div.Grenade Dump 8 a.m.	BLAVINCOURT.
	" Linen Store.	Linen.	2	BERNEVILLE Baths 9 a.m.	HERLENCOURT Area.
14th	Div. Train.	168th I.Bde.Group. Supplies.	8	AGNEZ Railhead, 8.30.a.m.	DENIER.
	"Bow Bells"	Baggage.	2	WARLUS: 1:p.m	HOUVIN.
	Div. Cinema.	"	1	WARLUS. 1.p.m.	LE CAUROY.
	A. D. M. S.	Medical Stores.	5	2/2nd Ldn.Fld.Ambce. AGNEZ. 8.a.m. and 1.p.m.	{GIVENCHY. (MK) GRAND RULLECOURT.
15th.	Div. Train.	167th I.Bde. Group. Supplies.	3	TINQUES Railhead.	MANIN.
	" "	169th I.Bde.Group. Supplies.	3	"	IZEL. {(MK)
	" "	Divl. Artillery. Supplies.	15	"	SIMENCOURT.
"A".	167th Inf. Bde.	Baggage.	3	WANQUETIN,Town Major's office, 2.p.m.	MANIN Area.
"B"	169th " "	"	3	BERNEVILLE Baths,2.p.m.	IZEL-LEZ-HAMEAU Area.
	G. R. E.	"	1	H.Q., WARLUS: 2 p.m.	HOUVIN.
	247th Emp.Coy.	"	1	" WARLUS: 8 p.m.	LE CAUROY.
	Divl. Hd.Qtrs.	"	5	" WARLUS: 9 a.m.	
	Div.Reception C.	"	2	" WARLUS: 2 p.m.	PENIN.
	Div. Arty.H.Q.	"	3	" WARLUS: 2 p.m.	HOUVIN - HOUVIGNEUL, Chateau GRAND RULLECOURT.
	A. D. M. S.	Medical Stores.	2	AGNEZ, 2 p.m.	

(2).

DATE. JULY.	UNIT.	Duty.	No. of lorries.	Rendezvous.	Destinations.
16th	Train.	Divl. Artillery. Supplies.	15	TINQUES Railhead.	SIMENCOURT.
	Div.Linen Store.	Linen.	2	BERNEVILLE Baths. 9 a.m.	BERLENCOURT.
	56th Bn.M.G.C.	Baggage.	2	WARLUS;No.1.Camp.9 A.m.	BERLENCOURT.
	" " "	Personnel.	25	WARLUS. 2 p.m.	LIENCOURT.
17th.	Div. Train.	Divl. Artillery. Supplies	17	TINQUES Railhead.	ETREE WAMIN.
	280th Bde.RFA.	Baggage.	5	BERNEVILLE Baths. 2 P.m.	BERLENCOURT Area.
	281st " "	"	5	SIMENCOURT. 2 p.m.	" " "
	T.M.Batteries.	"	8	" 2 p.m.	" " "
	D.A.C.	"	1	HOTEMESCOURT. 2 p.m.	" " "

REMARKS.

(AX). All lorries for one journey only unless otherwise stated.

(BX). Two journeys.

(CX). After completing journey with supplies to carry out "B" except those for Divl. Hd.Qtrs.

SECRET.   56th Division AQS/675.

ADMINISTRATIVE INSTRUCTIONS NO.3.
in connection with relief of the 56th Division.

1. **EMBUSSING.** (refce. 1/100000 Map Lens Sheet).

(a) The following Units will move by Bus on 15th instant.
    - 1/16th London Regt. ⎱ To PENIN.
    - Div. Reception Camp. ⎰
    - 169th Trench Mortar Battery. ⎱ To VILLERS-SIR-SIMON.
    - Div. Salvage Company. ⎰
    - 1/7th Middlesex Regiment. To AMBRINES.

   Units will enter the busses in the above order from the head of the convoy.

(b) <u>Embussing Point.</u>   WARLUS – WANQUETIN Road.
(c) <u>Head of Convoy.</u>   At BRIQUETERIE facing West.
(d) <u>Embussing Officer.</u> Major A.J.F. DAY, Commanding Div. Reception Camp.
(e) <u>Zero hour</u> (starting time) for Bus Convoy. – 6.30. a.m.
(f) The following will report to the Embussing Officer at Cross Roads in centre of WARLUS at 5.30.a.m.
   (i) Two guides from each unit who will be in possession of a state showing the embussing strength of their unit.
   (ii) A motor cyclist to be detailed by O.C., Signal Coy.
   (iii) A motor ambulance to be detailed by A.D.M.S.
   (iv) 4 Traffic Control police to be detailed by A.P.M.

(g) <u>Instructions.</u> Prior to embussing, units will wait in the area east or north of the BERNEVILLE – WARLUS – WANQUETIN Road. They must not cross to the area west or south of that road. Units will move on to the Embussing point as soon as their guides rejoin them. Guides will lead units to the portion of road space on which the busses allotted to them are, or will be, drawn up. Units will there be formed up clear of the right hand side of the road facing west, and will be equally distributed in parties of 6 groups for every 80 yards of road space, each group consisting of 25 for each bus and 20 for each seated lorry. All vehicles will be loaded simultaneously as soon as the vehicles and the troops are in position.

(h) Sections of the convoy will proceed to the villages in which units are billeted. Debussing will be carried out under the orders of the Senior Officer with each Village Section.

2. **MOVES OF TRANSPORT COLUMNS** on the 15th instant are given in Appendix "A" (attached).

3. **MOVES BY LIGHT RAILWAY.**
   167th and 169th Infantry Brigades (less the units named in para. 1.) and certain Units of Divisional Troops will move by Light and Metre Gauge Railways in accordance with the programme given in Appendix "B" (attached).

4. **BATHS.**
   The following baths will be run under Divl. arrangements from 14th instant, and will be stocked with clean linen. Bookings will be arranged with the N.C.O. in charge in each case.

	For troops billeted in:
IZEL-LES-HAMEAU.	IZEL-LES-HAMEAU, FARM DUFFINE, MANIN.
AMBRINES.	PENIN, VILLERS, AMBRINES, MAIZIERES, GIVENCHY.
BERLENCOURT.	MAGNICOURT, HOUVIN, ETREE WAMIN, LE CAUROY, BERLENCOURT, DENIER, SARS-LEZ-BOIS, LIGNEREUIL, LIENCOURT.

(2)

4. **BATHS.** (contd).

<u>For troops billeted in</u>

GRAND RULLECOURT.   GRAND RULLECOURT, BEAUFORT, BLAVINCOURT.

Swimming pools are situated at ETREE WAMIN near the trout ponds and BERLENCOURT near the baths.

5. **"BOW BELLS."** "Bow Bells" will perform for the last time in this area on the 13th instant.

Formations, and Units of Divisional Troops, requiring the "Bow Bells" for open-air performances should apply to this office.

6. Divisional Linen Store.   )
Divisional Waste Paper Dump.)
Divisional Tin Dump (for sheet)   VILLERS-SIR-SIMON.
                   tin)
Divisional Canteen.   )
Divisional Salvage Dump.   )

7. **SOLDER.** Solder kilns are established at the following places. Units will send their tins to the nearest kiln.

LE CAUROY, HOUVIN, PENIN, VILLERS, ETREE WAMIN, AMBRINES, LIENCOURT, MAIZIERES.

8. Soda Water Factory will remain at WANQUETIN for the present.

9. **SUPPLIES.**

Certain Units will draw supplies (and for the present fuel also) from Refilling Points, by First Line Transport, from day after arrival in the area.

A Supply Grouping Table is attached (Appendix "C").

10. Mobile Veterinary Section will be at VILLERS-SIR-SIMON.

                                                          Lieut-Colonel,

11th July, 1918.   A.A. & Q.M.G., 56th Division.

- DISTRIBUTION -

167th Inf. Bde.	A. P. M.	"G".
168th " "	D. A. D. O. S.	French Mission.
169th " "	Camp Commandant.	1st Canadian Div. "Q".
Divl. Artillery.	Div. M.T. Company.	2nd " " "Q".
56th Bn. M.G. Corps.	Div. Signal Coy.	Area Cdt. ARRAS.
1/5th Cheshire Regt.	247th Div. Employ. Coy.	" " DAINVILLE.
C. R. E.	D. A. D. V. S.	" " BERNEVILLE.
Divl. Train.	S.C.F. (C. of E).	" " WANQUETIN.
A. D. M. S.	S.C.F. (Non. C. of E).	" " LE CAUROY.
Offr. i/c S.A.A. Dump.	O.C., No.5.A. Sanitary Sec.	Div. Baths Officer.
Div. Water Service Officer.	Div. Burials Officer.	

APPENDIX "B" TO FOLLOW.

APPENDIX "A"

MOVES OF TRANSPORT COLUMNS ON 15th JULY, 1918.

Serial No.	UNITS.	Commander.	Starting Point.	Time.	ROUTE.	Destination.	Remarks.
1.	167th Infantry Bde. 416th Field Coy. R.E. 2/3rd London F.Ambce. (less minimum number of vehicles required for cooking breakfast for bus and L.R. parties, and vehicles which have been working after midnight). No. 2 Coy. Divl. Train.	To be appointed by B.G.Commdg. 167th Inf. Brigade.	WANQUETIN CHURCH.	7-30 A.M.	No restrictions. Not to move onto main BERNEVILLE—WARLUS—WANQUETIN—HAUTEVILLE Road until Bus Convoy has passed.	MANIN AREA.	Field Coy. to HOUVIN—HOUVIGNEUL.
2.	168th Infantry Bde. 513th Field Coy. R.E. 2/4th London F.Ambce. (less minimum number of vehicles required for cooking breakfast for bus and L.R. parties, and vehicles which have been working after midnight). No. 4 Coy. Divl. Train.	To be appointed by B.G.Commdg. 168th Inf. Brigade.	BRIQUETERIE (On WARLUS—WANQUETIN Road).	7-30 A.M.	Do.	IZEL—LEZ—HAMEAU AREA.	Field Coy. to HOUVIN—HOUVIGNEUL.
3.	Divisional Head Qrs. Divl. Signal Coy. (less Nos. 2,3,4 & 5 Sections). 2/1st London F.Ambce.	O.C. Signal Coy.	BRIQUETERIE (On WARLUS—WANQUETIN Road).	8 AM	No restrictions.	LE CAUROY—HOUVIGNEUL AREA.	Field Ambce. to join Column as it passes its transport lines

Serial No.	U N I T S.	Commander.	Starting Point.	Time	R O U T E.	Destination.	Remarks.
4.	Remaining vehicles of 167th Infantry Bde. Column.		As arranged by B.G.C. 167th I.Bde.		No restrictions.	---	---
5.	Remaining vehicles of 169th Infantry Bde. Column.		As arranged by B.G.C. 169th I.Bde.		MONTENESCOURT— HADARCQ.	---	---

Serial Nos. 1, 2 and 3 will halt from 9-30 A.M. to 10-30 A.M. to water and feed.

APPENDIX "3".

PROVISIONAL TRAIN ARRANGEMENTS FOR 15TH JULY. (Refce. 1/40000 Map, Sheet 51.C)

Detraining {(M) Metre Gauge. (L) Light Rly.

Serial No.	UNIT.	Strength, all ranks.	To be entrained by.	Entraining Point.	Detraining Point.	
1.	167th.I.Bde. H.Q.	115	4 a.m.	DAINVILLE WOOD (B.28.c.)	GIVENCHY ROAD (J.25.c)	(M) (AX)
2.	1st London Regt.	680	"	-- do --	-- do --	(M) (AX)
3.	167th T.M.Battery.	70	"	-- do --	-- do --	(M) (AX)
4.	8th Middlesex Regt.	700	"	-- do --	J.35.central.	(M) (AX)
5.	169th I.Bde. H.Q.	127	11 a.m.	DAINVILLE WOOD (L.23.c.)	HERMAVILLE ROAD SPUR. J.5.e.	(L)
6.	2nd London Regt.	304	"	-- do --	-- do --	(L)
7.	5th London Regt.	834	"	-- do --	-- do --	(L)
8.	416th Fld.Coy.R.E.	127	11.30.a.m.	DAINVILLE WOOD (L.23.c.)	ETREE WAMIN.	(M) (AX)
9.	56th Bn.M.G.Corps.	150	"	-- do --	LIENCOURT.	(M) (AX)
10.	513th Fld.Coy. R.E.	127	"	-- do --	ETREE WAMIN.	(M) (AX)
11.	2/1st. Ldn.Fld.Ambce.	152	To be notified later. After 3 p.m.	Road Crossing K.14.a.4.0.	ETREE WAMIN.	(M)
12.	Divl. Hd.Qtrs.	30	-- do --	-- do --	LE CAUROY	(M)
13.	247th Employ.Coy.	238	-- do --	-- do --	"	(M)
14.	2/3rd Ldn.Fld.Ambce.	152	-- do --	-- do --	GIVENCHY ROAD J.25.c.	(M)

PROVISIONAL TRAIN ARRANGEMENTS FOR 15TH JULY.

| 15. | 56th Bn.M.G.Corps. | 450 | 4 a.m. | DAINVILLE OOD. | LIENCOURT. | (M) (AX) |

All Units marked (AX) tranship at RIVER JUNCTION J.23.Central. from Light Railway to Metre Gauge.

P.T.O.

1.   Brigadier-General Commanding 167th Infantry Brigade will detail an Officer not below the rank of Captain to supervise the entraining of Serial Nos. 1 to 4. This Officer will travel with the last train of this series. Similarly an Officer will be detailed to supervise the transshipping at RIVER JUNCTION; this Officer will travel on the first train of this series.

2.   Brigadier-General Commanding 169th Infantry Brigade will similarly detail an Officer to supervise the entraining of Serial Nos. 5 to 7.

3.   O.C., Machine Gun Detachment serial no. 9 will be responsible for supervising the entraining and transshipping of serial Nos. 8 to 10.

4.   O.C., Employment Company will be responsible for supervising the entraining of serial Nos. 11 to 14.

5.   O.C., Machine Gun Battn. will detail an Officer to supervise the entraining and transshipping of serial Nos. 15.

APPENDIX "C".

SUPPLY GROUPING TABLE.

Supplies drawn from Refilling Point.	REFILLING POINTS.				REMARKS.
	167th Bde. Group.	168th Bde. Group.	169th Bde. Group.	Divl. Arty. Group.	
14/7/1918.	WANQUETIN	WANQUETIN	WANQUETIN	SIMENCOURT	There will be no alteration in existing Supply Groups except as shown below. Supplies for D.H.Q., C.R.E., C.R.A., Signals, Employt. Coy. Signal Co. R.E., M.V.S., D.A.D.O.S., 40th Bde. R.G.A., on 13th Bde. Refilling Point. Supplies for 56th Div. H.G.Bn. on Div. Arty. R.P. All supplies delivered from Refilling Points by Train Transport.
15/7/1918.	WANQUETIN	DENIER	WANQUETIN	SIMENCOURT	Supplies for Units on Refilling Points as on 14th. 168th Bde. Group supplies to be drawn by First Line Transport at ? A.M. All other supplies drawn from R.P. and delivered by Train Transport.
16/7/1918.	GIVENCHY LE NOBLE MANIN Road near MANIN	DENIER	VILLERS-SIR-SIMON	SIMENCOURT	Supplies for Div.Q., C.R.E., C.R.A., Signals, Employt. Coy. Sig. Coy. R.E., L.V.C., D.A.D.O.S., T.M.O., on 168th Bde. R.P. Supplies for other Units as on 15th. 137th, 138th & 169th Bde. Groups draw from R.P. by First Line Transport at ? A.M. Other Units by Train Transport.
17/7/1918.	GIVENCHY LE NOBLE MANIN Road near MANIN	DENIER	VILLERS-SIR-SIMON	SIMENCOURT	Supplies for 56th Div. H.G.Bn. on 168th Bde. R.P. Supplies of Other Units as on 13th. 137th, 138th & 139th Bde. Groups draw from R.P. by First Line Transport at ? A.M. Other Units by Train Transport.
18/7/1918 and subsequently.	GIVENCHY LE NOBLE MANIN Road Near MANIN	DENIER	VILLERS-SIR-SIMON	ETREE-WAMIN	Supplies for 415th, 2/1st Ldn. F.Ambce. on Div. Arty. R.P. C.R.E. and 2/1st Ldn. F.Ambce. on Div. Arty. R.P. Supplies of other Units as on 17th. Except Div. Arty. C.R.E. and Employt. Coy., all supplies will be drawn from R.P. by First Line Transport at ? A.M.

Fuel in New Area will be issued from Brigade Refilling Points until a Divisional Fuel Dump is established. Location of Divisional Fuel Dump will be indicated later.

SECRET.   56th Division AQS/675.

ALL FORMATIONS AND UNITS.

Reference Administrative Instructions No. 3.(AQS/675) dated 11.7.18.

(1)   Appendix "B". Provisional Train Arrangements, is confirmed.

(2)   Length of time for journey, Serial Nos. 1 to 10 (inclusive) is 4 to 5 hours.

(3)   Serial Nos. 11, 12, 13, 14, will be entrained by 4.30. p.m.

12th July, 1918.

Lieut-Colonel,
A.A. & Q.M.G., 56th Division.

SECRET.

56th Division AQS/675.

ALL FORMATIONS AND UNITS.

Addition to Administrative Instructions.

Field Post Offices.

Field Post Offices will be located at Refilling Points in the new area.

12th July, 1918.

Lieut-Colonel,
A.A. & Q.M.G., 56th Division.

App: E

SECRET.   56th Division AQS 675.

56th DIVISION.
LOCATIONS ON COMPLETION OF RELIEF.

Divisional Headquarters.	ROELLECOURT.
167th Inf. Bde. H.Q.	ORLENCOURT.
7th Middlesex Regt.	FREVILLERS.
8th Middlesex Regt.	OSTREVILLE.
1st London Regt.	MONCHY BRETON.
167th T.M.Bty.	ORLENCOURT.
168th Inf. Bde. H.Q.	CHELERS.
4th London Regt.	TINCQUES.
13th London Regt.	BAILLEUL AUX CORNAILLES.
14th London Regt.	CHELERS.
168th T.M.Bty.	TINCQUES.
169th Inf. Bde. H.Q.	DIEVAL.
2nd London Regt.	DIEVAL.
5th London Regt.	LA THIEULOYE.
16th London Regt.	LA COMTE.
169th T.M.Bty.	DIEVAL.
56th Battn. M.G.Corps.	MAGNICOURT.
1/5th Cheshire Regt.	AVERDOINGT.
247th (Divnl) Employment Co.	ROELLECOURT.
C.R.E.	BEUGIN.
416th Field Co. R.E.	MARESQUEL. (Corps School)
512th Field Co. R.E.	BEUGIN.
513th Field Co. R.E.	BEUGIN.
A.D.M.S.	ROELLECOURT.
2/1st London Field Ambulance.	HOUVELIN.
2/2nd London Field Ambulance.	AUBIGNY.
2/3rd London Field Ambulance.	LIGNY ST. FLOCHEL.
C.R.A.	
280th Brigade R.F.A.	
281st Brigade R.F.A.	
56th Div. Ammunition Column.	
Divisional Train H.Q.	ROELLECOURT.
No. 1 Company.	
No. 2 Company.	ROCOURT.
No. 3 Company.	TINCQUETTE.
No. 4 Company.	DIEVAL.
D.A.D.V.S.	ROELLECOURT.
Mobile Veterinary Section.	ROELLECOURT.
D.A.D.O.S.	ROELLECOURT.
Div. Baths Officer. }	TINQUES
Div. Claims Officer. }	
56th M.T.Co.	TINCQUETTE.
56th Divnl. Reception Camp.	BETHENCOURT.
Div. Gas Officer. }	ROELLECOURT
Div. Salvage Officer. }	
Div. Canteen.	TINQUES
Div. Ammunition Dump.	MONCHY BRETON.
Railhead for personnel.	TINCQUES.

TRANSPORT LINES are at same location as Unit concerned.

14th July 1918.

A.C. Dundas Major,
D.A.A.G., 56th Division.

SECRET.

War Diary App. F

AQS 375.

ADMINISTRATIVE INSTRUCTIONS No. 4
with reference to 56th DIVISIONAL ORDER No. 182.

1. The arrangements for embussing notified in para. 1 of Administrative Instructions No. 3 hold good with the exception of the destinations which are amended as shown below.

2. The entraining points and times notified in Appendix "B" of Administrative Instructions No. 3 hold good. Detraining points are amended as shewn below. All moves will be by Light Railway. Serial Nos. 11, 12 and 13 will entrain at BERNEVILLE R.1.c.7.2.

3. Moves of Transport Columns notified in Appendix "A" of Administrative Instructions No. 3 hold good. No restrictions as to routes. Destinations will be amended as shown below.

4. The amended detraining and debussing points and locations of units are as follows :-

UNIT.	DETRAINING or DEBUSSING POINT.	DESTINATION.
Divisional H.Q.		
Div. Employment Co.		
D.A.D.O.S.	U.8.c.	ROELLECOURT.
Train H.Q.		
A.D.M.S.		
167th Inf. Bde. Group.		
167th Bde. H.Q.	MONCHY BRETON.	ORLENCOURT.
1st London Regt.	" "	MONCHY BRETON.
8th Middlesex Regt.	" "	OSTREVILLE.
7th Middlesex Regt.	FREVILLERS. (by Bus)	FREVILLERS.
167th T.M.Bty.	MONCHY BRETON.	ORLENCOURT.
416th Field Co.	DIEVAL.	BEUGIN.
No. 2 Co. Train.		ROCOURT.
2/1st Field Ambce.	Road Crossing O.31.c.	HOUVELIN.
✶ 56th M.G.Bn.	U.8.c.	MAGNICOURT-EN-COMTE.
168th Inf. Bde. Group.		
168th Bde. H.Q.		CHELERS.
1 Battn.		"
1 Battn.		TINCQUES.
1 Battn.		BAILLEUL AUX CORNAILLES.
168th T.M.Bty.		TINCQUES.
512th Field Co.		BEUGIN.
No. 3 Co. Train.		TINCQUES.
2/2nd Field Ambce.		LIGNY St. FLOCHEL.
Div. Reception Camp.	BETHENCOURT. (by Bus)	BETHENCOURT.
Mob. Vet. Sec.		TINCQUES.
Pioneer Battn.		AVERDOINGT.

UNIT.	DETRAINING or DEBUSSING POINT.		DESTINATION.
169th Inf. Bde. GROUP.			
169th Bde. H.Q.	DIEVAL.		DIEVAL.
2nd London Regt.	"		"
5th London Regt.	Road Crossing N.30.a.		LA THIEULOYE.
✱ 16th London Regt.	LA COMTE.	(by Bus)	LA COMTE.
169th T.M.Bty.	DIEVAL.	(by bus)	DIEVAL.
513th Field Co.	DIEVAL.		BEUGIN.
No. 4 Co. Train.	------		DIEVAL.
2/3rd Field Ambce.	------		AUBIGNY. (Divisional Rest Station).
R.E.H.Q.,	------		BEUGIN.

✱ LA COMTE and MAGNICOURT will not be free before 9 pm 15th inst.

5. Supply Grouping Table will be issued later.

6. Area Commandants are located at :-

DIEVAL.
MAGNICOURT.
CHELERS.
ANVIN.

[signature]
Lieut. Colonel.
14. 7. 18. A.A. & Q.M.G., 56th Division.

- DISTRIBUTION -

167th Inf. Bde.	A.P.M.	"G".
168th Inf. Bde.	D.A.D.O.S.	French Mission.
169th Inf. Bde.	Camp Commandant.	1st Canadian Div. "Q".
Div. Artillery.	Div. M.T.Company.	2nd.Canadian Div. "Q".
56th Bn. M.G.Corps.	Div. Signal Coy.	Area Cdt. ARRAS.
1/5th Cheshire Regt.	247th Div. Employ Co.	" " DAINVILLE.
C.R.E.	D.A.D.V.S.	" " BERNEVILLE.
Div. Train.	S.C.F. (C of E.)	" " WANQUETIN.
A.D.M.S.	S.C.F. (Non C. of E)	" " LE CAUROY
Offr. i/c S.A.A. Dump.	O.C. No. 5A San. Sec.	" " DIEVAL.
Div. Baths Officer.	XVIIth Corps "Q".	" " MAGNICOURT.
Div. Water Service Officer.		" " CHELERS.
Div. Burials Officer.		" " ANVIN.

APPENDIX B.1. 56th Divn.
AQS/675.
War Diary

56TH DIVISION.

15th July. Light Railway.

Serial No.	UNIT.	Strength.	Time of departure.	Entraining Point.	Detraining Point.
1.	167th Inf. Bde. H.Q.	115	4 A.M.	DAINVILLE WOOD (L.28.c.)	MONCHY BRETON.
2.	1st London Regt.	680	"	---do---	---do---
3.	167th T.M. Battery.	70	"	---do---	---do---
4.	8th Middlesex Regt.	700	"	---do---	---do---
5.	169th Inf. Bde. H.Q.	127	11 A.M.	---do---	DIEVAL.
6.	2nd London Regt.	804	"	---do---	DIEVAL.
7.	5th " "	834	"	---do---	Road Crossing N.30.a.
8.	513th Fld. Coy. R.E.	127	11.30.A.M.	---do---	DIEVAL.
9.	Machine Gun Battn.	277	"	---do---	U.8.c. (for MAGNICOURT)
10.	Divl. Headquarters.	30	"	---do---	U.8.c. (for ROELLECOURT)
11.	2/1st London Fld. Amb.	152	9 P.M.	BERNEVILLE(B.6.)	O.31.c. (for HOUVELIN)
12.	247th Employ. Coy.	238	"	---do---	U.8.c. (for ROELLECOURT)

16th July. Light Railway.

Serial No.	UNIT.	Strength.	Time of departure.	Entraining Point.	Detraining Point.
13.	Machine Gun Battn.	450	4 A.M.	DAINVILLE WOOD.	U.8.c. (for MAGNICOURT)

All the above moves are by Light Railway throughout.
Officers to supervise entraining will be detailed by Brig-Genl. Commanding 167th Inf. Bde. for serials 1. to 4:
" " " " " " " " " " 169th " " " for " 5 to 7.
" " " " " " " " " " O.C., M.G.Battn. for serials 8. to 10.
" " " " " " " " " " Officer Commdg. Div. Employment Coy. for serials 11 and 12.
" " " " " " " " " " detailed by O.C., H.Q. Battn. for serial 13.

Appendix "B" issued with Administrative Instructions No.3. and Administrative Instructions No.4.
This table supersedes Appendix "B" issued with Administrative Instructions No.3. and Administrative Instructions No.4. where they differ from this table.

SECRET.   56th Division No. AQS/675.

ADMINISTRATIVE INSTRUCTIONS No. 5
with reference to 56th Divisional Order No. 182.

1. **SUPPLIES AND FUEL.**

   (A) For the present, supply grouping will remain normal.
   (B) Train Transport will continue to deliver supplies to units of 168th and 169th Brigade Supply Groups.
   (C) Units of 167th Brigade Supply Group will draw supplies from Refilling Point at ROCOURT, with First Line Transport, at 8-30 A.M. daily commencing 16th instant.
   (D) Fuel will be drawn from Refilling Points by Units' First Line Transport.
   Refilling Points are situated as follows:-
   167th Brigade Group.   ROCOURT.
   168th Brigade Group.   Near CROSS ROADS at TINQUES on
                           ARRAS - St. POL Road.
   169th Brigade Group.   No. 4 Coys' Lines DIEVAL.

2. Training Ammunition Dump will be established at MONCHY BRETON by 15th inst. Authority to draw from this dump will be obtained from Divisional Headquarters ("A & Q").

3. Baths are allotted to Brigade Groups as below:-

   167th Inf. Bde. Group.   ROCOURT   100 perhour
                            FREVILLERS   80   "
   168th Inf. Bde. Group.   TINQUES   100   "
   169th Inf. Bde. Group.   MAGNICOURT.   100   "

   These Baths will be run under Divisional arrangements as soon as personnel can be transferred to them from the LE CAUROY Area.

4. Leave parties on train at TINQUES at 8-20 A.M. on the day before sailing. They may stay overnight at the Divisional Reception Camp at BETHENCOURT

5. **LOCATIONS.**
   No. 3. Coy. Div. Train   TINCQUETTE (instead of TINQUES):
   Mobile Veterinary Section   ROELLECOURT (instead of TINQUES):
   Canteen   )
   Divl. Linen Store)   TINQUES.
   Sheet Tin Dump)
   Waste Paper Dump)   ROELLECOURT.

   SOLDER KILNS at TINQUES, CHELERS, BAILLEUL, AVERDOINGT, FREVILLERS,
         HOUVELIN, MONCHY BRETON, DIEVAL, LA THIEULOYE.

6. The "Bow Bells" and the Cinema will not re-open for the present.

7. **REDUCTION OF KIT.**

   In the event of the Division being required to move by Rail whilst in G.H.Q. Reserve it is practically certain that no lorries will be available for moving surplus kit to the new area. It is hoped that it will be possible to arrange for additional transport to convey
                                                                certain

                                                                P.T.O.

certain indispensable articles such as
- Additional Lewis Guns.
- Monkey puzzle anti-aircraft mountings.
- Kits of Officers supernumerary to establishment.
- Chauffeurs.
- Field Forges.
- Shoemakers' Tools.

to entraining stations for conveyance in Troop Trains.

Other Battle Stores must be carried on existing transport or "on the man".

It is essential that baggage such as Officers' Kits, Mess Stores, Office Stores etc., should be reduced at once to the absolute minimum. Formations and Units will report as early as possible how many lorry loads of baggage and stores can be dispensed with, and facilities will be provided for transporting them to the Divl. Dump at WAVRANS. Clothing etc., in Quartermasters' Stores should be kept down to the lowest possible working minimum.

Lieut-Colonel,
A.A. & Q.M.G., 56th Division.

14th July, 1918.

DISTRIBUTION.

167th Inf. Bde.	A. P. M.	"G"
168th Inf. Bde.	D. A. D. O. S.	French Mission.
169th Inf. Bde.	Camp Commdt.	1st Canadian Div. "Q"
Div. Artillery.	Div. H.T.Coy.	2nd " "
56th Bn. M.G.Corps	Div. Signal Coy.	Area Cdt. ARRAS.
1/5th Cheshire Regt.	247th D.Employt. Coy.	" " DAINVILLE.
C. R. E.	D. A. D. V. S.	" " BERNEVILLE.
Divl. Train	S.C.F. (C. of E.)	" " WANQUETIN.
A. D. M. S.	S.C.F. (Non C. of E.)	" " LE CAUROY.
O. i/c S.A.A.Dump.	O.C. No. 5A San. Sect.	" " DIEVAL
Baths Officer	XVIIth Corps "Q"	" " HAGNICOURT.
D.Water Service O.	Divl. Reception Camp	" " CHELERS.
D. Burials Officer		" " ANVIN.

App.-H-2 War Diary

56th Division AQS/675.

SCHEDULE. - LORRIES (2).

DATE JULY.	Serial Nos.	U N I T.	Duty.	No. of lorries.	Rendezvous.	Destination.
15th.	1.	416th Field Coy. R.E.	Personnel.	6	ARRAS, 5.30, A.M.	TINQUES Railhead. 8. A.M.
	2.	Divl. Train.	Supplies & Fuel.	7	TINQUES Railhead, 7. A.M.	RJCOURT.
				8	— do —	Cross roads, ARRAS-ST POL Road - TINQUES
						DIEVAL.
	3.	167th Inf. Brigade.	169th " Baggage.	7 8	— do — NANQUETIN (Town) Major's Office 9. A.M.	MONCHY BRETON Area.
	4.	O. R. E.	- do -	1	H.Q. WARLUS, 9 A.M.	BEUGIN.
	5.	247th Employ. Coy. } Divl. Hd.Qtrs. }	- do -	6	— do —(3 — 9 A.M) — do —(5 - 2 P.M)	ROELLECOURT. — do —
	6.	168th Inf. Brigade.	- do -	8	LIGNEREUIL, 2 P.M.	CHELERS Area.
	7.	169th "	- do -	8	BERNEVILLE Baths 2 P.M.	DIEVAL Area.
	8.	Div.Reception Camp.	- do -	2	No.1,Camp,WARLUS, 2,P.M.	BETHENCOURT.
	9.	1/5th Cheshire Regt.	- do -	1	GOUY-EN-TERNOIS, 2 P.M.	AVERDOINGT.
	10.	A. D. M. S.	Medical Stores	2	AGNEZ, 2 P.M.	CHELERS Area.

E M B U S S I N G   T A B L E.   Reference 1/40000 Map, Sheet 36.B.

Serial No.	Bus Group Commander.	Troops.	Embussing Point.	Head of Convoy.	Routes to Embussing Point.
1.	Brig-General Commanding 168th Infantry Brigade.	168th Inf. Brigade. 56th Bn.M.G.C.(less 2 Coys) Div. Hd.Qrs. H.Q. & No.1.Sec.Div. Signal Coy. H.Q.Div. R.E., 512th Fld.Coy. R.E., 2/2nd Ldn.Fld. Amb. Div.Reception Camp.	MONCHY BRETON - CHELERS Road.	CHELERS Cross Roads. (U.16.d.5.2.) facing East.	No restrictions.
2.	Brig-General Commanding 167th Infantry Brigade.	1/5th Cheshire Rgt. 1 Coy.M.G.Bn. 167th Inf. Bde. 416th Fld. Coy.R.E.(if available) 2/1st Ldn.Fld.Ambce. Div.Employment Coy. (including Traffic Control Police).	MONCHY BRETON - CHELERS Road.	Tail at MONCHY BRETON. Road Junction, U.1.a.9.9.	No restrictions.
3.	Brig-General Commanding 169th Infantry Brigade.	169th Inf. Brigade. 1 Coy. M.G.Battn. 513th Fld.Coy. R.E. Ldn.Fld.Ambce. 2/3rd	DEVAL - OURTON Road between Road Junction, I.34.c.38. and Road Junction. O.8.central.	May face in either direction.	Field Ambulance not to pass through either BAILLEUL, or MONCHY BRETON.

Units will embuss from the head of the convoy in the order given above.

E M B U S S I N G   T A B L E.   Reference 1/40000 Map, Sheet 51.C.

Serial No.	Bus Group Commander.	Troops.	Embussing Point.	Head of Convoy.	Routes to Embussing Point.
1.	Brig-General Commanding 168th Infantry Brigade.	168th Inf. Brigade. 56th Bn.M.G.Corps.(less 2 Coys.) Divl. Hd.Qtrs. Hd.Qtrs & No.1.Sect.Div. Signal.Coy. Div.R.E. Hd.Qtrs. 512th Fld.Coy. R.E., 2/2nd Ld.Fld.Ambce.	LIENCOURT STATION - BEAUFORT HALT Road.	Either at LIENCOURT STATION or at BEAUFORT HALT.	No restrictions.
2.	Brig-General Commanding 167th Infantry Brigade.	167th Inf. Brigade. 1 Coy. 56th Bn.M.G.C. 416th Fld.Coy.R.E. 2/1st Ldn.Fld.Ambce. Div.Reception Camp, Div.Employment Coy. (including Traffic Control Police).	MAGNICOURT-SUR-GANCHE - AMBRINES Road.	AMBRINES (Rd.Junction I.8.b.7.8) facing East.	Troops in BEAUFORT to move via MANIN. M.G.Coy. to move via DENIER. Employment Coy. to move via BERLENCOURT. Otherwise no restrictions.
3.	Brig-General Commanding 169th Infantry Brigade.	169th Inf. Brigade. 1 Coy. 56th Bn.M.G.G. 1/5th Cheshire Rgt. 513th Fld.Coy.R.E. 2/3rd Ldn.Fld.Ambce.	MAIZIERES - PENIN Road.	PENIN. (Road junction G.22.c.7.4.) facing East.	M.G.Coy. to move via SARS-LES-BOIS and MAIZIERES. No Units to pass through AMBRINES. Otherwise no restrictions.

Units will embuss from the head of the convoy in the order given above.

SECRET.   APPENDIX "A".

Instructions for Move of the Division (less Artillery)
by Bus whilst in G.H.Q. Reserve.

1.   Troops will be prepared to ombuss in accordance with the attached Embussing Table.

2.   On receipt of the order "Bus Move" the following action will be taken :-

(a) By all Units. Wire embussing strength (all ranks) to this office through the usual channels; and in the case of Divisional Troops repeat the wire to their Bus Group Commander.
(b) By Divl. Train. Return Baggage Wagons to Units.
(c) By all Units.   Load transport and park it ready to move at 1 hour's notice.
(d) By Infantry Brigades. Report to this office names and Units of Officers appointed Brigade Group   Embussing and Debussing Officers and O.C., Brigade Group Horse Transport Columns.
(e) By Infantry Brigades. Collect Billeting parties of their Bus Group and notify this office where a lorry should be sent to pick them up.
(f) By all concerned. Take action in accordance with the subsequent paragraphs of these instructions.

3.   A zero-hour for each convoy will be notified from Div.Hd.Qtrs. All Units will move to Embussing point under the orders of Bus Group Commanders. Moves of Units from billets will be timed so as to enable them to reach their sections of the embussing point at Zero - 30 minutes. Units will not actually move on to the Embussing point until their guides (see para.5) rejoin them.

4. Detailing of Personnel to Vehicles.

A Bus Convoy consists both of Busses which hold 1 Officer and 25 O.Rs and of Seated Lorries which hold 1 Officer and 20 O.Rs. When possible, information as to the arrangement of the two classes of vehicles in the convoy will be obtained in advance by these Headquarters and passed on to Bus Group Commanders. As soon as a Unit is informed of the class of vehicles which it will be allotted and their order in the convoy, personnel should be told off in groups accordingly; preferably before leaving billets. It may not however be possible to obtain this information before the Bus Convoy arrives on the Embussing Point.

5. Embussing arrangements.

Each Infantry Brigade will detail an Officer not below the rank of Captain to supervise the Embussing. This Officer, accompanied by at least two guides from each Unit of the Bus Group, who must know the latest embussing strengths of their Units, will be at the head of the embussing point at Zero - 1 hour. He will meet the O.C. Bus Convoy there as soon as the latter arrives. If the Embussing Officer is not already in possession of information as to the composition of the Bus Convoy he will obtain the information from O.C. Bus Convoy. When he knows the composition of the Convoy he will divide up the Embussing point into Unit Sections, allotting 80 yards for 6 vehicles, and will then despatch one guide to meet each Unit with instructions to lead the Unit on to its section of road space.

Guides must know the number and distribution of busses and seated lorries in their sections of the Convoy. After moving on to the Embussing point Units will be formed up clear of the road, on the right hand side if possible, and facing towards the head of the Convoy,

(2)

5. **Embussing arrangements (contd).**

the troops being equally distributed in parties of 6 groups (of 25 for a Bus and 20 for a lorry) for every 80 yards of road space. All vehicles will be loaded simultaneously as soon as the troops and the vehicles are in position. The Embussing Officer will travel on the last vehicle. Similarly each Infantry Brigade will detail an Officer to supervise the Debussing. This Officer will travel on the leading vehicle of the convoy. Embussing and Debussing Officers will wear the Blue arm-band whilst on duty, as a distinguishing badge.

6. The following will be detailed to report to Embussing Officers at the head of each Embussing point at Zero – 1 hour; and to Debussing Officers on arrival in the new Area.
   (a) 1 Motor Cyclist by O.C. Signal Company.
   (b) 1 Motor Ambulance by A.D.M.S.
   (c) 4 Traffic control police by A.P.M.

7. The following will be taken with the men in the busses :–
   (a) Machine Guns and at least 10 filled belts.
   (b) Lewis Guns and at least 20 filled Drums.
   (c) Stokes Mortars.

8. One lorry will be allotted to each Bus Group Commander for conveyance of billeting parties of the Group.

9. Infantry Battalions will move in Fighting Order. Their packs will be left in one dump in each Brigade area and guarded under Brigade arrangements. These Dumps will be cleared under Divisional arrangements. Locations of dumps will be notified to this office.

10. Horse Transport and Bicycles. Will move in columns constituted similarly to Brigade Bus Groups, and under the orders of Bus Group Commanders.
   M.G.Battn. Transport will move with Serial No.1. Bde. Group.
   Train H.Q. Transport " " " " " 2 " "
   Mob.Veterinary Sect. " " " " " 3 " "
   Train Companies will move with the Brigade Groups to which they are affiliated.
   Each Infantry Brigade will detail a Senior Officer to command the Brigade Group Transport Column.
A portion of the S.A.A. Section, D.A.C. will move with each Brigade Group Transport Column.

11. **Supplies.**

The unexpended portion of the current day's rations will be carried on the man. Rations for day of departure plus 1 will also be carried on the man if time permits of their being issued. In the event of the Bus party overtaking the Horse Transport party and arriving at their destination before the Horse Transport party, supplies which would ordinarily be refilled and delivered to Units by Horse Transport will be delivered to Units by M.T. in detail, under the direction of Supply Officers.
   The Horse Transport party will be rationed for day of departure; and, if time permits of issue, for day of departure plus 1 also; and will carry those rations.
   Rations of the Horse Transport party for consumption on day of departure plus 1 (if necessary), day of departure plus 2, and any following days, while still on the march, will be delivered on route, in detail, by M.T. under the direction of Supply Officer.
   If H.T. party reaches its destination before Bus Party, supplies for both Bus Party and H.T. party will be picked up from Refilling Points in the New Area in the normal manner.

12. **Motor Transport.** All Motor Cars, Motor Ambulances and Motor Cycles will move on the days on which the Units, to which they belong, embus.

War Diary

Amendment to Appendix "A" of "Instructions for Move of the Division (less Artillery) by Bus whilst in G.H.Q. Reserve.

Issued under this office No. G. 3/894 of 15/7/1918.

Cancel first sub-paragraph of para: 5 from "Each Infantry Bde. ———— Road space", and substitute:—

Each Infantry Brigade will detail an Officer not below the rank of Captain to supervise the embussing.

Each Unit of the Bus Group will detail an advance party, consisting of 1 Officer, 1 guide, and markers on the scale of 1 per Company or equivalent unit, to report to the Embussing Officer at the head of the convoy at Zero — 1 hour and to work under his orders. The O.C. party must know the latest embussing strength of his Unit.

The duties of the Embussing Officer will be.
(1) To keep in touch with the M.T. Officer commanding Bus Convoy.
(2) To ascertain from the O.C., Bus Convoy the composition of the convoy; if he does not know it already.
(3) When he knows the composition of the convoy to allot road spaces (6 vehicles = 80 yards of road space) or vehicles; if they have arrived, in accordance with the strength of Units.
(4) Hand over the allotted road space, or section of vehicles, to Units' advance parties.
(5) Instruct advance parties to act as follows:—
   (a) To send back a guide to the unit to lead it to its allotted section of vehicles or road space.
   (b) To sub-allot vehicles or road spaces to each company or equivalent unit and to post a marker at the head or tail of each company's area (according to the direction from which the unit is marching on to the embussing point) to point it out to the troops.
(6) Inform the O.C., Bus Convoy when the troops are all embussed, and ready to move.

SECRET.

APPENDIX "B" to 56th Divn. No. G.3/894 of 15.7.18.
Instructions for move of the Division by ~~Strategical~~ Train whilst in G.H.Q. Reserve.

56th Division AQS/677.

1. **STATIONS OF ENTRAINMENT.**
Units will entrain at stations as shewn in Table "C", under the orders of the Brig-Generals Commanding Brigade Groups and Divisional Artillery and of Divisional Headquarters in the case of Units of Divl. Troops not affiliated to Infantry Brigades.

2. **TIMES OF ENTRAINMENT.**
The order of entrainment is shown in Table "D" (to be issued later) Trains from each station will leave at 3 hour intervals.
All Transport will arrive at Stations of Entrainment 3 hours and personnel 1½ hours before the time of departure of the train in which they are to travel.

3. **LOADING PARTY.**
Each Infantry Brigade will detail a Company from their last train load as a loading party for all trains, except those conveying Units of Divisional Artillery, which leave their respective entraining stations. These Companies, with their cookers and rations, will report to the R.T.O., at the entraining station 4 hours before the first train is due to leave. They will travel by the last train of their Brigade Group.

4. **UNLOADING PARTY.**
Similarly each Infantry Brigade will detail a Company from their first train load as unloading party for all trains arriving at their respective detraining stations, except those conveying Units of Divl. Artillery. They will report to the R.T.O., immediately on arrival at the station of detrainment. They will be rationed by their own Unit and will rejoin their unit after the last train of their Brigade Group has been unloaded.

5. **DIVISIONAL ARTILLERY** will make their own arrangements for loading and unloading parties.

6. **FIELD COMPANIES.**
Each Field Coy. R.E., will detail 1 Officer and 60 O.Rs to assist the permanent loading and unloading parties at Stations of Entrainment and Detrainment in dealing with their own Transport. These parties will report to the Officers referred to in para. 7., 3 hours before the departure of the trains by which the Field Coys. travel, and to the Officers referred to in para. 8. on arrival.

7. **ENTRAINMENT OFFICERS.**
Each Infantry Brigade will detail two Officers, not below the rank of Captain, to report to the R.T.O., of their respective entraining station 4 hours before the first train is due to leave, to assist him in the general supervision of the entrainment of the Division (less Artillery). The Officers will work in two reliefs and will travel by the last train of their Brigade Group. The C.R.A. will make corresponding arrangements for Officers to assist in the entrainment of the Divisional Artillery.

8. **DETRAINMENT OFFICERS.**
Similarly each Infantry Brigade will detail 2 Officers to proceed by the first train, and report for the same purpose to the R.T.O. at the Station of Detrainment. Similar arrangements will be made by the C.R.A. for supervising the detraining of the Divisional Artillery.

(2)

9. O.C., Signal Coy. will detail a Motor Cyclist orderly for duty at each station of entrainment and detrainment. They will report to the Officers mentioned in paras. 7 and 8.

10. A.D.M.S. will detail an Ambulance Car to be on duty at each Railhead during the period of the entrainment and another Car to be on duty at each detraining station, during the period of detrainment.

11. ENTRAINMENT AND DETRAINMENT OFFICERS.
While Entrainment and Detrainment Officers are on duty they should wear the Blue Brigade armband as a distinguishing Badge.

12. DIVISIONAL STAFF.
An Officer from Division Headquarters will visit stations of entrainment and detrainment at frequent intervals.

13. POLICE.
For control of Traffic on the road approaches to each of the Entraining Stations the A.P.M. will detail 6 policemen to report to the Officers referred to in para. 7. four hours before the first train is due to leave. These policemen will travel by the last train and will rejoin Divl. H.Q. from the station of detrainment.
For the Control of Traffic on the roads leading from each of the detraining stations the A.P.M. will also detail 6 policemen to proceed by the first train from each station with orders to report to the Officers referred to in para. 8. on arrival. On completion of detrainment these policemen will rejoin Divl. H.Q. The A.P.M. will provide the necessary rations for those 36 policemen.

14. BAGGAGE and SUPPLY WAGONS.
Baggage and Supply Wagons will entrain with the Units for which they are carrying.
Baggage Wagons will join Units on receipt of orders to entrain. Supply Wagons will join Units before they entrain, as arranged in para. 17.

15. ENTRAINMENT.
(a) A Senior Officer from each Unit must be sent to report to the R.T.O. at Stations of Entrainment to receive detailed instructions, in sufficient time to permit of them being made known to all concerned before the arrival of the Unit at the Station.
This Officer will be provided with a complete Marching out State, showing the number of men, horses, G.S. and limbered G.S. and 2-wheeled wagons, and cycles, so that accommodation on the train can be checked by the R.T.O., at the beginning of the entrainment. Limbered G.S. wagons being counted as two 2-wheeled vehicles on the state.
(b) Units must provide a horse holder for each horse, also drag ropes for use as breast lines in the trucks. The Railway Authorities provide lashings for vehicles.
(c) No fused bombs or grenades are to be carried on any train.
(d) No lights will be lit in any train after dark. The fires of cookers will be drawn before entrainment.

16. MOTOR CARS, etc.
Unless orders to the contrary are issued, all Motor Cars, Motor Ambulances and Motor Cycles will proceed by road on the days on which the Units to which they belong entrain.

17. **SUPPLIES.**

(a) For a journey not exceeding 24 hours :-

Rations for consumption on the day of entrainment will be delivered in the normal manner, early on the day of entrainment minus 1.

Rations for consumption on the day of entrainment plus 1 will be sent to Units by Supply Wagons early on the day of entrainment minus 1, and the loaded Supply Wagons will proceed to, and remain with, Units until the completion of the move.

Rations for consumption on the day of entrainment plus 2, will be delivered as follows :-
  (1) For Units entraining before 12 noon, by Supply Column at Refilling Points in the new area, thence by Supply Wagons on day of entrainment, plus 1.
  (2) For Units entraining after 12 noon, by Supply Column lorries direct to Entraining Stations, where they should be taken over by representatives of Units by 12 noon on the day of Entrainment, and loaded by Units direct into their Railway Trains and not into Supply Wagons. Although in reality for consumption on day of entrainment plus 2, these rations should be consumed on day of entrainment plus 1, and the supplies already loaded on the supply wagons for consumption on day of entrainment plus 1 should be consumed on the day of entrainment plus 2.

(b) For a journey exceeding 24 hours special instructions will be issued.

18. Units will arrange for Lewis or Machine Guns to be kept in readiness for instant action during the train journey.

Ref. 56th Div. No. G.3/894 of 15/7/1918, Appendix "B"

Table "C", (Provisional).

Units will probably ontrain at the following stations:-

PERNES.	BRYAS.	TINQUES.
169th Infantry Bde.	167th Infantry Bde.	168th Infantry Bde.
56th M.G.Battn. (less 2 Coys)	1 Coy. M.G.Battn.	1 Coy. M.G.Battn.
Hd. Qrs. Divl. Engineers.	No. 2 Coy. Divl. Train	1/5th Cheshire Regt.
513th Fd. Coy. R.E.	416th Fd. Coy. R.E.	Divl. Reception Camp
No. 4 Coy. Divl. Train	Divl. Headquarters.	2/2nd Lond. Fd. Amb.
2/1st Lond. Fd. Amb.	Hd. Qrs. Divl. Train	Cable Section R.E.
½ S.A.A. Sect. D.A.C.	Hd. Qrs. & No. 1 Sig. Section R.E.	No. 3 Coy. Divl. Train
½ T.M.Batteries.	Divl. Employt. Coy.	512th Fd. Coy. R.E.
"A" & "C" Battys. 280th Bde. RFA	2/3rd Lond. Fd. Amb.	½ S.A.A. Sect. D.A.C.
"B" & "D" Battys. 281st Bde. RFA	Mob. Vety. Section	½ T.M.Batteries.
Part No. 1 & No. 2 Sect. D.A.C.	Hd. Qrs. Divl. Arty.	Hd. Qrs. 280th Bde. RFA
	No. 1 Coy. Divl. Train	"A" & 109th Battys. 281st Bde. RFA
	Head Qrs. D.A.C.	Part No. 1 & No. 2 Sect. D.A.C.
	93rd & "D" Batty. 280th Bde. RFA	
	Hd. Qrs. 281st Bde. RFA	
	Part No. 1 & No. 2 Sect. D.A.C.	

As the Railway Authorities cannot confirm the ontraining stations, Table "D" will not be issued at present. If the ontraining stations are altered the groupings may have to be altered.

SECRET.   AQS 678.

ADMINISTRATIVE INSTRUCTIONS No. 1 issued with reference to 56th DIVISION WARNING ORDER No. 183.

1. AREAS are allotted as shown below :-

    (a) Div. H.Q. - Div. Train H.Q. - H.Q. and No. 1 Section Div. Signal Co. - Div. Employment Co. - D.A.D.O.S..

    VILLERS CHATEL and MINGOVAL.

    Billets from Camp Commandant.

    (b) <u>167th Inf. Bde. Group.</u>

    <u>Troops.</u>

    167th Inf. Bde. - M.G.Bn. - Pioneer Bn. - No. 2 Co. Div. Train - 2/1st London Field Ambulance.

    <u>Villages.</u>   <u>Billets from.</u>

    CAMBLIGNEUL,   Bde. H.Q. T.M.By. and)
                      1 Battn.   )   Area Commandant
    GAUCHIN LEGAL.   M.G.Bn.   ) GAUCHIN LEGAL.
    CAUCOURT & HERIPRE. 1 Bn. & Train Co.)

    BETHONSART.   ) 1 Battn.   Area Commandant
    VILLERS BRULIN.)   SAVY.

    ESTREE CAUCHIE.   1 Battn. and Field)   Area Commandant
                                   Amboo.)   CAMBLAIN L'ABBE.

    <u>Restrictions.</u>

    M.G.Bn. to be at GAUCHIN LEGAL.
    Field Ambulance to be at ESTREE CAUCHIE (Field Amboo. site).
    Train Co. to be at CAUCOURT.

    (c) <u>168th Inf. Bde. Group.</u>

    <u>Troops.</u>
    168th Inf. Bde. - No. 3 Co. Div. Train.

    <u>Villages.</u>   <u>Billets from.</u>

    CHATEAU de la HAIE.   Bde. H.Q., T.M.Bty. &   Area Commandant
                          2 Battns.   CHATEAU de la HAIE

    MARQUEFFLES Fm.   1 Battn.   A.C. AIX-NOULETTE.

    ESTREE CAUCHIE.   Train Co. only.   A.C. CAMBLAIN
                                                        L'ABBE.

    (d) <u>169th Inf. Bde. Group.</u>

    <u>Troops.</u>

    169th Inf. Bde. - Div. R.E. (less 416th Field Co.) - No. 4 Co. Div. Train.

-2-

Villages.		No. 4 Co. Div. Train.	Billots from.
DIEVAL.	Bde. H.Q. - T.M.By. & 1 Battn.)		Area Commandant
ANTIGNEUL-CHATEAU.		)	
BAJUS.		)	
LA COMTÉ.	1 Battn.	)	DIEVAL.
BEUGIN.	1 Battn.	)	
FM. de HERLIN.		)	

(e) 2/2nd London Fd. Amboo. at AUBIGNY.
2/3rd London Fd. Amboo. and Div. Rest Station at LIGNY ST. FLOCHEL.

(f) **Divnl. Artillery.**

AUBIGNY - SAVY - BERLES - VANDELICOURT - AGNIERES.
Restrictions. No. 1 Co. Div. Train to be at SAVY.

2. Mobile Veterinary Section will be at BETHENCOURT.

3. Infantry Brigades will select sites for Training Ammunition Dumps in their Areas and report locations to this office. All units in Brigade Areas will draw from these Dumps. The Dumps will be replenished under Divisional arrangements on demand from Infantry Brigades.

4. Supply Railhead will remain at TINQUES. Supply Groups and Refilling Points will be notified later.

5. Canteen will be at MINGOVAL. Soda Water will be on sale there or at the Factory at WANQUETIN.

6. Waste Paper Dump and Sheet Tin Dump will be near D.A.D.O.S. Store at MINGOVAL.

7. Divisional Reception Camp will remain at BETHENCOURT.

ADundas Major,
for Lieut. Colonel,
A.A. & Q.M.G., 56th Division.

17.7.18.

DISTRIBUTION.

167th Inf. Bde.	A.P.M.	"Q".	
168th Inf. Bde.	D.A.D.O.S.	French Mission.	
169th Inf. Bdo.	Camp Commandant.	20th Division. "Q".	
Div. Artillery.	Div. M.T.Company.	Area Cdt. DIEVAL.	
56th Bn. M.G. Corps.	Div. Signal Co.	" " MAGNICOURT.	
1/5th Cheshire Regt.	247th Div. Employ Co.	" " CHELERS.	
C.R.E.	D.A.D.V.S.	" " GAUCHIN
Div. Train.	S.C.F. (C. of E)	" " LEGAL.
A.D.M.S.	S.C.F. (Non C. of E)	" " Chatuea
Offr. i/c S.A.A.Dump.	XVIIth Corps "Q".	de la HAIE.
Div. Baths Officer.		" " SAVY.
Div. Water Service Officer.		" " CAMBLAIN
Div. Burials Officer.		L'ABBE.
		" " AIX-NOULETTE.

SECRET.   56th Division AQS/678.

ADMINISTRATIVE INSTRUCTIONS NO.2.
issued with reference to 56th Division Order No.184.

1. SUPPLIES.

There will be no alteration in existing Supply Grouping, except that 2/3rd London Field Ambulance will be transferred to 169th Infantry Brigade Group as from issue on the 19th instant inclusive.

Refilling Points will be as follows :-

      167th Inf. Brigade Group. - CAUCOURT.
      168th "   "   " - ESTREE CAUCHIE.
      169th "   "   " - DIEVAL.

In the case of 167th Infantry Brigade Group, 1st Line Transport will draw from Refilling Points at 9 a.m. daily excepting day of move July 18th.

Rations for all other Units will be delivered by Train Companies.

Fuel will be available for 1st Line vehicles to draw from Brigade Refilling Points.

2. TRANSPORT.

All Train Baggage Wagons will be returned to Train Companies on arrival of Units in their new Billets.

3. LINEN STORE.

Divisional Linen Store will be at CAUCOURT.

                                                Lieut-Colonel,
17th July, 1918.   A.A. & Q.M.G., 56th Division.

- DISTRIBUTION -

167th Inf. Brigade.	A.P.M.	"Q".
168th " "	D.A.D.O.S.	French Mission.
169th " "	Camp Commandant.	20th Division "Q".
Div. Artillery.	Div. M.T. Company.	Area Cdt, DIEVAL.
56th Bn. M.G.Corps.	Div. Signal Coy.	" " MAGNICOURT.
1/5th Cheshire Rgt.	247th Div.Employ.Coy.	" " CHELERS.
C.R.E.	D.A.D.V.S.	" " GAUCHIN LEGAL.
Div. Train.	S.C.F. (Non.C.of E)	" " Chateau de la
A.D.M.S.	S.C.F. (C. of E.)	HAIE.
Offcr.i/c S.A.A. Dump.	XVIIth Corps "Q".	" " SAVY.
Div. Baths Officer.	Div. Burials Officers	" " CAMBLAIN
Div. Water Service Officer.		L'ABBE.
	Area Comdt. AIX-NOULETTE.	

SECRET.

App I4 W.[ar] Diary

Reference 56th Divn. No. G.3/894 of 15.7.1918.
Appendix "B".
Table "C" (Provisional).

The following amendments will be made :-

1. For PERNES read TINQUES.
    "   BRYAS   "   SAVY.
    "   TINQUES "   AUBIGNY.

2. 416th Field Coy. R.E. will entrain with 169th I.Bde. Group from TINQUES and 513th Field Coy. R.E. with 167th I.Bde. Group from SAVY.

3. 2/3rd London Field Ambulance will entrain with 169th I.Bde. Group from TINQUES and 2/1st London Field Ambulance with 167th I.Bde. Group from SAVY.

4. Delete reference to "Cable Section" with 168th I.Bde Group.

5. Div. Reception Camp now will travel with 169th I.Bde. Group from TINQUES.

18th July, 1918.

WAR DIARY

EMBUSSING TABLE. 56th Divn. No. G.3/894 dated 15.7.18.
Reference 1/40000 Map, Sheet 44.B. and 51.C.

Serial No.	Bus Group Commander.	Troops.	Embussing Point.	Head of Convoy.	Routes to Embussing Point.
1.	Brig-General Commanding 168th Infantry Brigade.	168th Inf. Brigade. Pioneer Battalion. M.G. Battn. (less 2 Coys.) 2/1st Ldn. Field Ambulance.	Gd SERVIN – VILLERS AU BOIS Road.	Fork road X.13.c.2.0. facing south east.	M.G.Battn. to move in rear of Pioneer Battn. Fld. Ambce. not to move on to Embussing Point until M.G.Bn. & Pioneer Bn. have passed.
2.	Brig-General Commanding 167th Infantry Brigade.	167th Inf. Brigade. 1 Coy. L.G.Bn. 416th Fld.Coy.,R.E.; Div.H.Q. H.Q. & No.1.Sec.Div. Signal Coyr Div. Employment Coy. Divl. Reception Camp, 2/2nd London Fld.Ambulance.	MINGOVAL – AUBIGNY Road.	Fork Roads, D.6.d.13. facing South.	2/2nd Ldn.Fld.Ambce. to move via VILLERS CHATEL & MINGOVAL. Any further restrictions considered necessary by Brig-Gen. Comdg. Inf. Bde. to be issued by him direct to Units of Bus Group.
3.	Brig-General Commanding 169th Infantry Brigade.	169th Inf. Brigade. 512th Fld.Coy. R.E. 513th " " " H.Q., Div.R.Engineers, 1 Coy. M.G.Battalion, 2/3rd Ldn.Fld.Ambce.	DIEVAL – OURTON Road between Road Junction, I.24.c.38. and Road Junction 0.8.central.	May face in either direction.	No restrictions.

Units will embuss from the head of the convoy in the order given above.

===== THIS CANCELS PREVIOUS TABLE =====

SECRET.   A.Q.S. 5

56th DIVISION
LOCATION TABLE.

Divisional Headquarters	VILLERS CHATEL.
167th Infantry Bde. H.Q.	VILLERS BRULIN.
7th Middlesex Regt.	CAMBLIGNEUL.
8th Middlesex Regt.	BETHONSART and VILLERS BRULIN.
1st London Regt.	CAUCOURT.
167th T.M.Battery	CAMBLIGNEUL.
168th Infantry Bde. H.Q.	VILLERS-AU-BOIS.
4th London Regt.	MARQUEFFLES FARM.
13th London Regt.	CANADIAN CAMP. ⎫ CHATEAU
14th London Regt.	St. LAWRENCE CAMP ⎬ de la
168th T.M.Battery	VANCOUVER CAMP. ⎭ HAIE.
169th Infantry Bde. H.Q.	DIEVAL.
2nd London Regt.	DIEVAL
5th London Regt.	BEUGIN.
16th London Regt.	LA COMTE
169th T.M.Bty	*DIEVAL*
56th Bn. Machine Gun Corps	GAUCHIN LEGAL
1/5th Cheshire Regt.	ESTREE-CAUCHIE.
247th (Divl.) Employment Coy.	MINGOVAL.
C. R. E.	BAJUS.
416th Field Coy. R.E.	"
512th Field Coy. R.E.	"
513th Field Coy. R.E.	"
H.Q., 56th Divl. Signal Coy.RE	VILLERS CHATEL.
A. D. M. S.	MINGOVAL
2/1st London Fd. Amboe.	GOUY-SERVINS.
2/2nd London Fd. Amboe.	AUBIGNY.
2/3rd London Fd. Amboe.	LIGNY-St-FLOCHEL.
C. R. A.	
280th Bde. R.F.A. ⎫	
281st Bde. R.F.A. ⎬	Detached.
56th Div. Ammn. Col. ⎭	
Divl. Train H.Q.	MINGOVAL.
No. 1 Coy. Divl. Train	SIMENCOURT.
No. 2 Coy. Divl. Train	HERIPRE
No. 3 Coy. Divl. Train	ESTREE-CAUCHIE.
No. 4 Coy. Divl. Train	DIEVAL
D. A. D. V. S.	MINGOVAL.
Mob. Vety. Section	BETHONCOURT.
D. A. D. O. S.	MINGOVAL.
Divl. Baths Officer ⎫	
Divl. Claims Officer ⎬	CAUCOURT
56 M.T.Coy.	TINCQUETTE.
Divl. Gas Officer	MINGOVAL
Divl. Salvage Officer	MINGOVAL
Divl. Reception Camp	AUBIGNY.
Divl. Canteen	MINGOVAL.
Divl. Ammn. Dump	MINGOVAL.
Railhead for personnel	FREVIN-CAPELLE.

Transport lines at same location as units concerned.

                                                              A.C.Dundas Major,
18/7/1918.   D.A.A.G., 56th Division.

56th Division AQS/677.

Reference 56th Divn. No. G.3/894 of 15.7.18. Appendix "A".
(Instructions for move by Bus).

(A). **Embussing Table.** Amend as follows:-
   Serial No. 2.
   Embussing Point.   ARRAS – ST POL Road, D.11.a.0.0. to E.13.b.5.0.
                       facing either direction.

   Routes to Embussing Points.
         Delete reference to 2/2nd London Fld. Ambce.
         and the word "further".

(B). Add:-
   Baggage and Advance Parties Lorries.

   Lorries for Machine Guns, Lewis Guns & Stokes Mortars.

1. Para. 7. of Appendix "A" to 56th Divn. G.3/894 of 15.7.18, is cancelled. These weapons and ammunition will not now be taken with the men on the busses.

2. As a general case lorries will be provided for baggage, advance parties, and for carrying the abovementioned Machine Guns, belt boxes, Lewis Guns, Magazines, and Stokes Mortars, as shown below. If it should happen that this number of lorries are not available those in Column "A" will be cut down.

UNIT.	Rendezvous.	A. Baggage.	B. Advance Parties.	C. M.G.	L.G.	S.M.
167th Inf. Bde. 5th Cheshire R. M.G. Battn.	Bde. H.Q. VILLERS BRULIN.	8 1 2	1.b.	2	3 (a)	2
168th Inf. Bde. 1 Coy. M.G. Bn.	Bde. H.Q. VILLERS AU BOIS.	8	1.b.	1	3	2
Divl. Hd. Qtrs. Div. Emp. Coy.	Div. H.Q. VILLERS CHATEL.	6 1	1.			
169th Inf. Bde. 1 Coy. M.G. Bn. H.Q. Div. Engrs.	Bde. H.Q. DIEVAL.	8 1	1.b.	1	3 (a)	2

(a) Lewis Guns and magazines of 1/5th Cheshire Regt. and Field Coys. will be taken on the busses with the men.
(b) Advance parties of Field Coys. and Field Ambces. will travel on these lorries according to the grouping given in "Embussing Table" dated 18.7.18.

Other Divisional Stores such as Linen Stores and Divl. Grenade Dump will be left behind under guard.

(2)

3. As soon as lorries mentioned in columns "A", "B" and "C" above are ready they will be ordered by Brigadier-Generals Commanding Infantry Brigades and Camp Commandant to move as follows:-

Column "A".
Lorries will draw up in the order in which they arrive, on the REBREUVE - OLHAIN road facing South West, head of column at entrance to OLHAIN. O.C., 1/5th Cheshire Regt. will appoint an Officer to take charge of the lorries on their arrival at this rendezvous. The lorries will stay at this point until further instructions are received from Divisional Headquarters.

Column "B".
Lorries will be despatched to the destination of Infantry Brigade Groups and Divisional Headquarters in the new area, independently, as soon as they are ready.

Column "C".
Lorries moving with 167th Infantry Brigade Group will rendezvous on the SAVY - AUBIGNY Road facing East, head of column at T. Road D.12.a.7.2.

Lorries moving with 168th Infantry Brigade Group will rendezvous on the FRESNICOURT-GD.SERVINS Road facing South East, head of column at entrance to GD. SERVINS.

Lorries moving with 169th Infantry Brigade Group will rendezvous on the OURTON-BAJUS Road facing North West, head of column at southern entrance to OURTON.

Lorries referred to in Column "C" will be despatched to their respective rendezvous with guides from the Infantry Brigades and M.G. Companies as soon as they are loaded and will move off in rear of the bus Group convoy carrying their Brigade Groups.

The following Roads must not be used by "Column C" lorries whilst moving to their rendezvous, in order to avoid clashing with the Bus Group Convoy.

AUBIGNY - CAMBLIGNEUL - 4-VENTS - GD.SERVINS.
ACQ - VILLERS AU BOIS.
BRYAS - DIVION.

Tom Buchan
for
Lieut-Colonel,
General Staff.

H.Q., 56th Divn.
20th July, 1918.

SECRET.   App L   56th Division AQS/677.

Reference 56th Division AQS/677 dated 20.7.18.

(1). Para. B.2.
 Rendezvous for 168th Infantry Brigade and 1 Coy. M.G. Battalion, delete "VILLERS-AU-BOIS" and substitute "T.road in X.1.C.(Sheet 44B). Number of Lorries, Column "C" - "M.G." amend to read with 167th Infantry Brigade Group 1, with 168th Infantry Brigade Group 2.

(2) Para. 3. - "Column 'A'" for facing South West read facing South East.

T.oy. Buchan hay
General Staff   Lieut-Colonel,
                       56th Division.

22nd July, 1918.

War Diary. App L1.

56th Division AQS/677.

Reference 56th Divn. AQS/677 of 20.7.18. para.(B) 2.

Cancel the lorry table there given and substitute the following:-

UNIT.	Rendezvous.	Number of lorries.				
		A. Baggage.	B. Advance Parties.	C. M.G.	C. L.G.	C. S.M.
167th Inf. Bde.) 1 Coy. M.G. Battn)	Bde. H.Q. VILLERS BRULIN.	8	1.(b)	1	3	2
168th Inf. Bde.) M.G.Bn.less 2 Coys) 5th Cheshire R.)	T. Road in X.1.C. Sheet 44.B.	8 2 1	1.(b)	2	3 (a)	2
Divl. Hd.Qtrs.) Div.Employ.Coy.)	Div. H.Q. VILLERS CHATEL.	6 1	1.			
169th Inf. Bde.) 1 Coy. M.G. Bn.) H.Q.,Div.Engrs.)	Bde. H.Q. DIEVAL.	8 1	1.(b)	1	3 (a)	2

22nd July, 1918.

M. Herald Capt
for Lieut-Colonel,
General Staff, 56th Division.

S E C R E T.   56th Division AQS/684/2.

ADMINISTRATIVE INSTRUCTIONS NO. 1.
in connection with the relief of the 1st Canadian Division in TELEGRAPH HILL Sector.

Issued with reference to 56th Division Order No. 186.

1. **Administration.**

    (a) Infantry Brigades will administer the area east of the line :-
    WAILLY - ACHICOURT Road as far north as Bridge at M.2.b.39, thence along the CRINCHON River into ARRAS.
    (b) The area west of that line is administered by Divisional Headquarters through the following Area Commandants and Town Majors.
    WAILLY.   -   Town Major. Lt. A.C. KEMMIS.   Address WAILLY.
    (There is accommodation for one Battalion in WAILLY and one Battalion in WAILLY WOOD (R.10.d). WAILLY Village is reported to be constantly shelled.)

			Address.
AGNY. ACHICOURT. DAINVILLE.	Area Commandant.	Lt. FILSHILL.	DAINVILLE.
RONVILLE and ST SAUVEUR CAVES.	Cave Majors to be appointed.		In the Caves.
WARLUS BERNEVILLE.	Area Commandant.	Lt.-Col. WILLIAMS.	BERNEVILLE.
WANQUETIN. SIMENCOURT.	"	Major ROSSITER.	WANQUETIN.
MONTENESCOURT.	"	Lt.-Col. BATTY.	GOUVES.

ARRAS is administered by XVIIth Corps through the Town Commandant.

2. **Wagon and Transport Lines and Quartermasters' Stores**, will be located in the same villages as they were in when the Division last occupied this sector. Formations and Units will apply for accommodation to the Area Commandants, who have been instructed to allot their old lines and Quartermasters' stores to units, as far as possible. The 167th Infantry Brigade lines at WANQUETIN will be vacated by 3rd Canadian Division on 30th instant. One Brigade Transport lines at BERNEVILLE will be available on the 31st inst. The other Brigade lines will not be available until the 1st August. Either the 168th or 169th Infantry Brigade Transport will therefore have to obtain other accommodation in BERNEVILLE for the night 31st July/1st August.

3. **Ammunition.**

    (a) Gun Ammunition.
    A.H.Ps at HORSESHOE (L.29.d.65) (51.C) and WAILLY WOOD, (R.10.d.56) (51.C) will be taken over by 56th Divisional Artillery at noon 31st instant.
    (b) Trench Munitions.
    Divisional T.M.Dump is X Dump at G.20.c.33.(51.B). It will be taken over by this Division at noon 31st instant. Application to draw from this Dump will be made to Divl.Headquarters ("A" & "Q").
    Right Brigade Main Dump is at M.15.c.43.(51.B)
    Centre   "   "   " " M.4.d.77. (51.B)
    The present Left Brigade Dump (CEMETERY Dump) will not be available for this Division and the Left Brigade will establish a new dump, drawing in the meantime upon the Centre Brigade Dump.

(2)

4. Baths.

The following baths will be run under Divisional arrangements. Bookings will be arranged with the N.C.O. in charge.

    WAILLY.   allotted to Right Brigade & Troops in WAILLY Area.
    ACHICOURT.   "   " Centre Brigade & Troops in ACHICOURT and AGNY Area.
XX   SCHRAMM BARRACKS, ARRAS. allotted to Left Brigade & Troops in ARRAS.
XX   WAGNONLIEU.   for troops in DAINVILLE Area.
XX   BERNEVILLE.   for Back Areas.

XX Will be stocked with clean clothing. The other Baths will be stocked as soon as the necessary accommodation can be provided.

5. Area, Billet & Trench Stores.

All Trench and Area Stores and Trench Ammunition will be taken over, and one copy of the receipted list given by Units of this Division will be forwarded through the usual channels so as to reach Div.H.Q., ("Q") within 24 hours of taking over.

Consolidated returns on A.F. W.3405 need not be forwarded. Special attention will be paid to checking Trench Stores, Trench Ammunition, Battle Equipment Ammunition and Stores, Gas Clothing, Preserved rations, Petrol tins both in the line and at transport lines and Area stores (including tents and trench shelters.)

Preserved Rations.

Attention is drawn to D.R.O. 2363 where it is pointed out that Units will be held responsible that the quantities shown on any receipts have been actually checked and that they agree with the articles under transfer.

6. Medical arrangements will be notified to all concerned by the A.D.M.S.

7. Locations of the following will be the same as when the Division was last in the Area :-

Divl. R.E. Dump, Divl. Reception Camp, Divl. Train, D.A.D.O.S., Mobile Veterinary Section, Canteen, Linen Store, Soda Water Factory, Gas Clothing Dip, Sock Drying Rooms, Solder Kilns, Waste Paper and Sheet Tin Dumps, Divl. Theatre, Cinema, Cemeteries.

29th July, 1918.
                                  Lieut-Colonel,
                            A.A. & Q.M.G., 56th Division.

- DISTRIBUTION -

167th Inf. Brigade.	Div. Water Service Offcr.	XVII Corps "Q".
168th " "	A.P.M.	Div. Burials Offcr.
169th " "	D.A.D.O.S.	"G".
Divl. Artillery.	Camp Commandant.	French Mission.
56th Bn. M.G.Corps.	Div. M.T. Coy.	1st Canadian Div.
1/5th Cheshire Regt.	Div. Signal Company.	"Q"
C.R.E.	247th Div. Employ. Coy.	Area Cdt. DAINVILLE.
Div. Train.	D.A.D.V.S.	" " BERNEVILLE.
A.D.M.S.	S.C.F. (P.C.Dept)	" " GOUVES.
Offcr. i/c S.A.A.Dump.	S.C.F. (D.C.G.Dept)	" " WANQUETIN.
Div. Baths Offcr.	Div. Reception Camp.	Town Major, WAILLY.

SECRET.   A.Q.S.5.

56TH DIVISION.

LOCATIONS ON COMPLETION OF RELIEF.

Divisional Headquarters. WARLUS.   Transport. WARLUS.

LEFT BRIGADE.	CENTRE BRIGADE.	RIGHT BRIGADE.
Bde.H.Q. G.28.a.9.8.	Bde. H.Q. G.27.b.8.3.	Bde. H.Q. M.8.c.7.0.

UNIT.	Headquarters.	Transport Lines.
167th Infantry Brigade.	--	WANQUETIN.
7th Middlesex Regt.	--	WANQUETIN.
8th Middlesex Regt.	--	- do. -
1st London Regt.	--	- do. -
167th T.M.Battery.	--	DAINVILLE.
168th Infantry Brigade.	--	BERNEVILLE.
4th London Regt.	--	- do. -
13th London Regt.	--	- do. -
14th London Regt.	--	- do. -
168th T.M.Battery.	--	- do. -
169th Infantry Brigade.	--	BERNEVILLE.
2nd London Regt.	--	- do. -
5th London Regt.	--	- do. -
16th London Regt.	--	- do. -
169th T.M.Battery.	--	- do. -
56th Battn. M.G.Corps.	WARLUS.	BERNEVILLE.
1/5th Cheshire Regt.	G.27.b.7.7.	WANQUETIN.
247th (Div) Employment Coy.	WARLUS.	--
C.R.E.	WARLUS.	WARLUS.
416th Field Coy. R.E.	WAILLY.	BERNEVILLE.
512th Field Coy. R.E.	G.28.a.7.6.	WARLUS.
513th Field Coy. R.E.	G.27.b.15.90.	WAGNONLIEU.
A.D.M.S.	WARLUS.	WARLUS.
2/1st London Field Ambce.	K.28.d.5.2.	WANQUETIN.
2/2nd London Field Ambce.	L.1.c.4.5.ACHICOURT.	WANQUETIN.
2/3rd London Field Ambce.	AVESNES LE COMTE.	AVESNES LE COMTE.
C.R.A.	WARLUS.	WARLUS.
280th Brigade R.F.A.	M.8.b.75.40.	BERNEVILLE.
281st Brigade R.F.A.	G.27.b.99.33.	SIMENCOURT.
56th Div. Ammn. Column.	MONTENESCOURT.	MONTENESCOURT.
Divisional Train.	WANQUETIN.	WANQUETIN.
No. 1. Company.	SIMENCOURT.	SIMENCOURT.
No. 2. Company.	WANQUETIN.	WANQUETIN.
No. 3. Company.	MONTENESCOURT.	K.21.d.34
No. 4. Company.	MONTENESCOURT.	K.21.d.34
D.A.D.V.S.	WARLUS.	
Mobile Veterinary Section.	MONTENESCOURT.	MONTENESCOURT.
56th M.T. Company.	TILLOY - LES - HERMAVILLE.	
D.A.D.O.S.	MONTENESCOURT.	--
Divl. Reception Camp.	AGNEZ-LES-DUISANS.	
Divl. Baths Officer.	WARLUS.	--
Divl. Claims Officer.	WARLUS.	--
Divl. Burials Officer.	WARLUS.	--
Divl. Canteen.	BERNEVILLE.	
"BOW BELLS."	WARLUS.	--
Divl. Cinema.	BERNEVILLE.	--
Railhead for personnel.	AGNEZ-LES-DUISANS.	

31st July, 1918.

A.C.Dundas
Major,
D.A.A.G., 56th Division.

UNIT.	STRENGTH. 1.7.18.		INCREASE.		DECREASE.		STRENGTH. 1.8.18.	
	O.	O.R.	O.	O.R.	O.	O.R.	O.	O.R.
Divisional Headquarters.	16	81	-	-	-	-	16	81
247th Employment Coy.	1	329	1	50	-	6	2	373
167th Infantry Bde.H.Q.	3	21	-	-	-	-	3	21
1/7th Middlesex Regt.	42	920	3	160	6	130	39	950
1/8th Middlesex Regt.	42	908	-	120	2	80	40	948
1/1st London Regt.	38	904	6	121	4	94	40	931
167th T.M. Battery.	4	46	-	-	-	-	4	46
168th Infantry Bde.H.Q.	2	19	1	1	-	-	3	20
1/4th London Regt.	43	909	2	114	3	125	42	898
1/13th London Regt.	41	931	3	64	5	70	39	925
1/14th London Regt.	45	956	6	131	8	162	43	925
168th T.M. Battery.	3	45	1	1	-	-	4	46
169th Infantry Bde. H.Q.	3	21	-	-	-	-	3	21
1/2nd London Regt.	38	899	2	58	3	66	37	891
1/5th London Regt.	38	997	-	74	3	82	35	989
1/16th London Regt.	40	926	5	100	3	67	42	959
169th T.M. Battery.	4	44	-	2	-	-	4	46
1/5th Cheshire Regt.	40	886	2	73	4	56	38	903
56th Battn. M.G.Corps.	45	907	6	12	4	38	47	881
56th Div. Artillery H.Q.	4	18	-	-	-	-	4	18
280th Brigade R.F.A.	32	765	3	35	3	21	32	779
281st Brigade R.F.A.	26	790	7	9	2	30	31	769
56th D.A.C.	16	572	1	10	1	13	16	569
56th Div. Engineers H.Q.	2	10	-	-	-	1	2	9
416th (Ediboro')Fld.Coy.RE.	7	210	-	8	-	8	7	210
512th (London)Fld.Coy.R.E.	7	220	-	2	-	14	7	208
513th (London)Fld.Coy.R.E.	7	214	1	6	-	13	8	207
56th Div. Signal Coy.	11	295	1	7	1	10	11	292
56th Divl. Train.	22	376	-	6	-	5	22	377
Medical Units.	22	548	-	3	-	12	22	539
Mobile Veterinary Section.	1	16	-	2	-	-	1	18

:-:-:-:-:-:-:-:-:-:-:-:-:-:-:-:-:-:-:

CASUALTIES -- JULY, 1918.

DATE. JULY.	UNIT.	OFFICERS Killed.	OFFICERS Wounded.	OFFICERS Missing.	O. Rs. K.	O. Rs. W.	O. Rs. M.	REMARKS.
1st	1st London Regt.	-	-	-	-	1	-	Includes 1 at Duty.
	13th "	-	-	-	-	1	-	
	14th "	-	-	-	-	3	-	
	2nd "	-	-	-	-	1	-	
	16th "	-	-	-	-	1	-	
2nd	2nd London Regt.	-	-	-	-	1	-	Injured S.I. cleaning rifle.
	16th "	-	-	-	-	3	-	At Duty.
	169th T.M.Battery	-	-	-	-	1	-	Injured - All at Duty.
	1/5th Cheshire Rgt.	-	-	-	-	5	-	
3rd	7th Middlesex Regt.	-	-	-	-	1	-	
	8th "	-	-	-	-	1	-	
	13th London Regt.	-	-	-	-	1	-	
	14th "	-	-	-	-	1	-	
4th	4th London Regt.	-	2/Lt. R.N. WILSON, 3/7/18.	-	-	1	-	
	13th "	-	-	-	1	1a	-	a At duty.
	14th "	-	-	-	-	3	-	
	2nd "	-	-	-	-	1	-	Injured - at Duty.
	1/5th Cheshire Rgt.	-	-	-	-	1	-	
5th	4th London Regt.	-	-	-	-	1	-	Injured accidentally by rifle.
	2nd "	-	-	-	-	1	-	
6th	7th Middlesex Regt.	Lt. I.H. GREENWOOD 26/7/18. (10th Mdlsx.Rgt.) (X)	-	-	-	1	-	(X) Died of Wounds.
	8th "	-	-	-	1	2	-	
	14th London Regt.	-	-	-	-	1	-	
	2nd "	-	-	-	-	1	-	
	16th "	-	-	-	-	1	-	
	1/5th Cheshire Rgt.	-	-	-	-	1	-	Injured - at Duty.

(2)

DATE. JULY.	UNIT.	OFFICERS. Killed.	Wounded.	Missing.	O. RS. K.	W.	M.	REMARKS.
7th	1st London Regt.	—	—	—	—	1	—	Injured.
	5th " "	—	—	—	1	1	—	
	16th " "	—	—	—	—	1	—	
	1/5th Cheshire Rgt.	—	—	—	1	1	—	Injured – At Duty.
8th	13th London Regt.	—	—	—	—	2	—	
	2nd " "	—	2/Lt. H.T. HARPER,7/7/18.	—	—	2	—	
9th	8th Middlesex Regt.	—	—	—	—	1	—	
	1st London Regt.	—	—	—	1	1	—	Injured.
	5th " "	—	—	—	—	1	—	
	16th " "	—	—	—	—	11	—	
	14th " "	—	—	—	1	1	—	
	513th(Ldn)Fld.Coy.R.E.	—	—	—	—	—	—	
10th	8th Middlesex Regt.	—	—	—	—	1	—	At Duty.
	5th London Regt.	—	—	—	—	1	—	
	2/1st Ldn.Fld.Amblce.	—	—	—	—	1	—	
11th	2nd London Regt.	—	—	—	—	1	—	At Duty.
12th	7th Middlesex Regt.	—	—	—	—	2	—	
	5th London Regt.	—	—	—	—	1	—	At Duty.
	16th " "	—	—	—	1	1	—	
	56th Battn. M.G.C.	—	—	—	—	1	—	
13th	16th London Regt.	—	—	—	1	1	—	
	5th Cheshire Rgt.	—	—	—	—	1	—	Injured.
14th	8th Middlesex Regt.	—	—	—	—	2	—	Includes 1 injured.
	2/2nd Ldn.Fld.Amblce.	—	—	—	—	1	—	
	16th London Regt.	—	—	—	—	—	—	
15th	281st Bde. R.F.A.	—	—	—	—	3	—	Premature.
16th	280th Bde. F.R.A.	—	—	—	—	1	—	
	1/5th Cheshire Rgt.	—	—	—	—	1	—	Injured.

(3)

DATE. JULY.	UNIT.	OFFICERS.			O. RS.			REMARKS.
		Killed.	Wounded.	Missing.	K.	W.	M.	
17th	1/5th Cheshire Regt.	-	-	-	-	1	-	Injured S.I. g.s.w. thumb.
19th	7th Middlesex Regt.	-	-	-	-	1	-	Injured.
18th	1/5th Cheshire Regt.	-	-	-	-	1	-	Injured.
20th	1st London Regt.	-	-	-	-	1	-	Injured.
21st	8th Middlesex Regt.	-	-	-	-	1	-	Injured.
	1/5th Cheshire Regt.	-	-	-	-	2	-	"
26th	14th London Regt.	-	-	-	1	6	-	Includes 1 at duty.
	Divl. M.M.P.	-	-	-	-	2	-	"
27th	1st London Regt.	-	-	-	-	1	-	Injured.
	1/5th Cheshire Rgt.	-	-	-	-	1	-	" – At Duty.
31st	7th Middlesex Regt.	-	-	-	-	1	-	
TOTALS FOR JULY:		1	2	-	6	95	-	

Secret.

Vol 31

War Diary

Administrative Branch

56th Division.

Period:- 1st to 31st August, 1918

Volume XXXI

Army Form C. 2118.

WAR DIARY
INTELLIGENCE SUMMARY

56th DIVISION "Q".   Volume XXXI.

(Erase heading not required.)

Instructions regarding War Diaries and Intelligence Summaries are contained in F.S. Regs., Part II. and the Staff Manual respectively. Title pages will be prepared in manuscript.

Place	Date	Hour	Summary of Events and Information	Remarks and references to Appendices
VILLERS-CHATEL.	1.8.18.		169th Inf. Bde. move from GAUCOURT Area to Centre sector of Divisional Front by Light Railway. Bde H.Q. RUE JEANNE D'ARC, ARRAS.	
WARLUS.	2.8.18.		Divisional Hd.Qtrs closed at VILLERS-CHATEL at 10 a.m. and opened at WARLUS at the same hour.	
WARLUS.	7.8.18.		Instructions received from XVIIth Corps that 3 Officers and 9 men can proceed to ENGLAND on leave from the Division per day. This triples the allotment previously in force.	
	14.8.18.		Instructions received from XVIIth Corps regarding move of Divisional Line to LE CAUROY Area and regarding relief by 15th Division.	APPX. I.
	15/16.8.18.		167th Inf. Bde. relieved by 44th Inf. Bde.	
	16/17.8.18.		169th Inf. Bde. relieved by 45th Inf. Bde. in centre section. 169th Bde. moved by Light Railway 45th Bde. by Bus.	
	17/18.8.18.		168th Inf. Bde. relieved. Divisional Hd.Qtrs closed at WARLUS at 10 a.m. 18th and opened at LE CAUROY at the same hour. Relief of the Division complete with the exception of Divisional Artillery which remained in the Line. Division in G.H.Q. Reserve.	APPX. II. (LOCATIONS)
LE CAUROY.	19.8.18.		169th Bde. move to ARRAS, to carry out collection of ammunition etc., in view of pending operations.	APPX. III. APPX. IV.
	20.8.18.		169th Bde. to AVESNES-LE-COMTE.	
	21.8.18. Evening		Division moved by march route to BAVINCOURT Area.	
BAVINCOURT.	22/23rd.		168th Bde. and 1st London Rgt. march to front trenches W. of BOYELLES. Div. H.Q. moved to BLAIREVILLE.	APPX. V.
BLAIREVILLE.	23.8.18.		168th Bde. and 1st London Rgt. attacked at 4.55 a.m. and reached all objectives by 8.30 a.m. Casualties Light.	APPX. VI.
	24.8.18.		167th Bde. continue the advance. Div. Hd.Qtrs. moved to BOISLEUX-AU-MONT.	(LOCATIONS)
BOISLEUX-AU-MONT.	27.8.18. to		Slight advance N. of CROISILLES. 169th Bde. heavily engaged. Casualties moderate.	
	28.8.18.		Attacks continued on CROISILLES.	
	29.8.18.		CROISILLES captured and BULLECOURT attacked.	
	30.8.18.		Line consolidated. Attacks continued on BULLECOURT and German counter-attacks repulsed. RearDiv. H.Q. moved up from BLAIREVILLE to BOISLEUX-AU-MONT.	APPX. VII. Lorry & Embussing Table.
	31.8.18.		Line consolidated. Advice of relief by 52nd (LOWLAND)Division received. Division relieved by 52nd (LOWLAND) Division. Brigades Headquarters established in BOISLEUX-AU-MONT - BOYELLES AREA. Divisional Headquarters remained at BOISLEUX-AU-MONT.	

Lieut-Colonel,
A.A. & Q.M.G., 56th Division.

APP. I.   War Diary

S E C R E T.   56th Division AQS/704/2.

In continuation of 56th Div. AQS/704/2 dated 14th instant.

Para. 6.   ACCOMMODATION.
follows:-   Field Ambulances will be included in Brigade Groups as

              167th Infantry Bde.   2/2nd London Field Ambulance.

              168th Infantry Bde.   2/1st London Field Ambulance.
              Restriction.   Field Ambce. to be at HOUVIN.

              169th Infantry Bde.   2/3rd London Field Ambulance.

                                              Lieut-Colonel
15/8/1918.   A.A. & Q.M.G., 56th Division.

                                                        P.T.O.

DISTRIBUTION.

167th Infantry Bde.	A. D. M. S.	S.C.F., D.C.G's Dept.
168th Infantry Bde.	A. P. M.	S.C.F., P.C's Dept.
169th Infantry Bde.	D. A. D. O. S.	"G"
Divl. Artillery,	Camp Commdt.	French Mission.
56th Bn. M.G.Corps.	56th M.T.Coy.	15th Division "Q"
1/5th Cheshire Regt.	Divl. Sig. Coy. R.E.	Area Commdt.
C. R. E.	247th D. Employt. Coy.	LE CAUROY.
Divl. Train	D. A. D. V. S.	S.A.C. MAIZIERES.
	Divl. Reception Camp.	" LIENCOURT.
		" VILLERS SIR SIMON.

SECRET.   56th Division AQS/704/2.

Administrative Instructions No. 1 in connection with relief
56th Division by 15th Division and the move to LE CAUROY Area.

(Issued with reference to 56th Division Order No. 189.)

1. **AREA, BILLET and TRENCH STORES.**
   Water Tins, Reserve Rations and Gas Clothing will be handed over as shewn on the attached Appendix "D". (Issued only to Formations and Units concerned).
   Gas underlinen, Washing Bowls, Aeroplane Tin Discs, Refuse Sprayers, Water Tins (Regimental Equipment) and Chaff Cutters and Soyer Stoves (except those taken over in this area) are Divisional Equipment and will NOT be handed over. Underlinen will be returned to the Divisional Linen Store.
   All Trench and Area Stores and Trench Ammunition will be handed over, and one copy of the Units' receipted list will be forwarded by all units in the Division, through the usual channels, so as to reach Divisional Headquarters "Q" within 24 hours of relief. Consolidated returns on A.F., W. 3405 need not be forwarded. Separate lists will be prepared for Trench Stores, Trench Ammunition, Battle Equipment Ammunition, Gas Clothing, Preserved Rations and Area Stores.
   Attention is drawn to D.R.O., 2363 where it is pointed out that the responsibility for, and onus of proof of, handing over rations rests with the outgoing unit; and that unit will be held responsible that the actual quantities shewn on any receipts given or taken, have been actually checked and that they agree with the articles under transfer.

2. **AREA EMPLOYMENT.**
   Personnel employed in the Area under Divisional control will be relieved on the 16th inst: in accordance with the arrangements notified in attached Appendix "C".

3. **TRANSPORT LINES.**
   Transport Lines and Quartermasters' Stores will be handed over as shewn below:-
   167th Infantry Bde. at (WAILLY
                          (WAILLY WOOD   to 44th Inf. Bde. on 15th
   168th Infantry Bde. at BERNEVILLE   to 46th Inf. Bde. on 17th
   169th Infantry Bde. at BERNEVILLE   to 45th Inf. Bde. on 16th
   416th Field Coy. R.E. at BERNEVILLE   to 91st Fd. Co. R.E. on 15th
   512th Field Coy. R.E. at BERNEVILLE   to 73rd Fd. Co. R.E. on 17th
   513th Field Coy. R.E. at WARLUS   to 74th Fd. Co. R.E. on 16th

   Other units will hand over transport lines to corresponding units of the 15th Division on the dates on which they are relieved.

4. **WORK in PROGRESS.**
   Formations and Units will hand over to relieving Formations and Units all details of work either projected or in progress. This particularly applies to schemes for improvement of Horse Standings, Water Supply and Baths.

5. **CERTIFICATES OF CLEANLINESS.**
   Particular attention is to be paid to handing over all Camps, Billets, Trenches and Horse Standings in a clean and sanitary condition. Certificates to this effect must be obtained from Area Commandants and advance parties of incoming units. Where necessary, rear parties must be left behind to hand over.

6. ACCOMMODATION.
The following areas are allotted in the LE CAUROY Area:-

Divl. Hd. Qrs.)
Divl. R.E. Hd. Qrs.)
Divl. Train Hd. Qrs.) LE CAUROY.   Billets from
Divl. Employt: Coy.)
                                             Camp Commdt.

Divl. Artillery (less) MAGNICOURT   Billets from
Headquarters).   ) SARS LES BOIS
No. 1 Coy. Divl. Train) BERLENCOURT
) ETREE WAMIN   Area Commdt.
) WAMIN   LE CAUROY.

167th Infantry Bde. Group.
Troops.   167th Inf. Bde. 416th Field Co. R.E., No. 2 Coy. Divl.
          Train. 1 Field Ambce. Mob. Vety. Section. Divl. Reception
          Camp.
Villages. IZEL LES HAMEAU   Billets from Sub Area Commdt.
           (Bde. H.Q. and
            2 Battns.)   VILLERS SIR SIMON.
           PENIN (1 Battn.)   do.
           VILLERS SIR SIMON   do.
           GIVENCHY LE NOBLE   )
           (Field Ambce.)   )   do.
Restrictions. DOFFINE FARM.
          Train Coy. to be at DOFFINE FARM and Field Ambce.
          at GIVENCHY LE NOBLE.

168th Infantry Bde. Group.
Troops.   168th Inf. Bde. M.G.Battn: Divl. Artillery Hd. Qrs.,
          512th Field Coy. R.E., No. 3 Coy. Divl. Train, 1 Field
          Ambce., D.A.D.O.S., Divl. Canteen.
Villages. MAIZIERES   Billets from Sub Area Commdt.
          (Bde. H.Q. and
           1 Battn.)   MAIZIERES.
          GOUY EN TERNOIS
          (Q Bn. & 1 Fd. Coy.)   do.
          HOUVIN-HOUVIGNEUL   Billets from A.C. LE CAUROY.
          AMBRINES.   Billets from S.A.C., MAZIERES.
Restrictions.
          Divl. Artillery Hd. Qrs. to be at HOUVIN HOUVIGNEUL.
          M.G.Battn: to be at AMBRINES.
          D.A.D.O.S. & Divl. Canteen do. AMBRINES.

169th Infantry Bde. Group.
Troops.   169th Inf. Bde. Pioneer Bn. 513th Field Coy. R.E.,
          No. 4 Coy. Divl. Train. 1 Field Ambce.
Villages. LIGNEREUIL   Billets from Sub Area Commdt.
          (Bde. H.Q. and one
           Bn.)   LIENCOURT.
          DENIER   do.
          LIENCOURT (1 Battn.)   do.
          GRAND RULLECOURT
          (1 Bn. & 1 Fd. Ambce.)   do.
          BEAUFORT   do.
          BLAVINCOURT   do.
Restrictions.
          Pioneer Battn.   to be at BEAUFORT.
          Field Ambce.   to be at GRAND RULLECOURT.

7. ATTACHMENT OF M.M.P.
M.M.P., will be attached to Headquarters for duty, accommodation and rations as shewn below:-

    167th Inf. Bde.   1 Sergt. and 4 Corporals from 15th instant.
    169th Inf. Bde.   1 Sergt. and 4 Corporals from 16th instant.
    168th Inf. Bde.   1 Sergt. and 4 Corporals from 17th instant.
    Divl. Artillery   1 Sergt. and 4 Corporals from 18th instant.

The senior N.C.O., will report to Brigade Headquarters for orders on the day before the attachment commences.

14th August, 1918.

                              Lieut-Colonel,
                A.A. & Q.M.G., 56th Division.

DISTRIBUTION.

167th Infantry Bde.
168th Infantry Bde.
169th Infantry Bde.
Divl. Artillery.
56th Bn. M.G.Corps.
1/5th Cheshire Regt.
C. R. E.
Divl. Train.
A. D. M. S.
A. P. M.
D. A. D. O. S.
Camp Commdt.
56th M.T.Coy.
Divl. Sig. Coy. R.E.
247th D.Employt. Coy.
D. A. D. V. S.
S.C.F., D.C.G's Dept.
S.C.F., R.C's Dept.
"G"

French Mission.
15th Division "Q"
Area Commdt. ARRAS.
  "   "   DAINVILLE.
  "   "   BERNEVILLE.
  "   "   WANQUETIN.
  "   "   MONTENESCOURT.
  "   "   LE CAUROY.
Sub. Area Commdt. MAIZIERES.
  "   "   "   LIENCOURT
  "   "   "   VILLERS SIR SIMON.

T.M. Wailly
Div Reception Camp

APPENDIX "G".
56th Divn. ACX.480/251.

AREA EMPLOYMENT TO BE RELIEVED UNDER DIVISIONAL ARRANGEMENTS ON 16TH AUGUST, 1918.

1. Serial No.	2. By whom employed.	3. Off.	NCOs.	Men.	4. Formation or Unit.	5. By whom rationed.	6. Nature of work.	7. Where reliefs report.	8. Rendezvous.
1.	Area Comdt. DAINVILLE.	—	1	6	247th Div. Employment Coy.	Area Comdt. DAINVILLE.	Billet wardens, Sanitary duties &c.		Office of A.Cdt. DAINVILLE 3.30 P.M. 16th.
2.	Cave Major, RONVILLE CAVES.	1	1	10	167th Inf. Bde.	Cave Major, RONVILLE CAVES.	Sanitary, Water & Gas duties. Officer detailed acts as Cave Major.		— do. — Guide will take relief on to ARRAS in lorry.
		1	1	5	168th " "				
		1	1	10	169th " "				
		1	1	10	Div.Gas Offr.				
3.	Town Major, WAILLY.	—	1	4	167th Inf. Bde.	Town Major, WAILLY.	Town Major & Staff WAILLY.		Office of A.Cdt. DAINVILLE 3.30 P.M. 16th.
4.	Offcr.i/c Div. Trench M'tion Dump.	1	2	10	Div. Artillery.	513th Fld. Coy. R.E.	Divl. Trench Munitions Dumps.		— ditto. —
5.	A. P. M.						Guarding u/mentioned bridges		— ditto. —
				3	167th Inf. Bde.		1. R.22.d.20.		
		1		3			2. R.22.b.30.65.		
							3. R.23.a.05.65.		
							4. R.23.a.20.67.		
				3			5. R.23.a.3.7.		
							6. R.17.d.5.5.		
							7. R.17.d.6.7.		
		1		4	A. P. M.		8. R.17.d.60.75.		
		1		4	— do. —		9. G.33.c.45.00.		
		1		4	— do. —		10. M.3.c.45.25.		
		1		3	169th Inf.Bde.		11. G.32.b.9.1.		
		1		4	A. P. M.		12. L.21.c.5.4.		
		1		4	— do. —		13. L.27.d.85.20.		
		1		4	— do. —		14. L.34.a.5.4.		
		1		5	169th Inf.Bde.		15. L.34.a.95.05.		
							16. M.2.b.35.50.		

P.T.O.

(2).   APPENDIX "G". (contd.)

1. Serial No.	2. By whom employed.	3. Off. NCOs. Men.	4. Formation or Unit.	5. By whom rationed.	6. Nature of work.	7. Where reliefs report.	8. Rendezvous.
6.	Water Service Officer.	1 - 4	Div.Employment Coy.	UNITS.	Water duties at:-	Div.Water Service Officer WARLUS 3 P.M. 16th.	
		1 - 5	Div. Artillery.		WARLUS.		
		1 - 4	" "		BERNEVILLE.		
		1 - 2	" "		SIMENCOURT.		
		1 - 2	" "		DAINVILLE.		
		1 - 2	" "		MONTENESCOURT.		
		1 - 4	A. D. M. S.		WANQUETIN.		
7.	Div. Baths Officer.	1 - 3	168th Inf.Bde.	Div.Baths Officer.	) Clothing Store at) BERNEVILLE.		
		1 - 6	247th Emp.Coy.				
		1 - 4	-- do. --		Baths BERNEVILLE.		
		1 - 3	-- do. --		" WAILLY.		
		1 - 2	-- do. --				
		1 - 1	167th Inf.Bde.		" WAGNONLIEU.		
		1 - 2	168th " "				
		1 - 3	247th Emp.Coy.)		" ACHICOURT.		
		1 - 1	167th Inf.Bde.)				
		1 - 2	247th Emp.Coy.)		" SCHRAMM BARRACKS, ARRAS.		
		-1 2	167th Inf.Bde.)				
		1 - 1	169th " "				
		1 - 1	167th " "		Sock Room, WANQUETIN.		
		1 - 2	168th " "				
		1 - 2	169th " "				
		1 - 3	169th " "		Ges Dip,WANQUETIN.		
		1 - 1	247th Emp.Coy.				
8.	Div. Burials Off.	- - 3	-- do. --	Area Comdt. DAINVILLE.	DAINVILLE CEMETERY.		- ditto. -
	-- ditto. --	- - 3	-- do. --	Town Major, WAILLY.	WAILLY CEMETERY.		- ditto -
9.	A. P. M.	- 4-49	A. P. M.	A. P. M.	Traffic Control. and M.P.'s	A.P.M. WARLUS. 3 p.m. 16th.	

APPENDIX "G". (contd.)

(3)

1. Serial No.	2. By whom employed.	3. Off. NCOs. Men.			4. Formation or Unit.	5. By whom rationed.	6. Nature of Work.	7. Where reliefs report.	8. Rendezvous.
10.	513th Fld. Coy.	-	-	4	169th Inf. Bde.	513th Fld. Coy.	Water patrol.		Office of A. Cdt. DAINVILLE, 3.30 P.M. 16th.
11.	A. P. M.	-	2	13	169th Inf. Bde.		Battle Straggler Posts.		
		-	2	13	168th " "		--- do. ---		
		-	3	12	169th " "				
12.	A. Cdt. BERNEVILLE.	-	1	10	168th Inf. Bde.		Village cleaning.		Daily party.
13.	" WARLUS.	-	1	10	169th " "		" "		" "
14.	T.M. WAILLY.	-	-	26	A. D. M. S. Div. Artillery.		Work on land " "		
15.	A.C. DAINVILLE.	-	-	8	A. D. M. S.		Potatoe digging.		
16.	Div. Salvage O.				To be arranged between Salvage Officers.				

Reference Serials No. 1. - 10. The Officer shown in Column 2 will be responsible for providing guides to meet reliefs at RENDEZVOUS and to take them to their duties. Personnel relieved will be instructed to return to their Units without delay.

Reference Serials Nos. 11 - 15. No parties will work after 16th instant. Parties will NOT wait until reliefs arrive, but rejoin Units in time to move with them.

SECRET.　　　　　　　　APP. II.　　　　　　　　War diary

Amendment to 56th Divn.
LOCATION TABLE at 10 A.M. 18th AUGUST.

UNIT.	Headquarters.	Wagon Lines.
C. R. A.	BERNEVILLE.	--
280th Brigade R.F.A.	BERNEVILLE.	BERNEVILLE.
281st Brigade R.F.A.	SIMENCOURT.	SIMENCOURT.
56th D. A. C.	MONTENESCOURT.	MONTENESCOURT.
No. 1. Coy. Div. Train.	WANQUETIN.	WANQUETIN.

17th August, 1918.

Captain,
for D.A.A.G., 56th Division.

War Diary

SECRET.

56th DIVISION.

LOCATION TABLE at 10 A.M. 18th AUGUST, 1918.

DIVISIONAL HEADQUARTERS. . . . . LE CAUROY.

UNIT.	HEADQUARTERS.
167th Inf. Brigade.	IZEL LES HAMEAU.
7th Middlesex Regt.	" " "
8th " "	PENIN.
1st London Regt.	IZEL LES HAMEAU.
167th T.M. Battery.	" " "
168th Inf. Brigade.	MAIZIERES.
4th London Regt.	HOUVIN-HOUVIGNEUL.
13th " "	GOUY-EN-TERNOIS.
14th " "	MAIZIERES.
168th T.M. Battery.	AMBRINES.
169th Inf. Brigade.	LIGNEREUIL.
2nd London Regt.	GRAND RULLECOURT.
5th " "	LIGNEREUIL.
16th " "	"
169th T.M. Battery.	DENIER.
56th Battn. M.G. Corps.	AMBRINES.
1/5th Cheshire Regt.	BEAUFORT.
247th (Div) Employment Coy.	LE CAUROY.
C. R. E.	LE CAUROY.
416th Field Coy. R.E.	VILLERS-SIR-SIMON. AMBRINES
512th " " "	DENIER.
513th " " "	LE CAUROY.
A. D. M. S.	HOUVIN-HOUVIGNEUL.
2/1st London Field Amblce.	GIVENCHY-LE-NOBLE.
2/2nd " " "	GRAND RULLECOURT.
2/3rd " " "	HOUVIN-HOUVIGNEUL.
C. R. A.	MAGNICOURT & SARS LES BOIS.
280th Brigade R.F.A.	BERLENCOURT.
281st " "	ETREE WAMIN.
56th D. A. C.	LE CAUROY.
Divl. Train.	ETREE WAMIN.
No. 1. Company.	DOFFINE FARM.
" 2 "	MAIZIERES.
" 3 "	DENIER.
" 4 "	LE CAUROY.
D.A.D.V.S.	DOFFINE FARM.
Mob. Veterinary Section.	AMBRINES.
D.A.D.O.S.	HABARCQ.
56th M.T. Company,	VILLERS-SIR-SIMON.
Divl. Reception Camp.	" " "
Divl. Baths Officer.	LE CAUROY.
Divl. Claims "	LE CAUROY.
Divl. Burials "	AMBRINES.
Divl. Canteen.	IZEL-LES-HAMEAU.
"Bow Bells."	Not showing at present.
Divl. Cinema.	TINQUES.
RAILHEAD for personnel.	

17th August, 1918.

[signature]
Captain,
for D.A.A.G., 56th Division.

App. III *War Diary*

SECRET.

56th Division AQS/677/2.

AMENDMENT NO.1. to
Standing Orders for Strategic Move of Division
(less Artillery) by Bus wilst in G.H.Q.Reserve.

Para. 11. line 4. After "M.G.Battn. Transport" insert " and
S.A.A. Section, D.A.C."

Erase lines 9 and 10.

[signature]
Lieut-Colonel,
A.A. & Q.M.G., 56th Division.

21st August, 1918.

- DISTRIBUTION -

167th Inf. Brigade.	1/5th Cheshire Regt.	Camp Commandant.
168th " "	56th M.G. Battalion.	Div. Claims Offcr.
169th " "	56th M.T. Company.	" Employment Coy.
Divl. Artillery.	Div. Reception Camp.	" Signal Coy. R.E.
S.A.A. SECT. D.A.C.	D.A.D.O.S.	S.C.F.(D.C.G's Dept.)
C.R.E.	Div. Salvage Offcr.	S.C.F. (P.C's Dept.)
A.D.M.S.	" Gas Officer.	French Mission.
Divl. Train.	A.P.M.	"Q".
	D.A.D.V.S.	

SECRET.   56th Division AQS/677/1.

Standing Orders for Strategic Move of the
Division (less Artillery) by Bus whilst in
G.H.Q. Reserve.

1. Troops will embuss in accordance with Embussing Tables which will be issued from time to time.

2. Definitions for the purpose of these Orders.

   <u>Brigade Group</u>. Troops who embuss at one Embussing point.

   <u>Brigade Bus Column</u>. Group of Vehicles carrying a Brigade Group.

   <u>Embussing Point</u>. Section of Road on which the Bus Column will be drawn up.

3. On receipt of the order "Strategic Bus Move" the following action will be taken:—

   (a) By all Units. Wire embussing strength (all ranks) to this office through the usual channels; and in the case of Divisional Troops repeat the wire to their Brigade Group Commander.
   (b) By Divl. Train. Return Baggage Wagons to Units.
   (c) By all Units. Load transport and park it ready to move at 1 hour's notice.
   (d) By Infantry Brigades. Report to this office names and Units of Officers appointed Brigade Group Embussing and Debussing Officers and O.C., Brigade Group Horse Transport Columns.
   (e) By Infantry Brigades. Collect Billeting parties of their Bde. Group at their Brigade Headquarters.
   (f) By all concerned. Take action in accordance with the subsequent paragraphs of these Instructions.

4. A zero-hour for each Bus Column will be notified from Divl. H.Q. All Units will move to Embussing point under the orders of Bde. Group Commanders. Moves of Units from billets will be timed so as to enable them to reach the vicinity of their sections of the embussing point at Zero – 30 minutes. Units will not actually move on to the Embussing point until their guides (see para.6) rejoin them.

5. <u>Detailing of Personnel to Vehicles</u>.

   A Bus Column consists both of Busses which hold 1 Officer and 25 O.Rs and of Seated Lorries which hold 1 Officer and 20 O.Rs. When possible, information as to the arrangement of the two classes of vehicles in the column will be obtained in advance by these Hd.Qtrs. and passed on to Brigade Group Commanders. As soon as this information is received, personnel of the whole Brigade Group (not of each unit separately) should be told off in groups accordingly; preferably before leaving billets. It may not however be possible to obtain this information before the Bus Column arrives on the Embussing Point.

6. <u>Procedure at Embussing Point</u>.

   Each Infantry Brigade will detail an Officer not below the rank of Captain to supervise the embussing.
   (Bde) Each Unit of the/Group will detail an advance party, consisting of 1 Officer, 1 guide, and markers on the scale of 1 per Company or equivalent Unit; to report to the Embussing Officer at the head of the column at Zero – 1 hour and to work under his orders. The O.C. party must know the latest embussing strength of his Unit.

                                                              P.T.O.

6. Procedure at Embussing Point. (contd).

The duties of the Embussing Officer will be.
(1) To keep in touch with the M.T. Officer commanding Bus Column.
(2) To ascertain from the O.C. Bus Column the composition of the Column; if he does not know it already.
(3) When he knows the composition of the column to allot road spaces (6 vehicles = 80 yards of road space) or vehicles (if they have arrived) in accordance with the strengths of Units.
(4) Hand over the allotted road space, or section of vehicles, to Units' advance parties.
(5) Instruct advance parties to act as follows:-
   (a) To send back a guide to the unit to lead it to its allotted section of vehicles or road space.
   (b) To sub-allot vehicles or road spaces to each Company or equivalent unit and to post a marker at the head or tail of each Company's area (according to the direction from which the unit is marching on to the embussing point) to point it out to the troops.
(6) Inform the O.C. Bus Column when the troops are all embussed and ready to move.

Guides must know the number and distribution of busses and seated lorries in their sections of the Column. After moving on to the Embussing Point, Units will be formed up clear of the road, on the right hand side if possible, and facing towards the head of the Column, the troops being equally distributed in parties of 6 groups (of 25 for a Bus and 20 for a lorry) for every 80 yards of road space. All vehicles will be loaded simultaneously as soon as the troops and the vehicles are in position. Kits should be taken off before the arrival of the Busses and troops should embuss carrying their kits. Officers should be distributed throughout the column on the drivers' seats.
The Embussing Officer will travel on the last vehicle.

7. Procedure at Debussing Point.

Similarly each Infantry Brigade will detail an Officer to supervise the Debussing. This Officer will travel on the loading vehicle of the column. Troops should not debus until the whole column has stopped.

They should debus without kits which should be handed out to them and put on outside the vehicles. As each Group debusses it should immediately clear off to the side of the road and not stand between the vehicles. Troops must remain off the road until the Bus Column has left the Debussing Point.

8. Embussing and Debussing Officers will wear the Blue arm-band whilst on duty, as a distinguishing badge.

9. The following will be detailed to report to Embussing Officers at the head of each Embussing point at Zero - 1 hour; and to Debussing Officers on arrival in the new Area.
   (a) 1 Motor Cyclist by O.C. Signal Company.
   (b) 1 Motor Ambulance by A.D.M.S.
   (c) 4 Traffic Control police by A.P.M.

10. Lorries will normally be allotted for conveyance of the following:-
(a) Surplus Baggage.
(b) Billeting parties of Brigade Groups.
(c) Machine Guns and 10 filled belts per gun.
   Lewis Guns of Inf. Battns. and 20 filled Magazines per gun.
   Stokes Mortars.

Lorry tables will be issued from time to time. Lewis Guns and Magazines of Pioneer Battn. and Field Coys. will be taken on the busses with the men.

11. **Horse Transport and Bicycles.** Will move in columns constituted similarly to Brigade Bus Groups, and under the orders of Brigade Group Commanders.

    M.G. Battn. Transport will move with Serial No. 1. Bde. Group.
    Train H.Q.   "   "   "   "   No. 2.   "   "
    Mobile Vet. Section   "   "   "   "   No. 3.   "   "

Train Companies will move with the Brigade Groups to which they are affiliated.

A portion of the S.A.A. Section, D.A.C. will move with each Brigade Group Transport Column.

Each Infantry Brigade will detail a Senior Officer to command the Brigade Group Transport Column.

12. **Supplies.**

The unexpended portion of the current day's rations will be carried on the man. Rations for day of departure plus 1 will also be carried on the man if time permits of their being issued. In the event of the Bus party overtaking the Horse Transport party and arriving at their destination before the Horse Transport party, supplies which would ordinarily be refilled and delivered to Units by Horse Transport will be delivered to Units by M.T. in detail, under the direction of Supply Officers.

The Horse Transport party will be rationed for day of departure; and, if time permits of issue, for day of departure plus 1 also; and will carry those rations.

Rations of the Horse Transport party for consumption on day of departure plus 1 (if necessary), day of departure plus 2, and any following days, while still on the march, will be delivered on route, in detail, by M.T. under the direction of Supply Officer.

If H.T. party reaches its destination before Bus party, supplies for both Bus Party and H.T. party will be picked up from Refilling Points in the New Area in the normal manner.

13. **Motor Transport.** All Motor Cars, Motor Ambulances and Motor Cycles will move on the days on which the Units, to which they belong, ombus.

14. These Standing Orders cancel all previous Divisional instructions on this subject. They are liable to modification for a Bus move not involving a Strategic move of the whole Division.

Lieut-Colonel,
A.A. & Q.M.G., 56th Division.

20th August, 1918.

- DISTRIBUTION -

167th Inf. Brigade.	1/5th Cheshire Rgt.	Camp Commandant.
168th " "	56th M.G. Battalion.	Div. Claims Offcr.
169th " "	56th M.T. Company.	" Employment Coy.
Divl. Artillery.	Div. Reception Camp.	" Signal Coy. R.E.
S.A.A. Sect. D.A.C.	D.A.D.O.S.	S.C.F.(D.C.G's Dept).
C.R.E.	Div. Salvage Offcr.	S.C.F. (P.C's Dept.)
A.D.M.S.	" Gas Officer.	French Mission.
Divl. Train.	A.P.M.	"G".
	D.A.D.V.S.	

S E C R E T.   APP. IV.   56th Division AQS/708/3.

AMENDMENT NO. 1. to
ADMINISTRATIVE INSTRUCTIONS NO. 1. IN CONNECTION with THISTLE.

Para. 6. regarding SUPPLIES is in abeyance for the present. The Second day's Mens' rations will not be delivered to the Units named this evening, or until further orders. First Line Transport of all Units will continue to draw Supplies from Refilling Points at 9 A.M. daily and not at 2 P.M.

20th August, 1918.

Lieut-Colonel,
A.A. & Q.M.G., 56th Division.

- DISTRIBUTION -

167th Inf. Brigade.	C. R. E.	D. A. D. O. S.
168th " "	Divl. Train.	Div. Reception Camp.
169th " "	A. D. M. S.	Div. Employ. Coy.
Divl. Artillery.	Divl. Signals.	"G".
M. G. Battn.	Camp Comdt.	A. P. M.
1/5th Cheshire Regt.		D. A. D. V. S.

SECRET.   56th Division A.Q.S/708/1.

ADMINISTRATIVE INSTRUCTIONS NO.1.
in connection with THISTLE.

Issued with reference to 56th Divn. Order No. 191.

1. DISPOSAL OF SURPLUS PERSONNEL, TRANSPORT AND BAGGAGE:

   Formations and Units will move from this Area on a strictly Fighting Scale as regards personnel, transport and baggage.
   (a) Personnel.
   (i) The Divl. Reception Camp will remain at VILLERS-SIR-SIMON with Headquarters at No. 2. Billet. Nucleus and Surplus personnel of 167th and 168th Infantry Brigades, and the Div. Employment Coy. (less Battle Employments), will be sent to the Divl. Reception Camp on the days on which their Formations move forward and will remain there. They will take rations for consumption on day of move plus 1.
   (ii) 2/2nd London Field Ambulance (less Bearers) will remain at GIVENCHY-LE-NOBLE.

   (b) Baggage.
   All baggage not actually required in action such as Officers' valises, men's packs, surplus office and mess Stores etc., will be left in one dump in each village in this area under guards to be detailed by Brigade Area Commanders from Infantry Nucleus personnel. Guards to be provided with 7 days' rations under Brigade arrangements. Locations of these dumps should be reported to this office.

   (c) Transport.
   Only essential transport will be taken forward. Any animals and vehicles which can be dispensed with will be attached to 2/2nd London Field Ambulance at GIVENCHY-LE-NOBLE and will report there on the day of the move, rationed for the following days consumption.

   (d) 169th Inf. Brigade.
   Nucleus and Surplus personnel and surplus baggage will be left behind in ARRAS under Brigade arrangements when that Brigade moves forward into action.

   (e) D.A.D.O.S. and Divl. Canteen will remain at AMBRINES. Clean Linen will not be taken forward.

   (f) The numbers of Officers, other ranks and horses being left behind in this Area in accordance with sub-paras. (a), (c) and (e) above will be reported to this office as soon as possible and repeated to O.C., Divl. Train. O.C., Divl. Reception Camp and O.C. 2/2nd London Field Ambulance.
   O.C. Divl. Train will arrange for them to be rationed for consumption on day of move plus two, onwards.

2. BUS MOVES.

   Troops will embus in accordance with the attached Embussing Table. The "Instructions for Move by bus" which were issued under this office No. G.3/894 of 15.7.18. will hold good for this move with the following exceptions.

P.T.O.

2. BUS MOVES. (contd).

(a) Para. 7. will be in abeyance. Lorries will be provided for the conveyance of Machine Guns and all Belts, Lewis Guns and all Magazines and Stokes Mortars to Battle Equipment Dumps in ARRAS. They will not be taken with the men in the busses, or in horse transport.

(b) Para. 10. Transport of the Pioneer Battn. and Mobile Veterinary Section will move with that of No. 2. Brigade Bus Group.

(c) Para. 11. Further instructions will be issued as to the arrangements made to ensure that supplies for day of move plus one shall arrive at Battle Equipment Dumps in ARRAS in time to allow of their being taken into the Line that night.

3. PREPARATIONS IN FORWARD AREA.

The proposals regarding Administrative Arrangements for THISTLE which were circulated under this office AQS/708 of 18.8.18. are confirmed and the necessary work is in hand under Divisional arrangements. Battle Stores, Extra Rations and Petrol tins will be distributed as soon as they are received.

4. ACCOMMODATION.

(a) "A" Echelon Transports of 3 Infantry Brigades, M.G.Battn. Pioneer Battn. and 3 Field Coys. R.E. will be accommodated in the Area, L.15, 16, 17, 21 and 22 (Sheet 51.C) on application to Area Commandant, DUISANS.

(b) "B" Echelon Transports & Q.M.Stores of the above Formations and Units will be accommodated in the AGNEZ-LES-DUISANS - GOUVES Area on application to the Area Commandants of those Villages.

(c) Divl. Train and Mobile Vet. Station will be accommodated in the HABARCQ - MONTENESCOURT Area on application to Area Commandants.

(d) It is improbable that much house accommodation will be available. Bivouac Shelters have been applied for.

5. STRAGGLER POSTS.

The A.P.M. will establish a line of Battle Straggler Posts East of RONVILLE CAVES and the entrances to ARRAS.

19th August, 1918.

Lieut-Colonel,
A.A. & Q.M.G., 56th Division.

6. SUPPLIES.

With reference to para. 2.(c) of the above instructions. O.C. Train is arranging to deliver Men's rations (but not Forage) for consumption on 22nd inst. to Inf. Bdes., M.G.Battn., Pioneer Battn., and Field Coys. to-morrow evening (20th). This will ensure 1 days rations for troops moving into the Line always being in possession of those Units and available for conveyance to the Line either "on the man" or on the empty Lewis Gun or Machine Gun Limbers. From 21st inst. onwards First Line Transport will draw from Refilling Points at 2 P.M. instead of at 9 A.M. daily. From consumption 23rd inst. the rations for the above Units will contain a high percentage of Preserved Meat and Biscuits.

- DISTRIBUTION. -

167th Inf.Bde.	C.R.E.	D.A.D.O.S.	Area Cdt.	LE CAUROY.
168th " "	Div.Train.	Div.Reception C.	" "	DUISANS.
169th " "	A.D.M.S.	" Employ. Coy.	" "	GOUVES.
Div.Arty.	Div.Signals.	XVIIth Corps "Q".	" "	AGNEZ-LES-DUISANS.
M.G.Battn.	A.P.M.	"G"	" "	HABARCQ.
1/5th Cheshire R.	D.A.D.V.S.	C.Cdt	Town Cdt., ARRAS.	

EMBUSSING TABLE.

Reference 1/100000. Map Sheet LENS 11.

Serial No.	Brigade Group Commander.	Troops.	Embussing Point.	Head of Convoy.	Routes to Embussing Point.
1.	Brigadier-General Commanding 167th Infantry Brigade.	167th Inf.Bde., L.G.Bettn. (less 2 Coys.), 416th Fld. Coy. R.E., 2/3rd Ldn.Fld. Amblce. (with bearers of 2/2nd Ldn.Fld.Amblce.), Divl.H.Q., R.E.H.Q., H.Q. and No.1.Sect.Signal Coy.	VILLERS-LA-SIMON - IZEL LES HAMEAU Road, Facing East.	Road Junction ½ mile North of M of IZEL-LES-HAMEAU.	No restrictions
2.	Brigadier-General Commanding 168th Infantry Brigade.	168th Inf. Bde., 2 Coys. M.G.Bettn.,512th Field Coy., R.E., 2/1st London Field Ablce., 1/5th Cheshire Regt., Divl. Employment Company.	GOUY-EN-TERNOIS - MAIZIERES Road, (Southern Road) Facing East.	Cross Roads ¼ mile South of S of MAIZIERES.	No restrictions

Units will embus from the head of the Convoy in the order given above.

:-;-:-;-:-;-:

SECRET.   56th Division AQS/710.

ADMINISTRATIVE INSTRUCTIONS
NO. 1. issued with reference to 56th Div. Order No. 193.

1. **S.A. Ammunition, Grenades, T.M.C. etc.**

   Dumps are situated as under:-
   Divisional. BLAIREVILLE. ... X.4.a.97.

   Other Dumps.
   Old Brigade Dump.   X.8.d.23
   " Battn. "   X.9.c.34.) Average Contents:-
   " " "   X.10.d.14.) 40 boxes S.A.A.
                       S.15.c.00.) 560 No. 23 Grenades.

   Purple Line Dumps. X.10.d.15.) Average contents:-
                           X.16.b.1.5.) 20 boxes S.A.A.
                           X.16.c.01.) 200 No. 23 Grenades.
                           X.17.a.33.)

   Battle equipment ammunition etc., will be drawn from Divl. Dump by Brigades etc. moving into action.

2. **Disposal of surplus personnel and Baggage.**

   (1) Before Brigades leave the BAVINCOURT Area for the Battle Area, Nucleus and Surplus personnel will be sent to the Divl. Reception Camp at GOUY EN ARTOIS where they will remain for the present.
   (2) Officers' valises and men's packs and other surplus baggage not required in action will be left in the BAVINCOURT Area and will not be taken forward to the Battle Area.
   Brigades will leave guards in charge of these dumps and will arrange to ration them.

3. First Line Transport of all Units moving forward to the Battle Area will be accommodated in the area between BLAIREVILLE and BRETENCOURT. To water at BLAMONT MILL and BRETENCOURT but not at BLAIREVILLE which is reserved for the Guards Division.

4. Divl. Prisoners' of War Cage. Will be at RANSART Cross Roads.

5. The Brigade in the Line will be responsible for establishing Straggler Posts.

6. Div. R.E. Dump will be at RANSART Cross Roads.

7. **Medical arrangements are as follows:-**

   Advanced Bearer Post at S.17.a.88.
   O.C. Bearers (Lt.-Col. A.C. DUCAT, 2/3rd Fld.Amb.)- BOISLEUX-AU-MONT.
   Walking Wounded Collecting Post. - S.2.b.80.
   Advanced Dressing Station. - M.31.b.28.

   Corps Main Dressing Station. - BAC DU SUD. - Q.32.a.71.(51c).

   The A.D.M.S. will arrange to reinforce Regtl. Stretcher Bearers with R.A.M.C. Bearers.

P.T.O.

(2)

Stores and Extra Rations.

(a) The following will be delivered to Units Q.M. Stores as they become available.
Pea Soup, Rum, Solidified Alcohol, Water Bottles, Pack Saddles, Tump Lines, Hedging Gloves.

(b) The following may be drawn from the Divl. S.A.A. Dump at BLAIREVILLE on application to Divl. H.Q. "A" & "Q" (Advanced).
Petrol tins, Wire cutters, Gas Stoves, Quicklime, Burial Discs.

9. All Administrative matters connected with operations will be dealt with at Divl. Hd.Qtrs. "A" & "Q" (Advanced).
Routine Administrative matters will be dealt with at Divl. H.Q., "A" & "Q" (Rear) at BASSEUX.
Correspondence should be addressed accordingly.

10. Div. Train Coys. & Field Ambulances will now leave Brigade Groups, and will work under the orders of O.C. Div. Train and A.D.M.S. respectively.

11. S.A.A. Section, D.A.C. will be located at BEAUMETZ.

12. Mobile Vet. Section will be at MONCHIET.

13. D.A.D.O.S. and Divl. Canteen will remain at BAVINCOURT for the present.

A.C. Dundas Major
for Lieut-Colonel,
A.A. & Q.M.G., 56th Division.

22nd August, 1918.

- DISTRIBUTION. -

167th Inf. Brigade.	1/5th Cheshire Regt.	A. P. M.
168th " "	56th Battn. M.G.Corps.	Camp Comdt.
169th " "	Divl. Train.	Div. Employ. Coy.
Divl. Artillery.	A. D. M. S.	Guards Divn. "Q".
S.A.A. Sect. D.A.C.	D. A. D. V. S.	52nd Divn. "Q".
C. R. E.	D. A. D. O. S.	VIth Corps "Q".
	Div. Signal Coy.	

S E C R E T.   **56th DIVISION.**   AQS/5.

Ref. Sheet 51.C.

LOCATION TABLE at 10 A.M. 24th AUGUST, 1918.

DIVISIONAL HEADQUARTERS.   BATTLE. BLAIREVILLE.
                            REAR.   BASSEUX.

UNIT.	Headquarters.	Transport Lines.
167th Infantry Brigade.	BLAIREVILLE, S.9.d.5.2.	BRETENCOURT.
7th Middlesex Regt.	)	-- do. --
8th " "	) LINE.	-- do. --
1st London Regt.	)	-- do. --
167th T.M. Battery.	)	-- do. --
168th Infantry Brigade.	BLAIREVILLE, S.9.d.5.2.	) "A" Echelon.
4th London Regt.	)	) R.27.c. & d.
13th " "	) LINE.	)
14th " "	)	) "B" Echelon.
168th T.M. Battery.	)	) BRETENCOURT.
169th Infantry Brigade.	BLAIREVILLE.	BRETENCOURT.
2nd London Regt.	-- do. --	-- do. --
5th " "	-- do. --	-- do. --
16th " "	-- do. --	-- do. --
169th T.M. Battery.	-- do. --	-- do. --
56th Battn. M.G.Corps.	BLAIREVILLE.	BRETENCOURT.
1/5th Cheshire Regt.	-- do. --	-- do. --
247th (Divl) Employment Coy.	BAILLEULVAL.	
C.R.E.	BATTLE.- BLAIREVILLE.	REAR.- BASSEUX.
416th Field Coy.R.E.	BLAIREVILLE.	BRETENCOURT.
512th " " "	BRETENCOURT.	-- do. --
513th " " "	BAILLEULVAL.	BAILLEULVAL.
A.D.M.S.	BASSEUX.	
2/1st Ldn.Field Amb.	SAULTY.	
2/2nd " " "	BAILLEULVAL.	
2/3rd " " "	SAULTY.	
C.R.A.	BATTLE. - BLAIREVILLE.	REAR. - BASSEUX.
280th Brigade R.F.A.	LINE.	WAILLY.
281st	LINE.	- do. -
56th D.A.C.(Less SAA.Sect.)	WAILLY.	S.A.A.Sect. BEAUMETZ.
Divl. Train.		
No. 1. Company.	BAVINCOURT.	
" 2. "	MONCHIET.	
" 3. "		MONCHIET.
" 4. "	BAVINCOURT.	
D.A.D.V.S.		MONCHIET.
Mob. Vet. Section.	MONCHIET.	
D.A.D.O.S.	-- do. --	
56th M.T. Company.	BAVINCOURT.	
Div. Reception Camp.	SOMBRIN.	
Divl. Baths Officer.	GOUY-EN-ARTOIS.	
Divl. Claims Officer.	BAVINCOURT.	
Divl. Burials "	-- do. --	
Divl. Canteen.	BAILLEULVAL.	
"Bow Bells."	BASSEUX.	
Divl. Cinema.	IZEL-LES-HAMEAU.	
RAILHEAD for personnel.	Not showing at present. GOUY-EN-ARTOIS.	

23rd August, 1918.

Major,
D.A.A.G., 56th Division.

(2)

As soon as lorries mentioned in columns "A", "B" and "C" overleaf are loaded and ready to move they will be ordered by Brigadiers-Generals Commanding Infantry Brigades and Camp Commandant to move as follows:-

Column "A".

Lorries will draw up in the order in which they arrive on the LIENCOURT - LE CAUROY Road facing West, head of the column clear of the East end of LE CAUROY. Lorries will wait at this point till instructions are received from Divisional Headquarters.

Column "B".

Lorries will be despatched to the destinations of Infantry Bde. Groups and Divisional Headquarters in the new Area, independently, as soon as they are ready.

Column "C".

Lorries moving with 167th Inf. Brigade Group will rendezvous on the VILLERS-SIR-SIMON - GIVENCHY Road facing South, head of column clear of the AMERINES - AVESNES main road.

Lorries moving with 168th Inf. Brigade Group will rendezvous on the LIGNEREUIL - GRAND RULLECOURT Road either North or South and clear of the AVESNES - LE CAUROY Road.

Lorries moving with 169th Inf. Brigade Group will rendezvous on the HAUTEVILLE - AVESNES-LE-COMTE Road facing West, head of column just clear of AVESNES - HABARCQ Road.

Lorries referred to in column "C" will be despatched to their respective rendezvous with guides from the Infantry Brigades and M.G. Companies as soon as they are loaded and will move off in rear of the bus column carrying their Brigade Groups.

A. Dundas Major
for Lieut-Colonel,
A.A. & Q.M.G., 56th Division.

21st August, 1918.

- DISTRIBUTION -

167th Inf. Brigade.	1/5th Cheshire Regt.	Camp Commandant.
168th " "	56th M.G. Battalion.	Div. Claims Offcr.
169th " "	56th M.T. Company.	" Employment Coy.
Divl. Artillery.	Div. Reception Camp.	" Signal Coy. R.E.
S.A.A. Sect. D.A.C.	D.A.D.O.S.	S.C.F.(D.C.G's Dept).
C.R.E.	Div. Salvage Offcr.	S.C.F. (P.C's Dept).
A.D.M.S.	" Gas Officer.	"G".
Divl. Train.	A.P.M.	French Mission.
	D.A.D.V.S.	

App. VII

56th Division AQS/677/3.

LORRY TABLE.
(Issued with reference to Bus Move Standing Orders, para.10).

Serial No.	UNIT	Rendezvous	Number of Lorries					
			"A" Baggage	"B" Baggage	"B" Advance Parties	M.G.	L.G.	S.A.A.
1.	167th Inf. Brigade. M.G. Bn. (less 2 Coys.)	167th Inf.Bde. H.Q. IZEL-LES-HAMEAU.	8 2		1	- 2	3 1	2 -
2.	Divl. Headquarters Div. Employment Coy. Hd.Qtrs. R.E.	Divl. H.Q. LE CAUROY.	6 1 1		1	- - -	- - -	- - -
3.	168th Inf. Bde. 2 Coys. M.G. Battn.	168th Inf.Bde. H.Q. LIGHEREUIL.	8 -		1	- 2	3 -	2 -
4.	169th Inf. Brigade. 1/5th Cheshire Regt.	169th Inf.Bde. H.Q. AVESNES-LE-COMTE.	8 1		1	- -	3 -	2 -

EMBUSSING TABLE.

56th Divn. A.S/677/3.

(Issued with reference to Bus Move Standing Orders, para.1.) Ref. Map LENS EL. 1/100,000.

Serial No.	Brigade Group Commander.	Order of Embussing.	Embussing Point.	Head of Column.	R outes to Embussing Point.
1.	Brigadier-General Commanding 167th Inf. Brigade.	167th Inf. Bde. M.G.Bn.(less 2 Coys). 416th Field Coy. R.E. Div. Reception Camp. 2/3rd Ldn.Fld. Amblce.	AMBRINES – GIVENCHY LE NOBLE Road.	Fork roads immediately N.E. of Y in GIVENCHY facing SOUTH EAST.	Under orders of Brig-Genl. Comdg 167th Inf. Bde.
2.	Brigadier-General Commanding 168th Inf. Brigade.	Div. H.Q.; H.Q. R.E. H.Q. & No.1.Sec. Div. Signal Coy. Employ.Coy. 168th Inf. Brigade. 2 Coys. M.G. Battn. 512th Fld.Coy. R.E. 2/1st Ldn.Fld. Amblce.	AVESNES LE COMTE – LIENCOURT Road.	Immediately N. of L. in LIENCOURT facing WEST.	Under orders of Brig-Genl. Comdg. 168th Inf. Bde. Restrictions :– 2 Coys.M.G.Bn. to move via DENIER and BLAVINCOURT.
3.	Brigadier-General Commanding 169th Inf. Brigade.	169th Inf. Brigade. 1/5th Cheshire Regt. 513th Fld.Coy. R.E. 2/2nd Ldn.Fld.Amblce.	AVESNES LE COMTE – HABARCQ Road.	Cross Roads 700 yards North of 1st E. of LATTRE ST QUENTIN, facing NORTH EAST.	Under orders of Brig-Genl. Comdg. 169th Inf. Brigade.

Units will embus from the head of the column in the order shown above.

UNIT	STRENGTH 1.8.18. O. O.R.	INCREASE O. O.R.	DECREASE O. O.R.	STRENGTH 1.9.18. O. O.R.
Divisional Headquarters.	16 81	- -	- -	16 81
247th Employment Coy.	2 373	- 3	- 28	2 348
167th Inf.Brigade H.Q.	3 21	1 1	- -	4 22
1/7th Middlesex Regt.	39 950	8 99	12 373	35 676
1/8th Middlesex Regt.	40 948	10 145	12 306	38 787
1/1st London Regt.	40 931	2 77	15 395	27 613
167th T.M. Battery.	4 46	- -	- -1	4 45
168th Inf.Brigade H.Q.	3 20	1 -	- -	4 20
1/4th London Regt.	42 898	5 125	15 313	32 710
1/13th London Regt.	39 925	3 102	18 344	24 683
1/14th London Regt.	43 925	- 78	13 455	30 548
168th T.M. Battery.	4 46	- -	1 6	3 40
169th Inf.Brigade H.Q.	3 21	- -	- -	3 21
1/2nd London Regt.	37 891	5 108	15 400	27 599
1/5th London Regt.	35 989	4 41	14 361	25 669
1/16th London Regt.	42 959	- 33	15 415	27 577
169th T.M. Battery.	4 46	- -	2 4	2 42
1/5th Cheshire Regt.	38 903	3 22	1 38	40 887
56th Battn. M.G.Corps.	47 881	3 94	8 136	42 839
56th Div. Artillery H.Q.	4 18	- -	- -	4 18
280th Brigade R.F.A.	32 779	- 15	2 24	30 770
281st Brigade R.F.A.	31 769	- 4	4 67	27 706
56th D.A.C.	16 569	1 -	- 76	17 493
56th Div. Engineers H.Q.	2 9	- -	1 1	1 8
416th (Edin)Fld.Coy.RE.	7 210	- 2	- 17	7 195
512th (Ldn) Fld.Coy.RE.	7 208	- 2	- 2	7 208
513th (Ldn) Fld.Coy.RE.	8 207	- 3	- 5	8 205
56th Divl. Signal Coy.	11 292	1 -	- 2	12 290
56th Divisional Train.	22 377	- 5	- 3	22 379
Medical Units.	22 539	2 3	3 11	21 531
Mobile Vet. Section.	1 18	- 2	- -	1 20

:-:-:-:-:-:-:-:-:-:

Third Army "A".
XVIIth Corps "A".
"G" Branch,

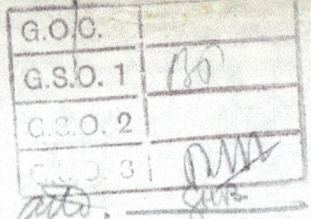

Herewith amendments to Casualties reported for period 23rd to 31st August, 1918.

List No. A.C.241 of 27.8.18. as amended by A.C.248 of 3.9.18.
1/13th London Regt. 2 O.Rs reported missing 23/8/18 now reported wounded and NOT missing.

List No. A.C.243 of 29.8.18. as amended by A.C.247 of 2.9.18.
1/8th Middlesex Regt. Of 4 O.Rs reported missing 24/8/18, 2 O.Rs now reported killed.
    Of 8 O.Rs reported missing 26/8/18, 2 O.Rs now reported killed.
1/1st London Regt. Of 15 O.Rs reported missing 24/8/18, 5 O.Rs now reported killed and 4 O.Rs wounded and NOT missing
    (Includes 1 O.R. Wounded (Gas).)

List No. A.C. 245 of 31.8.18.
1/1st London Regt. 2/Lt. E.T. COLLENS reported missing 30/8/18 now reported Died of wounds.

List No. A.C. 246 of 1.9.18.
56th Battn. M.G.Corps. 1 O.R. reported missing 29/8/18, now reported killed.

List No. A.C. 247 of 2.9.18.
1/7th Middlesex Rgt. Of 13 O.Rs reported missing 30/8/18. 4 O.Rs now reported killed and 3 O.Rs wounded and NOT missing.
    Of 5 O.Rs reported missing, 31/8/18, 4 O.Rs now reported wounded and NOT missing.
1/8th Middlesex Rgt. 1 O.R. reported missing 29/8/18, now reported evacuated sick.
1/1st London Regt. Of 113 O.Rs reported missing 30/8/18, 12 O.Rs now reported killed and 20 O.Rs wounded and NOT missing.
    3 O.Rs reported missing 31/8/18, now reported wounded and NOT missing.
1/2nd London Regt. Of 6 O.Rs reported missing 27/8/18, 4 O.Rs now reported killed.
1/5th London Regt. 6 O.Rs reported missing 26/8/18, now reported wounded and NOT missing.
    3 O.Rs reported missing 27/8/18, now reported killed.
    Of 15 O.Rs reported missing 28/8/18, 2 O.Rs now reported killed and 10 O.Rs wounded and NOT missing.
    Of 4 O.Rs reported missing 29/8/18, 2 O.Rs now reported killed and 1 O.R. wounded and NOT missing.
1/16th London Regt. Of 13 O.Rs reported missing 28/8/18, 4 O.Rs now reported killed.
    Of 17 O.Rs reported wounded and missing 28/8/18, 12 O.Rs now reported killed and 2 O.Rs wounded and NOT missing.

List No. A.C. 248 of 3.9.18.
1/4th London Regt. Of 10 O.Rs reported missing 31/8/18, 1 O.R. now reported killed and 4 O.Rs wounded and NOT missing.
1/13th London Regt. Of 7 O.Rs reported missing 29/8/18, 3 O.Rs now reported killed and 1 O.R. wounded and NOT missing.
1/14th London Regt. 3 O.Rs reported missing 29/8/18, now reported killed
    Of 5 O.Rs reported missing 31/8/18, 3 O.Rs now reported killed and 2 O.Rs wounded and NOT missing.

A.Dundas Major
for Brigadier-General,
Commanding 56th Division.

16th Septr., 1918.

AMENDED CASUALTIES.

for

PERIOD 23rd to 31st AUGUST, 1918.

UNIT.	KILLED.		WOUNDED.		MISSING.		INJURED.		TOTAL.	
	O.	O.R.	O.	O.R.	O.	O.R.	O.	O.R.	O.	O.R.
167th Infantry Bde.										
1/7th Middlesex Rgt.	2	53	5	217	1	18	-	1	8	289
1/8th Middlesex Rgt.	4	42	4	168	-	8	-	-	8	218
1/1st London Regt.	5	56	8	186	-	91	-	-	13	333
Brigade Totals.	11	151	17	571	1	117	-	1	29	840
168th Infantry Bde.										
1/4th London Regt.	4	35	8	153	1	5	-	-	13	193
1/13th London Rgt.	5	47	10	208	-	3	-	-	15	258
1/14th London Rgt.	1	62	11	242	1	2	-	1	13	307
Brigade Totals.	10	144	29	603	2	10	-	1	41	758
169th Infantry Bde.										
1/2nd London Regt.	1	43	11	225	-	12	-	2	12	282
1/5th London Regt.	3	42	10	243	-	4	-	-	13	289
1/16th London Rgt.	4	66	9	265	-	12	-	-	13	343
169th L.T.M.Bty.	-	-	2	2	-	-	-	-	2	2
Brigade Totals.	8	151	32	735	-	28	-	2	40	916
56th Battn.M.G.Corps.	3	14	5	71	-	2	-	-	8	87
1/5th Cheshire Regt.	-	-	-	4	-	-	-	3	-	7
Divisional Artillery.										
280th Bde. R.F.A.	-	4	3	41	-	-	-	-	3	45
281st Bde. R.F.A.	1	1	1	38	-	-	-	-	2	39
X/56th M.T.M.Bty.	-	-	-	1	-	-	-	-	-	1
Totals.	1	5	4	80	-	-	-	-	5	85
Divisional Engineers.										
416th(Edin)Fd.Coy.RE.	-	-	-	1	-	-	-	1	-	2
56th Div.Signal Coy.	-	-	-	1	-	-	-	-	-	1
Totals.	-	-	-	2	-	-	-	1	-	3
R.A.M.C.										
2/1st Ldn.Fld.Ambce.	-	1	-	3	-	-	-	-	-	4
2/2nd Ldn.Fld.Ambce.	-	1	-	2	-	-	-	-	-	3
2/3rd Ldn.Fld.Ambce.	-	1	-	3	-	-	-	-	-	4
Totals.	-	3	-	8	-	-	-	-	-	11
247th (Div)Employ.Coy.	-	-	-	1	-	-	-	-	-	1
DIVISIONAL TOTALS.	33	468	87	2075	3	157	-	8	123	2708

"G" Branch.

For information.

17th September 1918

D.A.A.G. Major, 56th Division.

G.O.C.	
G.S.O. 1	BP.
G.S.O. 2	
G.S.O. 3	

CASUALTIES. - AUGUST, 1918.

DATE AUGUST.	UNIT.	OFFICERS Killed.	OFFICERS Wounded.	OFFICERS Missing.	O.RS. K.	O.RS. W.	O.RS. M.	REMARKS.
1st	7th Middlesex Rgt.					1		At duty.
	14th London Regt.					1		
2nd	7th Middlesex Rgt.				1			
	1st London Regt.					2		Includes 1 injured.
3rd	2nd London Rgt.					2		Includes 1 injured.
	5th " "					4		Injured.
	16th " "					1		"
Add1.2nd	13th " "					1		Gassed.
4th	7th Middlesex Rgt.					2		
	13th London Rgt.					1		
	16th " "					1		
Ad'l.2nd	56th M.G. Battn.					1		Injured.
	4th London Regt.					1		"
5th	8th Middlesex Regt.					1		
	1/4th Ldn.Rgt.attd) 168th T.M.Bty.)					1		Injured.
	5th London Regt.					1		At duty.
Ad'l.2nd	4th London Regt.					5		Gassed.
6th	13th London Regt.					1		Injured.
	A.E.D.&attd. 1/5th London Regt.							Rev. J.M.DUNCAN, C.F.(6.8.18.)
	5th Cheshire Regt.					1		Injured.
	56th M.G. Battn.					1		"

(2)

DATE AUGUST.	UNIT.	OFFICERS Killed.	OFFICERS Wounded.	OFFICERS Missing.	O.Rs. K.	O.Rs. W.	O.Rs. M.	REMARKS.
7th	8th Middlesex Regt.				2x	1	-	x Includes 1 Died of Wounds.
	2nd London Regt.				-	1	-	
	16th "				-	1	-	
	280th Bde. R.F.A.				-	3	-	At duty.
	512th (Ldn)Fld.Coy.RE.				-	1	-	
	13th London Regt.				-	1	-	Injured.
8th	8th Middlesex Regt.				-	1	-	By Bayonet Injured.
	2nd London Regt.	(X)Capt.W.R.RAWLE,7/8/18.	2/Lt.E.M.D.MACKIE.7/8/18.		1	1	-	(X) Died of Wounds
	5th "				-	3	-	
	16th "				-	-	-	
	56th M.G. Bn.				-	2	-	
	56th Div.Signal Coy.				-	1	-	
	13th London Regt.				-	1	-	Injured.
9th	7th Middlesex Regt.		Lt. W.C. FIELDER. 9/8/18. 2/Lt. E.J. OWEN, 9/8/18.		-	1	-	
	1st London Regt.				-	1	-	
	4th "				-	4.	-	All at duty.
	14th "				-	2	-	
	5th "				-	1	-	
10th	8th Middlesex Regt.				2	1	-	
	1st London Regt.				-	1	-	
	13th "				-	1	-	Injured.
	5th Cheshire Regt.				-	1	-	
11th	7th Middlesex Regt.				-	2	-	Gas.
	2nd London Regt.				-	2	-	Includes 1 at Duty.
	5th "				-	1	-	At Duty.
	16th "				-	1	-	Injured by pick.
	5th Cheshire Regt.				-	1	-	
	280th Bde. R.F.A.				-	2	-	Includes 1 at duty.

(3)

DATE AUGUST.	UNIT.	OFFICERS Killed.	OFFICERS Missing.	OFFICERS Wounded.	O.Rs. K.	O.Rs. W.	O.Rs. M.	REMARKS.
12th	13th London Regt.	-	-	-	-	1	-	
	14th " "	-	-	-	-	2	-	Injured by pick.
	2nd " "	-	-	-	-	1	-	" "
	16th " "	-	-	-	-	1	-	
13th	1st London Regt.	-	-	-	-	3	-	Incl. 1 injured.
	14th " "	-	-	-	-	2	-	
	5th " "	-	-	-	-	2	-	
	56th M.G. Bettn.	-	-	-	-	2	-	At duty.
	280th Bde. R.F.A.	-	-	-	-	1	-	
14th	8th Middlesex Regt.	-	-	-	-	1	-	Injured by explosion of
	5th Cheshire Regt.	-	-	-	-	1	-	(Grenade.
	56th M.G. Bettn.	-	-	-	-	1	-	
15th	1st London Regt.	-	-	-	-	3	-	Incl. 2 Injured.
	4th Ldns attd 168th TMBty.	-	-	-	-	1	-	
	13th London Regt.	-	-	-	2	5	-	
	14th " "	-	-	-	1	43x	-	x Inc.38 ORs Wndd.Gas.
	5th " "	-	-	-	-	2	-	
	5th Cheshire Regt.	-	-	-	-	1	-	Injured at Duty.
	X/56th T.M.Bty.	-	-	-	-	1	-	
16th	13th London Regt.	-	-	-	-	2	-	Injured.
	16th " "	-	-	-	-	1	-	
	56th M.G. Bettn.	-	-	-	-	1	-	Incl. 1 at Duty.
	280th Bde. R.F.A.	-	-	-	-	2	-	
17th	14th London Regt.	-	-	Capt. W.M. JAMES, 14/8/18. X 2/Lt. G.G. MILNE, -do- X	-	-	-	X Gassed.
	56th M.G. Bettn.	-	-	Lt. B.M. WILSON. @ 15/8/18.	-	5X	-	@ Injured. Thrown from horse.
18th	1st London Regt.	-	-	-	-	1	-	Injured.
	4th " "	-	-	-	-	1	-	"
19th	56th M.G. Bettn.	-	-	-	-	1	-	Gassed 17/8/18.

(4)

DATE	UNIT	OFFICERS			O. Rs.				REMARKS.
		Killed.	Wounded.	Missing.	K.	W.	M.	I.	
AUGUST.									
20th	16th London Rgt.	—	—	—	—	1	—	—	
21st	8th Middlesex Rgt.	—	—	—	—	4	—	—	Injured in Train Smash, ST POL.
	14th London Regt.	—	—	—	—	1	—	—	Injured by pick.
14th	"	—	—	—	—	5	—	—	Wounded(Gas.)
23rd	2nd London Regt.				K.	W.	M.	I.	
	281st Bde. R.F.A.	—	—	—	—	—	—	1	(& 1 gassed)
	280th	—	—	—	—	—	—	—	. Includes 1 at duty)
	1st London Regt.	—	2/Lt.(A/Cpt)G.W.ROWLANDS,MC, 2/Lt.(A/Cpt) R.S.B. SIMMONDS-(20th Ldns)	—	1	5x	—	—	Gassed.
4th	"	—	Lt.(A/Cpt)H.A.T.HEWLETT, 2/Lt.A.F.POTTER(7th Ldns)			6			x Inc.13 ORs Gassed
	"		" F.S.C.TAYLOR,(20th Ldns)						
	"		" T. YOXALL.						
	"		" A.W.CHIGNALL.		18	81x			x " 8 ORs Gassed
13th	"	—	Capt.(A/Lt/Col.R.E.F.SHAW,MC, Lt.(A/Cpt)F.J.B.GODDARD.	—	12	83x	2	—	x Inc.29 ORs Gassed
	"	—	2/Lt. R.N. WILSON.						
	"	—	Lt.(A/Cpt)F.R.ROSEVEAR.(X)						(X) Died of Wounds
	"		" E.A. SHERWOOD.(9th Ldns)						
	"		2/Lt. E. SHENON.						
	"		" W.V. FOOT. (15th Ldns).						
14th	"	—	" B.L. LELLIOTT.	—	23	99x	1	—	x Inc.44 ORs Gassed.
	"		Lt. G. WOODCOCK.						
	"		2/Lt. G.H. STEWART.						
	56th M.G. Battn.	2/Lt. F.G. BRIGHT.	—	—	9	19	1	—	
24th	7th Middlesex Rgt.	—	Capt. A.T.SHIPTON,M.G.	—	16	93	4	—	Lx x By discharge of (rifle.
8th	"	—	Lt. H.H. MUMMERY.						
	"	—	Capt.R.F.M. BULLER.	—					
	"	—	" H.F. DAMPNEY.						
	"	—	Lt.(A/Cpt)G.J.KEEPING.	—	29	120x	4	—	x Inc.1 at Duty.
	"	—	" W.H. FULLER.						
	"	—	2/Lt. E. CHILD.						
	"	—	2/Lt. W.J. THORNE.						
	"	— G.E. COUSENS.							
	1st London Rgt.	Lt. O.H. GARRUD,(8th Ldns)	Capt. F.H.C.WILTSHIRE.	—	20a	90	15c	—	a Inc.1 Died of Wnds
	"	—	Lt.(A/Cpt)A.G.HERBERT,M.C.						c 1 Wnd & M'ing.
	"	Capt. J.K. MEWS.(X)	Lt. G.S. SMALLMAN						
	"	—	" A.T.G. NIBBS.						
	"	—	2/Lt. H.E. WHITBREAD.						(X) Died of Wounds.

(5)

DATE.	UNIT.	OFFICERS.			Missing.	O. Rs.				REMARKS.
		Killed.	Wounded.			K.	W.	M.	I.	
AUGUST.										
24th contd.	1st London Rgt.		2/Lt. G.W. ANGRAVE.				1			
	13th "						6			
	16th "		2/Lt. A.T. SHORTER.				1a		1b	a At duty. b By pick.
	56th M.G. Battn.						3			
	5th Cheshire Rgt.		Lt. E.L.WOOD.(at duty)				1			
	280th Bde.R.F.A.						1			
	281st "						1			
	2/1st Ldn.Fd.Amb.									
	2/2nd "									
25th	7th Middlesex Rgt.	Lt. G.E. ADAMSON. x				1	6			x Died of Wnds.
	8th "	2/Lt. R. COX. x					2			x "
	1st London Regt.					2x	7			x "
	5th "					1	3			
	16th "						12			
	56th M.G. Battn.						3g			g Gassed.
	5th Cheshire Rgt.						2			"
	280th Bde. R.F.A.					1	4g			g "
	281st "						2			
26th	7th Middlesex Rgt.		2/Lt. G.E. BREWER.(7th Ldns). 2/Lt. F.A. PEARSON.			8	60		2	(of Wnds. x Inc. 3 ORs Died
	8th "					13x	3			
	1st London Regt.		2/Lt. L.J. SKINNER.			1	14		4	g 1 OR Gassed
	4th "						2g		1	
	14th "									
	2nd "	2/Lt. E. FREY.					6			
	5th "					1	13d			d Inc.1 OR At duty
	56th M.G. Battn.						23			
	280th Bde. R.F.A.		2/Lt. F.R. GROOM.				3			
	281st "						1g			g Gassed
	2/2nd Ldn.Fld.Amb.						1g			g Gassed.
	2/3rd "					1	2g			g Gassed Inc.1 OR Gassed

(6)

DATE AUGUST.	UNIT.	OFFICERS Killed.	OFFICERS Wounded.	Missing.	O. RS. K.	O. RS. W.	O. RS. M.	O. RS. I.	REMARKS.
27th	8th Middlesex Rgt.				7	20			
	4th London Regt.	2/Lt. E.H.GARNER.			1	10			
	2nd "	" G.H.MERRIKIN.	2/Lt. W.A. COUSINS.		32	169	6	1b	b By Bayonet.
	" "		Capt. E.J. HARRINGTON.						
	" "		2/Lt. F.P. DEERE.						
	" "		" L. MAY. (7th Ldns.)						
	" "		" W.J. THOMAS.(20th Ldns)						
	" "		" G.W. GONOLEY. (13th Ldns)						
	" "		" A. WILLSON.						
	5th "	2/Lt.S.F.J.CAMPBELL.(6th Ldns)	2/Lt. W.G. LEAN.		14	63	3		
	" "		" E.F. BYLES. (15th Ldns)						
	16th "	Lt. F.W.RUSSELL, M.G.	" J.W. GRINDEY.		3	17		X	X 7th Ldns attd
	169th T.M.Bty.		" O.M. POWER.(20th Ldns)			2		-0	-0 2nd Londons.
	56th M.G. Battn.		" A.J.HASSLACHER. X			10			
			" J.H. BULOW.						
			" E.G. CAVE.						
	5th Cheshire Rgt.		" J.W.K. MORTON.						
	280th Bde. R.F.A.					1g		1a	1a gassed
	281st "					1g		a	a Sprained ankle.
			2/Lt. T.W. WEST.			1			g gassed.
28th	8th Middlesex Rgt.					5		g	g Inc.3 ORs gassed.
	1st London Regt.					2			
	4th "	Lt. J.F. BAKER.			1	10g	8	g	g Inc.10 ORs gassed.
	13th "		2/Lt. (A/Cpt) H.D. PRATT.		6	37	8		
	14th "		2/Lt. R.N. MORLEY.		7	82	15		
	2nd "		Capt. G.B. VAILE.			1			
	5th "		Lt. (A/Capt) R. COPE.						
	" "		2/Lt. V.W.R. CRANE.						
	16th "	Lt. L.P. HARROW, D.C.M.	2/Lt. (A/Cpt) F.E. WHITBY, M.G.		37	99	30q	q	q Inc.17 ORs Wnded
	" "	2/Lt. G.G.WARREN.(21st Ldns)	Lt. R.R. CALKIN.						& Missing.
	" "	" J.C.GOADEY.(13th Ldns)	2/Lt. A.J. PHILIP.						
	" "		" B. WADE.						
	" "		" W.E. TODD.						
	" "		" A.H. CHAPLIN.						
	" "		" L.W. FRIEND. (9th Ldns)						

(8)

DATE AUGUST.	UNIT.	OFFICERS Killed.	OFFICERS Wounded.	OFFICERS Missing.	O.Rs. K.	O.Rs. W.	O.Rs. M.	REMARKS.
30th	7th Middlesex Rgt.				10	20	13	
	8th " "					8		
	1st London Rgt.	Lt.(A/Cpt)G.H. LE TALL.	2/Lt. J. HEARN.	Lt. E.T.COLLENS.X	1	22	113	X Wnded & Missing.
	4th " "				1	2		
	14th " "					6		
	2nd " "					2		
	5th " "				1	7		Since reptd. Killed in Action
	16th " "		2/Lt. P.R.S. SPETTIGUE.					k Inc 2 ORs Died of Wds
	280th Bde. R.F.A.		Capt. V.E.O. WELCH. X		3k	1		sed
	281st " "					1g		g gassed.
	-X/56th T.M.Bty.	2/Lt. W. WILLIAMS.				21x	1	x Inc.3 at duty & 3 Gas
	416th (Edin)Fd.Co.RE.					1g		g gassed.
	56th Div.Signal Co.					1		By fall.
	247th Employ.Coy.					1		
31st	7th Middlesex Rgt.		Capt. C.F. CHALLEN.		14	30	5	
	" "		" P.W. LIMBREY.		1	6		
	8th " "				1	4	3	
	1st London Rgt.				2	8		
	280th Bde. R.F.A.							
	4th London Rgt.	Lt. V.R.OLDREY.	2/Lt,W.G.HOOK.(9th Ldns) 2/Lt.R.T.STEVENSON. (5th Londons) A. HOLLOWAY.		13	41	10	
	13th " "					2		
	14th " "		Lt.(A/Cpt)F.G.BISHOP. at Duty. 2/Lt. G.M.W.DAVIES. " J. McNAUGHTON.		11	54	5	
	2nd " "					10		
	16th " "				1			Died of Wounds
	2/1st Ldn.Fd.Amb.				1	2g		g Inc.1 OR Gassed.
	2/2nd " "					1		
	2/3rd " "							
TOTALS FOR AUGUST.		32	94	4	415	2179	279	8

DATE AUGUST.	UNIT.	OFFICERS Killed.	OFFICERS Wounded.	OFFICERS Missing.	O.Rs K.	O.Rs W.	O.Rs M.	O.Rs I.	REMARKS.
28th	16th London Rgt.	-	2/Lt. T.W.R. PROCTER.	-	-	-	-	-	
	169th T.M.Bty.	-	2/Lt.(A/Cpt) S. du PLESSIS. (7th Ldns attd. 5th Ldns)	-	-	-	-	-	(Gassed
	56th M.G. Bttn.	-	-	-	2	14g	-	-	g Inc. 3 ORs Gassed
	5th Cheshire Rgt.	-	-	-	-	1x	-	-	1x By Barbed wire.
	280th Bde. R.F.A.	-	-	-	1	16x	-	-	x Inc. 5 Ors Gassed.
29th	7th Middlesex Rgt.	-	-	-	1	1	-	-	
	8th	-	-	-	1	4	-	-	
	1st London Rgt.	Lt. D.F. HUGGINS.	-	-	1	1x	-	-	x Gassed.
	280th Bde. R.F.A.	-	-	-	-	1x	-	-	
	281st	-	-	-	-	7	-	-	
	416th (Edin)Fld.Co.	-	-	-	1	1	-	-	
	4th London Rgt.	-	-	-	-	3	-	-	
	13th	Lt. W.E.SMITH,M.G.	2/Lt. G.G. LEWIS.(1st Londons)	-	31	111	7	-	
	"		" G.J. DENYER.						
	"		" G.B. CAMERON.						
	"		" F.F. MILTON.						
	"		" A.E.E. PHILLIPS.						
	"		" L.B. HUTCHINSON.(6th Ldns)						
	"		" H.A. DAVIES.						
	14th	2/Lt.W.S. McLACHLAN.	" A.A. BEARDMORE.	2/Lt.J.S.L.BAYFIELD.(X)	22	80a	3	-	a Inc. 2 ORs (x)Wnd & M'Ing
	"		Lt. W.C. NEEDS.						
	"		" E.L. REID.						
	"		" J. ALLARDYCE,DSO,MM.						At duty.
	2nd	-	2/Lt. W.P. ANDREWS.	-	1	1	-	-	
	"		Lt. A.S. JARVIS.						
	5th	-	2/Lt. A.G. WILDING.(20th Ldns)	-	12	58	4	-	(Died of Wnds.
	"		Lt.(A/Cpt)T.E.BURROUGHS,M.G.						d Inc 2 ORs
	"		2/Lt. W.A. HOUGHTON.						
	16th	Major J. LECKIE,M.C.	(d)	-	4d	111	-	-	d Died of Wnds
	56th M.G.Bettn.	2/Lt. T.H.CHALKLEY.	-	-	2	16	2a	-	a Inc L OR Wndd & Missing.

<u>Secret.</u>

War Diary

Administrative Branch

<u>56th Division</u>

Period :- 1st to 30th Septr. 1918.

Vol :- <u>XXXII</u>

Army Form C. 2118.

WAR DIARY
or
INTELLIGENCE SUMMARY.
(Erase heading not required.)

56 DIVISION
VOLUME XXXII

Place	Date	Hour	Summary of Events and Information	Remarks and references to Appendices
BOISLEUX-au-MONT	1 Sept 1918		Division resting and reorganizing after BATTLE of the day. Single German on	
"	2		Division rest a half Showers. Weather warm & fine	
"	3		Still resting. Reconnaissance carried out to find sector the newly captured Territory. Apparent sabotage.	
"	4		Order received that Division will relieve 52nd (LOWLAND) DIVISION in support to 1st ARMY	
"	5		H.Q. at SUSMIT. One Brigade and other Divnl. Arts. Engineers will relieve 1st DIVISION (XVII Corps) FIRST ARMY) in the line with H.Q. at LES FOSSES FARM. AA.16.a.6.5. ans. DUNS reconnoitre new area	
"	6		168th Inf. Bde. move to join 1st Division same GUEMAPPE (D.16) AA.26.c.16.a. 3.6 relief of troops up to 29/8/18 completed by 12 mn.	
"	7		169th Inf. Bde. Right Brade. in position relieves near GUEMAPPE 168 L.J. in Reserve into Line ans. Relieves 2nd Brigade. 1st Div. HQ at AA.16.C.3.5 RESERVE BRIGADE FEUCHY. 169 Inf. Brigade H.Q. 167th Inf. Bde. in reserve. Div relieves 1st Brigade 1st Div. at A.15.2.8.4. 167 H.Q. Arras. into line (RIGHT SECTOR) and relieve 1st Brigade at 10 am.	
"	8		Div. 948 H.Q.C to LES FOSSES FARM, opening at 10 am	
LES FOSSES FARM	9		Div. at LES FOSSES FARM	
"	10		— " —	
"	11			

WAR DIARY or INTELLIGENCE SUMMARY

Army Form C. 2118.

Place	Date September	Hour	Summary of Events and Information	Remarks and references to Appendices
LES FOSSES FARM	12		168th Infantry Bde. relieved by 167th Inf. Bde. in Left Sector. 168th Inf. Bde. moved into reserve to relief to FEUCHY-BLANGY area. 167th Inf. Bde HQ at P.19.a.5.6., 168th Inf. Bde HQ at M.25.a.6.3.	
	13 14 15		Bde at LES FOSSES FARM.	
	16		Warning order received that 4th (British) Div. will relieve Left Brigade (167th) & 56th Div. & that 58th Div. will extend its front to the Right on the night of 18/19th Sept & that 58th Div. will extend its front to the Right on the front held by 3rd Canadian Div. from the present southern boundary L.W.c.2.6. relief to be completed by 10 a.m. 19th Sept. 20x. Div. at LES FOSSES FARM.	
	17 18		167th Infantry Bde. relieved by 10th Inf. Bde. (4th (British) Div.) on night 18/19th. 167th Inf. Bde. relieved 169th Inf. Bde. on its present frontage (1st Formerly Right Sector of Div. Front) - Bde HQ remains to same position. 165th Inf. Bde. again moved to Div. Rn. Enclosed in position. HQ at O.11.d.6.5.50. Bde on Bdes in rest of area. V.25. 0.13.b. - 0.13.d.	
	19		168th Infantry Bde. moved by bus from BLANGY-TILLOY and LYS-EN-ARTOIS & proceeded to and taking over line of 8th Can. Inf. Bde. (2nd Can. Div.) 167th Inf. Bde. extended its front to the Right, taking over frontage hitherto by Left Battn. 8th Can. Inf. Bde. - Bde. HQ remaining in same position. 168th Inf. Bde. takes over frontage held by Right Bn. 8th Can. Inf. Bde with Bde. HQ at P.34.a.2.9. 169th Inf. Bde. in Div. Reserve moves to a position Left Bn with Bde. HQ at O.35.c.7.3. One Battn. in rest of area V.25. 0.29.b., 0.29.c.	

Army Form C. 2118.

WAR DIARY
or
INTELLIGENCE SUMMARY.
(Erase heading not required.)

Place	Date	Hour	Summary of Events and Information	Remarks and references to Appendices
LES FOSSES FARM	19th Septr		Boundaries between 167th & 168th Inf Bdes readjusted to conform to following:- Northern Bn Boundary :- K 27 central - P.12 central - P.11 & 4 - P.15 cent. Western Bn W E CAMBRAI RD. Southern Bn Boundary :- W.6 central - W.4 c.2.6. - N.2 central - Y.6 central - P.26.a.13 - thence along CAMBRAI RD. Inter-Brigade Boundary :- P.12 central - P.16.a.6.9 - thence following the HIRONDELLE RIVER to P.19.c.H.O - SAUDEMONT VILLAGE (inclusive to left Bn) - P.2H.c.5.0 - thence W to the CAMBRAI RD.	
	20		Bn at LES FOSSES FARM.	
	21		Active measures taken by Div - moved /Rec four in an attack on the XVII Corps front - line of forming up troops - completely camouflaged provision to meet an	
	22		"	
	23		"	
	24		"	
	25			
	26		Arrangements in connection with operations on 27th but completed. Advanced Divl HQ opened at V.3 b.2.7. Zero hour for operations Tomorrow is 5.20 AM	
	27th		Following G.S. Wagon were ordered to report to a rendezvous at) CRE at R.E. dump V.6a.72 ARRAS-CAMBRAI Road at 6 am today :- 29 G.S. wagon from Divl Train and 20 from DAC. This wagon was required for taking bays to Cork Bridges in connection with bridge which are being constructed over Canal du NORD. 165th & 166th Bde R.E.a attached N.W.I to ARRAS - CAMBRAI Road rainfall 4 gradually. Estimated Casualties 3 offrs 5 OR. per Battn.	

Army Form C. 2118.

WAR DIARY
or
INTELLIGENCE SUMMARY.
(Erase heading not required.)

Place	Date	Hour	Summary of Events and Information	Remarks and references to Appendices
LES FOSSES Fm	27	(cont'd)	Number of Prisoners passed through Div'n PoW Cage ; 112 Offrs 501 ORs.	
VILLERS LEZ CAGNICOURT	28		A and Q moved to C.Hqrs VILLERS LEZ CAGNICOURT. 169th Bde Remaining in line.	
	29		167th Bde ordered to move into reserve area South of VIS en ARTOIS	
	30		No change.	

M. [signature]
Lieut.-Col:
A.A. & Q.M.G. 56th Division.

SECRET.   56th Division AQS/734/1.

ADMINISTRATIVE INSTRUCTIONS
in connection with forthcoming operations.
Issued with reference to 56th Divn. Order 205.

1. **TRENCH MUNITION DUMPS.**

   Advanced Trench Munition Dumps under Divisional control are situated as under :-

   V.3.b.7.3.
   P.36.b.8.9.

2. **NUCLEUS PERSONNEL** of 169th Infantry Brigade will be accommodated at Brigade Transport Lines. Canvas shelters will be issued for this personnel.
   This personnel will remain under Divisional control and will not be drawn upon without reference to Divisional Headquarters.

3. **FIRST LINE TRANSPORT.**

(a) All concerned are reminded that in the present type of warfare the whole of Units' First Line Transport remains under control of Formations and Units. In the event of operations developing in such a manner that ammunition, tools etc., have to be drawn from Transport Echelons instead of from Dumps, those Echelons (A) would be located near the fighting troops and directly under their control, and the reserved Echelons (B) would then be controlled by Divisional Hd.Qtrs. This reversion of "B" Echelon Transports to Divisional control would however only take place as the result of definite orders to that effect from Divisional Headquarters.
(b) The following areas are suggested as being (or likely to become) suitable for First Line Transport during these operations and may be used if desired :-

   (i) U.5. and U.11.
   (ii) V.3.c. & d. V.10.
   (iii) V.18. W.13 and 14.

Any moves of First Line Transports and Qr.Mtr's Stores must be IMMEDIATELY reported to this office and O.C. Divl. Train.
(c) The C.R.E. will arrange to develope the water/facilities in (ing) areas (b) (ii) and (iii) as the tactical situation permits.

4. **ACCOMMODATION.**

   In the event of moves, Tents, Trench Shelters, Tarpaulins and other canvas accommodation will be dealt with as follows :-
(a) Formations and Units (or portions of Units such as Wagon and Transport Lines), who vacate an area and receive orders from Divl. Headquarters to hand over the same area to other troops, will hand over all canvas in situ to the troops who replace them. Receipts for this canvas will be taken and copies forwarded to this office. Demands for fresh canvas for the new area will be submitted to Div. Headquarters.
(b) Formations and Units (or portions of Units such as Wagon and Transport Lines), who vacate an area and do not receive orders from Divl. Headquarters to hand over that area to other troops, will either
(i) If moving into action or into an area where canvas accommodation is not required, collect the canvas into dumps, under guards, and report the locations of dumps to Divl. Headquarters, who will issue instructions as to disposal,
or
(ii) If moving into an area where canvas accommodation is required, move forward the canvas into the new area.

P.T.O.

5. PRISONERS OF WAR CAGE.

The Divisional Prisoners of War Cage will be at V.3.b.3.7.

6. MEDICAL.

	LEFT BRIGADE.	RIGHT BRIGADE.
Bearer Posts	P.24.a.4.9	P.36.b. central.
Car Posts	P.24.d.6.0	Q.26.d.5.2
Advanced Dressing Stations	P.21.a.7.2	P.34.d.4.4
	(DURY)	(TANNERY Buildings).

WALKING WOUNDED COLLECTING POST   O.24.c.3.2
MAIN DRESSING STATION Hospital St. Jean ARRAS.   G.21.d.central.
Headquarters, O.C., Bearers   O.24.c.3.2

7. VETERINARY.

An advanced Veterinary Collecting Station will be established in the vicinity of VERT-EN-ARTOIS on the 26th instant.

8. STRAGGLER POSTS.

Will be established under Brigade arrangements.

9. SUPPLEMENTARY TRANSPORT FOR 169th INFANTRY BRIGADE.

167th and 168th Infantry Brigades will each hand over 18 pack animals (complete turn-outs) to 169th Infantry Brigade to supplement their Transport establishment whilst they are in the Line.

Transfers of these turn-outs and their rations will be arranged direct between Brigades.

10. BATTLE STORES will be issued as follows:-

Formations.	Pack Saddles.	Tump Lines.	Wire Cutters.
167th Inf. Bde.	20	—	—
168th Inf. Bde.	20	30	—
169th Inf. Bde.	20	30	50
S.A.A. Sect. D.A.C.	20	—	—

11. BATTLE RATIONS.

Pea Soup will be issued as follows :-

        167th Inf. Bde.   100 rations.
        168th " "   400   "
        169th " "   1500   "

A special issue of Rum for these operations in proportion to the number of troops actively engaged in the forward area will be made to

    Each Infantry Brigade.
    M.G.Battalion. (including attached Companies).
    Divnl. Artillery. (including attached Brigades).
    R.Es. and Pioneers.
    R.A.M.C.

12. BATTLE EQUIPMENT.

ammunition will be delivered to 169th Infantry Brigade in its present area, under Divisional arrangements. Other Brigades will draw Battle Equipment ammunition from their own Brigade dumps.

13. DIVISIONAL HEADQUARTERS.

All matters immediately connected with the operations will be dealt with at Divisional Headquarters "A & Q" (Advanced). Matters not immediately connected with the operations will be dealt with at Divisional Headquarters "A & Q" (Rear). Correspondence should be addressed accordingly.

                                            Lieut. Colonel,
                               A.A. & Q.M.G., 56th Division.

23rd September 1918.

DISTRIBUTION.

167th Inf. Bde.	5th Cheshire Regt.	D.A.D.O.S.
168th " "	C.R.E.	D.A.D.V.S.
169th " "	Div. Train.	Senior Chaplain
Div. Arty.	A.D.M.S.	(D.Cs. Dept.)
M.G.Battn.	D.A.P.S.	Senior Chaplain
	"G"	(R.Cs. Dept).

SECRET.   56th DIVISION.   A.Q.S.5.

Ref. Sheets 51.B. & 51.C.
LOCATION TABLE AT 12 NOON, 22ND SEPTEMBER, 1918.

```
                   Divisional Headquarters.    LES FOSSES FARM. N.12.a.0.4.
UNIT.                              Headquarters.        Transport Lines.
167th Infantry Bde.                P.19.b.8.5.          Area N.18 a & b.
   7th Middlesex Regt.             Q.20.b.6.5.          -- do. --
   8th     "        "              P.24.a.4.8.          -- do. --
   1st London Regt.                P.15.b.3.2.          -- do. --
   167th L.T.M. Battery.           P.33.a.0.2.
168th Infantry Bde.                P.34.a.2.9.          Area N.18. a & b.
   4th London Regt.                Q.20.a.6.5.          -- do. --
   13th   "     "                  P.28.c.2.3.          -- do. --
   14th   "     "                  Q.25.d.6.0.          -- do. --
   168th L.T.M. Battery.           P.34.a.2.9.
169th Infantry Bde.                O.35.c.7.3.          Area O.13.a.
   2nd London Regt.                V.2.a.25.60.         -- do. --
   5th   "     "                   O.29.b.9.1.          -- do. --
   16th  "     "                   O.29.c.5.2.          -- do. --
   169th L.T.M. Battery.           O.29.b.9.1.

56th Battn. M.G. Corps.            N.12.a.0.4.          N.3.d.
1/5th Cheshire Regt.               N.11.b.9.5.          N.3.d.
247th (Div) Employment Coy.        O.7.a.5.5.
C.R.E.                             LES FOSSES FARM.
   416th Field Coy. R.E.           O.14.b.7.3.          O.13.a.
   512th   "    "    "             O.23.b.2.2.          -- do. --
   513th   "    "    "             O.32.d.4.5.          -- do. --
A.D.M.S.                           LES FOSSES FARM.
   2/1st Ldn. Fld. Amblce.         HOSPICE ST JEAN, ARRAS.   ARRAS.
   2/2nd   "    "     "            O.24.c.3.2.          N.11.b.
   2/3rd   "    "     "            COLLEGE des JEUNES FILLES, ARRAS.  ARRAS.
C.R.A.                             LES FOSSES FARM.
   280th Bde. R.F.A.               P.21.a.8.2.          O.25.d. O.27.c.
                                                        O.27.d. O.28.c.
   281st  "    "                   P.34.b.20.80.        N.33.b.5.2.
                                                        O.19.b.9.5.
56th D.A.C. H.Q. (less SAA.SECT) N.15.a.central.  SAA.Sect. N.24.c.5.2.
Attached.
   282nd A.F.A. Bde.               P.27.c.00.60.        U.2.a.2.9.
   293rd Army Bde. R.F.A.          P.28.b.40.70.        O.21.d.20.30.
Divisional Train.                  TILLOY. M.6.b.2.6.
   No. 1. Company.                    "    M.6.a & b.
    "  2.    "                        "       "
    "  3.    "                        "       "
    "  4.    "                        "       "
D.A.D.V.S.                         LES FOSSES FARM.
   Mobile Vet. Section.            TILLOY.
D.A.D.O.S.                         ST SAUVEUR.
56th M.T. Company.                 O.20.a.8.8.
Div. Reception Camp.               ETRUN.
NUCLEUS PERSONNEL.                 ETRUN.
Div. Baths Officer.                TILLOY. H.31.d.2.3.
  "  Claims    "                      "
  "  Burials   "                   O.7.a.1.6.
  "  Salvage   "                   O.7.d.2.2.
  "  Canteen.                      TILLOY. H.31.d.2.3.
RAILHEAD for Personnel.            AGNEZ-LES-DUISANS.
```

21st Septr., 1918.   A.C. Dundas
                                                   Major,
                                      D.A.A.G., 56th Division.

SECRET. 56th Divn. AQS/734/1.

AMENDMENT TO ADMINISTRATIVE INSTRUCTIONS
in connection with forthcoming operations.
Issued under AQS/734/1 dated 23.9.18.

Para. 3 (a). line 7.

For "reserved" road "rearward".

24th Septr., 1918.

Lieut-Colonel,
A.A. & Q.M.G., 56th Division.

War Diary

SECRET.   A.Q.S.5.

LOCATIONS.

Please make the following amendments to Location Table dated 21st September 1918. :-

7th Middlesex Regt.	For Q.20.b.6.5.	Read P.18.c.8.3.
8th Middlesex Regt.	For P.24.a.4.8.	Road P.15.d.60.40.

A C Dundas
Major,
D.A.A.G., 56th Division.

22nd Septr., 1918.

War Diary

SECRET.   56th DIVISION.   A.Q.S.5.

Ref. Sheet 51.B.
LOCATION TABLE at 10 A.M. 11th SEPTR., 1918.

DIVISIONAL HEADQUARTERS. ... LES FOSSES FARM. N.12.a.0.

UNIT.	Headquarters.	Transport Lines.
167th Infantry Brigade.	G.21.d.9.0.	
7th Middlesex Regt.	H.13.a.0.1.	ARRAS.
8th " "	H.21.c.4.6.	H.13.a.
1st London Regt.	H.26.central.	H.21.c.
167th T.M. Battery.	G.30.d.0.2.	H.26.
168th Infantry Brigade.	P.14.c.3.3.	
4th London Regt.	P.8.d.1.8.	
13th " "	P.11.a.7.1.	} N.18.a.7.7.
14th " "	P.3.a.0.0.	
168th T.M. Battery.	P.14.c.3.5.	
169th Infantry Brigade.	P.15.b.8.4.	
2nd London Regt.	P.15.d.5.4.	
5th " "	P.12.c.5.5.	} AREA. O.13.a.
16th " "	P.15.c.9.4.	
169th T.M. Battery.	P.21. Area.	
56th Battn. M. G. Corps.	N.12.a.0.4.	H.3.d.
1/5th Cheshire Regt.	N.11.b.9.5.	H.3.d.
247th (Div) Employment Coy.	O.7.a.1.6.	
C. R. E.	LES FOSSES FARM.	
416th Field Coy. R.E.	O.9.b.9.6.	
512th " " "	O.9.c.3.3.	} O.13.a.
513th " " "	O.18.c.	
A. D. M. S.	LONDON CAVE, ST SAUVEUR.	
2/1st Ldn.Fld.Amblce.	HOSPICE ST JEAN, ARRAS.	ARRAS.
2/2nd " " "	LES FOSSES FARM.	H.3.b.
2/3rd " " "	COLLEGE des JEUNES FILLES, ARRAS.	ARRAS.
C. R. A.	LES FOSSES FARM.	
280th Brigade R.F.A.	P.21.b.1.4.	
281st " "	P.14.c.8.4.	} CHERISY.
56th D. A. C.	N.15.a.5.5.	O.33. a & b.
Divisional Train.		
No. 1. Company.	TILLOY. H.6.b.2.6.	
" 2. "		
" 3. "	} TILLOY.	
" 4. "	H.3.a. & b.	
D. A. D. V. S.	LONDON CAVE, ST SAUVEUR.	
Mobile Vet. Section.	TILLOY.	
D. A. D. O. S.	ST SAUVEUR.	
56th M.T. Company.	Near PORTE BAUDIMONT, ARRAS.	
Divl. Reception Camp.	ETRUN.	
NUCLEUS PERSONNEL.	ETRUN.	
Divl. Baths Officer.	TILLOY. H.31.d.2.3.	
" Claims "		
" Burials "	O.7.a.1.6.	
" Salvage "	O.7.d.2.2.	
" Canteen.	TILLOY. H.31.d.2.3.	
RAILHEAD for Personnel.	ACHEZ-LES-DUISANS.	

10th September, 1918.

B.E.Pocock Capt.
for Major,
D.A.A.G., 56th Division.

SECRET.　　　　　　　56th DIVISION.　　　　　　　A.Q.S.5.

Ref. Sheet 51.B.

LOCATION TABLE at 10 A.M. 9th SEPTR., 1918.

DIVISIONAL HEADQUARTERS.　　　LES FOSSES FARM.

UNIT.	Headquarters.	Transport Lines.
167th Infantry Brigade.	C.21.d.9.0.	ARRAS.
7th Middlesex Regt.	H.13.a.0.1.	H.13.a.
8th " "	H.21.c.4.6.	H.21.c.
1st London Regt.	H.26.central.	H.26.
167th T.M.Battery.	2 RUE ST CLAIRE, ARRAS.	
168th Infantry Brigade.	P.14.c.3.3.	)
4th London Regt.	-- do. --	)
13th " "	-- do. --	) O.19.a & b.
14th " "	-- do. --	)
168th T.M.Battery.	-- do. --	)
169th Infantry Brigade.	P.15.b.8.4.	)
2nd London Regt.	P.15.d.5.4.	) AREA
5th " "	P.12.c.5.5.	) O.13.a.
16th " "	P.15.c.9.4.	)
169th T.M.Battery.	P.21.Area.	
56th Battn. M.G.Corps.	H.12.a.0.4.	N.3.d.
1/5th Cheshire Regt.	H.11.b.9.5.	N.3.d.
247th (Div) Employment Coy.	H.12.a.5.0.	--
C.R.E.	LES FOSSES FARM.	
416th Field Coy. R.E.	O.9.b.9.6.	--
512th " " "	O.9.c.3.3.	N.3.d.
513th " " "	O.18.c.	O.19.
A.D.M.S.	LES FOSSES FARM.	O.13.
2/1st Lan. Fld. Amblce.	HOSPICE ST JEAN, ARRAS.	ARRAS.
2/2nd " " "	LES FOSSES FARM.	N.3.b.
2/3rd " " "	COLLEGE des JEUNES FILLES, ARRAS.	ARRAS.
C.R.A.	LES FOSSES FARM.	--
280th Brigade R.F.A.	P.21.a.7.9.	) AREA, N.17, N.27,
281st	WANCOURT AREA.	) & N.28.
56th D.A.C.(less S.A.A.SECT)	N.9.c.	S.A.A. Sect. N.9.c.
Divisional Train.		TILLOY.
No. 1. Company.	)	
" 2. "	)	TILLOY
" 3. "	)	M.6.a & c.
" 4. "	)	
D.A.D.V.S.		
Mobile Vet. Section.	-	LONDON CAVE, ST SAUVEUR.
D.A.D.O.S.		TILLOY.
56th M.T. Company.		TILLOY.
Div. Reception Camp.		BOISLEUX AU MONT.
NUCLEUS PERSONNEL.		AGNEZ-LES-DUISANS.
Divl. Baths Officer.		-- do. --
" Claims "		TILLOY.
" Burials "		"
Divl. Canteen.		T.18.b.3.2.
"Bow Bells".		TILLOY.
Div. Cinema.		IZEL-LES-HAMEAU.
RAILHEAD for personnel.		Not showing at present. AGNEZ-LES-DUISANS.

8th September, 1918.

D.A.A.G., 56th Division.

CASUALTIES. — SEPTEMBER, 1918.

DATE SEPT.	UNIT	OFFICERS Killed	OFFICERS Wounded	Missing	O.R.s K.	O.R.s W.	O.R.s M.	O.R.s I.	REMARKS
1st	13th London Regt.							1	
	5th Cheshire Regt.	Lt. B. EDWARDS.							Burns on hand.
	281st Bde. R.F.A.							1	
2nd	280th Bde. R.F.A.					1		1	Gassed.
	2nd London Regt.							1	Unloading Revolver.
	2/2nd Ldn.Fld.Amb.					1			Gassed.
	2/3rd " " "					1			At duty.
4th	247th Employment Coy.							1	Sprained ankle.
	2nd London Regt.					1			
	280th Bde. R.F.A.				1	2			
	281st " "				1	2			
5th	5th Cheshire Regt.		Capt. J.H. ROWLANDS,4/9/18.		2	18			
	U.S.M.O.R.C.		1/Lt. R.J. MILLER, (X)4/9/18.						(X)M.O. attd.5th Cheshire R.
	280th Bde. R.F.A.				1	1			
	416th (E)Fd.Co.RE.				4	3			
	56th Div.Sig.Co.RE.					1			
	167th I.Bde. H.Q.		Capt. C.W. HAYDON.(at duty.)4/9/18.						
6th	2nd London Regt.		2/Lt. G.W.AVENS,M.M. (X)					1	Lighting fire.
	16th " "		Lt. A.C.W.FISKEN,M.C. (5/9/18)		8	7			(X)Injured by runaway horse
	281st Bde. R.F.A.		Lt. J.C. POWELL,M.C. (5/9/18)						
7th	168th I.Bde. H.Q.		Lt. A.O.COLVIN,M.C. (7.9.18)						Intelligence Officer
	56th Div. Train.		Lt. G.R.T.MAYNE. (7.9.18)						
8th	56th Bn. M.G.C.					1			
	13th London Regt.					2x			x Gassed.

(2)

DATE SEPT.	UNIT	OFFICERS Killed	OFFICERS Wounded	OFFICERS Missing	O.R.S. K.	O.R.S. W.	O.R.S. M.	L.	REMARKS
9th	4th London Regt.	-	-	-	-	1	-	-	
	5th Cheshire Regt.	-	-	-	-	1	-	2x	x Includes 1 at duty.
	56th M.G. Battn.	-	-	-	-	1	-	-	
	281st Bde. R.F.A.	-	-	-	-	1	-	-	
7th	8th Middlesex Rgt.	-	-	-	-	1	-	1	By german hand grenade.
	13th London Regt.	-	-	-	-	7x	-	-	x Gassed.
10th	5th London Regt.	-	-	-	1	-	-	-	
	281st Bde. R.F.A.	-	-	-	-	2	-	-	
	512th Fld.Coy.RE	-	-	-	-	1	-	-	
11th	13th London Regt.	-	-	-	-	1x	-	-	x Gassed.
	14th "	-	-	-	-	1	-	-	
	5th "	-	-	-	-	1	-	-	At duty.
	281st Bde. R.F.A.	-	-	-	-	1	-	-	
12th	4th London Regt.	-	-	-	-	1	-	-	
	14th "	-	-	-	1	2	-	-	
	5th London Regt.	-	Lt. B.F.SAWBRIDGE. 11/9/18.	-	-	-	-	-	
	280th Bde. R.F.A.	-	-	-	-	2	-	1x	x Fell from cycle.
	2/2nd Lan.Fd.Amb.	-	-	-	-	1x	-	-	x Gassed.
13th	4th London Regt.	-	-	-	-	1	-	-	
	2nd "	-	-	-	-	1	-	-	
	5th "	-	-	-	1	6	-	-	
	16th "	-	2/Lt. J.P.GEE. 13/9/18.	-	-	2	-	-	
7th	280th Bde. R.F.A.	-	-	-	-	2x	-	-	x Gassed.
14th	13th London Regt.	-	-	-	-	2	-	-	
	16th "	-	-	-	-	1	-	1x	x By entrenching tool.
	2/2nd Lan.Fld.Amb.	-	-	-	-	1	-	1	
15th	7th Middlesex Regt.	-	-	-	-	1	-	-	
	16th London Regt.	-	-	-	-	1	-	-	
	56th Battn. M.G.Corps.	-	-	-	1	-	-	-	

(3)

DATE SEPT.	UNIT.	Officers Killed.	Officers Wounded.	Officers Missing.	O.RS. K.	O.RS. W.	O.RS. M.	O.RS. I.	REMARKS.
16th	8th Middlesex Regt.	-	-	-	-	1	-	-	1. By bayonet.
	2nd London Regt.	-	-	-	-	1	-	-	At duty.
	5th Cheshire Regt.	-	-	-	-	2	-	-	
	56th Bn. M.G. Corps.	-	-	-	-	-	-	-	
	56th D.A.C.	-	-	-	-	3	-	-	
	512th Fld.Coy.RE.	-	-	-	-	1	-	-	
	2/2nd Ldn.Fld.Amb.	-	-	-	-	1	-	-	Gassed.
17th	7th Middlesex Regt.	-	-	-	-	1	-	1x	1x At duty. x By burns.
	X/56th T.M.Battery	-	-	-	-	4x	-	-	x Gassed.
14th	13th London Regt.	-	-	-	-	1x	-	1x	x "
12th	14th " "	-	-	-	-	1	-	-	1 By fall.
6th	" " "	-	-	-	-	4	-	-	
17th	2nd " "	-	-	-	-	2	-	-	Includes 1 at duty.
	5th " "	-	-	-	-	10 X	-	-	X Gassed.
27/8/18	56th Bn. M.G.C.	-	2/Lt. S.H. HARGREAVES - 16/9/18(X)	-	-	-	-	1	1 Indian. By German grenade.
2/9/18	280th Bde. R.F.A.	-	-	-	-	-	-	1	1 By German Grenade.
18th	8th Middlesex Regt.	-	-	-	-	1	-	1	1 By fall.
	1st London Regt.	-	-	-	-	1	-	1	1 By rifle.
	13th " "	-	-	-	-	2	-	-	Inc. 1. at duty.
	5th " "	-	-	-	2	4	-	-	
	16th " "	-	-	-	2	2	-	-	
	169th T.M.Battery.	-	Capt. A.V.HEAL, M.C.-18/9/18.	-	-	1	-	-	
	280th Bde. R.F.A.	-	Lieut. A.H.ZOBEL. 18/9/18	-	-	-	-	-	
	281st " "	-	-	-	-	-	-	-	
28/8/18	" " "	-	-	-	-	3	-	-	Gassed.
19th	7th Middlesex Regt.	-	-	-	-	2	-	-	
	16th London Regt.	-	-	-	-	1	-	-	
	56th D.A.C.	-	-	-	-	-	-	2	2 Indians. Believed by land mine.
20th	7th Middlesex Regt.	-	2/Lt. A. CARTMELL,(1st ldns)20/9/18.	-	-	1x	-	-	x Gassed.
	4th London Regt.	-	" W.P. ANDREWS, 20/9/18.	-	-	3x	-	-	x From Listening post.
	14th " "	-	-	-	-	-	-	-	

(4)

DATE SEPT.	UNIT.	OFFICERS Killed.	OFFICERS Wounded.	OFFICERS Missing.	O.RS. K.	O.RS. W.	O.RS. M.	REMARKS.
21st	7th Middlesex Regt.				1	2		
	1st London Regt.		2/Lt. S.W. NEVILLE.(7th Ldns)21/9/18.			1		
	4th " "					3		
	13th " "				1	1		At duty.
	56th Bn. M.G. Corps.					3		
22nd	4th London Regt.				1	2		
	14th " "				1	6		
	5th Cheshire Regt.				1	3		
	280th Bde. R.F.A.					2		
	281st " "				1	1		At duty.
23rd	1st London Regt.				2	9		
	4th " "		2/Lt. S.R. CATTERALL.23/9/18.		1			At duty.
	14th " "						3	By cordite. near fire.
	5th Cheshire Regt.						1	Sprained ankle.
24th	1st London Regt.		2/Lt. R.D. SIMMONS.(7th Ldns)23/9/18.					
	4th " "					4	5x	x Sentry Group to Outpost
	13th " "					5		
	16th " "						1x	x By German Grenade.
	56th Bn. M.G. Corps.					4		
25th	8th Middlesex Regt.					2		
	4th London Regt.					1		
	13th " "					4x		xInc. 3 ORs Gassed.
	14th " "					2	1x	x Sprained ankle.
	2nd " "				1	3		
	5th " "		2/Lt. W.A. CHRISP. 24/9/18.			2		
	56th Bn. M.G. Corps.					1		
	281st Bde. R.F.A.					1		At duty.

(5)

DATE	UNIT	OFFICERS Killed	OFFICERS Wounded	OFFICERS Missing	O.Rs. K.	O.Rs. W.	O.Rs. M.	O.Rs. I.	REMARKS
SEPT.									
26th	4th London Regt.	—	—	—	—	1	—	—	
	13th " "	—	—	—	—	1	—	—	
	14th " "	—	—	—	1	1	—	1x	x Scalded whilst cook'g
	56th Bn. M.G.Corps.	—	—	—	—	—	—	—	
	5th Cheshire Regt.	—	Lt. J.H.L.GIBSON. 25/9/18.	—	—	—	—	—	
	2nd London Regt.	—	—	—	—	—	—	—	
	5th " "	—	(2/Lt. G.D.HILDER. " H. CROSS.	—	1x	—	—	1x	x By detonator.
27th	4th London Regt.	—	—	—	1	1	—	—	
	13th " "	—	—	—	1	1	—	—	
	14th " "	—	—	—	—	1	—	—	
	280th Bde. R.F.A.	—	—	—	1	1	—	—	
	X/56th T.M.Battery.	—	—	—	1	4	—	—	
	Y/56th T.M.Battery.	—	—	—	2	2	—	2	
	8th Middlesex Regt.	—	2/Lt. A.S. QUIRKE, M.C.	—	2	2	—	—	
	56th Bn. M.G.Corps.	—	—	—	2	28	—	—	
	5th London Regt.	—	Lt. A.J. WHITTLE. 2/Lt. J.C. SUMMERS.	—	6	46	—	—	
	2nd " "	—	S.H. CLIFFORD. (6th Ldns) 2/Lt. J.R. PIJNKETT (9th Ldns)	—	—	—	—	—	
	16th " "	Capt. W.C.M. McRAE, (ASC) 2/Lt. C. SHEPPARD " J.C.B. PRINCE. (9th Ldns) " A.A.W. RITCHINGS. (11th Ldns)	—	—	16	47	—	1	
28th	8th Middlesex Regt.	—	—	—	—	2	—	—	Gassed.
	5th Cheshire Regt.	—	—	—	—	3	—	—	Inc. 1 O.R. gassed.
	280th Bde. R.F.A.	—	—	—	—	2	—	—	
	4th London Regt.	—	—	—	—	4	—	—	
	13th " "	—	—	—	—	12	—	—	Inc. 1 at duty.
	168th T.M.Battery.	—	—	—	—	1	—	—	
	2nd London Regt.	—	—	—	—	6	—	—	
	5th " "	2/Lt. J. ADAMS. X	—	—	1x	1	—	—	X Died of wounds.
	416th Fld.Coy. R.E.	—	—	—	—	1	—	—	
	512th " "	—	—	—	—	3	—	—	
	513th " "	—	—	—	—	—	—	—	

(6)

DATE	UNIT	OFFICERS Killed	OFFICERS Wounded	OFFICERS Missing	O.RS. K	O.RS. W	O.RS. M	O.RS. I	REMARKS
SEPT. 29th	7th Middlesex Regt.				1	38x			x Inc. 34 Gassed.
	8th " "		2/Lt. C.E. CROSS.				12		
	" " "		" H.J.P. HULL. (X)						(X) Gassed.
	" " "		" H.J. BOWYER. (X)						(X).
	5th Cheshire Regt.				3	20x	4		x Inc. 2 ORs at duty.
	280th Bde. R.F.A.				1				
	281st " "				1	1			
	2nd London Regt.					14x	1		x Gassed.
	5th " "				1	2			
	16th " "				1	1		1	At duty.
	416th Fld. Coy. R.E.								
	512th " " "								
30th	5th London Regt.		2/Lt. N. CRAIG. (X)			16x		1	(X) Gassed.
	5th Cheshire Regt.				1	7		1	x Inc. 15 gassed.
	56th Baktn. M.G.C.				1				By pick.
	281st Bde. R.F.A.				1	1			
	2/3rd Ldn. Fd.AmbIce.								
TOTALS FOR SEPTEMBER.		8	29		72	465	25	31	

UNIT.	STRENGTH. 1.9.18. O. O.R.		INCREASE. O. O.R.		DECREASE. O. O.R.		STRENGTH. 1.10.18. O. O.R.	
Divisional Headquarters.	16	81	-	1	-	-	16	82
247th Employment Coy.	2	348	-	11	-	19	2	340
167th Inf.Brigade H.Q.	4	22	-	-	-	1	4	21
1/7th Middlesex Regt.	35	676	12	284	4	95	43	865
1/8th Middlesex Regt.	38	787	6	221	3	144	41	864
1/1st London Regt.	27	613	16	107	3	63	40	657
167th T.M. Battery.	4	45	-	4	-	3	4	46
168th Inf.Brigade H.Q.	4	20	-	-	-	-	4	20
1/4th London Regt.	32	710	9	100	4	105	37	705
1/13th London Regt.	24	683	20	118	3	110	41	691
1/14th London Regt.	30	548	7	175	6	101	31	622
168th T.M.Battery.	3	40	1	10	-	6	4	44
169th Inf.Brigade H.Q.	3	21	1	-	-	-	4	21
1/2nd London Regt.	27	599	10	291	6	173	31	717
1/5th London Regt.	25	669	16	92	9	158	32	603
1/16th London Regt.	27	577	14	113	10	130	31	560
169th T.M.Battery.	2	42	-	3	-	6	2	39
1/5th Cheshire Regt.	40	887	5	69	4	130	41	826
56th Battn. M.G.Corps.	42	839	11	91	4	84	49	846
56th Divl. Artillery H.Q.	4	18	-	-	-	-	4	18
280th Brigade R.F.A.	30	770	4	15	6	31	28	754
281st Brigade R.F.A.	27	706	3	84	4	27	26	763
56th D. A. C.	17	493	5	5	2	75	20	423
56th Divl. Engineers H.Q.	1	8	-	-	-	-	1	8
416th (Edin)Field Coy. R.E.	7	195	-	16	-	10	7	201
512th (Ldn.)Field Coy. R.E.	7	208	-	6	-	10	7	204
513th (Ldn.)Field Coy. R.E.	8	205	-	3	-	14	8	194
56th Divl. Signal Company.RE.	12	290	-	8	-	2	12	296
56th Divisional Train.	22	379	2	7	4	6	20	380
Medical Units.	21	531	4	18	6	7	19	542
Mobile Veterinary Section.	1	20	-	-	-	2	1	18

:-:-:-:-:-:-:-:-:-:-:-:-:-:

Cover for Documents.

October 1918.

Nature of Enclosures.

War Diary

A.A. & Q.M.G.

56th Division

Notes, or Letters written.

Army Form C. 2118.

WAR DIARY
or
INTELLIGENCE SUMMARY.
(Erase heading not required.)

Instructions regarding War Diaries and Intelligence Summaries are contained in F. S. Regs., Part II. and the Staff Manual respectively. Title pages will be prepared in manuscript.

Place	Date	Hour	Summary of Events and Information	Remarks and references to Appendices
VILLERS LEZ CAGNICOURT	1		167th Inf Brigade moved to forward area South of SAUDEMONT	
	2		No change	
	3		"	
	4		"	
	5		167th Inf Brigade relieve the 168th Inf Bde in line, in the Left Sector.	
	6		No change	
	7		"	
	8		"	
	9		"	
	10		"	
	11		The 168th Inf Bde extends its front to FRESSIES	
	12		The 168th Inf Bde. captured FRESSIES with 8 M/Gs and 32 OR prisoners. Casualties. the Brigade were 1 killed & 8 wounded. 168th Inf Bde relieved the 189th Bde in the Right Section of the Canadian Corps at 5°pm today. 56th Div was transferred to Canadian Corps at 5°pm today. Night 11/12. 1st Canadian Div. captured HAMEL and the trench system to the north. The 167th Inf Bde has to extend its front to join the 1st Cdn Div N of ARLEUX. 167th and 189th Inf Bde carried out minor operation during night to clear enemy West of the SENSEE Canal. Administrative Instruction No 1. Canadian bde pending relief of Div by 4th Cdn Div. issued.	A
	13.		168th Inf Brigade captured AUBIGNY au BAC this morning with 200 prisoners. Village was later recaptured. C.R.E. is ordered to construct bridges over the SENSEE. 10th Cdn Inf Bde is moved from ARRAS to SAUCHY LESTREE Area and comes under order of G.O.C 56 Div. Administration Instruction No 2 issued	B

Army Form C. 2118.

WAR DIARY
or
INTELLIGENCE SUMMARY.
(Erase heading not required.)

Instructions regarding War Diaries and Intelligence Summaries are contained in F. S. Regs., Part II. and the Staff Manual respectively. Title pages will be prepared in manuscript.

Place	Date	Hour	Summary of Events and Information	Remarks and references to Appendices
VILLERS LES CAGNICOURT	14		169th Inf Bde relieved in line by 10th Cdn Inf Bde. 168th Inf Bn entrain MARQUION for ARRAS at 8pm night 14/15.	
	15		169th Inf Brigade leave for HAUTE AVESNES area by train from MARQUION - detraining AGNEZ les DUISANS. 167th Inf Bde relieved in line by 11th Cdn Bde.	
ETRUN	16		167th Inf Bn entrain MARQUION for Y HUTS MAROEUIL. Divnl HQ opened at 10.00 d'ETRUN. Of remainder Relief of the Divn Complete except Divnl Arty who remain under Canadian J of 4th Cdn Divn. Divnn was in first Army Reserve. Administrative instructions issued in event of a General Advance taking place.	
	17.			
	18 19 20 21 22		No change	
	23 24 25 26			
	27 28		No change. Bon Beds open in Theatre ARRAS Cinema at HAUTE AVESNES. Owing to few cases of influenza epidemic occurring in the Divn measures in civilian billets have been observed. As many men as possible put into huts.	

WAR DIARY
or
INTELLIGENCE SUMMARY.

(Erase heading not required.)

Army Form C. 2118.

Place	Date	Hour	Summary of Events and Information	Remarks and references to Appendices
ETRUN	29		Owing to the changes of command that are being made there are quite a number of minor moves to be carried out. Our will be transferred to XVII Corps & will move forward on the 31st. Following new [attached] Divisional Administrative Instruction AQS/753/1 - AQS/753/2 & Administrative Instructions AQS/753/4.	
	30		Div moved by bus to BARASTRE and later joined N.E of CAMBRAI). Thr moved by road staying night 31/1 at IMRDION	
	31		Div HQ open at BARASTRE morning 31/12.	

Hugh [Sutton?]
Lieut.-Col.
A.A. & Q.M.G. 56th Division.

Appendix A — War Diary

SECRET.   A.Q.S.5.
Ref.Sheet 51B.
56th DIVISION.

LOCATION TABLE AT 12 NOON, 3RD OCTOBER, 1918.

Divisional Headquarters. ... V.3.b.2.7.

LEFT BRIGADE.		RIGHT BRIGADE.	
Bde. H.Q.	Q.36.a.2.5.	Bde. H.Q.	X.1.c.1.5.
Right Bn.	Q.23.b.3.4.	Right Bn.	R.25.d.0.3.
Left Bn.	Q.23.a.5.0.	Left Bn.	R.25.c.5.3.
Resve.Bn.	Q.34.b.4.2.	Suppt.Bn.	P.31.central.
T.M. Bty.	Q.35.b.7.3.	T.M. Bty.	--

RESERVE BRIGADE.

Bde. H.Q.	P.34.a.2.9.
"A" Battn.	Q.25.d.6.0.
"B" "	P.35.b.9.2.
"C" "	Q.31.a.4.0.
T.M. Bty.	P.33.a.1.2.

UNIT.	Headquarters.	Transport Lines.
167th Infantry Bde.	--	V.10.b.8.8.
168th " "	--	V.10.c.9.5.
169th " "	--	V.10.b.1.9.
56th Battn. M.G. Corps.	V.3.b.2.7.	U.5.a.4.3.
1/5th Cheshire Regt.	P.26.d.6.3.	V.2.a.9.6.
247th (Div) Employment Coy.	VILLERS-LEZ-CAGNICOURT.	--
C. R. E.	V.3.b.2.7.	
416th Field Company R.E.	W.16.a.5.9.	V.6.c.7.8.
512th " " "	W.16.a.5.8.	W.13.d.7.9.
513th " " "	Q.20.c.7.1.	P.32.d.3.7.
A. D. M. S.	P.32.d.central.	--
2/1st London Field Amblce.	HOSPICE ST JEAN, ARRAS.	
2/2nd " " "	W.9.d.9.3.	P.31.b.2.3.
2/3rd " " "	P.34.d.4.3.	VIS-EN-ARTOIS.
C. R. A.	V.3.b.2.7.	
280th Brigade. R.F.A.	Q.30.d.3.3.	V.15.a.8.5.
281st " "	Q.30.c.3.2.	V.4.c.8.8.
56th D.A.C.(less SAA.Section)	O.28.c.central.	SAA.Sect. V.16.a.
Attached		
282nd Army Bde. R.F.A.	Q.20.b.95.15.	
Divl. Train.	O.27.c.2.3.	
No. 1. Company.	O.27.c.	
" 2. "	O.25.c.central.	
" 3. "	O.27. a & b.	
" 4. "	O.27.c.	
D. A. D. V. S.	P.32.d.central.	
Mobile Vet. Section.	O.22.a.1.6.	
D. A. D. O. S.	VILLERS-LEZ-CAGNICOURT.	
56th M.T. Company.	G.20.a.8.8.	
Div. Reception Camp.	ETRUN.	
Nucleus Personnel.	ETRUN.	
Divl. Baths Officer.	VILLERS-LEZ-CAGNICOURT.	
" Claims "	" " "	
" Burials "	" " "	
" Salvage "	" " "	
" Canteen.	" " "	
RAILHEAD for Personnel.	AGNEZ-LES-DUISANS.	

4th October, 1918.

R. Dundas, Major,
D.A.A.G., 56th Division.

SECRET.   *Appendix B*

AQS/746.

ADMINISTRATIVE INSTRUCTIONS in connection with
relief of the Division by 4th Canadian Division.

Issued with reference to 56th Division WARNING ORDER
No. 215.

12th October 1918.

1. AREA and TRENCH STORES.

The following will be handed over to 4th Canadian Division :-

All Trench Stores except Aeroplane Discs & Refuse Sprayers.
Trench Ammunition.
Petrol tins surplus to Units' equipment.
Gas clothing (50 sets at A.D.S., 50 sets at M.D.S., 300 sets by D.A.D.O.S.)
Tents and Trench Shelters as shown below (to be handed over in situ where they are already pitched).

	Tents.	Trench shelters
167th Inf. Bde. Transport Lines.	—	75.
168th " " " "	2.	75.
169th " " " "	8.	79.
Reserve Inf. Bde. Area.	—	120.
5th Ches.Regt. (Pioneer Bn).	—	33.
Divnl. Arty.	—	20.
M.G.Bn.	2.	33.
Div. Grenade Dump.	—	14.
Camp Commandant.	5.	15.
D.A.D.O.S.. (in stores).	—	155.
Div. Employment Co.	—	10.

100 Gum Boots by D.A.D.O.S.

Receipts will be taken in all cases and one copy of the Units' receipted list will be forwarded by all units in the Division through the usual channels so as to reach Divnl. H.Q. "A & Q" within 24 hours of relief. Consolidated returns on A.F.W.3405 need not be forwarded.

2. INFANTRY TRANSPORT LINES will be handed over as shown below :-

168th Inf. Bde. at V.10.c.9.5. to 11th Can. Inf. Bde. on 14th.
167th " " at V.18.b.8.8. to 10th Can. Inf. Bde. on 13th.
     (10th Can. I.B. and 167th I.B. transports
     to double up until 13th.)
169th " " at V.10.b.1.9. to 12th Can. Inf. Bde. on 16th.

3. AREA EMPLOY.

The following will be relieved on 15th inst. and will send guides to Divnl. H.Q. "A & Q" at noon on that date to meet their opposite numbers.
Traffic Control - Area Commandants - Baths - Salvage - SAA and Grenade Dump - Cemetery Wardens.

-1-

4. Details regarding handing over of accommodation for Headquarters and Transport Lines of Pioneer Battn., Field Coys., and M.G.Bn. will be arranged direct between Commanders concerned.

5. O.C.Train, A.D.M.S. and D.A.D.V.S. will arrange reliefs of Units under their command direct with their opposite numbers in the 4th Canadian Division. They will move to the new area independently after relief.

6. C.R.E., O.C.Pioneer Bn., and O.C.M.G.Bn., will notify this office at the earliest possible moment their requirements in Busses. The following information is required :-

    Place, date and time at which it is desired to embuss.
    Numbers (all ranks) to be conveyed.

Arrangements will then be made in this office for the personnel to travel by the most convenient of the available Bus convoys. If a Staging area is required after relief and prior to embussing, application for it should be made to this office.

7. Arrangements for Embussing, Moves of Transport Columns and Baggage Lorries and Information regarding the new area, will be notified as soon as possible.

8. Bow-Bells, Canteen, Linen Store and Ordnance Store will close in the present area after the 14th inst.

                                              Lieut. - Colonel,
                             A.A. & Q.M.G., 56th Division.

-:DISTRIBUTION:-

167th Inf. Bde.	O.C.Train.	D.A.D.V.S.
168th Inf. Bde.	A.D.M.S.	S.C.F. D.C.G.
169th Inf. Bde.	A.P.M.	S.C.F. P.C.
Div. Arty.	D.A.D.O.S.	"G"
M.G.Bn.	Camp Commandant.	French Mission.
C.R.E.	56th M.T.Co.	A.C. SAUCHY LESTREE.
5th Cheshire R.	Div. Sig. Co.	A.C. RUMAUCOURT.
	Div. Employment Co.	4th Canadian Div. "Q".

Appendix C War Diary

SECRET.   56th Divn. AQS/746/2.

ADMINISTRATIVE INSTRUCTIONS NO.2.
in connection with relief of the Division by 4th Canadian Divn.

Issued with reference to 56th Division Order No. 217.

1. ACCOMMODATION.

Accommodation in the new Area is allotted as shown below:-

Formation.	Area.	Billets vacated by.	Billets from.	Restrictions.
Divisional H.Q.	ETRUN.			
167th Inf. Bde.	Y. Huts. 51C/L.2.c.cont.	11th C.I.B.	T.Major, DUISANS. (Billet Warden at Y. Huts.)	Existing site Ambloo for 1 Fld.Amb.
168th Inf. Bde.	ARRAS.	10th C.I.B.	Town Cmdt.	NIL.
169th " "	HAUTE-AVESNES.	12th C.I.B.	" Major	NIL.
56th Bn.M.G.C.	ANZIN.	4th Bn.M.G.C.	" "	NIL.
Div. R.E. H.Q. 3 Field Coys. 5th Cheshire R.	MAROEUIL.	4th Bdo.C.E.	" "	Accommodation to be sub-allotted by C.R.E. Ambulance site to be allotted to Field Ambulance.
Train H.Q.	ETRUN.		Camp Comdt.	
3 Train Coys.	51C/A.26.c & d.	4th C.Div.Train.	—	
A.D.M.S.	ETRUN.		Camp Comdt.	
1 Field Amb.	Y. Huts.		167th Inf.Bde.	
1 " "	ECOIVRES.		Town Major.	
1 " "	MAROEUIL.		C. R. E.	
Mob.Vet.Section.	51B/G.8.a.2.5.		T.Maj. ANZIN.	
D.A.D.O.S.	MAROEUIL.		Town Major.	
Div.Employ.Coy.	ETRUN.		Camp Comdt.	

13th October, 1918.

ACDundas Maj
p/ Lieut-Colonel,
A.A. & Q.M.G., 56th Division.

** DISTRIBUTION. **

167th Inf. Brigade.	O.C. Div. Train.	D.A.D.V.S.
168th " "	A.D.M.S.	S.C.F.(D.C.G.)
169th " "	D.A.P.M.	S.C.F.(P.C.)
Divl. Artillery.	D.A.D.O.S.	"G"
56th M.G. Battn.	Camp Comdt.	French Mission.
C.R.E.	56th M.T. Company.	A.C. SAUCHY LESTREE.
5th Cheshire Regt.	Div. Signal Coy.	A.C. RUMAUCOURT.
Div.Reception Camp.	Div.Employment Coy.	4th Canadian Div. "Q".
Town Major, ETRUN.		
" " DUISANS.		
" " ARRAS.		
" " HAUTE AVESNES.		
" " ANZIN.		
" " MAROEUIL.		
" " ECOIVRES.		

Appendix D — War Diary

SECRET. A.G.S.5.

56th DIVISION.
LOCATION TABLE.

UNIT.	Headquarters & Transport Lines.
Divisional Headquarters.	Chateau, ETRUN.
167th Infantry Bde. & Battalions.	Y. HUTS.
168th " " " "	ARRAS.
169th " " " "	HAUTE AVESNES.
56th Battn. M.G.Corps.	ANZIN.
1/5th Cheshire Regiment.	CHINESE Camp, MAROEUIL.
C.R.E.	
416th Field Company R.E.	MAROEUIL.
512th " " "	F.27.a.5.9.
513th " " "	Chateau, MAROEUIL.
A.D.M.S.	ETRUN.
2/1st London Field Amblce.	Hospice St JEAN, ARRAS.
2/2nd " " "	MAROEUIL.
2/3rd " " "	ECOIVRES.
C.R.A.	MAROEUIL.
280th Brigade, R.F.A.	Detached.
281st " " "	" "
56th D.A.C. (less S.A.A. Section)	" "
S.A.A. Section.	ANZIN.
Divl. Train H.Q.	ETRUN.
No. 1. Company.	Detached.
" 2 "	STUART CAMP. L.17.central.
" 3 "	MADAGASCAR Corner. A.26.c.32
" 4 "	STUART CAMP.
D.A.D.V.S.	ETRUN.
Mobile Veterinary Section.	ANZIN.
D.A.D.O.S.	MAROEUIL.
56th M.T. Company.	"
Divl. Reception Camp.	AGNEZ-LES-DUISANS.
247th (Divl) Employment Company.	ETRUN.
Divl. Baths Officer.	"
" Claims "	"
" Burials "	"
" Salvage "	"
" Canteen.	"
RAILHEAD for Personnel.	AGNEZ-LES-DUISANS.

18th October, 1918.

ADundas Major,
D.A.A.G., 56th Division.

Appendix E   War Diary

SECRET.   56th Division AQS/748.

ADMINISTRATIVE INSTRUCTIONS IN CONNECTION WITH A GENERAL ADVANCE.

1. The existing instructions for the working of certain administrative services during Mobile Warfare are as follows :-
(a) Field Service Regulations. Whilst the general principles are applicable to the present type of warfare, the details have to be modified to suit modern conditions and organisation.
(b) Memoranda issued during the German Offensive in March, April and May 1918.
During this period the initiative was with the enemy and the suddenness and weight of his attacks made it difficult for Formations and Units actually engaged to control their own rearward administrative services, and there was a tendency for this control to revert to higher formations, who were more conveniently situated for dealing with the rearward echelons of the fighting Formations and Units.

2. Neither of the types of instructions referred to above are quite suited to the type of operations now contemplated. The instructions in the following paragraphs are issued in anticipation of operations of a semi-mobile nature in which the fighting troops commence and continue the advance in contact with the enemy, and in which the depth of the advance will be limited by the tactical situation. Administrative Staffs of the fighting Formations and Units will however be in a position to control their own Administrative services.

3. The following administrative services will be worked by Brigade Groups :-
    Distribution of Rations, R.E.Material, Mails and Ordnance
                                                        Stores.
    Billeting.

    In the orders for the advance the General Staff would notify what Units or portions of Units of Divisional Troops (including Divl. Artillery) will be under the tactical control of Brigadier-Generals Commanding Infantry Brigades, and those Units (irrespective of their arm of the Service) will constitute the Infantry Brigade Group.
    The Divl. Artillery group will consist of all Units or portions of Units of Divisional Troops (including Artillery) which have not been placed under the tactical control of a Brigadier-General Commanding an Infantry Brigade.

4. Supply of ammunition of all natures, (Artillery, Infantry and Machine Gun) will be worked by Arms of the Service and not by Brigade Groups; the   channel of supply being the normal one, viz, D.A.C. to Batteries, Infantry Brigade Reserve and M.G. Battalion Reserve.

5. The outstanding difficulty in all the administrative services referred to in paras. 3 and 4 will be that of intercommunication between the troops and the echelons in rear which supply them. The system of interchange of orderlies between the forward and rear echelons has been found not to be satisfactory, as if the two echelons both move at the same time all touch is lost. Prior to the advance, therefore, the Administrative Staff of each Brigade Group will fix a "Meeting Point" or "Rear Report Centre" as far forward as possible on the probable line of advance. This point will serve as a rendezvous for all maintenance services. The locations of this Rear Report Centre will be notified to Brigade Supply Officer, Brigade Post Office, Brigade Ordnance Warrant Officer, S.A.A. Section D.A.C., Divisional Headquarters "A" & "Q".

                                                            P.T.O.

A suitable number of guides from each Unit of the Brigade Group and from the S.A.A. Section D.A.C. will proceed to and be maintained at this Report Centre for the purpose of transmitting demands for ammunition from Units, and for guiding convoys of Ammunition, Rations, R.E.Material, Mails and Ordnance Stores to Units. When this Report Centre is moved forward a guide to the new location should be left there until all concerned have been informed of the new location.

6. The principle of intercommunication by means of a fixed report centre will also be adopted by the Divisional Artillery and M.G. Battalion for the purpose of Ammunition Supply. When possible these Report Centres should be the same as those fixed by Infantry Brigades

Additional guides for ammunition duties alone will be stationed at these report centres by Artillery Brigades, M.G.Battalion and D.A.C. (S.A.A. Section in the case of M.G.Battalion).

7. It should be noted that "B" Echelon First Line Transports will not be controlled by Divisional Headquarters. The Administrative Staff of each Infantry Brigade will control the "B" Echelon First Line Transports of all Units of its Brigade Group.

8. Moves of the S.A.A. Section D.A.C. will be controlled by Divl. Headquarters and normally the Section will be kept intact and not distributed amongst Infantry Brigades and M.G.Battalion.
Infantry Brigades and M.G. Battalion will maintain communication with the S.A.A. Section by means of their fixed Report Centre referred to in paras. 5 and 6; and will draw direct upon the S.A.A. Section to keep their "on the man" and "on wheel" Echelons up to establishment.
It must be distinctly understood that no ammunition surplus to the establishment authorized to be carried "on the man" or "on wheel" is to be demanded from the D.A.C. The function of this Unit is to replenish empty authorized Echelons, and no more.

9. Attention is drawn to the instructions for collection of baggage in the event of an advance issued under this office letter AQS.735/3 of 28.9.18. Necessary amendments to suit different Areas will be notified from time to time.

17th October, 1918.

Lieut-Colonel,
A.A. & Q.M.G., 56th Division.

** DISTRIBUTION **

167th Infantry Bde.
168th   "   "
169th   "   "
Divl. Artillery.
S.A.A.Section D.A.C.
C. R. E.
1/5th Cheshire Regt.

56th Battn. M.G.Corps.
56th Divl. Train.
A. D. M. S.
D. A. D. V. S.
D. A. D. O. S.
D. A. P. M.
Camp Commandant.

"G".

Appendix to Wardiary

SECRET.

AQS 753/1.

PROVISIONAL ADMINISTRATIVE INSTRUCTIONS issued in connection with 56th Divnl. WARNING ORDER No 247.

30th October 1918.

ADVANCE PARTIES. 25 All ranks Advance Party of each Brigade Group will travel on the first lorry of each Bus Column. O i/c Buses is arranging for these Busses to move off independently as soon as they are loaded.

BLANKETS. Each man will carry one blanket folded on the top of his pack. No lorries will be provided for blankets.

BUSSES. The number of vehicles in each Bus Column will be notified later. 25 All ranks will be carried on each vehicle.

MACHINE GUNS. Four lorries will report at H.Q. M.G.Battn. at 0800 hours 31st to carry surplus bolt boxes etc. These will move to the new area under orders of O.C.M.G.Battn. No other lorries will be provided for the M.G.Battn.

LEWIS GUNS and
STOKES MORTARS. Five lorries will report at the H.Q., of each Infantry Brigade at 0800 hours 31st. Three of these are for Lewis Guns and Magazines, and two for Stokes Mortar handcarts etc. Each Group of five lorries will move independently to the new area as soon as loaded, under orders of B.G.C., Infantry Brigade.

SURPLUS BAGGAGE. Lorries as under will be provided on 31st October or November 1st for one journey each :-

```
        Div. H.Q.    6.     Each Infantry Bde.   2.
        Emplyt.Co.   1.     5th Cheshire Rgt.    1.
        Div. Recep.         H.Q., R.E.           1.
        Camp.        2.     D.A.D.O.S.           6.
```

SUPPLIES. Instructions regarding Supplies will be issued later.

for A.A.& Q.M.G., Major,
56th Division.

** DISTRIBUTION **

167th Inf. Bde.   Camp Comdt.   M.G. Battalion
168th " "   French Mission.   5th Cheshire Rgt.
169th " "   Employment Coy.   56th M.T. Company
H. R. E.   D.A.P.M.   D.A.D.O.S.
Div. Train.   Sen.Chaplain D.C.G's Dept.   D.A.D.V.S.
A.D.M.S.   P.C's Dept.   "G".
                   Div. Reception Camp.

Serial No.	Bde. Group Cdr.	Order of Embussing.	Strength All Ranks.	Embussing Point and time of Embussing.	Debussing Point	Route to Embussing Point.	Restrictions.
1.	B.G.C. 168th Inf. Bde.	168th Bde. H.Q. 168th T.M.By. 4th Lon:Regt. 13th Lon:Regt. 14th Lon:Regt. M.G.Bn. 512th Co.R.E. 2/1st Fd.Amboo. Div. Grenade Dump. No.3 Co. Train.	93. 65. 596. 420. 600. 747. 108. 127 11. 6.	ST.POL – ARRAS Rd. Head of Column G.21.a.4.6. (Sheet 51b) Facing East 0900 hours.	DOUGHY – NOYELLES Rd. I.28.d. (Sheet 51a.) Length of journey about 5 hours.		M.G.Bn. and 512th Field Co.R.E. not to use Main ST.POL – ARRAS Rd. West of G.20.b.7.8.

P.T.O.

Serial No.	Bde. Group Comdr.	Order of Embussing	Strength all ranks.	Embussing Point and time of Embussing.	Debussing Point and time of Debussing.	Route to Embussing Point.
2.	B.G. 167th Inf. Bde.	167th I.Bdo.H.Q. 167th T.M.Bty. 7th Middlesex Rgt. 8th " " 1st LoNDoN" 416th Field Coy.RE. 5th Choshire Rgt. No. 2. Coy. Train. 2/2nd Ldn.Fld.Ambloe. Divl. Hd. Qtrs. R.E. Hd. Qtrs. Employment Coy. H.Q. & No. 1. Sect. Div. Signal Coy.	202 54 671 632 586 104 617 10 145 20 10 122 51	ST POL - ARRAS Rd. head of column L.2.c.5.5. (Sheet 51.A.) facing EAST. 0900 hours.	DEUCHY - NOYELLES Rd. I.28.d. (Sheet 51.A.) Length of journey about 5 hours. PAVE DE VALENCIENNES.	As ordered by Brig-Genl. Comdg. 167th Inf. Bdo.
3.	B.G.C. 169th Inf. Bde.	169th I.Bdo.H.Q. 169th T.M. Bty. 2nd London Rgt. 5th " " 16th " " 513th Fld.Coy.RE. 2/3rd Ldn.Fld.Amboe. No. 4. Coy. Train. Div. Reception Camp.	96 41 474 521 497 107 126 8 50	ST POL - ARRAS Rd. head of column E.25.c.6.1. (Sheet 51.C.) facing EAST. 0900 hours.	DOUCHY - NOYELLES Rd. I.28.d. (Sheet 51.A.) Length of journey about five hours.	As ordered by Brig-Genl. 169th Inf. Bde.

Appendix to War Diary

SECRET.

56th Division   AQS/753/2.

PROVISIONAL ADMINISTRATIVE INSTRUCTIONS
issued in connection with 56th Division Order No. 218.

1. SUPPLIES.

Rations for consumption on November 1st by all personnel of Units proceeding to new area on October 31st will be drawn at ARRAS Railhead by lorry on the morning of Oct. 31st. These rations will be delivered by such lorries direct to the Brigade Group billeting areas, where they will be issued under direction of Brigade Supply Officers on the afternoon of the 31st. Units should arrange to get into touch with Supply Officers on the lorries immediately on arrival, and inform him where they require their rations to be dumped. They should also be ready to provide ration carrying parties if necessary.

Rations drawn this morning at Railhead will be carried by Train Supply Wagons to the new area and will be issued on the evening of the 1st November for consumption on the 2nd November. The rations required for consumption on November 1st by the personnel proceeding by road with the transport, and the forage necessary for consumption on that day, will be issued to them by the A.S.C. Coy. attached to their Brigade Group immediately on arrival at the staging point (MARQUION) 31st October. Officers Commanding Transport Columns of Units will give receipts to Officers Commanding A.S.C. Companies for men's rations and also for forage drawn at MARQUION.

There will be no forage available for issue in the DOUCHY – NEUVILLE – NOYELLES Area to-morrow (Oct. 31st).

2. BAGGAGE WAGONS will join Units on the evening of 30th inst.

3. BAGGAGE LORRIES.

Lorries will be provided for baggage on 31st instant. for the following
These lorries are available for one journey only and must be off-loaded by 1430 and despatched to their Units. Under no circumstances may these lorries be retained for any purpose after that hour.

One guide from

    Camp Commandant.
    Div. Employment Coy.
    Div. Reception Camp.
    167th Infantry Bde.
    169th   "   "
    1/5th Cheshire Regt.
    H.Q. Royal Engineers.

will report to the D.A.Q.M.G. at the junction of the ETRUN Road with ST.POL – ARRAS Road, L.8.b.3.9. at 0645 hours. Unless guides are punctual lorries will not be able to be retained.

Two lorries will report at H.Q. 168th Infantry Bde. at 0700 hours.

30th October, 1918.

for A.A. & Q.M.G., Major, 56th Division.

DISTRIBUTION as for AQS/753/1.

P.T.O

S E C R E T.
56th Division AQS/753/3.

REFERENCE: PROVISIONAL ADMINISTRATIVE INSTRUCTIONS
NO. AQS/753/1 & 2. ISSUED IN CONNECTION WITH DIVL. WARNING
ORDER NO. 247 AND DIVISIONAL ORDER NO. 218.

These are now confirmed with the following amendment:—

Time of Embussing for all parties will be 0830 instead of 0900 hours.

30th October, 1918.

for A.A. & Q.M.G., Major,
56th Divn.

DISTRIBUTION as for AQS/753/1.

S E C R E T.   56th Division AQS/753/4

ADMINISTRATIVE INSTRUCTIONS ISSUED IN
connection with 56th Divisional Order No. 218.

1. **ACCOMMODATION.**

The following is the accommodation available in the New Area:-

	Vacated by.	Billets from.
Div. Head Qrs. BASSEVILLE	51s Div. H.Qrs.	Camp Commdt.
187th Inf. Bde. Group		
Head Qrs. DOUCHY.	154th Inf. Bde.	Town Major
T.M.Bty.)		
1 Battn.) DOUCHY	do.	" "
1 Battn. THONVILLE. I.12.a	do.	
1 Battn. MOULIN I.11.a.	do.	
416th Field Co. R.E. NOYELLES		T.M. thro' C.R.E.
2/2nd L.Field Ambce. NEUVILLE	49th Div. Field A.	Town Major
1/5th Cheshire R. NEUVILLE	Bn. 152nd Inf. Bde.	Town Major
No. 2 Coy. D.TRAIN PAVE	No. 2 Coy. 51st D.T.	
168th Inf. Bde. Group.		
Head Qrs. DOUCHY.	152nd Inf. Bde.	Town Major
T.M.Bty. &)		
3 Battns.) DOUCHY		Town Major
512th Field Coy. R.E. NOYELLES		T.M. thro' C.R.E.
2/1st L.Field Ambce. DOUCHY	51st Div. Field A.	Town Major
56th Bn. M.G.Corps.BASSEVILLE		Camp Commdt.
No. 3 Coy. D.Train. PAVE	No. 3 Coy. 51st D.T.	
S.A.A.Sect. D.A.C. DOUCHY.	S.A.A.Sect.	Town Major
I.23.a.6.7	51st D. A. C.	
169th Inf. Bde. Group.		
Head Qrs. LIEU St.AMAND	153rd Inf. Bde.	Town Major
T.M.Bty. &) LIEU St.AMAND		
3 Battns.) and N.5.b.		
513th Field Coy. R.E. PAVE		
2/3rd L.Field Ambce. NEUVILLE	51st Div. Field A.	Town Major
Div. Recep. Camp. BASSEVILLE		Camp Commdt.
No. 4 Coy. D.Train. PAVE.	No. 4 Coy. 51st D.T.	
Mob. Vety. Section. PAVE.	51st Div. M.V.S.	
D.A.D.O.S. BASSEVILLE.		Camp Commdt.
247th (D) Employ. Coy. BASSEVILLE		Camp Commdt.
Canteen and PAVE.		
Linen Store H.36.b.8.2.		

30th October, 1918.

DISTRIBUTION AS FOR AQS/753/1.

AWDundas
Major,
for A.A. & Q.M.G., 56th Divn.

CASUALTIES. OCTOBER 1918.

DATE. OCTBR. 1918.	UNIT.	OFFICER'S Killed.	OFFICER'S Wounded.	Missing.	K.	W.	M.	O.Rs	REMARKS.
1st	4th London Rgt.	-	-	-	-	1	-	-	
	13th " "	-	-	-	1	3	-	-	
	14th " "	2/Lt. F.A. BAKER, M.M.	-	-	-	-	-	-	
	2nd " "	-	-	-	1	1	-	-	
	5th " "	-	-	-	1	1	-	-	
	5th Cheshire R.	-	-	-	3	-	-	-	
	280th Bde. RFA.	-	-	-	-	2	-	-	2 { 1 by explosion in fire / 1 by fall of log.
	281st " "	-	-	-	-	5	-	-	
	56th Div. Train.	-	-	-	-	-	-	-	
	8th Middlesex Rgt.	-	-	-	-	26x	-	-	x Gassed.
2nd	4th London Regt.	-	-	-	-	1	-	-	
	13th " "	-	-	-	1	2	-	-	
	2nd " "	-	-	-	-	2	-	-	
	5th " "	- Lt. E.P. HUDSON, M.C.	-	-	1	1	-	-	
	280th Bde. RFA.	- T/Capt. C.B. BUDDLE,	-	-	-	1	-	-	
	8th Middlesex R.	-	-	-	1	2	-	-	Gassed.
3rd	4th London Rgt.	-	-	-	-	1	-	-	At duty.
	13th " "	-	-	-	-	2	1x	-	x Not returned from patrol.
	14th " "	- Capt. H.L. CHURTON,	-	-	-	1	-	-	
	5th Cheshire Rgt.	-	-	-	-	-	-	-	
4th	13th London Regt.	-	-	-	-	1	-	-	
	14th " "	-	-	-	-	1	-	-	
	2nd " "	-	-	-	-	7	1x	-	xDid not returned from patrol.
	5th " "	-	-	-	-	1	-	-	
5th	1st London Rgt.	-	-	-	1	6	-	-	
	14th " "	2/Lt. E.R.C. MISSEN,(4/10/18)	-	-	-	-	-	-	
	2nd " "	-	-	-	1	8	-	-	
	56th Bn. M.G.C.	-	-	-	1	1	1x	-	1x Cleaning rifle.

(2)

DATE	UNIT	OFFICERS				O. Rs				REMARKS
		Killed	Wounded	Missing		K.	W.	M.	I.	
OCT.										
6th	8th Middlesex R.	-	-	-		-	1	-	-	
	4th London Rgt.	-	-	-		-	1	-	-	
	280th Bde. RFA.	-	-	-		-	3	-	-	x Gassed.
	56th Bn. M.G.C.	-	-	-		-	3x	-	-	x Gassed.
7th	13th London Rgt.	-	-	-		-	3	-	1	Chopping wood.
	5th "	-	-	-		-	1	-	1	At duty.
	5th Cheshire Rgt.	-	-	-		-	-	-	-	
	56th Bn. M.G.C.	-	-	-		-	4x	-	-	x Inc. 3 gassed.
8th	7th Middlesex Rgt.	-	-	-		-	3	-	1	"Inc."1 gassed.
	8th "	-	-	-		1	2	-	1x	x Explosion in fire
	4th London Rgt.	-	-	-		1	1	-	1	Ay duty.
	13th "	-	-	-		-	1	-	-	
	14th "	-	-	-		-	3	-	2	T by pick l; playing football.
	5th Cheshire Rgt.	-	-	-		-	-	-	-	
	280th Bde. R.F.A.	-	-	-		-	2x	-	-	x Gassed.
9th	7th Middlesex Rgt.	-	-	-		-	1	-	-	
	45th London Regt.	-	-	-		2	1	-	-	
	14th "	-	-	-		-	4*	-	1	x Gassed * Inc 3.
	5th Cheshire Rgt.	Lt. S.P.FERDINANDO.	-	-		-	-	-	3	"2 by fall 1 by barbed wire Gassed.
	280th Bde. R.F.A.	-	-	-		-	8x	-	-	x Inc. 6 gassed.
	281st "	-	-	-		-	2	-	-	x Gassed.
	13th London Rgt.	-	-	-		-	3x	-	-	x Gassed.
10th	7th Middlesex R.	-	-	-		-	4x	-	1@	1 Gassed @ By discharge of German rifle
	1st London Regt.	-	-	-		-	2	-	-	
	8th Middlesex Rgt.	-	-	-		-	1	-	-	x Gassed.
	4th London Rgt.	2/Lt.(A/Capt) L. WATTS,	-	-		-	2x	-	1x	x By jam tin.
	13th "	-	-	-		-	-	-	-	

(3)

DATE	UNIT	OFFICERS			O.Rs			REMARKS
		Killed.	Wounded.	Missing.	K.	W.	M.I.	
11th	7th Middlesex Rgt.	—	—	—	1	2	1x	1x By German Bomb
	8th "	—	—	—	—	1	—	
	13th London Rgt.	—	—	—	3	16	—	2x x Both kicked by
	5th Cheshire Rgt.	—	—	—	—	1	—	1 Indian By rifle
	280th Bde. R.F.A.	—	—	—	—	1	—	bullet.
	56th Bn. D.A.C.	—	—	—	—	—	—	
12th	8th Middlesex Rgt.	—	—	—	1	—	—	
	4th London Regt.	—	—	—	—	2x	—	Inc 1 gassed.
	13th "	—	Capt. J.B. FARRER, M.O., 11/10/18.	—	1	—	—	
	14th "	—	—	—	1	5	—	
	5th "	—	Capt. S.T. HOSKING,* (11/10/18)	—	2	2	—	* 7th Ldns attd.
			2/Lt. A. Mc DONALD, 11/10/18.					
	56th Bn. M.G.C.	—	—	—	—	1	—	
	281st Bde. RFA.	—	—	—	1	—	—	1 Recoil of gun.
13th	7th Middlesex Rgt.	—	—	—	—	8	—	Inc 1 'at' duty
	8th "	—	Lt. H. WOLFENDER, 13/10/18	—	—	4	—	
	13th London Rgt.	—	—	—	—	1	—	By German revolver
	14th "	—	—	—	—	1	—	Sprained ankle
	416th Field Coy. RE.	2/Lt. J.E. ARNOLD, 13/10/18	—	—	—	—	—	
	512th "	—	2/Lt. H.J.B. TALLING, 13/10/18	—	—	—	—	
	16th London Rgt.	—	—	—	1	1	—	
	4th "	—	—	—	1	1	—	Gassed.
	5th "	—	—	—	—	2	—	
	169th T.M. Battery.	—	Lt. H.F. JAMES, 13/10/18. 2/Lt.J.N.W.WATSON,13/10/18	—	1*	1	1	*Wounded & Missing
	2nd London Rgt.	—	Lt. A.W. DOLMAN 13/10/18	—	8	51	56x	x Inc 9 ORs Wnd &
								M'ing

(4)

DATE	UNIT	OFFICERS			O.Rs			REMARKS
		Killed	Wounded	Missing	K.	W.	M.	
OCT.								
14th	7th Middlesex Rgt.	-	2/Lt. R.J. HAYNES. 13/10/18.	-	-	2	-	
	8th " "	-	-	-	3	9x	-	x.Inc.2 at duty.
	1st London Regt.	-	-	-	-	1	-	
	5th " "	2/Lt. J.D. KEEP. 13/10/18.	Lt.(A/Capt)S.COLEMAN.14/10/18.	-	1	4x	-	x Inc.1 at duty.
	16th " "	-	-	-	4	5x	-	x Inc.2 at duty.
	56th Bn.M.G.C.	-	-	-	1	3	-	
	416th(Edin)Fd.Co.RE	-	-	-	1	4	-	
	512th (Ldn.) "	-	-	-	1	1	-	
	2/3rd Ldn.Fd.Amb.	-	-	-	-	1	-	
	2nd London Rgt.	-	-	-	1	8	-	
15th	16th London Rgt.	-	-	-	-	1	-	
	5th Cheshire Rgt.	-	-	-	-	1	-	
	56th Bn.M.G.Corps.	-	-	-	-	1	-	
	7th Middlesex Rgt.	-	-	-	-	5x	-	x Gassed.
17th	A.O.C. attd. 167th I.B.	-	-	-	-	1	1	Petrol Burns.
19th	5th London Rgt.	-	-	-	-	1	1	Scalded.
24th	13th London Rgt.	-	-	-	-	1	1	Slipped on nail.
	X/56th T.M.Bty.	-	-	-	-	1	1	German Automatic Pistol.
25th	5th Cheshire Rgt.	-	-	-	-	1	1	BY fall.
26th	2nd London Rgt.	-	-	-	-	1	1-	By fall.
27th	13th London Rgt.	-	-	-	-	1	1	Kicked in eye.

(5)

DATE.	UNIT.	OFFICERS.		Missing.	O.Rs.				REMARKS.
		Killed.	Wounded.		K.	W.	M.	I.	
OCT.									
28th	A.S.C. attd.169th I.Bde.	-	-	-	-	-	-	1	Kicked by horse.
30th	4th London Regt.	-	2/Lt. J.A.VOSKULE (7th Ldns) (Injured)	-	-	-	-	-	Fractured finger at football
	"	-		-	-	-	-	-	1 Died of injuries knocked down by lorry.
31st	280th Bde. R.F.A.	-	-	-	-	1	-	-	
	281th " "	-	-	-	-	1	4	-	-
TOTALS FOR OCTOBER.		5	14	1	44	278	59	28	

UNIT.	STRENGTH. 1.10.18. O. O.R.		INCREASE. O. O.R.		DECREASE. O. O.R.		STRENGTH. 1.11.18. O. O.R.	
Divisional Headquarters.	16	82	-	-	-	-	16	82
247th Div. Employment Coy.	2	340	-	5	-	17	2	328
167th Inf. Brigade H.Q.	4	21	-	1	-	-	4	22
1/7th Middlesex Regt.	43	865	5	93	5	95	43	863
1/8th Middlesex Regt.	41	864	3	90	8	141	39	813
1/1st London Regt.	40	657	3	107	3	52	40	712
167th T.M. Battery.	4	46	-	3	-	3	4	46
168th Infantry Bde. H.Q.	4	20	-	1	-	-	4	21
1/4th London Regt.	37	705	5	110	4	94	38	721
1/13th London Regt.	41	691	8	81	3	123	46	649
1/14th London Regt.	31	622	5	144	2	61	34	705
168th T.M. Battery.	4	44	-	3	-	2	4	45
169th Inf. Brigade H.Q.	4	21	-	-	-	-	4	21
1/2nd London Regt.	31	717	10	134	6	250	35	601
1/5th London Regt.	32	603	6	99	5	71	33	631
1/16th London Regt.	31	560	2	127	4	75	29	612
169th T.M. Battery.	2	39	-	-	-	6-	2	33
1/5th Cheshire Regt.	41	826	3	53	3	76	41	803
56th Bn. M.G.Corps.	49	846	3	77	4	48	48	875
56th Divl. Artillery H.Q.	4	18	-	-	-	-	4	18
280th Brigade, R.F.A.	28	754	-	68	-	58	28	764
281st Brigade, R.F.A.	26	763	2	17	3	26	25	754
56th D. A. C.	20	423	-	10	2	4	18	429
56th Divl. Engineers H.Q.	1	8	-	2	-	-	1	10
416th (Edin)Field Coy. R.E.	7	201	-	12	1	16	6	197
512th (Ldn.)Field Coy. R.E.	7	204	1	15	-	20	8	199
513th (Ldn.)Field Coy. R.E.	8	194	1	19	1	7	8	206
56th Div. Signal Coy. R.E.	12	296	2	8	2	9	12	295
56th Divisional Train.	20	380	2	10	-	8	22	382
Medical Units.	19	542	10	17	6	16	23	543
Mobile Veterinary Section.	1	18	-	-	-	-	1	18

****

Secret

War Diary

Administrative Branch

56th Division

Period: 1st to 30th November 1918.

Vol: XXXIV

Army Form C. 2118.

Vol XXIV Page 1

WAR DIARY
or
INTELLIGENCE SUMMARY.
(Erase heading not required.)

Place	Date	Hour	Summary of Events and Information	Remarks and references to Appendices
BOISSEUILLE	1/11/18		Administrative Instructions in connection with Relief of 49th Division & subsequent operations issued & attached Appendix "A". Our Railhead is today at ARRAS a distance of 30 to 40 miles from the Div. the curtailing considerable difficulties with M.T.	
MONCHAUX			Relief of 49th Div in the line taken place today. 168th & 169th Inf Bde go into line, 167 Bde in support. Amb Wks open on movement & 1500 hours. Administrative Instructions Appendix "B".	

Army Form C. 2118.

WAR DIARY
or
INTELLIGENCE SUMMARY.
(Erase heading not required.)

Instructions regarding War Diaries and Intelligence Summaries are contained in F.S. Regs., Part II. and the Staff Manual respectively. Title pages will be prepared in manuscript.

Place	Date	Hour	Summary of Events and Information	Remarks and references to Appendices
SAULTAIN	6.11.18		Weather very wet and road situation in consequence rather difficult. Work on crafts blown up by the enemy carried on by R.E. and Pioneers. Un is being much of Curtain waggons hauled by spare animals from various units. Attack in. on this morning met with strong opposition and line was not advanced materially. D.H.Q. remained at SAULTAIN. The division is now retaining about 16000 Civilians in various villages. Some of this work in the forward areas was done by the handful of 168 + 169 Inf. Bdes.	
SEBOURG	7.11.18		Attack this morning made good progress and it was decided to Moved Div.H.Q. to SEBOURG, 15 km at 3 P.M. Heavy rain continued to fell during the night. Railhead yesterday was at Aubigny au Bac and should be at ANZIN today. COYPATE situation in forward area anonymous on P.M. + Divis Reservists of the North in Front line (167 Inf.Bde.) By another	
"	8.11.18		The despatching of Rations by Curtain was curtailed so unnecessary. The advance of the division continued without much opposition and it was directed to Moved H.Q. to FRANC tonument. Railhead was moved to ANZIN yesterday but owing to some mistake the Push train that was held at RAISMES and had was not returned with it until late in the day. Weather showery + finally milder.	

Army Form C. 2118.

Page 3

WAR DIARY
or
INTELLIGENCE SUMMARY.
(Erase heading not required.)

Instructions regarding War Diaries and Intelligence Summaries are contained in F.S. Regs., Part II. and the Staff Manual respectively. Title pages will be prepared in manuscript.

Place	Date	Hour	Summary of Events and Information	Remarks and references to Appendices
FAY T. le FRANC	9/11/18		D.H.Q. opened at 10 A.M. Road situation is still difficult and is holding up the advance of Infantry owing to difficulty of supplies. The enemy continued his retirement and on reaching the Red Castle opposition. The enemy has done his demolition work most effectively. Craters are blown at road junctions and rendu roads impassable especially in Forthuin. From the rim of the crater comes in many cases, up to the walls of the houses. Culverts are blown on main roads, and a particularly difficult blockage is present in one place by blowing a bridge across a road and stream so that all the materials amounting to many tons fell across the road and in the river. One Bde (?) Immediately set Transport used for road repairs. Weather fine but cold — Fine and bright but colder.	
" "	10/11/18		Weather continues fine but cold. Road situation still difficult but the enemy front line has been given to one division (63rd) with 11th + 56th following behind. This Div. and the situation. 118 + 169 Inf. Bdes are supplying large working parties for roads under C.R.E. and Transport is being supplied by S.A.A. Section + No. 1 & 2 Sections D.A.C. It has been decided to dump surplus S.A.A. + Bombs etc at this railway.	
" "	11/11/18		Hostilities ceased at 11 A.M. today. N/66 Div. train moved off 15 this morning today. Considerable difficulty was experienced in getting the Train down through the Pierre road in manner and very greasy army is made and Lorries skidded off and got bogged. These roads which would be perfectly serviceable for any traffic when clean (i.e. with...	

Army Form C. 2118.

WAR DIARY
or
INTELLIGENCE SUMMARY.
(Erase heading not required.)

Instructions regarding War Diaries and Intelligence Summaries are contained in F. S. Regs., Part II. and the Staff Manual respectively. Title pages will be prepared in manuscript.

Page 4.

Place	Date	Hour	Summary of Events and Information	Remarks and references to Appendices
Fayt le Franc	12/11/18		When reached by rail) a day and in daylight are almost impossible when greasy + in the dark impossible as long as long as much mud is being made. The Batte., lorries stairs hicks + blankets and other dumped stores +DADOS are being brought to this village. Application for M.T. from Corps to bring up ligger stores etc. then been met with some ill. It was certainly that there was been between the SMTS considered the lorries could do also ferrying stores they can hardly do so, and have any out any to the condition of the roads. Refilling point at FAYT le FRANC (sic) and arrangements for Nos 2 + 3 Coys to go to SARS la BRUYERE, the tam buses have had very long runs ample, and their will give them a chance to put into condition again. The Division has notified that it will go forward to the Rhine by easy marches. Marching days and resting days to be dispersed and unless it attained to be dumped and attained to have seen completed out district and arr slight rain making the roads pricey. Weather dull.	Appendix... See Appendix A
"	13/11/18		Fine bright day. Nos 2 + 3 Co. Div Train moved up to SARS LA BRUYERE. Fine at night. Arrangements to form companies termorrow. Transport Livers try and work return all brought up. Reception arrangements will permit so no men will come from ill units. All reinforcements from Reception Camps + depots + England. The first lot of 7,150 Cms of in Europe today.	See Appendix A. Ammunition exfunt... No. 11 (Marches the Rhine) issued today location Table delib.
"	14/11/18		Weather fine bright + cool. Frost at night. Orders for the MDNS Corps to be in position Army Commander... received from Corps in the morning in MDs by 10 A.M. down Battle order with Steel Helmets. B.G.C. 169 Bde. commands.	See Appendix A A.Q. X. 1499

WAR DIARY
or
INTELLIGENCE SUMMARY

Army Form C. 2118.

Page 5

Place	Date	Hour	Summary of Events and Information	Remarks and references to Appendices
Fayt le Franc	15.11.18		The troops of the division attending. The troops moved to Mons by Buses. All men have now got their packs and are [illegible].	
"	16.11.18		Weather still fine, ie light & cold. Buses were later, lots of embussing points and Pom Points to join the convoy army (a system hitherto a potent difficulty). Troops moved at their [illegible] of positions in time... 1/6 Field Co. R.E. moved billets from P.9.c.40 to Sars la Bruyère Area 1/7 Bn 148 Bde and Divisionals Fayt le France. 2 new allotment Bdes at Sars la Bruyère 149 Bde and Div artillery Fayt le France. Received today advance Officers from S.B.6.52. Two special O.R. returns are allotted daily.	
"	"		Fine bright weather and very cold. Roads first found in early morning. Rich motoring convoy traffic. The road from Buvrinnes to Fayt le France is not already the types will the part is sinking, [illegible] than the shells of the days between which farming carts which are gradually becoming more constant. AA + QMG + DAQMG attended conference at XXII Corps. this morning have practically being cleared + brought up to units by lorry or Lorries known available within from the M.T. Cos as supplied by XXII Corps.	
"	17.11.18		Sunday. The G.O.C. attended on a special Thanksgiving Service held by the S.C. Fr the Schools, then the divisional Band marched the Mouns Church from the Te Deum was chanted by the Curé.	

Army Form C. 2118.

WAR DIARY
or
INTELLIGENCE SUMMARY.
(Erase heading not required.)

Page 6

Instructions regarding War Diaries and Intelligence Summaries are contained in F.S. Regs., Part II. and the Staff Manual respectively. Title pages will be prepared in manuscript.

Place	Date	Hour	Summary of Events and Information	Remarks and references to Appendices
Fayt le France	17.11.18		The weather is still cold and the country is rapidly becoming frost bound. As a scheme is being proposed to bring up supplies all the way from Railhead (Bouchain) up to unit by lorry transport in relays due in in the event of the roads becoming impassable for horses owing to weather conditions. Any DIvnl Details needed to come 2 U.K.	
	18.11.18		A thaw set in today and some rain in the afternoon. Preliminary instructions for the of Horse Transport to stuff Rail head XH places of horses if in the event of the roads becoming unsuitable for horse transport. The changes over Railhead to 2nd Army.	
	19.11.18		From 1200 hrs 18th Nov 1918. Corps Schools the 15 units Railhead was changed to ANZIN and to BOUCHAIN YT / DR(?). Arrival of BOUCHAIN YT / DR(?) could not be definitely ascertained but Since 15 Lorries are required on the journey at them VR but permits Refreshment to Fayt to the Rather hopeful in moment in with BOUCHAIN in France as actually from to Fayt. ...the back from the DRC at NEUVILLE. For the best findings been pursued etc. ...has been used shortly by lorries unit tabulated to Bryas. ... arrived today Clara Bouras 4. the Militar. City of 1st Ninth p R. DAGGER. U. Div. Chaplains Gard.	
	20.11.18		Arrangements were made in the 19th Instant supplies of Clothing materials in Armies Baths. Absence to suit the first unit allotment each Sunday Officer. Athletics moved by next Corps to Charge available at trained from BOUCHAIN to	

Army Form C. 2118.

WAR DIARY
or
INTELLIGENCE SUMMARY.
(Erase heading not required.)

Instructions regarding War Diaries and Intelligence Summaries are contained in F. S. Regs., Part II. and the Staff Manual respectively. Title pages will be prepared in manuscript.

Page 1

Place	Date	Hour	Summary of Events and Information	Remarks and references to Appendices
FAYT LE FRANC 20.11.18			Received orders to take over the arrangements of the Nov. 21 ascertainments (Sic) and that the Brass Band [illegible] with the band of the 39 Bn Honnoduste (?) to attend. DRO 15 SOMAIN on arrival and rendered conference.	
" "	21.11.18		In 2nd Corps summary Comminication to Corps HQ. transports to join RAISINES as instructed (point of arrival + departure of leave personnel. Orders received from XXII Corps late last night to the effect that the XXII Corps would Entrain to the following 81220 22 W. The Army does not proceed to the Rhine. In the same order an area of Mons was allotted to the division for Billets. Westler Bright + Cold - Forty nights.	
" "	22.11.18		The letting DAA & QMG'S [illegible] = [illegible] of the out area which is shewn along to 56 DIV GA 509 dated 22.11.18. The policy in the reserve area is to billet troops in houses owning of the cost of cells, and chiefumas are to use their own rooms. Schools etc for recreation + educational training. Hearty fires for fuel. As the tram or fuel to the hewn area. Railhead was probably be at Mons and horse transport will ride be used from Railhead. Lorries will probably be unnecessary but there are no roads reduced. the roads in the hewn area are showing signs of wear - the heart sinking in the levels of Lorries.	

Army Form C. 2118.

Page 5

WAR DIARY
or
INTELLIGENCE SUMMARY
(Erase heading not required.)

Place	Date	Hour	Summary of Events and Information	Remarks and references to Appendices
FAYT-LE-FRANC	23/11/18		With C.R.A. RO.S Reminder of 63rd Div. came to D.H.Q. this morning to [?] information of this area as they will take over billets here in [?]. H.R. XXII Corps should have spared at Mons today like the move to our proposed area to 24th. Administrative instruction Not [?] with move to HARVENG. War moved today and 56 Div Order No 24 [?] Mined Table for move. D.H.Q. moved 23/11/18 to HARVENG	Admin instn not [?] Mov to HARVENG Appendix A.
"	24/11/18		H.Q. 22 Corps moved 6 mons today. Reinforcements (524 ranks) arrived at [?] [?] for inspection and arranged to supply short tours [?] the division of 16 [?] to animals and some under by the Q.M.C. [?] to [?]. Conference at SARS-la-BRUYÈRE today with [?] [?] [?] by Commission of [?]. [?] to discuss [?], [?], Reveries, Billeting [?] and other [?] in 56 DIV & HQ [?] [?] of units and Furniture material offers and further [?] [?]. [?] [?] [?] [?] with XXII Corps. Rect Baths opened at Blangies & [?].	
"	26/11/18		169 Bde group moved to its new area today with Company Rlle HQ at HARVENG [?]. [?] [?] Rochfort the [?] and [?] [?] [?] QUEVY-le-GRAND [?] [?] out with 2 Coys at [?] [?] moving [?] moving a relief, Smyth [?] [?] [?] [?] Com [?]	

Army Form C. 2118.

WAR DIARY
or
INTELLIGENCE SUMMARY.
(Erase heading not required.)

Page 9.

Instructions regarding War Diaries and Intelligence Summaries are contained in F. S. Regs., Part II. and the Staff Manual respectively. Title pages will be prepared in manuscript.

Place	Date	Hour	Summary of Events and Information	Remarks and references to Appendices
FAYT-le FRANC.	27/11/18		Move of Division to new area was continued today - 169 Bde group moving into the area. It has been arranged for the Div. Cinema to show for the benefit of the troops about ATH's tomorrow afternoon, it will be then move into the new area.	
HARVENG.	28/11/18		Div. HQ. moved to HARVENG today. Railhead is still at ANZIN. Divisional reception Camp was moved to RAISMES yesterday and reinforcements are being channelled thence from SOMAIN. Another wet and long mile. There are still considerable numbers of Corps Troops & 63rd Div details in the area & until they are moved the accommodation is rather cramped. The Billeting Policy is so that men shall be in houses & horses in stables & barns and at present there is not provision in all cases. Any better schools etc are to be used for recreation & educational purposes.	
	29/11/18		A new Car (Vauxhall) was received today, this makes 3 for the HQ. and will ease the situation. London letter issued (A.Q.S.S.) 169 Bde. analysed their billeting arrangements by moving 16 London. from BOUGNIES to GENLY. General Lock proceeded on leave to Paris 30th to 7th Dec. He on which return will go to AMIENS will return with Gen. Freeth.	Appendix A Location table AR.S.C.

Army Form C. 2118.

WAR DIARY
or
INTELLIGENCE SUMMARY.
(Erase heading not required.)

Page 10

Place	Date	Hour	Summary of Events and Information	Remarks and references to Appendices
HARVENG.	30/11/18		175 Bde R.F.A. and 277 A Bde R.F.A. moved out of HARMIGNIES and EVRY respectively today and 169 Bde H.Q. moved into its final H.Q. at Nouvelles. There are still one Snr. Corps hosp. and 4 D.A. (Asquiths) in the area. Additional officers have been vacancy for alternate days starting 1st December are allotted to this Division.	

Wm Collins R.Lt.Col.
A.A. & Q.M.G. 56 Div

13/XII/18

Appendix A   *War Diary*

S E C R E T.　　　　　　　　　　　　　　　　56th Division AQS/755/1.

ADMINISTRATIVE INSTRUCTIONS
in connection with 56th Divn. G.280 dated 1st November/18.

1. **TRANSPORT.**

   Transport Lines will be located as follows:-

167th Inf.Bde. Group.	J.21.clear of THIANT.
168th　"　"　"	J.22. clear of THIANT.
169th　"　"　"	J.28. clear of MONCHAUX.
56th M.G. Battn.	J.34.c & d. clear of MONCHAUX.
1/5th Cheshire Regt.	J.15.c.
S.A.A. Section.	DOUCHY.

   Divl. Train will remain in present sites.

2. **AMMUNITION.**

   All ammunition will be drawn from mobile reserves. Supplies will not be available for the formation of Brigade dumps.
   Requirements for small arms ammunition, grenades, etc. will be wired to Divl. "Q". Indents will state the location at which the ammunition is to be delivered and the time by which it is required.
   There will not be any Divisional Grenade Dumps.
   Battle equipment ammunition will be available for issue at Halting places on the 2nd instant for 3 Infantry Brigades. Brigades will notify Halting places to this office.

3. **SURPLUS BAGGAGE.**

   Attention is called to AQS/735/3 of 28.9.18. paras. 1,4,5,10. Guards over these dumps may be counted as Nucleus personnel.

4. **NUCLEUS PERSONNEL** will be sent to Transport Lines of Units.

5. **WATER.**

   The C.R.E. will detail an Officer to exploit the water supplies and cause wells to be marked as soon as water has been tested.

6. **MEDICAL.** Medical arrangements will be issued separately.

7. **VETERINARY.** Mob.Vet.Section will be at PAVE de VALENCIENNES.

   　　　　　　　　　　　　　　　　　A.E.Dundas Major,
   1st November, 1918.　　　　　　for A.A. & Q.M.G., 56th Divn.

   * DISTRIBUTION *

167th Inf. Bde.	D. A. D. V. S.	56th M.T. Company.
168th　"　"	D. A. D. O. S.	56th Bn. M.G.Corps
169th　"　"	D. A. P. M.	1/5th Cheshire Rgt.
C. R. A.	French Mission.	Div.Reception Camp.
C. R. E.	Camp Commandant.	S.C.F.(D.C.G's Dept)
Div. Train.	Div.Employment Coy.	S.C.F. (P.C's Dept)
A. D. M. S.	"G".	

Appendix B   War diary

SECRET.   56th Division AQS/755/2.

ADMINISTRATIVE INSTRUCTIONS
in connection with 56th Divn. G.280 dated 1st November 1918.(contd)

8. MEDICAL.

    2/1st Ldn.Field Ambloe. Advanced Dressing Station at J.15.c.6.4.
    2/3rd   "   "   "   Main Dressing Station   at I.29.d.9.3.
    2/2nd   "   "   "   Divl. Rest Station   at I.30.a.2.1.
    Corps Walking Wounded Centre.   HASPRES. (Sheet 51a.P.13.central)
War posts will be pushed forward to points which will be notified to all concerned.

9. P.O.W.   The Divisional Prisoners of War Cage will be at MAING.

10. In para. 1. after "1/5th Cheshire Regt." for "J.15.c." substitute "PYRIMIDS DE DENAIN". Erase the word "Group" after "Infantry Brigades".

11. The 3 Field Companies will be located at THIANT in accommodation vacated by Field Companies of 49th Division.

                                                         Dundas
                                                         Major,
2nd November, 1918.   for A.A. & Q.M.G. 56th Divn.

DISTRIBUTION as for AQS/755/1 dated 1.11.18.

"G" War Diary

56th Division AQX.1493.

ADMINISTRATIVE INSTRUCTIONS NO.1.
Issued in connection with the March to the Rhine.

Issued with reference to 56th Divn. No. G.A.288 of 13.11.18.

1. The present policy should be
   (a) To get troops and transport as smart and serviceable as possible.
   (b) To re-equip up to a mobile establishment.
   (c) To get as mobile as possible.

2. (a) Endeavours are being made to obtain cleaning material from PARIS. Any which is obtained will be sold on allotment through the Divl. Canteen.
   (b) Vehicles will be released from R.E. work as soon as possible. They must then be cleaned.
   (c) It is considered that there will be time to paint vehicles if the work is put in hand at once. In any case vehicles should be thoroughly cleaned and touched up with paint, and all Divisional and Unit signs should be re-painted.
   Attention is drawn to G.R.O. 4809.

3. The Corps have been asked to arrange for demands for horses, vehicles, equipment etc., to be met as soon as possible; or, alternatively, to arrange for transfers from Divisions not advancing, if replacements from the usual source cannot be expedited.

4. (a) Packs, Steel helmets, and Box respirators will be carried on the man.
   (b) Rifle grenade dischargers and pouches, Rifle grenade cup attachments, Very Pistols, Binoculars and Compasses must be carried "on the man" or on Units' transport.
   (c) Additional transport will be provided for one blanket per man, Leather Jerkins, 1 change of underlinen per man, a limited amount of surplus baggage and stores, and for Trench Mortars.
   (d) The second blanket will not be issued until the march is completed.

5. The following stores and equipment will be dispensed with forthwith.
   They will be handed in to the D.A.D.O.S. at BLAUGIES whence they will be evacuated to the Base under D.A.D.O.S' arrangements.
   Tents and Trench Shelters.   Gloves Anti Gas   G.R.O.5419.
   Anti Aircraft L.G.Mountings.   Goggles, night firing
   Gas Rattles.   Stretchers ambulance 2 per Bn.
   Arty. Emergency Ammunition Carriers.   Gloves Hedging.
   Carriers, Grenade bucket pattern.
   All Lewis Guns surplus to 20 per Battn. with corresponding number of magazines, canvas carriers and magazine boxes.
   All Lewis Gun Chests.   32 sets Packsaddlery per M.G.Bn.
   Periscopes.   Signal Stores of Units as notified by O.C. Divl. Signal Company.
   3 Range Finders per Battn.   Telescopic Sighted Rifles.
   Wire Breakers,   Wire Cutters.
   All hand-carts,   Water can crates.

   Units wishing to dump any stores other than those mentioned above will communicate at once with Div. H.Q. "Q" through the usual channels.

P.T.O.

6. One dump on a good lorry route should be formed in each Brigade Area for reception of Salvage.
Location of those dumps should be notified to this office.
Guards need not be left on those dumps.

13th November, 1918.

Lieut-Colonel,
A.A. & Q.M.G., 56th Division.

* DISTRIBUTION *

As for Area Instructions.

AQX. 1494.

167th Inf. Bde.	Div. Artillery.	5th Cheshire Rgt.
168th " "	C. R. E.	A. D. M. S.
169th " "	56th M.G. Battn.	"G".

A party is required to represent this Division at the Official entry of the Army Commander into MONS on the 15th instant.

The party will be composed as stated below and will be conveyed by bus in groups as shown.

The proportion of Officers to O.Rs will be 1 to 25.

Embussing Point.

"A" Group.
167th Inf. Bde.	240 all ranks.)	Head of column at W.14.d.9.7.
R.E.	60 " ")	Sheet 45. facing South East.
M.G. Corps.	90 " ")	

"B" Group.
168th Inf. Bde.	240 all ranks.)	Tail of column at D.2.a.1.7.
Div. Artillery.	180 " ")	Sheet 51. facing North.
5th Cheshire Regt.	100 " ")	

"C" Group.
169th Inf. Bde.	240 all ranks.)	Tail of column at C.8.d.9.2.
R.A.M.C.	50 " ")	Sheet 51. facing North.

The name of the Senior Officer proceeding with the party from each formation or unit will be notified to this office by 1600 on the 14th instant.

Further details will be issued later.

13.11.18.

(S'gd) A.C. DUNDAS, Major,
D.A.A.G., 56th Division.

Copies to :-
    XXII Corps "A". (for information).
    D. A. P. M.

War Diary

S E C R E T.   L O C A T I O N   T A B L E.   56th Div.AQS/5.

Ref. Sheet 51. 1/40000.

Divisional Headquarters.	FAYT LE FRANC.
U N I T.	Headquarters.
167th Infantry Bde.	D.6.a.3.2. QUEVY le PETIT.
7th Middlesex Regt.	BOUGNIES.
8th " "	E.2.b.5.8.
1st London Regt.	BOUGNIES.
168th Infantry Bde.	SARS-le-BRUYERE.
4th London Regt.	D.1.d.4.5.
13th " "	D.8.d.8.8.
14th " "	D.9.d.4.0.
169th Infantry Bde.	ATHIS.
2nd London Regt.	
5th " "	ERQUENNES.
16th " "	ATHIS.
56th Battn. M.G.Corps (less 1 Coy.)	QUEVY le PETIT.
1/5th Cheshire Regt.	ATHIS.
247th (Div)Employment Coy.	FAYT LE FRANC.
C. R. E.	"
416th Field Coy. R.E.	D.9.c.4.0.
512th " " "	D.7.b.2.7.
513th " " "	B.18.a.5.4.
A. D. M. S.	B.12.c.2.3.
2/1st Ldn.Fld.Ambloe.	D.6.d.2.5.
2/2nd " " "	VALENCIENNES.
2/3rd " " "	C.7.central.
C. R. A.	FAYT LE FRANC.
280th Brigade R.F.A.	BLAREGNIES.
281st " " "	QUEVY le PETIT.
56th D.A.C. H.Q.(less SAA.Section) ONNEZIES.	SAA.Sect. FAYT LE FRANC.
Divl. Train. H.Q.	FAYT LE FRANC.
No. 1. Company.	"
" 2. "	SARS le BRUYERE.
" 3. "	"
" 4. "	FAYT LE FRANC.
D. A. D. V. S.	"
Mobile Vet. Section.	"
D. A. D. O. S.	BLAUGIES.
56th M.T. Company.	MARLY.
Divl. Reception Camp.	NEUVILLE.

P. T. O.

U N I T .	Headquarters.
Div. Baths Officer.	FAYT LE FRANC.
" Claims "	" " "
" **Burials** "	" " "
" Salvage "	" " "
" Canteen, "	" " "
" Linen Store.	" " "

RAILHEAD for Personnel. — BOUCHAIN.
167th Inf. Bde. Transport Lines. — RUINSETTE.
Other Transport Lines. — With Units.

15th November, 1918.

S.H. Brunner Capt.
for Major,
D.A.A.G., 56th Division.

SECRET. A.Q.S.5.

The following amendments will be made to Location Table issued under this office AQS/5 dated 13th November, 1918.

8th Middlesex Regt.	QUEVY le PETIT.
56th Bn. M.G.Corps.	BLAUGIES.
416th Field Coy.R.E.	SARS LE BRUYERE. D.2.a.5.6.
167th Inf.Bde. Transport Lines.	With Unit.

16th November, 1918.

S H Bunney Capt
for Major,
D.A.A.G., 56th Division.

War Diary

56th Division AQX.1493.

ADMINISTRATIVE INSTRUCTIONS NO. 2.
issued in connection with the March to the Rhine.

Issued with reference to 56th Divn. No. G.A.286 of 13.11.18.

1. Superstructures on water carts will not be removed at present and water tins will be retained by Units.

2. Infantry and Pioneers will only carry 60 rounds of S.A.A. per man. Ammunition at present being carried on the man surplus to this will be returned forthwith to the "Depot. FAYT LE FRANC". B.18.b.7.8.

15th November, 1918.

Lieut-Colonel,
A.A. & Q.M.G., 56th Division.

* DISTRIBUTION. *

As for Area Instructions.

SECRET.   56th Div. AQS/762/1.
         ADMINISTRATIVE INSTRUCTION NO. 1.
         in connection with the move to the HARVENG Area.

         Issued with reference to 56th Div. Order No. 224.

1. BILLETING GROUPS. On completion of the move will be as follows:-

   167th Inf. Bde. Group.   167th Inf.Bde. 281st Bde. R.F.A. 416th Field
                            Coy. R.E., No. 2 Coy. Div. Train. 2/1st London
                            Field Amblce.

   168th Inf. Bde. Group.   168th Inf. Bde. 280th Bde. R.F.A. 512th Field
                            Coy. R.E. No. 3. Coy. Div. Train. 2/2nd London
                            Field Amblce.

   169th Inf. Bde. Group.   169th Inf. Bde. Army Bde. R.F.A.   513th Field
                            Coy. R.E. No. 4 Coy. Div. Train.   2/3rd London
                            Field Amblce.

   Areas allotted to Infantry Brigade Groups are shown on the tracing issued with 56th Div. Order No. 224.

   Divl. H.Q. Group will be constituted and located as shown below.

   Divl. H.Q. Divl.R.A. H.Q. Divl. R.E. H.Q.   ⎫
   Divl. Train H.Q. Div.Employ.Coy. and details.   ⎬ HARVENG.
   Machine Gun Battalion.   VILLERS GHISLAIN.
   1/5th Cheshire Regt. (Pioneers).   SPIENNES.
   D.A.C., No.1.Coy. Div.Train, and attached transport. CIPLY & MESVIN.
   Mobile Veterinary Section.   to be notified later.

2. ALLOTMENT OF BILLETING AREAS.

   The following factors should be taken into consideration when arranging billeting areas :-

   (a) Men to be billeted in Houses.
   (b) Horses to be in Stables and Barns.
   (c) Suitable Halls or Barns to be reserved in each area for "Bow Bells" and Cinema.
   (d) Accommodation to be provided for Battalion Officers' Messes, Sergeants' Messes, Corporals' Messes, Mens' dining and recreation rooms, Lecture Rooms.(Village schools are suggested for this purpose).
   (e) Train Coys to be billeted in that part of the Area which is the shortest distance from MONS by means of a good road.
   (f) Field Ambulances to take over hospital (but not billeting) accommodation from outgoing Field Ambulances.

3. BATHS.

(a) Baths now run by 167th Inf. Bde. at BOUGNIES will be handed over in situ to 169th Inf. Brigade.
(b) 168th Inf. Bde. will move their present Baths from LA DESSOUS to their new area under their own arrangements.
(c) 169th Inf. Bde. will remove their Baths from ATHIS and will hand them over to 167th Inf. Bde. who will establish them in their new area.
(d) Further instructions will be issued regarding the existing Baths at NOIRCHAIN.

                                                          P. T. O.

4. FIELD POST OFFICES will remain with Train Companies.

5. 2/2nd London Field Ambulance will move to GIVRY independently on the 27th instant and will come under the orders of 168th Infantry Brigade on arrival at GIVRY. This ambulance will take over the existing arrangements of the 63rd Division for reception of released Allied Prisoners of War.

6. The C.R.A. will arrange with C.R.A. 63rd Division for Echelon Ammunition of S.A.A. Sections to be dumped at present locations and exchanged. The S.A.A. Section will rejoin the D.A.C. when that Unit moves to the CIPLY - MESVIN Area.

7. TRANSPORT FOR BLANKETS AND SURPLUS KIT.

  (a) C.R.A. will allot to 169th Inf. Brigade the equivalent of 23 G.S. Wagons from the S.A.A. Section, D.A.C.
  (b) C.R.A. will arrange with 168th Inf. Brigade for a maximum of 23 G.S. Wagons from the D.A.C. to be attached to them for their move.
  (c) 167th Inf. Brigade will move with the transport now at their disposal.

8. SURPLUS KIT FROM ARRAS DUMP which has been asked for by Units will be delivered to the Tramway Depot at E.3.a. on the 28th instant under Divisional arrangements. It may be drawn from there by Units after that date.

    The remainder of the kit from this dump will be brought up into the new area in due course.

9. SOUP KITCHENS for the benefit of French refugees and the poorer inhabitants will be run under Inf. Brigade Group arrangements in their areas.

10. LEAVE. The arrangements for despatch of leave parties notified in "G" Area Instruction No. 46 will hold good in the new area.

[signature]

23rd November, 1918.
                                Lieut-Colonel,
                           A.A. & Q.M.G., 56th Division.

DISTRIBUTION.

167th Inf. Brigade.	1/5th Cheshire Rgt.	S.C.F. (D.C.G's Dept)
168th " "	Divl. Train.	S.C.F. (P.C's Dept).
169th " "	A.D.M.S.	Camp Commandant.
C.R.A.	D.A.D.V.S.	Div. Employment Coy.
C.R.E.	D.A.P.M.	63rd Division "Q".
56th Bn. M.G.Corps.	D.A.D.O.S.	French Mission.
	56th Div. M.T.Company.	

S E C R E T.

56th Division AQS/762/2.

ADMINISTRATIVE INSTRUCTIONS NO.1.
in connection with move to the HARVENG Area.

Issued with reference to 56th Div. Order No.224.

Amendment to para. 1. Billeting Groups.

280th Bde. R.F.A. will be in 167th Inf. Brigade Group.
281st   "   " " " "   168th "   "   "

instead of as previously stated.

24th November, 1918.

Lieut-Colonel,
A.A. & Q.M.G., 56th Division.

DISTRIBUTION: As for AQS/762/1 dated 23/11/18.

UNIT	STRENGTH. 1.11.18. O. O.R.		INCREASE. O. O.R.		DECREASE. O. O.R.		STRENGTH. 1.12.18. O. O.R.	
56th Divisional Headquarters.	16	82	-	-	-	3	16	79
247th (Divl)Employment Coy.	2	328	-	10	-	6	2	332
167th Infantry Bde. H.Q.	4	22	1	1	-	-	5	23
1/7th Middlesex Regt.	43	863	6	95	6	106	43	852
1/8th Middlesex Regt.	39	813	3	64	2	97	40	780
1/1st London Regt.	40	712	3	28	2	35	41	705
167th T.M.Battery.	4	46	-	-	1	1	3	45
168th Infantry Bde. H.Q.	4	21	1	1	-	-	5	22
1/4th London Regt.	38	721	9	87	4	146	43	662
1/13th London Regt.	46	649	2	95	6	144	42	600
1/14th London Regt.	34	705	5	70	6	149	33	626
168th T.M.Battery.	4	45	-	-	-	2	4	43
169th Infantry Bde. H.Q.	4	21	-	1	-	-	4	22
1/2nd London Regt.	35	601	15	82	9	177	41	506
1/5th London Regt.	33	631	14	157	7	195	40	593
1/16th London Regt.	29	612	13	57	4	182	38	487
169th T.M.Battery.	2	33	-	12	-	-	2	45
1/5th Cheshire Regt.	41	803	1	56	3	81	39	778
56th Bn. M.G.Corps.	48	873	5	50	4	46	49	879
56th Divl.Artillery H.Q.	4	18	-	-	-	-	4	18
280th Brigade R.F.A.	28	764	3	5	2	22	29	747
281st Brigade R.F.A.	25	754	3	8	1	27	27	735
56th D. A. C.	18	429	-	3	-	19	18	413
56th Divl. Engineers H.Q.	1	10	-	-	-	-	1	10
416th (Edin)Fld.Coy.RE.	6	197	-	12	-	2	6	207
512th (Ldn.)Fld.Coy.RE.	8	199	-	11	-	4	8	206
513th (Ldn.)Fld.Coy.RE.	8	206	-	6	-	4	8	208
56th Divl.Signal Coy.RE.	12	295	-	2	-	2	12	295
56th Divl. Train.	22	382	-	4	2	12	20	374
Medical Units.	23	543	2	5	5	20	20	528
Mobile Vet. Section.	1	18	-	-	-	2	1	16

....

CASUALTIES. NOVEMBER, 1918.

DATE.	UNIT.	OFFICERS Killed.	OFFICERS Wounded.	Missing.	O.Rs. K.	O.Rs. W.	O.Rs. M.	REMARKS.
NOVBR.								
1st	8th Middlesex Regt.	-	-	-	-	1	-	Fell out of window
	280th Bde. R.FWA.	-	-	-	-	1	-	
2nd	1st London Regt.	-	-	-	-	1	1	Brushed by motor lorry.
	16th do. do.	-	-	-	-	1	-	
	5th Cheshire Regt.	-	-	-	-	1	-	
	280th Bde. R.F.A.	-	-	-	-	8	-	Inc. 2 gassed.
3rd	4th London Regt.	-	-	-	4	17	1	
	13th do. do.	-	-	-	-	1	-	Sprained ankle.
	16th do. do.	-	-	-	2	1	-	
4th	4th London Regt.	-	2/Lt. A.M. BULLOCH,(15th Ldns) 2/Lt. G.H.SYLVESTER *	-	2	14	1	*Died of Wounds.
	13th do. do.	-	-	-	-	2	-	
	14th do. do.	-	-	-	1	1	-	
	2nd do. do.	-	-	-	1	2	-	
	5th do. do.	-	-	-	3	22	1	
	16th do. do.	-	2/Lt. F.H.B.MOORE,(9th Ldns). 2/Lt. I.P.McEWAN (ASC)	-	20	50	1	
5th	4th London Regt.	2/Lt. W. OSBORN.	2/Lt.H.W.TAYLOR.(18th Ldns)	-	5	22	-	
	13th do. do.	Lieut. J. HYSLOP.	2/Lt.J.H.M.WRIGHT.	-	2	5	-	
	14th do. do.	-	-	-	3	17	-	
	do. do. do.	-	Lt.(A/Capt) R. WHITE, M.C.	-	-	-	-	
	2nd do. do.	-	2/Lt. G.T. GILL. (20th Ldns).	-	-	7	-	
	do. do. do.	-	" W. TOWNSEND. (18th Ldns)	-	-	-	-	
	5th do. do.	-	" C.M. KING. (18th Ldns).	-	6	40	-	
	16th do. do.	2/Lt. H.R. SMITH.(9th Ldns)	-	-	2	2	-	
	169th T.M. Battery.	-	-	-	-	5	-	
	280th Bde. R.F.A.	-	-	-	-	1	-	
	5th Cheshire Regt.	-	-	-	-	1	-	

- 2 -

DATE. NOVB.	UNIT.	OFFICERS. Killed.	Wounded.	Missing.	O. Rs K.	W.	M.	I.	REMARKS.
6th	7th Middlesex Regt.				-	2	2	-	
	8th do. do.				3	13	2	-	
	#st London Regt.		Lt. E.W. HAZELDINE.		-	1	-	1	Hit by missile.
	4th do. do.				-	-	-	-	
	13th do. do.		Lt.(A/Capt)H.D.PERRY@ 2/Lt. W.T.SNOOK (Inj)		8	24b	2	-	b Inc. 1 gassed.
	14th do. do.				11	56	-	-	* Sprained ankle.
	168th T.M.Battery.				-	1	-	-	
	2nd London Regt.		2/Lt. D.H. MARSHALL, 2/Lt. J.M.STOTESBURY@ (19th Ldns)		7	71	28x	-	x Inc. 5 Wnd. & Missing.
			# F.E. POWELL,						
	5th do. do.		2/Lt. E. BARNES@(18th Ldns) Lt. O.P.DARRINGTON.		6	51	15	-	
	do. do. do.		# D.C.COCKERILL. 2/Lt. E.A.THIEDE(#as)						
			# H. STEVENS.(Gas)(18th Ldns)						
	16th do. do.				2*	23	-	-	* Inc. 1 died of wds.
	56th Bn. M.G.Corps.	2/Lt.J.BOOTH,MC.(5/11/18) 2/Lt. F.C.EDWARDS.			-	9	-	-	
	280th Bde. R.F.A.		Lieut. G.S. JONES.(at duty)		-	1	-	+	
	2/3rd Ldn.Fld.Amb.		(2/2 F.A) Lt. E.R.MONIER.(USA.M.O.R.C.)*		-	1	-	-	* Gassed.
7th	7th Middlesex Regt.		Lt. H.G. SHILCOCK.		-	16	1	-	
	do. do. do.		2/Lt. T.E. JONES.		5	17	-	-	
	8th do. do.				-	1	-	-	
	1st London Regt.		2/Lt. P.M. COOKE,(7th Ldns)		-	3	-	-	
	56th Bn. M.G.Corps.				-	1	-	-	
	2/1st Ldn.Fld.Amblce.				-	5	-	-	
	2/3rd # #				-	1	-	-	
	4th London Regt.				-	-	-	-	
8th	7th Middlesex Regt.		2/Lt. S. HEATH.		-	12	-	-	
	do. do. do.		# F.T.M. MERRETT.		2	12a	-	1b	a.Inc.2 gassed.
	8th do. do.				2	1	-	-	b fell into ditch.
	5th Cheshire Regt.				-	3	-	-	
	56th Bn. M.G.Corps.		2/Lt. G.F. GRIFFITHS.		# 1	2	-	-	Inc. 1 at duty.
	280th Bde. R.F.A.				1	5	-	-	
	13th London Regt.				-	2	-	-	Gassed.

- 5 -

DATE. NOVR.	UNIT.	OFFICERS. Killed.	OFFICERS. Wounded.	OFFICERS. Missing.	O.Rs K.	O.Rs W.	O.Rs M.	REMARKS.
9th	8th Middlesex Regt.	-	-	-	1	1	-	
	2/1st Ldn.Fd.Amblce.	-	-	-	2	1	-	
10th	1st London Regt.	-	-	-	2	9	-	
	8th Middlesex Regt.	-	1	-	1	2	-	
	16th London Regt.	-	-	-	-	-	1	Sprained ankle.
	284st Bde. R.F.A.	-	-	-	-	2	-	
11th	56th Bn. M.G.Corps.	-	-	-	-	1	-	
13th	13th London Regt.	-	-	-	-	-	-	1 Discharge of revolver
	5th Cheshire Rgt.	-	-	-	-	-	-	10 Explosion caused by lighting fire.
14th	2nd London Regt.	-	-	-	-	-	-	1 Slipped down iron staircase.
15th	16th London Regt.	-	-	-	+	-	-	1 At football.
18th	13th London Regt.	-	-	-	-	-	-	1 At football.
TOTALS FOR NOVEMBER.		9	24	1	104	567	53	20

"A" Form
MESSAGES AND SIGNALS.

Army Form C. 2121
(In pads of 100)

No. of Message.

Prefix....Code....m,	Words.	Charge.	This message is on a/c of:	Recd. at....m.
Office of Origin and Service Instructions	Sent			Date......
	At....m.		....Service.	From......
	To......			By......
	By......	(Signature of "Franking Officer.")		

TO { Arq

Sender's Number.	Day of Month.	In reply to Number.	AAA
S468	13		

Please send total list of
casualties during period
Nov 1 to Nov 12

G

Herewith

18/11/18.   field
                             cashier
                             to shaf

From G
Place
Time

The above may be forwarded as now corrected.   (Z)

Censor.   Signature of Addressor or person authorised to telegraph in his name.

* This line should be erased if not required.
(7981) Wt. W492/M1647 130,000 Pads 5/17 D. D. & L. E1187

56th DIVISION.

CASUALTIES FOR PERIOD 1st to 12th NOVEMBER, 1918.

UNIT.	Killed. O.	Killed. O.R.	Wounded. O.	Wounded. O.R.	Missing. O.	Missing. O.R.	Injured. O.	Injured. O.R.	TOTAL. O.	TOTAL. O.R.
167th Inf. Bde.										
7th Middlesex Rgt.	-	2	4	30	-	3	-	-	4	35
8th " "	-	11	1	45	-	2	-	2	1	60
1st London Rgt.	-	2	1	10	-	-	-	2	1	14
Bde. Totals.	-	15	6	85	-	5	-	4	6	109
168th Inf. Bde.										
4th London Rgt.	2	11	1	55	-	1	-	-	3	67
13th " "	2	10	1	31	-	2	1	1	4	44
14th " "	1	15	1	74	-	2	-	-	2	91
168th T.M.Bty.	-	-	-	1	-	-	-	-	-	1
Bde. Totals.	5	36	3	161	-	5	1	1	9	203
169th Inf. Bde.										
2nd London Rgt.	-	8	4	80	1	28	-	-	5	116
5th " "	2	15	4	113	-	16	-	-	6	144
16th " "	2	26	1	77	-	1	-	1	3	105
169th T.M.Bty.	-	-	-	5	-	-	-	-	-	5
Bde. Totals.	4	49	9	275	1	45	-	1	14	370
Pioneer Battn.										
5th Cheshire R.	-	-	-	2	-	-	-	10	-	12
56th Bn. M.G.C.	1	1	2	15	-	-	-	-	3	16
Divl. Artillery.										
280th Bde. RFA.	-	1	1	14	-	-	-	-	1	15
281st " "	-	-	-	2	-	-	-	-	-	2
Ambulances.										
2/1st Ldn.Fd.Amb.	-	2	-	2	-	-	-	-	-	4
2/3rd " "	-	-	-	6	-	-	-	-	-	6
DIVISIONAL TOTALS.	10	104	21	562	1	55	1	16	33	737

"B" Form. Army Form C 2122.

MESSAGES AND SIGNALS.

Prefix **y** Code **2009** m.

Office of Origin and Service Instructions. Words. **4f**

29

TO { **APM** }

Sender's Number **G 747** Day of Month **16** AAA

Please forward the nos of Officers and OR captured during period Nov 1 to Nov 11 to this office as soon as possible

HQ 56 Divn
10 Officers 228 ORs

                                    CAPTAIN.
17/11/18   A.P.M. 56 DIVISION.

From **56 Divn**

na 21.00 p.
na 28.00 p.

"A" Form.
MESSAGES AND SIGNALS.

Army Form C. 2121.
(In pads of 100.)

TO 73rd Corps.

Sender's Number	Day of Month	In reply to Number	
G 734	14	GA 880	AAA

One 77 m.m. gun aaa 46 heavy and light m.g's approx aaa One German mtr. lorry aaa 3 British Tanks with German markings

From 56 Div

"G" Form.
MESSAGES AND SIGNALS.

Army Form C. 2123.
(In books of 100.)

No. of Message

Prefix — Code 52A Words 56

Received. From — By Belling

Sent, or sent out. At ... m. To ... By ...

Office Stamp. SIGNALS

Charges to Collect

Service Instructions.

Handed in at GHO Office 5.30 m. Received 1.54 m.

TO /6 J

Sender's Number.	Day of Month	In reply to Number.	AAA
BM 791	14		
Captured	war	material	aaa
GHO	1	77	mm
field	piece	left	in
position	sheet	51	A 18 a 5.6
aaa	GEDA	German motor	
lorry	sheet	51	D 9 c 5.1
1 Heavy MG		sheet	51
B 17 c 8.8 aaa	2 EJ 1	1 light	
MG sheet	4	M 12 c 2.2	

FROM

TIME & PLACE

*This line should be erased if not required.

"C" Form.
MESSAGES AND SIGNALS.

Army Form C. 2123.
(In books of 100.)

No. of Message

Prefix......Code......Words......
Charges to Collect
Service Instructions.

Received. From...... By......

Sent, or sent out. At......m. To...... By......

Office Stamp.

Handed in at......Office 1520 m. Received 1520 m.

TO M7

Sender's Number.	Day of Month	In reply to Number.	AAA
1	Heavy	MG	sheet
45	WHA7.2	aaa	nos
of	all	guns	not
taken			

FROM
TIME & PLACE Ju 30

This line should be erased if not required.

"C" Form.
MESSAGES AND SIGNALS.

Army Form C. 2123.
(In books of 100.)

Prefix AM 1323 Code Words 46

Charges to Collect

Service Instructions.

Received From YK7K By Sllin

Sent, or sent out. At... To... By

Office Stamp. SIGNALS 14/2/18

Handed in at GuQA Office 13£ Received ...m.

TO 56 Divn

Sender's Number	Day of Month	In reply to Number	AAA
SCR18	14	yB23	

13 time 4 heavy and 3 light mg at about A6a and c sheet 51 several of both types in house in ANGRE estimated number 9 aaa none removed DF 14 Aug 26 mg east of ANGRE aaa none returned to DADOS

955
1415

FROM GuQA (168)
TIME & PLACE

"C" Form.
MESSAGES AND SIGNALS.

Army Form C. 2123.
(In books of 100.)

No. of Message

Prefix........ Code........ Words 13

Charges to Collect

Service Instructions.

Received. From _____ By _____

Sent, or sent out. At _____ To _____ By _____

Office Stamp.

Handed in at _____ Office 3:09 m. Received 13:13 m.

TO Y & S (953)

*Sender's Number.	Day of Month.	In reply to Number.	AAA
VM 41	14	G 723	

3 British Tanks with German markings

13.45

to all material reported

FROM
TIME & PLACE 169 SB

*This line should be erased if not required.
100,000.—John Rissen, Ltd.—3/17.—5141. Forms C2123.

"B" Form.
MESSAGES AND SIGNALS.

Army Form C2122.
(In pads of 150.)

No. of Message............

Prefix....Code....m.		Received	Sent	Office Stamp.
Office of Origin and Service Instructions.	Words	At........m. From.... By....	At........m. To.... By....	14.XI [stamp] SIGNAL

TO — copy 1/20 95?

Sender's Number.	Day of Month.	In reply to Number.	AAA
MM 794	14	G7?	

War material September 1st
to 11th .... nov
now nil

From ..... (56 Bn HQ)
Place
Time

* This line (except **AAA**) should be erased if not required.

"A" Form
MESSAGES AND SIGNALS.

Army Form C. 2121
(In pads of 100.)

No. of Message............

Prefix	Code	m	Words	Charge	This message is on a/c of :	Recd. at......m
Office of Origin and Service Instructions			Sent		...............Service.	Date.............
			At ....m			From ....
			To			
			By	(Signature of "Franking Officer")		By............

TO— 56 Div G

Sender's Number.	Day of Month.	In reply to Number.	AAA
L137	14/11	G723 2/3	
	NIL aaa		
		956	
		14.15	

From 56 DA

Place

Time

The above may be forwarded as now corrected. (Z)

.... Censor. Signature of Addressor or person authorised to telegraph in his name

* This line should be erased if not required.

Order No. 1625. Wt. W8253/ P 511. 27/2. H. & K., Ltd. (E. 2634).

"B" Form.
MESSAGES AND SIGNALS.

Army Form C2122 (In pads of 150)

Sender's Number.	Day of Month.	In reply to Number.	AAA
G 880	13		

Wire by 1400 not to detailed list of war material captured for period 1st to 11th Nov both inclusive aaa Cavalry Corps 16 forward reptl.

From: 22 Corps
Place:
Time: 12.40

SECRET.

WAR DIARY - ADMINISTRATIVE BRANCH, 56th DIVISION.

Period 1/12/1918 to 31/12/1918.

Volume:-   XXXV

WAR DIARY
or
INTELLIGENCE SUMMARY.
(Erase heading not required.)

Army Form C. 2118.

Vol XXXV   Page 1

Place	Date	Hour	Summary of Events and Information	Remarks and references to Appendices
HARVENG.	30/11/18		175 A Bde R.F.A. and 277 A. Bde R.F.A. moved out of the area yesterday and from HARMIGNIES and CIVRY respectively and today 16 Bde H.Q. moved into its final H.Q. NOUVELLE. There are still Corps troops and 4th D.A. in the area. An additional been usual was allotted to the division on alternate days starting 1st December.	
	1/12/18		M. Alberti (French marsien) reported on the results of his enquiries made at Aubigny on the possibility of the purchase of Christmas fare for the Troops. His report showed that large quantities of Turkeys could be obtained at about 19 frs kilo, fresh vegetables can also be obtained. Lorries have been arranged to bring up a supply of the latter weekly. Weather fair & mild. Belgian Mission sent say that all schools would be required by the civil people. This will seriously affect Education & Recreation Institutions.	
	2.12.18		4 DIV. artillery moved out of the area today, leaving them Corps in Artillery and giving us a little more room. Weather fair and mild.	
	3.12.18		A cinema show was arranged for the M.G. Bn at Bruy, the mine owners putting their apparatus and hall at our disposal and us providing the films. The D.A.C. moved into their new billets at OBIY from Dinegies yesterday so as to be prepared for the arrival of Railhead to MONS about the 7th. This will supplies will have to be drawn by Horse Transport.	

Army Form C. 2118.

WAR DIARY
or
INTELLIGENCE SUMMARY.
(Erase heading not required.)

Place	Date	Hour	Summary of Events and Information	Remarks and references to Appendices
HARVENG	5/12/18		H.M. the King passed through the Lines to see the troops informally. Representatives of all groups were assembled at 3 points on the route and cheered the King as he passed. At 100 yards H.M. stopped and spoke to officers & men. Weather fine — bright on the A.M. but cloudy later. Location little altered today.	See Appendices A. Location table.
	6/12/18		Weather fair and mild. D.A.A.G. returned from leave.	
	7/12/18		Supply question is not entirely satisfactory, we got behind hand with supplies the Artillery. Caught up to the tail of last train about the 11th. The Conveyance is that then to as reserve of supplies at the Railing points and it is consequently impossible to replace consumed rations immediately. Railhead is still at ANZIN, so that a certain fuel short to has been established at NOUVELLE, so that all fuel coming up is pushed.	
	8/12/18		Orders have been received for Major. Dundas D.A.A.G. to report for duty at H.Q. L. of C. Capt. Scott A. & S.H. S.17th Capt.184 Bde. is to run the duties of D.A.Q.G. Temporarily until the return from England of Capt. Head Ches.R.	
	9/12/18		D.A.Q.M.G. proceeded on leave (30 days to U.K.) and Capt. Bishop Staff Capt. 169 Bde took up the duties of D.A.Q.M.G. today. Weather fair & mild.	

Army Form C. 2118.

WAR DIARY
or
INTELLIGENCE SUMMARY.
(Erase heading not required.)

Place	Date	Hour	Summary of Events and Information	Remarks and references to Appendices
HARVENG.	10/12/18	—	D.A.A.G. Major Dundas proceeded to take up appointment as D.A.A.G. h.o.f.C. and Major A Scott A.Q. & S. Hrs reported to take over the duties of D.A.A.G. The first batch of Miners are in due to depart tomorrow under the demobilization scheme. Considerable difficulty has been experienced in getting the party together owing to the movement by units of the special forms required. In the case of some units the form has not been received and they men will therefore not be able to proceed. Railhead is still at Anzin and the last had him has not yet been made i.e. we are still 24 hours behind with supplies. The train now comes in to Railhead in our hit hours are not available to clear & feed him per day. Weather hot & mild. A suggestion has been made that one of the Brigades should be moved to MONS.	
"	11/12/18		The first party of Miners proceeded to Concentration Camp today 70 O.R. and 1 Officer conducting. This Corps Concentration Camp opens on the 14th. The British today proceeded to Tournai.	
"	12/12/18		Party of about 70 D.R. (columns) proceeded to Concentration Camp Tournai Today. Same in route for England and the present details by this Division for the 22 Corps Concentration Camp (Demobilization) at Valenciennes also left. Reinforcements continue to arrive. Railhead is likely to move forward on the 14th to Mons. Then a scheme for drawing by H.T. from Rail Head will come into operation. Application has been made to XXII Corps, for a Lorry service. Personnel from the returning supply lorries will no longer be able to convey to Railhead the personnel and stores of Divisions available. It will be some considerable time before the personnel and stores L. of MONS.	

Army Form C. 2118.

WAR DIARY
or
INTELLIGENCE SUMMARY.
(Erase heading not required.)

Place	Date	Hour	Summary of Events and Information	Remarks and references to Appendices
Harveng	13/12/18		The third party of Minenwerfen demonstration proceeded today strength about 50. They went by lorry to the Concentration Camp, Tournai. The XXII Corps Comp. Tuns at Valenciennes tomorrow. Todays Pritch practically close off the moven, a few proceed tomorrow (6) under with consignments to MONS. Weather mild and damp. R. Eng. Gy football match has been arranged for tomorrow at GIVRY between the Division and South African Bde. H.A.	
	14/12/18		Packard moves from ANZIN to VALENCIENNES tomorrow, this relieves the problem of the MT Company by about 2 miles, lorries for Christmas Fare were asked for, to be at Antwerp 15th int. Long talk Educational situation to our on its way up from BOULOGNE and has broken down at TOURNAI and MT Co. has been informed by wire tonight. The Car situation is quite – only one Car is on the road (Wolseley) at present the G. Vauxhall's below deen yesterday. The Crane lorry badly smashed – A key on the Cadam Gluff sheared – it is being informed by the drivers the long journeys and angle roads account for the heavy repairs.	
	15/12/18		Sunday. Weather fair and mild. B.Drivers proceeded today to VALENCIENNES Concentration Camp in route for England.	

Army Form C. 2118.

WAR DIARY
or
INTELLIGENCE SUMMARY.
(Erase heading not required.)

Instructions regarding War Diaries and Intelligence Summaries are contained in F. S. Regs., Part II. and the Staff Manual respectively. Title pages will be prepared in manuscript.

Place	Date	Hour	Summary of Events and Information	Remarks and references to Appendices
HARVENG	Dec 16		Capt G.H. BRUNNER proceeded on 14 days leave to ENGLAND. Weather fair. 28 miners proceeded to TOURNAI Concentration Camp en route for ENGLAND. Bow Bells opened at GENLY for 169 Infy Bde.	
do	17		Weather showery. Meeting of CANTEEN committee in Div'l H.Q.	
do	18		Weather stormy. Despatch of miners for demobilization temporarily in abeyance pending move of personnel nearer to Mons. Pack train sent late supplies him a day behind in time of arrival as Railhead. Weather showery.	
do	19			
do	20		Arrangements made for 157 Bde to move to Mons about Dec 27th. Preparations being made to open Bow Bells Xmas Pantomime in Mons on Dec 26th. Weather still showery.	
do	21		Mons opened as Railhead for BOULOGNE leave personnel. Party of 33 miners and partially men collected at G.H.Q under supervision of Town Major ready to proceed to Mons Railhead on 22d instant, morning.	
	22		Stormy afternoon. 36 coalminers demobilised despatched to Mons	

A6345 Wt. W14422/M1160 350,000 12/16 D. D. & L. Forms/C./2118/14.

WAR DIARY
or
INTELLIGENCE SUMMARY.
(Erase heading not required.)

Army Form C. 2118.

Place	Date	Hour	Summary of Events and Information	Remarks and references to Appendices
HARVENG	Dec 22		A further party collected at CIPLY for despatch in following day. Orders received to prepare a return of numbers of Officers and OR in each unit on Dec 28th to be demobilized arranged according to dispersal areas and Industrial groups.	
	23		Christmas fare arrived from AUBIGNY. A supply of BEER obtained from MONS. Both BEERS moved to CHIEN VERT Cinema Theatre MONS, to start showing with Xmas Panto on 27th inst. Stormy day. AA & QMG attended Conference at Corps HQ. int GOC	
	24		Demobilization fever, including 2000 turkeys, distributed to units. Weather fair.	
	25		Christmas day at Officers closed at 1200. Division engaged in Christmas dinners and festivities. Party of 14 miners and demobilizees despatched to MONS	
	26		Stormy day.	
	27		Both BEERS opened at MONS. Corps Commander & GOC present	

WAR DIARY
or
INTELLIGENCE SUMMARY.

(Erase heading not required.)

Army Form C. 2118.

Place	Date	Hour	Summary of Events and Information	Remarks and references to Appendices
HARVENG	Dec 27		Further batch of miners & demobilizers despatched to Concentration Camp at VALENCIENNES via MONS. Wet day.	
	28		Got proceed on leave to ENGLAND. Brigadier General R.J.G. BARINGTON. CMG. DSO. CRA 5th E. Divison assumes command of Division. Winter still very bad. Supply of rations rendered with difficulty owing to bad state of MT Supply Columns which by 1st July has been on bad roads from RELLEN to VALENCIENNES. 167 Inf. Bde moved to billets in MONS.	
	29		DIVL CINEMA moved to CEMENT FACTORY HARMIGNIES. Weather continues wet.	
	30		Lorries arranged to take troops from 168 & 169 Bdes to Pow Belly at Mons. Weather fair.	
	31		Supply situation still bad. Parkeal expected to move to Mons on January 3rd. The following Holiday despatch was received in Sir Douglas Haigh for service rendered in last year ending Sept 25th 1918:-	

Army Form C. 2118.

WAR DIARY
or
INTELLIGENCE SUMMARY.
(Erase heading not required.)

Place	Date	Hour	Summary of Events and Information	Remarks and references to Appendices
MARVENG	Dec 31		LT. COL. W.H. SUTTON, M.C., MAJOR A.C. DUNDAS, + MAJOR T.O.M. BUCHAN. Strength of Division on 31st Dec. 1918.	8.

Lieut.-Col.
A.A. & Q.M.G. 56th Division.

UNIT.	STRENGTH. 1.12.18. O. O.R.	INCREASE. O. O.R.	DECREASE. O. O.R.	STRENGTH. 1. 1.19. O. O.R.
56th Divisional Headquarters.	16. 79.	- 4.	1. 3.	15. 80.
247th (Div.) Employment Co.	2. 332.	- -	- 13.	2. 319.
167th Infantry Bde. H.Q.	5. 23.	- -	- -	5. 23.
1/7th Middlesex Regt.	43. 852.	7. 47.	3. 45.	47. 854.
1/8th Middlesex Regt.	40. 780.	4. 160.	1. 36.	43. 904.
1/1st London Regt.	41. 705.	2. 65.	2. 39.	41. 731.
167th T.M. Battery.	3. 45.	- -	- -	3. 45.
168th Infantry Bde. H.Q.	5. 22.	- -	- -	5. 22.
1/4th London Regt.	43. 662.	7. 58.	3. 46.	47. 674.
1/13th London Regt.	42. 600.	8. 145.	6. 19.	44. 726.
1/14th London Regt.	33. 626.	4. 70.	2. 35.	35. 661.
168th T.M. Battery.	4. 43.	- -	- -	4. 43.
169th Infantry Bde. H.Q.	4. 22.	- -	- 2.	4. 20.
1/2nd London Regt.	41. 506.	- 121.	2. 27.	39. 600.
1/5th London Regt.	40. 593.	5. 163.	7. 57.	38. 699.
1/16th London Regt.	38. 487.	6. 53.	8. 40.	36. 500.
169th T.M. Battery.	2. 45.	- -	- 1.	2. 44.
1/5th Cheshire Regt.	39. 778.	1. 28.	2. 41.	38. 765.
56th Bn. M.G.C.	49. 879.	1. 67.	2. 78.	48. 868.
56th Divnl. Arty. H.Q.	4. 18.	- -	- -	4. 18.
280th Brigade R.F.A.	29. 747.	- 9.	3. 11.	26. 745.
281st Brigade R.F.A.	27. 735.	- 19.	3. 16.	24. 738.
56th Div. Ammn. Column.	18. 413.	- 17.	- 10.	18. 420.
56th Div. Engineers H.Q.	1. 10.	- -	- -	1. 10.
416th (Edinboro') Fd. Co. R.E.	6. 207.	- -	- 12.	6. 195.
512th (London) Fd. Co. R.E.	8. 206.	- -	1. 8.	7. 198.
513th (London) Fd. Co. R.E.	8. 208.	- -	- 8.	8. 200.
56th Div. Signal Co. R.E.	12. 295.	- 7.	1. 4.	11. 298.
56th Divnl. Train.	20. 374.	- 20.	- 22.	20. 372.
Medical Units.	20. 528.	- 3.	7. 13.	13. 518.
Mobile Vet. Section.	1. 16.	- 2.	- -	1. 18.

Original

Vol 36

Headquarters 56th Division

A.H.-Q. M. G.

WAR DIARY

January 1919

Army Form C. 2118.

WAR DIARY
or
INTELLIGENCE SUMMARY.
(Erase heading not required.)

Instructions regarding War Diaries and Intelligence Summaries are contained in F. S. Regs., Part II. and the Staff Manual respectively. Title pages will be prepared in manuscript.

Place	Date	Hour	Summary of Events and Information	Remarks and references to Appendices
HARVENG	Jan 1/19	12⁰	By order of Army all officers clocks at 1200 hrs were synchronised.	
	2		New Year's Honours Gazette received. Following Officers received awards. Lt Col W N SUTTON M.C. to D.S.O. MAJOR W ASCOTT DAVIS to OBE and Rev. W LEONARD C.F. Senior Chaplain (Principal Chaplain's Dept) OBE	
			M.C. T MM to R A. SCOTT M.C. to the D.S.O.	
	3		News allowed for demobilization received at rate of 80 per day commenced with despatch to Concentration Camp in 5th most Divisional Reception Camp moved to MONS.	
	4		Major A. SCOTT DSO MC. DAAG proceeded on 14 days leave to ENGLAND. Duties of DAAG taken over by LT. R.H. FRANKLIN 3 Cops of French Interps arrived in Divisional Area and visited J- VIEUX RENG VILLERS - SIRE-NICOLE & BETTIGNIES to set to French Guards on Franco- Belgian boundary. Weather fine.	
	5		Party of 67 men and 1 Officer proceeded to Concentration	

WAR DIARY
or
INTELLIGENCE SUMMARY

Army Form C. 2118.

Place	Date	Hour	Summary of Events and Information	Remarks and references to Appendices
MARVENG	Jan 1919 5		Cont. of Demobilization.	
	6		Further despatch of men for demobilization. Weather showery.	
	7		Supply situation very difficult. Pork Gan 48 hours late. Division concerned in drawing full quantities & prepared Return from Field Supply Depot. Weather Showery.	
	8		Grants renewed opening up for groups for demobilizing men Group (1) Agriculture (14) Fishermen (10) Building trade (22) Railmaking (30) Building trade (33) Horse Carters (35) Employees of public Works Authorities. Present supplies of men expected considerable reduction in leave allowance expected. Only 2 Officers and 29 Other ranks per day, all via CALAIS. to commence on 12th Jan. New allotment of 135 OR & 4 Officers per day for demobilization received deaprted commenced 10th inst. Instructions received for all Armies to be inspected by Pres. under D.A.D.V.S. and classified for demobilization. Weather Showery.	

Army Form C.2118/14.

Army Form C. 2118.

WAR DIARY
or
INTELLIGENCE SUMMARY.
(Erase heading not required.)

Instructions regarding War Diaries and Intelligence Summaries are contained in F. S. Regs., Part II, and the Staff Manual respectively. Title pages will be prepared in manuscript.

Place	Date	Hour	Summary of Events and Information	Remarks and references to Appendices
HAVRE	Jan 9/19		Draw pay of 135 OR & 14 Officers under new allotment dispositions	
	10		Nominal for Demobilization. Information received that Col. Major Bohem Sir C.R.A. still detained in ENGLAND for present duty in connection with demobilization disturbances at SPROTCLIFFE and R.A.S.C. depots at home. Demobilization Allotment from 11 Inclusive increased to 177 OR & 5 Officers per draw.	
	11		Major W. ASCOTT O.B.E. D.A.D.V.S. awarded MEDAILLE de la RECONNAISSANCE 3rd Class (French). Division ordered to billet 27 Squadron R.A.F. at QUEVY-LE-PETIT. Arrangements made for now BEDS to visit PARIS from 15th to 20th for first performance at THEATRE RÉJANE in aid of French Red Cross. Reports amateur aerial locaters fair. Daily service of buses commences from GENLY, GIVRY, POESME, THULIN and VILLERS-SIRE-NICOLE to MONS. MAJOR T.F.C.H. P.P.N.S. handed extension of leave to 24th Jan.	

Army Form C. 2118.

WAR DIARY
or
INTELLIGENCE SUMMARY.
(Erase heading not required.)

Instructions regarding War Diaries and Intelligence Summaries are contained in F.S. Regs., Part II. and the Staff Manual respectively. Title pages will be prepared in manuscript.

Place	Date	Hour	Summary of Events and Information	Remarks and references to Appendices
HARVENG	1919 Jan 12		Parts of 177 O.R and 5 Officers departed for demobilization. Instructions received to dispose of animals which is to commence in near future. Weather showery	
	13		Further party of 133 men & 4 Officers departed for demobilization. Weather indifferent. Information received that all Schools in Area may be evacuated by Jan 22nd.	
	14		Orders received for further parties to be transported to 98 Division Second Army. Party of 133 Officers & O.R. despatched for demobilization but held up in Mons owing to lack of transport. MAJOR T.F. CHIPP. M.C.	
	15		Did MG returned from leave. Orders received for London Scottish to entrain at Mons on 16 D. man. no 1530 Div Division informed that additional recommendations may now be made for the "Peace" despatch. Bearded "frim" but Observery	
	16		Demobilization expected until 20th pending removal of	

A16945 Wt. W11422/M1160 350,000 12/16 D.D.& L. Forms/C/2118/14.

Army Form C. 2118.

WAR DIARY
or
INTELLIGENCE SUMMARY.
(Erase heading not required.)

Instructions regarding War Diaries and Intelligence Summaries are contained in F. S. Regs., Part II. and the Staff Manual respectively. Title pages will be prepared in manuscript.

Place	Date	Hour	Summary of Events and Information	Remarks and references to Appendices
	1919			
HARENG	Jan 15		Corps Concentration Camps from VALENCIENNES to MONS.	
	16		Weather fine with bright sun. Demobilization allotment for period ending 20th rec'd	
			amounting to a Total of about 235 per day. 14th London B proceeded to 9th Div today.	
	17th		Weather dull, cloudy, slight showers. Demobilization of Nurses – a warning that received	
			that about 500 Female should be earmarked for demobilization at an early date.	
	18th		The question of mobility of units in demobilization of Horses his been raised and	
			B.Gen L. Conolly Divrnen and ADC attended conference at Army Headquarters. Their question	
			of moving out A.D. Demobilization and other matters were discussed.	
	19th		Sunday. Fine but cloudy.	+ Scotland
	20th		Reduced allotment for demobilization received. The reduction is mainly for Company Group	
			Vaccines for which are not required in Egypt. Numbers for this Group. Major Scott (DAPG) returned from leave.	
	21st		Cold Frosty day. 470 All ranks of the division proceeded for demobilization.	
	22nd		No impact on Rosen proceeded. Evidently today is Saturday	
			and consists of 2 days leave. Considered the division played St. Pol Div at	
			Football. Rugby rules at Quvery the officers and two by two tries 6 pts to 0	
	23rd		Answer: whereas that today to Brussels moved start on 29th.	

A6945 Wt. W11422/M1160 /350,000 12/16 D.D. & L. Forms/C/2118/14.

Army Form C. 2118.

WAR DIARY
or
INTELLIGENCE SUMMARY.
(Erase heading not required.)

Place	Date	Hour	Summary of Events and Information	Remarks and references to Appendices
HARVENG	Jan 23		Cold, frost weather. Bow Bells returned from PARIS.	
	24		Frost continues. Particulars received of proposed Corps Race Meeting on Feb 10th.	
	25		Two officers and 179 O.R. despatched to MONS for demobilization. Major General Sir C.F.A. HULL, K.C.B. returned from leave. No train arrived on Railheads yesterday, supplies being drawn from Field Depot. Weather continues cold & frosty.	
	26		Snowy morning. One officer & 178 O.R. despatched for demobilization. First parties of animals despatched.	
	27		Cold frosty weather. Further party of 8 officers & 178 O.R. despatched to Concentration Camp, including Capt. Col. BRUNNER.	
	28		G.O.C. & AA & QMG with representatives from units of the division attended Ball given by XXII Corps at BRUSSELS. Further party despatched for Demobilization of 6 offrs & 177 O.R. No leave train left MONS today owing to traffic Congestion at CALAIS. Frost continues.	

Army Form C. 2118.

WAR DIARY
or
INTELLIGENCE SUMMARY.
(Erase heading not required.)

Place	Date	Hour	Summary of Events and Information	Remarks and references to Appendices
HARVENG	Jan 29		Thos. part of 50 OR (from 166 Bn) left for 3 days w/ Y.M.C.A. BRUSSELS. V.C. awarded to Spr. J. McPHIE late #6 Field Coy R.E. for conspicuous bravery during the early morning of 14th Oct 1918 while in charge of a party of sappers maintaining a cork float bridge across the CANAL DE LA SENSÉE near AUBENCHEUL AU BAC during a British attack. Supply situation acute owing to trouble with R.O.D. personnel in CALAIS. All leave via CALAIS suspended until further notice; neither home nor trains running. Party of 6 Officers from continues to be deputised to Concentration Camp. Moves of 179 OR despatched to Concentration & 171 OR and demobilization. New allotment of 6 Officers Feb 1st received for convoy work commencing Feb 1st.	
	30		Allotment for demobilisation returned by 39 per day from Feb 2nd. Cold weather continues. Supply situation improved. Lock trains now running from HAVRE.	
	31		Colder weather continues. Conference held at Div. H.Q. to	

Army Form C. 2118.

WAR DIARY
or
INTELLIGENCE SUMMARY.
(Erase heading not required.)

Instructions regarding War Diaries and Intelligence Summaries are contained in F. S. Regs., Part II. and the Staff Manual respectively. Title pages will be prepared in manuscript.

Place	Date	Hour	Summary of Events and Information	Remarks and references to Appendices
MARVENGT.	Jan. 9.		Meeting proposed Divisional Race meeting on Feb. 15th	
			Alcott major staff	
			for Lieut. Colonel	
			A.A. & Q.M.G. 58th Division	

War Diary

LIST OF AWARDS IN THE NEW YEAR'S HONOURS DESPATCH.

C. B.

Brigadier General G.H.B. FREETH, C.M.G., D.S.O.

C. M. G.

Lieut-Colonel C.H. PARK, D.S.O., T.D.   Middlesex Regiment.
A/Lieut-Colonel W.R. GLOVER, D.S.O.   London Regiment.

O. B. E. (Class 4).

A/Major J. ASCOTT,   D..D.V.S.
Captain & Qr.Mr. J.D. CHAPMAN. R.A.S.C.

BREVET COLONEL.

Brigadier General E.S. D'E CUFF, C.M.G., D.S.O.

BREVET MAJOR.

Captain (Temp.Lt.Col) E.D. JACKSON, D.S.O.   London Regiment.

D. S. O.

Brigadier General G.G. LOCH, C.M.G.
T/Lt. Col. C.M. SUTTON, M.C.
T/Major A. SCOTT, M.C.

M. C.

A/Captain C. ROBINSON.	D.T.M.O.
T/Captain W.C. GRANT.	R.F.A.
A/Captain W.A.R. BOURNE.	R.E.
A/Major R.L. HULME.	M.G.Corps.
The Revd. W.W. LEONARD.	A.C. Dept.
The Revd. S.F.L. GREEN.	A.C. Dept.
T/Captain H.G.L. BRYENE.	London Regt.
T/Captain E.F. COKE.	Canadian Inf.Btn.
A/Captain L.T. ELVY.	London Regt.
Captain A.T. TAYLOR.	" "
A/Captain V.C. VON BERG.	" "
T/Captain F. BISHOP.	Cheshire Regt.

D. C. M.

546721. Cpl. H.G. LATARCHE.	R.E.	
7321. C.S.M. J. WATTS.	M.G.C.	
42119. Corpl. W. MOTHERSHAW.	"	
205105. C.Q.M.Sgt. L. NEVILLE.	Middlesex Regt.	
200068. C.S.M. C.W. SLATER.	London Regt.	
280605. Sergt. R.C. CLAIBER, M.M.	" "	
514111. Corpl. W.G. CALDER.	" "	attd.T.M.Bty.
510816. A/Sgt. C. USHER.	" "	
253433. A/Cpl. S.J. LA THWOOD.	" "	
300184. L/Cpl. P.D. CHARLES.	" "	

P.T.O.

M. S. M.

DIVISIONAL ARTILLERY.
930270. Fitter Q.M.Sgt. T.C.MOORCROFT.
940008. Bty.Sgt.Major. P.J.McCARTNEY.
37470. Bty.Q.M.Sergt. T.ROWLANDS.

925070. Ftr.Corpl. A.C.G. GUNTHORPE.

DIVISIONAL ENGINEERS.
422459. C.Q.M.S. J.A.SWANSTON.   548032. Sergt. E.C. MILLER.
16160. Sergt. C.J.BUTCHER. L.M.

CHESHIRE REGIMENT.
5587. R.S.M. J.F. WILCOCK.   240176. R.Q.M.S. T.WHITEHEAD.
240031. C.S.M. E.A. CORBETT.

M. G. CORPS.
71442. Sergt. J.N. BUCK.

R.A.S.C.
T4/238640. T.S.S.M. A.Y.D. JONES.   TS/7431. Sadler S.Sgt. R.MALLETT.
T/29620. T/C.Q.M.Sgt. J.THEXTON.

M. T. Coy.
935331. Sergt. G.P. HANCOCK. R.F.A.

R.A.M.C.
512191. A/Q.M.S. W.H.STEVENS.   503238. L/Cpl. F.W. CHARMAN.

R.A.O.C.
0842. A/Condr. J.H. LEWIS.

LABOUR CORPS.
224327. Corpl. H.R. COCKERTON.

167th INFANTRY BRIGADE.
240063. R.Q.M.S. S. KING.   Middlesex Regiment.
F/233. C.S.M. H.C. BEAR. D.C.M.   "   "
200093. Sergt. P.H. WESTON.   "   "
200412. L/Sgt. E.G. CARTER.   "   "
200103. Corpl. G.G. MARSHALL.   "   "
200861. R.Q.M.S. F.FORSDYKE.   London Regiment.
200164. Sergt. F.S. SEARLE.   "   "
200020. Sergt. H. CARNEHIE.   "   "

M. S. M. -contd-

168th INFANTRY BRIGADE.

280555.	R.Q.M.S.	L.T. DAVIES.	London Regiment.
280128.	C.S.M.	A.D. McLAREN.	" "
493602.	C.Q.M.S.	A.S. SKIPPER.	" "
510472.	Sig.Sgt.	D. NISBET.	" "
510043.	Sergt.	W.T. PIRIE.	" "
510346.	Sergt.	G. REID.	" "
490390.	Sergt.	W. ANDERSON.	" "
510729.	A/L.Sgt.	H.B. COATES.	" "
490848.	Private.	E.A. EVIS.	" " attd Div.H.Q.

169th INFANTRY BRIGADE.

554573.	C.S.M.	. ESSAM.	London Regiment.
550414.	C.Q.M.S.	A.E. FINBOW, M.M.	" "
300110.	C.Q.M.S.	A.A. FROST.	" "
232858.	Sergt.	M. SAMUELS.	" "
550034.	Sergt.	W.B. GREEN.	" "
551207.	Sergt.	G.O. MEECH.	" "
230205.	Corpl.	H. NOTTINGHAM.	" "
300933.	Corpl.	R. ROGERS.	" "
390604.	Corpl.	M.H.A. JONES.	" " attd.T.M.Bty.

MENTIONED IN DESPATCHES.

Major-General Sir AMYATT HULL, K.C.B.
Brig-General G.H.B. FREETH, C.B., C.M.G., D.S.O.
Brig-General G.G. LOCH, C.M.G., D.S.O.
Brig-General E.S. D'E COKE, C.M.G., D.S.O.
T/Lieut-Colonel W.H. SUTTON, D.S.O., M.C.
Major A.C. DUNDAS.
T/Major T.O.L. BUCHAN, M.C.
T/Major W. ASCOTT, O.B.E.
T/Major A. SCOTT, D.S.O., M.C.

Divisional Artillery.

A/Capt. A.V. HEAL, M.C.
Capt. R.W. MARTELL.
Lieut. T.U. ODELL.
2/Lt. W.L. EVANS.
940815 B.Q.M.S. F.C. BEDLOE.
930320 Sergt. D.A. REGAN.
947555 Sergt. R.A. ROBSON.

Divisional Engineers.

A/Major A.J. RANSFORD.
A/Capt. A.W. BILES.
546513 Sergt. F. BENNETT.

Cheshire Regiment.

Capt. H.L. CHURTON.
Lieut. J.H.L. GIBSON.
241639 A/Sgt. G.E. KING.

Machine Gun Corps.

A/Major J. COLQUHOUN.
25074 C.Q.M.S. E.G. EDWARDS.

R.A.S.C.

Capt. C.B. BUDDLE.
S26R/04585 A/Sgt. A.E.L. PONTON.
M2/130868 Pte. J.R. ANDERSON.

R.A.M.C.

Major A.B. MURRAY.
A/Major N.L. FERGUSSON.
Capt. & Q.M. J.D. CHAPMAN, O.B.E.
528073 Corpl. J. YEOMAN.

R.A.O.C.

O.2997 Sub Condr. W. SPENCER.

P.T.O.

(4)

MENTIONED IN DESPATCHES (contd).

167th Infantry Brigade.

Lieut-Col. C.H. PANK, C.M.G., D.S.O., T.D.	Middlesex Regt.
A/Lieut-Col. W.R. GLOVER, C.M.G., D.S.O.	London Regt.
A/Lieut-Col. M. BEEVOR.	E.Kent Regt. attd. Middlesex Rgt.
Capt. C.F. CHALLEN.	Middlesex Regt.
A/Capt. H.R. HOARE.	do. do.
2/Lt. C.W. ANGRAVE.	do. do.
2/Lt. W. WILKES.	London Regt.
240367 C.Q.M.S. F.J. REDDING.	do. do.
200036 Sergt. E.T. LILL.	Middlesex Regt.
262929 A/Cpl. G.H. SIMS.	do. do.
200757 Pte. F.H. HOLLOWAY.	do. do.
200278 Sergt. R. HAMILTON.	London Regt.

168th Infantry Brigade.

T/Lieut-Colonel E.D. JACKSON, D.S.O.	London Regt.
A/Capt. H.N. WILLIAMS, M.C.	do. do.
Lieut. V.T. FARRANT.	do. do.
Lieut. D.H. WHITELAW.	do. do.
2/Lt. H.J. KADWILL.	do. do.
2/Lt. F.A. BAKER, M.M.	do. do.
81182 T/R.S.M. J. JACQUES.	do. do.
490047 Sergt. D.T. JONES.	do. do.
510616 L/Cpl. E.F. COPPARD.	do. do.

169th Infantry Brigade.

T/Lieut-Colonel S.R. SAVILL, D.S.O. M.C.	London Regt.
A/Lieut-Colonel J.P. KELLETT, D.S.O., M.C.	do. do.
A/Lieut-Colonel C.D. BURNELL.	do. do.
A/Capt. S. du PLESSIS.	do. do. attd. T.M.Bty.
Lieut. & Q.M. A. DENNY.	London Regt.
550093 C.S.M. F.G. WESTON.	do. do.
231782 Sergt. G.E. WALKER.	do. do.
300198 L/Cpl. A.E. BRYER.	do. do.
318061 L/Cpl. E.J. CHAPMAN.	do. do.

War Diary

56th DIVISION.
LOCATION TABLE.

A.Q.S.5.

Ref. Sheets 45 & 51. 1/40000.

	UNIT.	Headquarters.
1.	56th Divisional Headquarters.	HARVENG.
2.	167th Infantry Bde. H.Q.	QUEVY-LE-GRAND.
3.	7th Middlesex Regt.	"
4.	8th " "	QUEVY-LE-PETIT.
5.	1st London Regt.	GOEGNIES-CHAUSSEE.
6.	167th T.M. Battery.	QUEVY-LE-GRAND.
7.	168th Infantry Bde. H.Q.	GIVRY.
8.	4th London Regt.	VILLERS-SIRE-NICOLE.
9.	13th " "	do. do.
10.	14th " "	GIVRY.
11.	168th T.M. Battery.	"
12.	169th Infantry Bde. H.Q.	NOUVELLES.
13.	2nd London Regt.	HARMIGNIES.
14.	5th " "	do.
15.	16th " "	GENLY.
16.	169th T.M. Battery.	NOUVELLES.
17.	1/5th Cheshire Regt.	SPIENNES.
18.	56th Divl. Artillery H.Q.	HARVENG.
19.	280th Brigade, R.F.A.	GOEGNIES-CHAUSSEE.
20.	281st " "	VIEUX RENG.
21.	282nd A.F.A. Brigade, R.F.A.	NOIRCHAIN.
22.	C.R.E. H.Q.	HARVENG.
23.	416th Field Coy. R.E.	QUEVY-LE-PETIT.
24.	512th " " "	VILLERS-SIRE-NICOLE.
25.	513th " " "	ASQUILLIES.
26.	A.D.M.S.	HARVENG.
27.	2/1st London Field Ambulance.	QUEVY-LE-PETIT.
28.	2/2nd " " "	GIVRY.
29.	2/3rd " " "	ECOLE NORMALE, MONS.
30.	56th Div. Ammn. Column (less S.A.A.Sect)	CIPLY.
31.	S.A.A. Section.	HARVENG.
32.	56th Batt. M.G. Corps.	VILLERS ST GHISLAIN.
33.	56th Divl. Gas Officer.	HARVENG.
34.	56th Divl. Train H.Q.	"
35.	Divl. Reception Camp.	RAISMES.
36.	" Baths Officer.	HARVENG.
37.	" Claims "	"
38.	" Salvage "	"
39.	D.A.D.O.S.	The Depot. E.3.a. Brasserie Co-operative. (W.2.d.0.5.)
40.	D.A.D.V.S.	
41.	247th (Divl) Employment Coy.	HARVENG.

5th December, 1918.

[signature]
Captain,
for D.A.A.G., 56th Division.

56th DIVISION.
LOCATION TABLE.

A.Q.S.5.

Ref.Sheets 45 & 51. 1/40000.

	UNIT.	Headquarters.
1.	56th Divisional Headquarters.	HARVENG.
2.	167th Infantry Bde. H.Q.	QUEVY-LE-GRAND.
3.	7th Middlesex Regt.	"
4.	8th " "	QUEVY-LE-PETIT.
5.	1st London Regt.	GOEGNIES-CHAUSSEE.
6.	167th T.M. Battery.	QUEVY-LE-GRAND.
7.	168th Infantry Bde. H.Q.	GIVRY.
8.	4th London Regt.	VILLERS-SIRE-NICOLE.
9.	13th " "	do. do.
10.	14th " "	GIVRY.
11.	168th T.M. Battery.	"
12.	169th Infantry Bde. H.Q.	NOUVELLES.
13.	2nd London Regt.	HARMIGNIES.
14.	5th " "	do.
15.	16th " "	GENLY.
16.	169th T.M. Battery.	NOUVELLES.
17.	1/5th Cheshire Regt.	SPIENNES.
18.	56th Divl. Artillery H.Q.	HARVENG.
19.	280th Brigade, R.F.A.	GOEGNIES-CHAUSSEE.
20.	281st " "	VIEUX RENG.
21.	282nd A.F.A. Brigade, R.F.A.	NOIRCHAIN.
22.	C.R.E. H.Q.	HARVENG.
23.	416th Field Coy. R.E.	QUEVY-LE-PETIT.
24.	512th " " " "	VILLERS-SIRE-NICOLE.
25.	513th " " " "	ASQUILLIES.
26.	A.D.M.S.	HARVENG.
27.	2/1st London Field Ambulance.	QUEVY-LE-PETIT.
28.	2/2nd " " "	GIVRY.
29.	2/3rd " " "	ECOLE NORMALE, MONS.
30.	56th Div. Ammn. Column (less S.A.A.Sect)	CIPLY.
31.	S.A.A. Section.	HARVENG.
32.	56th Batt. M.G. Corps.	VILLERS ST GHISLAIN.
33.	56th Divl. Gas Officer.	HARVENG.
34.	56th Divl. Train H.Q.	"
35.	Divl. Reception Camp.	RAISMES.
36.	" Baths Officer.	HARVENG.
37.	" Claims "	"
38.	" Salvage "	
39.	D.A.D.O.S.	The Depot. E.3.a. Brasserie Co-operative. (W.2.d.9.5.)
40.	D.A.D.V.S.	
41.	247th (Divl) Employment Coy.	HARVENG.

5th December, 1918.

Captain,
for D.A.A.G., 56th Division.

War Diary

56th DIVISION
LOCATION TABLE.

A.C.S.5.

Ref. Sheets 45 & 51. 1/40000.

UNIT.	Headquarters.
1. 56th Divisional Headquarters	HARVENGT.
2. 167th Inf. Brigade H.Q.	155 BOULEVARD DOLEZ, MONS.
3. 7th Middlesex Regt.	42 RUE de NIMY, MONS.
4. 8th Middlesex Regt.	96 BOULEVARD DOLEZ, MONS.
5. 1st London Regt.	JEMAPPES.
6. 167th L.T.M. Battery.	RUE de ARQUELIESIERES, MONS.
7. 168th Inf. Brigade H.Q.	GIVRY.
8. 4th London Regt.	VILLERS-SIRE-NICOLE.
9. 13th London Regt.	GIVRY.
10. 168th L.T.M. Battery.	GIVRY.
11. 169th Inf. Brigade H.Q.	NOUVELLES.
12. 2nd London Regt.	HARMIGNIES.
13. 5th London Regt.	HARMIGNIES.
14. 16th London Regt.	GENLY.
15. 169th L.T.M. Battery.	NOUVELLES.
16. 1/5th Cheshire Regt.	SPIENNES.
17. 56th Divl. Artillery H.Q.	HARVENGT.
18. 280th Brigade, R.F.A.	GOEGNIES-CHAUSSEE.
19. 281st Brigade, R.F.A.	ROUVEROY.
20. 282nd A.F.A. Bde., R.F.A.	NOIRCHAIN.
21. 56th Divl. Ammunition Column.	CIPLY.
22. C.R.E., H.Q.	HARVENGT.
23. 416th Field Company, R.E.	MONS, 0.13.b.15.00.
24. 512th Field Company, R.E.	VILLERS-SIRE-NICOLE.
25. 513th Field Company, R.E.	ASQUILLIES.
26. A.D.M.S.	HARVENGT.
27. 2/1st London Field Ambulance.	QUEVY-LE-PETIT.
28. 2/2nd London Field Ambulance.	GIVRY.
29. 2/3rd London Field Ambulance.	ECOLE NORMALE, MONS.
30. 56th Bn. Machine Gun Corps.	VILLERS-ST-GHISLAIN.
31. 56th Divisional Train H.Q.	HARVENGT.
32. 56th Divisional Train No. 1. Coy.	CIPLY.
33. 56th Divisional Train No. 2. Coy.	RUE de PASSAGE, MONS.
34. 56th Divisional Train No. 3. Coy.	MESVIN.
35. 56th Divisional Train No. 4. Coy.	NOUVELLES.
36. Divisional Reception Camp.	ATHENEE ROYALE, 12 RUE de la STATION, MONS.
37. Divl. Baths Officer.	HARVENGT.
38. Divl. Claims Officer.	HARVENGT.
39. Divl. Salvage Officer.	The DEPOT, E.3.a.
40. D.A.D.O.S.	Brasserie, V.2.c.9.5.
41. D.A.D.V.S.	HARVENGT.
42. 247th (Divl) Employment Coy.	HARVENGT.
43. 56th M.T. Company.	12 RUE de la PRISON, MONS.

23rd January, 1919.

Major,
D.A.A.G., 56th Division.

War Diary

56th DIVISION.
LOCATION TABLE.

A.F.S.5.

Ref. Sheets 45 & 51. 1/40000.

UNIT.	Headquarters.
1. 56th Divisional Headquarters	HARVENGT.
2. 167th Inf. Brigade H.Q.	155 BOULEVARD DOLEZ, MONS.
3. 7th Middlesex Regt.	42 RUE de NIMY, MONS.
4. 8th Middlesex Regt.	96 BOULEVARD DOLEZ, MONS.
5. 1st London Regt.	JEMAPPES.
6. 167th L.T.M. Battery.	RUE de ARQUELINIERES, MONS.
7. 168th Inf. Brigade H.Q.	GIVRY.
8. 4th London Regt.	VILLERS-SIRE-NICOLE.
9. 13th London Regt.	GIVRY.
10. 168th L.T.M. Battery.	GIVRY.
11. 169th Inf. Brigade H.Q.	NOUVELLES.
12. 2nd London Regt.	HARMIGNIES.
13. 5th London Regt.	HARMIGNIES.
14. 16th London Regt.	GENLY.
15. 169th L.T.M. Battery.	NOUVELLES.
16. 1/5th Cheshire Regt.	SPIENNES.
17. 56th Divl. Artillery H.Q.	HARVENGT.
18. 280th Brigade, R.F.A.	GOEGNIES-CHAUSSEE.
19. 281st Brigade, R.F.A.	ROUVEROY.
20. 282nd A.F.A. Bde., R.F.A.	NOIRCHAIN.
21. 56th Divl. Ammunition Column.	CIPLY.
22. C.R.E., H.Q.	HARVENGT.
23. 416th Field Company, R.E.	MONS, O.13.b.15.00.
24. 512th Field Company, R.E.	VILLERS-SIRE-NICOLE.
25. 513th Field Company, R.E.	ASQUILLIES.
26. A.D.M.S.	HARVENGT.
27. 2/1st London Field Ambulance.	QUEVY-LE-PETIT.
28. 2/2nd London Field Ambulance.	GIVRY.
29. 2/3rd London Field Ambulance.	ECOLE NORMALE, MONS.
30. 56th Bn. Machine Gun Corps.	VILLERS-ST-GHISLAIN.
31. 56th Divisional Train H.Q.	HARVENGT.
32. 56th Divisional Train No. 1. Coy.	CIPLY.
33. 56th Divisional Train No. 2. Coy.	RUE de PASSAGE, MONS.
34. 56th Divisional Train No. 3. Coy.	MESVIN.
35. 56th Divisional Train No. 4. Coy.	NOUVELLES.
36. Divisional Reception Camp.	ATHENEE ROYALE, 12 RUE de la STATION, MONS.
37. Divl. Baths Officer.	HARVENGT.
38. Divl. Claims Officer.	HARVENGT.
39. Divl. Salvage Officer.	The DEPOT, E.3.a.
40. D.A.D.O.S.	Brasserie, W.2.c.9.5.
41. D.A.D.V.S.	HARVENGT.
42. 247th (Divl) Employment Coy.	HARVENGT.
43. 56th M.T. Company.	12 RUE de la PRISON, MONS.

23rd January, 1919.

Major,
D.A.A.G., 56th Division.

UNIT	STRENGTH 1.1.19 O.	O.R.	INCREASE O.	O.R.	DECREASE O.	O.R.	STRENGTH 1.2.19. O.	O.R.
56th. Divisional H.Q.	15	80	–	4	–	16	15	68
247th. Employt. Coy.	2	319	–	–	–	39	2	280
167th. Infantry Bde. H.Q.	5	23	–	–	–	3	5	20
1/7th. Middlesex Regt.	47	854	1	10	12	252	36	612
1/8th. Middlesex Regt.	43	904	–	9	4	254	39	659
1/1st. London Regt.	41	731	–	13	4	203	37	541
167th. L.T.M. Battery.	3	45	–	–	1	15	2	30
168th. Infantry Bde. H.Q.	5	22	–	–	–	1	5	21
1/4th. London Regt.	47	674	3	19	7	231	43	462
1/13th. London Regt.	44	726	–	11	2	288	42	449
168th. L.T.M. Battery.	4	43	–	2	1	21	3	24
169th. Infantry Bde. H.Q.	4	20	–	1	–	3	4	18
1/2nd. London Regt.	39	600	2	17	5	168	36	449
1/5th. London Regt.	38	699	2	8	8	215	32	492
1/16th. London Regt.	36	500	–	13	6	168	30	345
169th. L.T.M. Battery.	2	44	–	1	–	8	2	37
1/5th. Cheshire Regt.	38	765	–	13	13	236	25	542
56th. Battn. M.G. Corps.	48	868	1	13	12	190	37	691
56th. Divl. Arty. H.Q.	4	18	–	–	–	12	4	6
280th. Brigade R.F.A.	26	745	–	–	6	104	20	641
281st. Brigade R.F.A.	24	738	1	–	3	75	22	663
Divl. Ammunition Col.	18	420	–	31	2	21	16	430
56th. Divl. Engineers H.Q.	1	10	1	–	–	3	2	7
416th (Edinboro') Fd. Co. R.E.	6	195	–	4	2	66	4	133
512th (London) Fld Co. R.E.	7	198	–	–	–	75	7	123
513th (London) Fld. Co. R.E.	8	200	–	–	2	85	6	115
Divisional Signal Coy.	11	298	–	–	1	60	10	260
56th. Divisional Train.	20	372	2	4	3	11	19	365
Medical Units.	13	518	1	–	1	90	3	428
Mobile Veterinary Section.	1	18	–	–	–	–	1	18

****

Original

War Diary for
month of February 1919

A.A. & Q.M.G. Branch

56th Division

Army Form C. 2118.

WAR DIARY
or
INTELLIGENCE SUMMARY.
(Erase heading not required.)

Instructions regarding War Diaries and Intelligence Summaries are contained in F. S. Regs., Part II. and the Staff Manual respectively. Title pages will be prepared in manuscript.

Place	Date	Hour	Summary of Events and Information	Remarks and references to Appendices
HARVENG	Jan 31 1919		Duties of troops Entrained Leave Party for 15th Army filled during night of 31/12/15 continued today. Two first trains arrived today & unloaded supplies until 4th mail party of 6 officers & 1171 OR departed for demobilization. Major T.F. CHIPP M.C. BATMS left for demobilization & was replaced by Capt. H.G.L. PRYNNE M.C. Staff Captain 167 Infy Bde. Capt. T.C. HEARD D.S.O.³ also departed for demobilization. New regulations received re demobilization to come into operation on 10th Feby this date home released under 37 and enlisted after 1 Jan 1916 except protables A.F.Z.62 & W.112.3 wound stripes. Gas day. Post continues. Employment situation normal.	
	2		Instructions received that leave trains would re-commence on 3rd inst. 6 officers & 151 OR despatched for demobilization. Brig General H. Day H.Q. on disposal of Inmate.	
	3		Cold weather continued. No first train arrived today.	

A6945 Wt. W14422/M1160 350,000 12/16 D.D. & L. Forms/C/2118/14.

Army Form C. 2118.

WAR DIARY
or
INTELLIGENCE SUMMARY.
(Erase heading not required.)

Place	Date	Hour	Summary of Events and Information	Remarks and references to Appendices
MARVENG	Jan 4		No men despatched for demobilization today. Frost continued.	
	5.		Lt. Col. W.M. SUTTON D.S.O. M.C. proceeded on 8 days leave to ENGLAND. MAJOR A. SCOTT acting as A/H. C.O.N.G in his absence. Snow fell during day. Instructions received for 5 O.Rs & 150 O.Rs of 8th Middx to join 18th Middx 33rd Div.	
	6.		Orders received from 3rd Echelon for 100 O.Rs & 200 O.Rs of 13th London 16th London & 5th Cheshire to join 18th KRRC 20th KRRC & 117th Cheshire in Second Army. Slight thaw but followed by further fall of snow. Supply situation normal. All units returns of days reserve rations in QM Stores. 6 O.Rs & 152 O.Rs demobilised.	
	7		Instructions received to make parts from 8th Middx to go to 18th Middx up to 10 O.Rs & 300 O.Rs if possible. Frost continues. Fine weather but receiving cases parts of 6 O.Rs & 151 O.Rs sent for demobilization. Army Order XIV of 29 Jan 1919. received consequently changing	

WAR DIARY
or
INTELLIGENCE SUMMARY
(Erase heading not required.)

Army Form C. 2118.

Place	Date	Hour	Summary of Events and Information	Remarks and references to Appendices
HARVENG	Feb 7		Regulations for dispatch of men for demobilization. Very few officers now releasable and only men over 37 yrs of age or enlisted prior to 1 Jan 1916. New rules known into force Feb 10th.	
	8		Very own night 7/8th. 6 Officers and 152 ORs sent for demobilization.	
	9		No park train arrived, but supply vehicles still good. Further Army of Occupation & 152 ORs demobilised. Cash paid under old rules. Group four companies.	
	10		Park of Supps & 185 ORs sent for demobilization. Instructions received to prepare Nominal Rolls of all Group volunteers for Army of Occupation of those whom under A.O. 14 of 1919 for entrance with unabated seniority. Bow Bells opens at Mons THEATRE with a Variety Show. Troops strengthened by new members from former 169 Infy Bde Troupe.	
	11.		Ten Officers & 200 ORs of 5th Middx despatched to 18th Middx	

WAR DIARY
or
INTELLIGENCE SUMMARY.
(Erase heading not required.)

Army Form C. 2118.

Place	Date	Hour	Summary of Events and Information	Remarks and references to Appendices
MARVENG	Feb 11		33rd Div. ABANCOURT area, entraining at MORS at 0010 hrs. 17th week. Fair weather. Good shell release. Instructions received to send all available men for returning in army from 1st Bns and 4th Bn to 2/23rd Bns. 30th Div and from 5th Bns and 2nd Bns to 2/16th Bns.	
	12.		30th Div. CALAIS at an early date. Frost continued. Lecture by Earl of DENBIGH at MONS on "Germany's attempt for World Dominion". Instructions received for M.G. Bn to send draft of 4 officers 150 ORs to 200" M.G. Bn.[?]	
	13.		Cloud weather maintained with slight statement[?] of previous severity. 6 officers and 114 ORs despatched for demobilisation. Slow commenced with some rain. Nominal Rolls despatched to AG. GHQ of all officers who do not volunteer for army of Occupation. Those who do not volunteer. Sea officers and 110 ORs despatched for demobilisation.	
	14.		Information received that Machine Gun are to transferred to 41st Div.	

WAR DIARY
or
INTELLIGENCE SUMMARY.
(Erase heading not required.)

Army Form C. 2118.

Place	Date	Hour	Summary of Events and Information	Remarks and references to Appendices
HARVENG	Feb 14		in the Second Army	
	15		Party of N.C.O's have departed to Paris by Auto-bus. For refreshment to England. Weather fine and warm. "Pan Bells" performed for last time at MON'S THEATRE. An entirely new performance for demonstration an excellent last performance was attended by the G.O.C. and a crowded and enthusiastic audience.	
	16		Very enjoyable fine day warm its afternoon. Two officers and 105 O.Rs departed to demonstration than tomorrow but into force for 10 days.	
	17		Part of 101 ORs denetined today. Weather fine & warm.	
	18		Warm day in morning but stuck mist came later.	
	19		First draft of animals to Belgium taken at GIVRY. Good horses were obtained, averaging 1000 francs	

WAR DIARY
or
INTELLIGENCE SUMMARY.

Army Form C. 2118.

Place	Date	Hour	Summary of Events and Information	Remarks and references to Appendices
HARVENG	Oct 19		For a horse and 800 francs for a mule; all the animals sent 2" or low grade. Finals of the XVII Corps Boxing Competition at MONS. Major General Sir C.R.A. Hull K.C.B. forwarded the prizes. Weather fine. 300 horses V.S. despatched to Base.	
	20		Glorious fine morning. Party of 9 one officer 107 other ranks despatched for demobilization.	
	21		Showery day. Leave allotment considerably reduced. All personnel or volunteers officers + men kept not eligible. Party of 1 officer and 95 O.R. sent for demobilization. Weather showery. Semi-final of the 56th Divl. Football Competition. 1/5 Cheshire vs. 2/3 Edw Fused Counties. Won for Cheshire 6-0.	
	22		Party of 4 officers and 71 O.R. despatches for demobilization. Dull day - no rain. 1 Off. and 70 O.R. sent for demobilization.	
	23		Orders received for moves of 7th Middlesex to 2nd Army on 25".	
	24		Capt Osgoine, g.R.M.b. awarded 6 days leave to England - his dept being taken over by Capt Bentall, 166 Bde. C.R.D. Moses, Divl F.O. amalgamated.	

A6945 Wt. W11422/M1160 350,000 12/16 D. D. & L. Forms/C./2118/14.

Army Form C. 2118.

WAR DIARY
or
INTELLIGENCE SUMMARY.
(Erase heading not required.)

Instructions regarding War Diaries and Intelligence Summaries are contained in F. S. Regs., Part II. and the Staff Manual respectively. Title pages will be prepared in manuscript.

Place	Date	Hour	Summary of Events and Information	Remarks and references to Appendices
HARVENGT	Feb. 24 (Contd)		78 O.R. proceeded on demobilization.	
	25		Dull day - no news. Trial of Divinl football competition 5" Cheshire v. 280 Bde R.F.A. resulting in a draw. To be replayed on 28th.	
	26		7 Mid'sex proceeded to join the 2nd Army. Train left Mons 1345 hours. Showery day + colder. Successful sale of 2 horses at GIVRY, good prices being obtained, 132 Animals disposed of.	
	27		69 O.R. sent for demobilization. Draft of 5 off. + 79 o.r. of 1st LONDON REGT. left for transfer to 1/23 LONDON REGT. Supply situation normal. 40 Y Mans sent to Base for repatriation. Final replay of the Divnl Football competition - won by 5" Cheshires by 2 goals to nil. Cups provided by Maj. Gen. Sir A. Hall, K.C.B. All available men for demobilization to be	
	28		sent to Cuesmes Camp by Mar 3rd. Daily train service then likely to cease.	

Wm Lukin. Lt.Col.
A/A QMG 56th Divn.

1/3/19.

UNIT.	STRENGTH 1/2/19		INCREASE.		DECREASE.		STRENGTH. 1/3/19.	
	O.	O.R.	O.	O.R.	O.	O.R.	O.	O.R.
56th.Divl.H.Q.	15	68	2	19	3	10	14	77
247th.Employt.Co.	2	280	-	-	-	135	1	145
167th.Inf.Bde.H.Q.	5	20	-	3	2	7	3	16
1/8th.Middsx.Rgt.	39	659	1	-	14	443	26	216
1/1st.London Rgt.	37	541	2	4	17	374	22	171
168th.Inf.Bde.H.Q.	5	21	-	-	1	1	4	20
1/4th.London Rgt.	43	462	2	1	8	227	37	236
1/13th.London Rgt.	42	449	-	1	12	161	30	289
169th.Inf.Bde.H.Q.	4	18	-	1	2	1	2	20
1/2nd.London Rgt.	36	449	2	-	4	176	34	273
1/5th.London Rgt.	32	492	2	-	7	224	27	268
1/16th.London Rgt.	30	345	1	-	6	128	25	217
1/5th.Cheshire Rgt.	25	542	-	1	6	263	19	280
56th.Bn.M.G.Corps.	37	691	-	1	13	284	24	408
56th.Div.Arty.H.Q.	4	6	2	4	2	2	4	8
280th.Bde.R.F.A.	20	641	-	-	6	67	14	574
281st.Bde.R.F.A.	22	663	-	-	4	67	18	596
282nd.Bde.R.F.A.	-	-	-	-	1	15	24	540
Div.Ammn. Col.	16	430	-	39	1	59	15	410
56th.Div.Engineers H.Q.	2	7	1	-	1	1	2	6
416(Edinboro') Fld.Co.R.E.	4	133	-	-	1	53	3	80
512(London) Fld. Co. R.E.	7	123	1	-	4	41	4	82
513(London) Fld. Co. R.E.	6	115	-	-	-	37	6	78
Div.Signal Coy.	10	260	-	1	2	111	8	150
56th.Div.Train.	19	365	-	9	3	39	16	335
Medical Units.	13	428	-	-	1	96	12	332
Mobile Vet.Sect.	1	18	-	-	-	1	1	17

****

Vol 38

Original

56th Division

A A and Q M G

War Diary

March 1919

Army Form C. 2118.

WAR DIARY
or
INTELLIGENCE SUMMARY.
(Erase heading not required.)

Instructions regarding War Diaries and Intelligence Summaries are contained in F. S. Regs., Part II. and the Staff Manual respectively. Title pages will be prepared in manuscript.

Place	Date	Hour	Summary of Events and Information	Remarks and references to Appendices
	Mar			
HARVENG	1		Lt.Col. Sutton DSO, MC, DA.Q.M.G, returned 6duty on completion of leave & attendance at a Conference at VALENCIENNES. Draft of 5 offs & 91 O.R. of 1st/4th London Regt. left at 0215 hours MONS.	
	2		This morning to join 2/2/3rd London Regt. 116 O.R. proceeded to Concrete Camp for demobilization. 5 OFF & 60 O.R. of 5th LONDONS left MONS at 2330 as Draft for 2/16 London 3 officers 400 O.R. of 13th LONDONS left at 0715 from MONS for LAPUGNOY for	
	3		BETHUNE guard. 3 Officers & 181 O.R. sent for demobilization. 5/6th Divnl. Race Meeting. Fine morning but heavy rain in the afternoon. No news from demobilization to be sent to Concrete Camps given this date till further notice, numbers available to be sent to Camps daily.	
	4		Draft of 5 OFF and 69 O.Rs of 2nd Londons left MONS at 22.55 hours for CALAIS to join	
	5		2/16 London Regt. Sale of "Z" horses at GIVRY. Good prices obtained, averaging 1000 frs each for the 128 animals to sale.	
	6		Capt Payne, M.C, D.A.Q.M.G. returned from leave, took over from Capt Bootall, M.C. 375 Z Horses despatched sent to ROUEN for sale	
	7		Final figures asked for by Corps of all relevant officers and O.R's separated from Cadre Establishment.	

Army Form C. 2118.

WAR DIARY
or
INTELLIGENCE SUMMARY.
(Erase heading not required.)

Instructions regarding War Diaries and Intelligence Summaries are contained in F. S. Regs., Part II. and the Staff Manual respectively. Title pages will be prepared in manuscript.

Place	Date	Hour	Summary of Events and Information	Remarks and references to Appendices
HARVENG	Mar 8		Lt. Col. Sutton DSO, MC, left for duty as DA & QMG with 61st Divn.	
	9		7 officers & 72 O.Rs of 15" Cheshires left MONS at 2300 hours to join 1/7 Cheshire. Fine morning, rain in the afternoon. 100 text "Z" horses left MONS for BOULOGNE. 236 Other Ranks left Concent. I for demobilization.	
	10		XXII Corps Race Meeting, - well attended and racing good.	
	11		170 "X" horses sent to COLOGNE and 100 to mons. for sale. No 4 Coy Train moved from HOUDENG & CIPLY.	
	12		300 ORs awaiting orders for demobn. to Concent. I for demobilization. Orders received for Maj. Gen Sir A Hull, KCB (to proceed) as G.O.C. 6th Divn.	
	13		Orders received that officers over 37 and 50% of men enlisting or commissioned in 1914 can be released as soon as can be spared. Bns must apply to Offr Cmdg Staff, RASC or RCOD. Battln of 100 more or two more special classes. 13" Londons Regt (BETHUNE's guard) returned for draft to 30 "Devon's buring	
	14		Party of 5 offr. & 100 men (BETHUNE's guard) returned for draft to 30 "Devon's buring on the 17. 376 horses sent to COLOGNE & 80 to Base for repatriation. Concentration of troops near Railhead commences. 261 Bde R.F.A. to MESVIN	
	15		Nos 2 & 3 Coys of Divn. Train to CIPLY. from MESVIN 30 X horses sent to the Base for repatriation. Maj. Gen. Sir A Hull	

Army Form C. 2118.

WAR DIARY
or
INTELLIGENCE SUMMARY.
(Erase heading not required.)

Instructions regarding War Diaries and Intelligence Summaries are contained in F. S. Regs., Part II. and the Staff Manual respectively. Title pages will be prepared in manuscript.

Place	Date	Hour	Summary of Events and Information	Remarks and references to Appendices
HARVENG	Nov 15"		Left for the 6th Divn. Orders received for Brig-Gen G.S.L.XIII, 166 Bde, to proceed	
			to take command of a Bde in 9th Divn by 18th and Brig Gen G.H.B. Trench, 167 Bde,	
	16		to a Bde in the 32nd Divn by same date.	
	17		Draft of 140 ORs from 56 M.G. Btn. left MONS at 19.45 for the 29th Divn.	
			2 Officers + 98 ORs of the 1/13 London left as draft for the 2/13 London 30 Divn.	
	18		8th Wn ame moved to JEMAPPES from MYON.	
			1st Bde reserved from QUIVY to JEMAPPES. 2/1st London Fd Amb moved from QUEVY-LE-PETIT to JEMAPPES.	
	19		2/2nd Field Amb moved to CUESMES. RE: 513 Field Coy moved from ASQUILLIES to JEMAPPES.	
			30 Z horses sent to MONS for sale.	
	20		Preliminary instructions received under which Orders will be issued.	
			to the Base, shipped to England and disposed of. Conference at	
			Corps HQrs to discuss the closing off + concentration of Corps.	
	21		1/5 Cheshires moved from SPIENNES to JEMAPPES + 280 Bde to FLENU	
			Orders received to Bde to move the 2nd Londons and 3rd Londons Co	
			QUAREGNON on 23rd and 24th also the 1st-1/16 Londons.	
	22		Brig Gen E.M.S. D'e COKE, CMG DSO assumed command of 6th Divn.	
			Brig Gen R.J. PINKINGTON CMG DSO proceeded on leave. Orders received	
			that every horse in the Divn must be away by 29th Nov except 60 for	
			food + police horses. All troops suspended owing to fear of strikes in England.	
			for demob, leave & movement of cadres.	

Army Form C. 2118.

WAR DIARY
or
INTELLIGENCE SUMMARY.
(Erase heading not required.)

Instructions regarding War Diaries and Intelligence Summaries are contained in F. S. Regs., Part II. and the Staff Manual respectively. Title pages will be prepared in manuscript.

Place	Date	Hour	Summary of Events and Information	Remarks and references to Appendices
HARVENGT	Mar	23	1/5 London Regt (L.R.B.) moved from HARMIGNIES. 1/6 London (Q.W.R.) both to QUAREGNON. 50 "2" Horses sent to the Base. Leave for officers + O.R.s suspended until further notice except in cases of serious illness of parent, wife or child.	
"	"	24	Restrictions as to leave, demobilizations etc removed. 2nd Londons moved from HARMIGNIES to QUAREGNON. 135 animals sent to the Base. Draft of O.R.s from 1st Londons 42, 4th Londons 30, 13th Lons 30, 16th Lons 40 and 1 offr. from 13th Lons, left Mons at 0700 hours for CALAIS to 30th Divn to Care of small pox in H.Q. BTn, JEMAPPES, pleave "Out of Bounds" + movement of Civilians to that town stopped till further orders	
"	"	25	During	
"	"	26	Cases of small-pox found. Sub Chatelton, Emburg, + Jemappes removed.	
"	"	27	170 "Y" Horses sent to the Base.	
"	"	28	510 "D" 13" Horses left Mons for repatriation in England.	
"	"	29	56th Divn Hdqrs, A.D.M.S. H.Q. 56 Divn Train, Mobile Vet. H.Q.C.R.E., 247 Emp. Coy., 169 Bde. Hdqrs, 247 Engs. Coy, moved to JEMAPPES. All remaining horses sent to the Base, leaving a pool of 60 + establishment for D.A.P.M.	
JEMAPPES	"	30	167 Bde. H.Q. moved from MONS to JEMAPPES.	
"	"	31	NIL	

A. Clark, Major
A.A. + Q.M.G., 56 Div

14/4/19

UNIT.	STRENGTH 1/3/19.		INCREASE.		DECREASE.		STRENGTH. 1/4/19.	
	O.	O.R.	O.	O.R.	O.	O.R.	O.	O.R.
56th.Div.Headquarters.)	14	77						
56th.Div.Engineers H.Q.)	2	6	-	-	8	-	8	83
247th.Employt. Coy.	1	145	-	22	-	82	1	85
167th.Inf. Bde. H.Q.	3	16	-	-	1	2	2	18
8th.Middlesex Rgt.	26	216	-	-	9	133	17	83
1st.London Regt.	22	171	1	2	7	73	16	100
168th.Inf. Bde. H.Q.	4	20	-	-	2	14	2	16
4th.London Regt.	37	236	1	-	14	153	24	83
13th.London Regt.	30	289	-	-	9	189	21	100
169th.Inf. Bde. H.Q.	2	20	-	-	-	3	2	17
2nd. London Regt.	34	273	1	-	16	164	19	109
5th. London Regt.	27	268	-	-	17	185	10	83
16th.London Regt.	25	217	1	-	17	150	9	67
1/5th.Cheshire Regt.	19	280	-	1	11	195	8	86
56th. Bn. M.G.Corps.	24	408	-	-	17	189	7	119
56th.Div.Artillery H.Q.	4	8	-	-	-	7	4	1
280th. Brigade R.F.A.	14	574	2	11	4	286	12	299
281st. Brigade R.F.A.	18	596	-	10	3	244	15	362
282nd. Brigade R.F.A.	24	540	-	-	3	142	21	398
Divl. Ammunition Col.	15	410	-	1	1	130	14	281
416th(Edinboro')Fld.Co.RE	3	80	-	-	-	7	3	73
512th.(London) Fld.Co.RE	4	82	-	1	1	15	3	68
513th.(London) Fld.Co.RE	6	78	-	-	4	7	2	71
Divl. Signal Coy.	8	150	-	-	2	44	6	106.
56th.Div.Train No.1 Coy.)								
56th.Div.Train No.2.Coy.)	16	335	-	-	5	164	11	171
56th.Div.Train No.3.Coy.)								
56th.Div.Train No.4.Coy.)								
2/1st.London Fld.Amblce.)								
2/2nd.London Fld.Amblce)	12	332	1	3	±	153	13	182
2/3rd.London Fld.Amblce.)								
Mobile Veterinary Section	1	17	-	-	-	2	1	15

Army Form C. 2118.

WAR DIARY
or
INTELLIGENCE SUMMARY.
(Erase heading not required.)

HQ ATO 56 D

Place	Date	Hour	Summary of Events and Information	Remarks and references to Appendices
JEMAPPES	Apl. 1		Draft of 26 O.R.'s from 1/13 Londons + 16 O.R.'s various units left MONS at 20.15 hours for 2/16 Londons, 30th Divn. Orders received for Major A. Scott, Sto.K.C, D.A.G.S. to proceed to Army HQ Rhine. Application made to EHQ for the appointment to be cancelled, Major Scott to remain with Divn. pending result.	
	2		24 officers + 36 O.R's sent to cover 7 pr December. (1 off 23 ors Special Service)	
	3		Nil	
	4		Draft of 27 O.R's from field Coys sent to CRE 9" Lowland Divn. 28 ORs M.G. Bttn. 6. 29 + 13th M.G.C. 20 ors 5" Cheshires to 7" Cheshires 1st Divn. 7 ors 6 N'um to 7" N'um 41st Divn.	
	5		Draft of 4 ors 1st Cdrs to 2/23 Lotus 30 Divn.	
	5/30		Notice before Division down to cease payment preventing to entirem for time.	

H. Plagma Capt.
D.A.T.O. 56 Division

WAR DIARY
or
INTELLIGENCE SUMMARY. May 1919

Army Form C. 2118.

56 DIVISION

Place	Date	Hour	Summary of Events and Information	Remarks and references to Appendices
JEMAPPES	1/3 1st		Nothing to Report. First cadres leave for UK Div H.Q. Cadre entrain Jemappes in tiworth via ANTWERP.	

M Payne
Capt.
D.A.Q.M.G 56TH DIVISION

UNIT	STRENGTH 1/4/19.		INCREASE		DECREASE		STRENGTH 1/5/19.	
	O.	O.R.	O.	O.R.	O.	O.R.	O.	O.R.
56th.Divl. Headquarters) 56th.Div.Engineers H.Q.)	8	83	–	4	3	36	5	51
167th.Infantry Bde.H.Q.	2	18	–	–	–	9	2	9
8th.Middlesex Regt.	17	83	–	1	8	30	9	54
1/1st.London Regt.	16	100	–	–	8	44	8	56
168th.Infantry Bde.H.Q.	2	16	–	–	1	3	1	13
1/4th.London Regt.	24	83	1	3	7	35	18	51
1/13th.London Rgt.	21	100	–	2	2	63	19	39
1/2nd.London Regt.	19	109	–	2	6	71	13	40
1/5th.London Regt.	10	83	–	11	3	65	7	29
1/16th.London Rgt.	9	67	–	3	4	29	5	41
1/5th.Cheshire Regt.	8	86	–	3	4	42	4	46
56th. Bn. M.G.Corps.	7	219	–	2	2	73	5	148
56th.Divl. Arty.H.Q.	4	1	–	–	2	–	2	1
280th.Brigade RFA.	12	299	–	–	5	88	7	211
281st. Brigade RFA.	15	362	–	–	6	115	9	247
282nd.Brigade RFA.	21	398	–	–	7	68	14	330
Divl. Ammn. Column.	14	281	–	6	5	24	9	263
416th.Field Co.R.E,	3	73	–	–	1	17	2	56
512th.Field Co.R.E.	3	68	–	–	1	12	2	56
513th.Field Co.R.E.	2	71	–	–	–	6	2	65
Divl. Signal Coy.	6	106	1	–	3	39	4	67
56th.Div.Train No.1 Coy.) 56th.Div.Train No.2 Coy) 56th.Div.Train No.3 Coy) 56th.Div.Train No.3 Coy)	11	171	–	–	5	65	6	106
2/1st.London Fld.Ambl.) 2/2nd.London Fld.Amb.) 2/3rd.London Fld.Amb.)	13	182	1	3	8	56	6	129
Mobile Veterinary Sect.	1	15	–	–	–	8	1	7

www.ingramcontent.com/pod-product-compliance
Lightning Source LLC
Chambersburg PA
CBHW081424300426

44108CB00016BA/2293